W9-CZX-465

Japan's
Administrative
Elite

WITHDRAWN

Japan's Administrative Elite

Theodore Lownik Library
Illinois Benedictine College
Lisle, Illinois 60532

B. C. Koh

UNIVERSITY OF CALIFORNIA PRESS
Berkeley • *Los Angeles* • *Oxford*

354.52
K79j

University of California Press
Berkeley and Los Angeles, California
University of California Press, Ltd.
London, England
© 1989 by
The Regents of the University of California

LIBRARY OF CONGRESS
Library of Congress Cataloging-in-Publication Data

Koh, Byung Chul.
    Japan's administrative elite / B.C. Koh.

        p.   cm.
    Bibliography: p.
    Includes index.
    ISBN 0-520-06314-7 (alk. paper)
        1. Civil service—Japan.   2. Bureaucracy—Japan.   I. Title.
    JQ1647.K63 1989
    354.52006—dc19   88-22737
                                                                CIP

Printed in the United States of America
9 8 7 6 5 4 3 2 1

For Eui Soon and Bong Jin Lee

Contents

Figures and Tables

Preface

The recent surge of interest in Japan on the part of scholars and the general public alike is due to its phenomenal track record in economic development. In the space of a few decades, Japan transformed itself from a defeated nation ravaged by war and occupied by its erstwhile enemy into an industrial giant whose gross national product was surpassed only by those of the two superpowers, the United States and the Soviet Union. In the past decade or so Japan has become the world's premier trading nation, flooding the world market with high-quality but competitively priced products ranging from automobiles to wrist-watches. In the process it has accumulated huge trade surpluses with virtually every trading partner.

Just how Japan, a resource-poor and overcrowded country, has managed to perform such a feat is a complex story about which volumes have already been written and will no doubt continue to be written in the years ahead. One thing that seems quite plain is that the government has played a part in Japan's success story. The expansion of the Japanese economy has occurred not in a climate of laissez-faire but in a controlled environment—one in which carefully formulated and skillfully executed government policies have helped to minimize fallouts from adverse currents abroad while maximizing conditions for growth in strategic industries at home.

In other words, Japan's civil servants cannot be divorced from their country's accomplishments in the economic field as well as in other public-policy areas, such as crime control, environmental protection, and social welfare. A study of how the elite among the Japanese civil servants are recruited, trained, promoted, and rewarded; how they interact among themselves and with other individuals; and how the structure and functioning of Japanese-government bureaucracy as a whole have changed over the years will, then, go a long way toward elucidating that extraordinary phenomenon that is Japan.

Another function that a study of Japan's administrative elite may perform is to help the reader assess the strengths and weaknesses of the Japanese model of management. Although much attention has been paid to the Japanese model in the private sector by those who aspire to decipher Japan's secret of success, analysis of the Japanese model as it operates in the governmental domain has barely begun. We need to build a reliable data base before we can make appreciable headway. This study may help us move in that direction.

If there is a conceptual framework that has informed this study, it may be called the life cycle of the adminstrative elite. The stages through which elite administrators progress in their career, from induction to retirement, are its principal components. The precise order in which the key stages are examined in this book, however, is not necessarily chronological. For example, although the most significant part of the elite administrator's socialization occurs both before and immediately after induction, it is discussed after the promotion process has been analyzed. For a scrutiny of the latter allows us to identify the principal subset of the administrative elite whose preentry socialization experience merits special attention.

The genesis of this study may be traced to my first trip to Japan in the spring of 1972, when I explored the possibility of conducting research on the social background of Japanese higher civil servants. Since then, I have made eight more trips, each lasting from several days to a few weeks, during which I tried to collect material on the Japanese civil service from all accessible sources—public libraries (notably, the National Diet Library and the Tokyo Metropolitan Library), bookstores, scholars, and civil servants. The short duration of my visits, however, dictated by my failure to obtain any research grants from funding agencies, has necessarily prolonged the gestation period of this study, which has lasted an incredible fifteen years.

I hasten to add that I did receive two small grants during that period—a thousand-dollar grant from the Campus Research Board of the University of Illinois at Chicago (UIC) that enabled me to hire two Japanese students to code biographical data in 1976, and a research travel grant from the Northeast Asia Council (NEAC) of the Association for Asian Studies that allowed me to spend two weeks at the Library of Congress in Washington, D.C., in 1983. Three journal articles have resulted from these endeavors. I am grateful to the UIC and the NEAC for their timely assistance in preventing my research project from withering away.

A number of institutions have contributed to this project indirectly. All those institutions that have invited me to scholarly conferences in South Korea during the past fifteen years have unwittingly subsidized this project in some small way, for I have made a point of stopping over in Tokyo on my way to or from Seoul. I am therefore deeply indebted to Drs. Chungwon Choue, Chairman of the Committee for International Exchanges, Kyung Hee University; Sung-joo Han, former Director of the Asiatic Research Center, Korea University; Robert J. Myers, President of the Carnegie Council on Ethics and International Affairs, New York; Jae Kyu Park, President of Kyungnam University; and Robert A. Scalapino, Director of the Institute of East Asian Studies, University of California at Berkeley.

That this project has been sustained for so long and finally brought to a successful completion, however, is due to the unstinting support of my sister, Eui-Soon, and my brother-in-law, Dr. Bong Jin Lee, who is currently employed as senior development engineer and general manager of the Production Technology Laboratory of Fanuc Ltd. in Yamanashi prefecture, Japan. They have been a constant and reliable source of all manner of help—procuring books and magazines, clipping newspaper articles, coming to the rescue when my funds were depleted—during the past fifteen years.

Many other persons have also assisted me in collecting material for this study. Mr. Tsutsui Tetsuro, a former classmate of my brother-in-law at the University of Tokyo and an engineer with Ohkawara Ka-kohki Co., has sent me magazine articles and newly published books on Japanese bureaucracy for more than a decade without even being asked. Mrs. Tokudome Kinue, a former student of mine, has not only shared her copy of the Japanese daily *Asahi shinbun* with me for the past three years but also helped me learn the correct pronunciation of Japanese names and words on numerous occasions. Her editing of my letters to Japanese government officials has been particularly helpful.

For their generous assistance and warm hospitality during my visits to Japan, I am deeply indebted to Professors Hanai Hitoshi of Tsukuba University, Ichikawa Masaaki of Aomori University, and Nagano

Nobutoshi of Tokai University; Dr. Ch'oe Suh Myun, Director of the Tokyo Institute for Korean Studies; Dr. Kim Sam-Kyu, Director of the Institute for National Problems, Tokyo, and his assistant, Ms. Choy Il-Hae; Mr. Hirota Takao of the Japan Foundation; and Mr. Asakawa Koki of Izumi Junior College. Professor Hanai has been singularly generous, inviting me to stay in his apartment, giving me access to his personal library, and introducing me to other scholars.

For opening their doors to a stranger without proper introductions, giving generously of their time, and supplying me data, including unpublished documents, I am most grateful to officials of the National Personnel Authority, especially Mr. Ono Seinosuke, former secretary general, and Ms. Nakajima Sachiko, currently chief of the Legal Affairs Section of the Bureau of Administrative Services.

I have also incurred a lasting debt to Mr. Thaddeus Y. Ohta of the Japanese Section, Asian Division, the Library of Congress, for giving me free access to the stacks, helping me find obscure material, and sharing his considerable knowledge of Japanese affairs with me during my two-week visit to the library in the summer of 1983. My bosom friend, Yong Keun Cha, a senior civil servant in his own right, has cheerfully served as my unpaid research assistant, copying vast amounts of material at the Library of Congress and sending it to me at his own expense. Dr. Sung Yoon Cho, assistant chief of the Far Eastern Law Division, the Library of Congress, has also assisted me in locating and duplicating back issues of *Kanpo* (Official Gazette).

Professor Yung H. Park of California State University at Humboldt has kindly provided me copies of his articles on Japanese policy making. Mr. and Mrs. Oishi Koichirō and Mr. Lee Kyung Won have performed the tedious chore of coding biographical data with remarkable efficiency. Mr. Lee has also handled the data entry and analysis of the 1986 sample.

At various times, four colleagues have helped me to obtain lodging at the International House of Japan in Roppongi: Professors Soon Sung Cho of the University of Missouri at Columbia; Hong Nack Kim of West Virginia University; Chae-Jin Lee, dean of the School of Social and Behavioral Sciences, California State University at Long Beach; and Jung Suk Youn, director of the Institute of Area Studies, Chung-Ang University, Seoul. Professor Youn, a Japan specialist himself, has kindly given me access to his personal library, thus saving me many hours of work in public libraries.

In the earlier stage of this project I had the good fortune of working with Jae-On Kim, professor of sociology at the University of Iowa. His sharp mind and incomparable methodological skills made our collaboration a most rewarding learning experience for me.

The helpful comments of those who have evaluated my manuscript for the University of California Press have saved me from many errors and improved both the substance and style of this book. I express my profound appreciation to Professor Robert M. Spaulding of Oklahoma State University and the two anonymous readers. Because their recommendations have not been fully implemented, however, either because of the lack of data or because of my disagreement with them, I am solely responsible for any errors of fact and judgment that may still remain.

Last but not least, my wife, Hae Chung, and my two children, Michelle Suhae and Christopher Seung-bom, have sustained me all these years with their love, support, and understanding. Although this book cannot even begin to compensate for the neglect and inconvenience they have endured as a result of my preoccupation with this and other research projects, I hope it will at least show that my time away from them has had its own rewards and that perseverence does pay.

Finally, a few words on romanization and translation are in order. The romanization of Japanese words and names in this book is based on Kenkyusha's *New Japanese-English Dictionary,* 4th edition (Tokyo, 1974). As for translation of terms, notably *kachō, buchō,* and *kyokuchō,* I have decided not to follow *Organization of the Government of Japan* (Tokyo: Institute of Administrative Management, 1986), as one of the anonymous readers has recommended, but to use translations that seem prevalent in the literature in the field. Hence *kachō* is rendered as "section chief," *buchō* as "division chief," and *kyokuchō* as "bureau chief." In view of the fact that translations in *Organization of the Government of Japan* have not remained consistent over the years, I feel that maintaining consistency with the major works in the field should take precedence over all other considerations.

Byung Chul Koh
January 1988
Glencoe, Illinois

CHAPTER ONE

Administrative Elite in a Developmental State

A universally shared attribute of contemporary polities is the prepotent role of the government bureaucracy. No matter what the configuration of a polity may be, the formal state bureaucracy invariably occupies a strategic position in it. On the other hand, the bureaucracy's relative importance varies depending on such factors as historical legacy, the prestige and power of competing political structures, the caliber of its personnel, and the nature of nexus between state and economy.

Of particular relevance is the last-mentioned factor. As Chalmers Johnson points out, "all states intervene in their economies for various reasons," hence what matters most are the purpose and mode of state intervention. On the basis of these, Johnson differentiates between a "developmental state" and a "regulatory state." In the former, of which Japan is a prime example, the state has a predominantly "developmental orientation," taking an active part in setting "such substantive social and economic goals" as "what industries ought to exist and what industries are no longer needed." By contrast, the latter, exemplified by the United States, eschews explicitly developmental goals, concerning itself instead with the "forms and procedures . . . of economic competition." A developmental state, in Johnson's words, is "plan rational," whereas a regulatory state is "market rational."[1]

---

1. Chalmers Johnson, *MITI and the Japanese Miracle: The Growth of Industrial Policy, 1925–1975* (Stanford: Stanford University Press, 1982), pp. 18–19.

Unlike the situation in a Soviet-type command economy, which according to Johnson is "plan ideological," the plan-rational, developmental state employs "market-conforming methods of state intervention in the economy." Nonetheless, the degree of state intervention is necessarily greater in a developmental state than it is in a regulatory state. And the greater the degree of state intervention in the economy, the more salient is the government bureaucracy, a quintessential embodiment of state power. A "natural corollary of plan rationality," in Johnson's words, is the "existence of a powerful, talented, and prestige-laden economic bureaucracy."[2] We should add that it is not just economic bureaucracy but the entire state bureaucracy whose role is magnified in a developmental state.

Inasmuch as power tends to be concentrated at the upper rungs of bureaucratic organizations, we may be justified in focusing our attention on members of the "administrative elite"—those who occupy relatively high positions in the government bureaucracy. Operationally, however, "administrative elite" can be defined in a dual sense: in a narrow sense, it refers to those bureaucrats who actually occupy designated positions, say section chiefs (*kachō*) and above in the national government; in a broad sense, the concept encompasses not only current incumbents of such designated positions but also candidates for promotion to such positions.

If Japan's administrative elite, broadly defined, merits scrutiny, what is the general state of the literature on the subject? Looking at the English-language literature first, we find that the subject has indeed received a substantial amount of attention from students of Japanese politics, society, and history. Nonetheless, the list of monographs dealing either exclusively or primarily with the subject is surprisingly short. The earliest study one can find is Robert M. Spaulding, Jr.'s *Imperial Japan's Higher Civil Service Examinations.*[3] By meticulously documenting the long, difficult process by which the merit principle, a sine qua non of modern government bureaucracy, was introduced into prewar Japan, Spaulding sheds an important light not only on the formation of Japan's administrative elite but on that country's modernization process as well.

The first comprehensive study of Japanese higher civil servants in the postwar period was published two years later. *Higher Civil Servants in Postwar Japan,* by Akira Kubota, presents a statistical analysis of 1,353

2. Ibid., pp. 18, 317, 21.
3. Princeton: Princeton University Press, 1967.

Japanese civil servants with the rank of section chief or above in the national government for the period from 1949 to 1959.[4] His analysis of the social origins, educational backgrounds, and career patterns of Japan's postwar administrative elite provides irrefutable empirical evidence of their elitist character as well as the striking continuity of prewar patterns and practices.

The first and thus far the only in-depth study of a major government agency in Japan is Chalmers Johnson's book on *MITI and the Japanese Miracle,* cited at the outset of this chapter. His is not simply a detailed chronological analysis of a pivotal bureaucratic organization but a penetrating study of the Japanese political economy as well. It presents a convincing argument that the Japanese miracle owed much to the planning, leadership, and "administrative guidance" of the Ministry of International Trade and Industry, in both its prewar and postwar incarnations.

The latest addition to the English-language monographic literature on Japanese bureaucracy is Yung H. Park's *Bureaucrats and Ministers in Contemporary Japanese Government.*[5] Based on interviews with nearly two hundred politicians, bureaucrats, scholars, and other individuals in Japan, the study makes a persuasive case for the revision of conventional wisdom that relegates LDP politicians to an ornamental role in policy making; it shows that the era of manifest bureaucratic supremacy is being replaced by one in which politicians are becoming increasingly assertive in the policy arena.

Several monographs that focus on policy making in Japan are worth mentioning, for they help to illuminate, either directly or indirectly, the role of the government bureaucracy in the formulation and implementation of Japanese public policy. They are, in the order of publication, *How the Conservatives Rule Japan,* by Nathaniel B. Thayer;[6] *Party in Power: The Japanese Liberal-Democrats and Policy-making,* by Haruhiro Fukui;[7] Japan's *Parliament: An Introduction,* by Hans H. Baerwald;[8] *Contemporary Japanese Budget Politics,* by John C. Campbell;[9] and *Patterns of Japanese Policymaking: Experiences from Higher Education,* by T. J. Pempel.[10]

4. Princeton: Princeton Unviersity Press, 1969.
5. Berkeley: University of California, Institute of East Asian Studies, 1986.
6. Princeton: Princeton University Press, 1969.
7. Berkeley: University of California Press, 1970.
8. London: Cambridge University Press, 1974.
9. Berkeley: University of California Press, 1977.
10. Boulder, Colo.: Westview Press, 1978.

There are a number of anthologies that contain studies on various aspects of Japanese bureaucracy. One of the most useful is *Modern Japanese Organization and Decision-Making,* edited by Ezra F. Vogel.[11] It contains studies on government bureaucracy, economic organizations, newspapers, and an institution of higher learning. Also noteworthy is *Public Administration in Japan,* edited by Kiyoaki Tsuji.[12] It presents brief overviews of a wide range of topics in Japanese public administration, from administrative guidance to local administration and finance, by Japanese scholars. Finally, *Policymaking in Contemporary Japan,* edited by T. J. Pempel,[13] contains a literature survey, conceptual syntheses, and a number of case studies.

Studies of Japanese bureaucracy or administrative elite are also found in anthologies of a more general nature[14] as well as in various scholarly journals. Some of the journal articles, along with most of the works listed above, will be cited later in this study. In sum, there is a sizable body of works of varying lengths on nearly all important aspects of the subject. Nonetheless, a reasonably up-to-date and moderately comprehensive monograph on either Japanese government bureaucracy as a whole or on its higher civil service (or administrative elite) is conspicuously lacking. The monograph that comes closest to fitting the preceding description, Kubota's study of higher civil servants in postwar Japan, presents data up to 1959.

When we turn to the Japanese-language literature, we are struck by a staggering quantity of books, articles, and government publications. Although most of the books and articles can be characterized as either scholarly or journalistic, some of them defy classification. For example, there are a number of books by former bureaucrats that purport to be more than memoirs, containing information of a general nature as well as commentaries on various aspects of government bureaucracy.[15]

To cite a few examples of scholarly monographs, we may note *Shinpan Nihon kanryōsei no kenkyū* (A Study of Japanese Bureaucracy,

11. Berkeley: University of California Press, 1975.
12. Tokyo: University of Tokyo Press, 1984.
13. Ithaca: Cornell University Press, 1977.
14. To cite but two examples: Yoshinori Ide and Takeshi Ishida, "The Education and Recruitment of Governing Elites in Modern Japan" in Rupert Wilkinson, ed., *Governing Elites: Studies in Training and Selection* (New York: Oxford University Press, 1969), pp. 108–134, and T. J. Pempel, "Organizing for Efficiency: The Higher Civil Service in Japan" in Ezra N. Suleiman ed., *Bureaucrats and Policy Making: A Comparative Overview* (New York: Holmes and Meier, 1984), pp. 72–106.
15. Examples of this genre include Sakakibara Eisuke, *Nihon o enshutsu suru shin kanryō-zō* [A Portrait of New Bureaucrats Who Direct Japan] (Tokyo: Yamade Shobō,

New Edition), by Tsuji Kiyoaki;[16] *Sengo Nihon no kanryōsei* (Postwar Japan's Bureaucratic System), by Muramatsu Michio;[17] *Kanryō no kenkyū: Fumetsu no pawa, 1868–1983* (A Study of Bureaucrats: Immortal Power, 1868–1983), by Hata Ikuhiko;[18] and *Ōkura kanryō shihai no shūen* (The End of Domination by Finance Ministry Bureaucrats), by Yamaguchi Jirō.[19]

Tsuji's book consists of a series of essays on various aspects of Japanese bureaucracy by a leading authority on the subject. It presents an orthodox view, in which the phenomenon of bureaucratic dominance is both explained and evaluated. Muramatsu's work departs from Tsuji's both in methodology and in conclusion. Using the survey research method, Muramatsu finds the orthodox view of bureaucratic dominance to be divorced from the reality, which, he argues, is marked by a significant increase in the power of the ruling-party politicians.

Hata, a bureaucrat-turned-academic, presents a wealth of statistical data on the evolution of bureaucracy from the Meiji period to the early 1980s. Particularly useful are his data on the social background of higher civil servants and the results of the higher civil-service examinations in both the prewar and postwar periods. He does not, however, directly address the issue of the changing balance of power between bureaucrats and politicians.

Yamaguchi represents a new breed of political scientists who are taking a critical look at conventional wisdom. Inspired by the work of Muramatsu, Yamaguchi sets out to analyze the changing complexion of Japanese bureaucracy. Through theoretically guided case studies, he attempts to explain when and how the erosion of the power base of bureaucracy began. His basic argument, nonetheless, is not that bureaucrats have become powerless but that they have become partners of politicians in the policy arena.

As examples of journalistic works, we may list *Nihon no kanryō* (Japan's Bureaucrats), by Tahara Sōichirō;[20] *Ōkura-shō shukei-kyoku*

1977); Hayashi Shūzō, *Nihon kanryō kenkoku ron* [On State Building by Japanese Bureaucrats] (Tokyo: Gyōsei Mondai Kenkyūjo, 1982); Katō Eiichi, *Kanryō desu, yoroshiku* [I Am a Bureaucrat, Pleased to Meet You] (Tokyo: TBS Buritanika, 1983); and Ōkita Saburō, *Nihon kanryō jijō* [Conditions of Japanese Bureaucrats] (Tokyo: TBS Buritanika, 1984).

16. Tokyo: Tōkyō Daigaku Shuppankai, 1969.
17. Tokyo: Tōyō Keizai Shinpōsha, 1981.
18. Tokyo: Kōdansha, 1983.
19. Tokyo: Iwanami Shoten, 1987.
20. Tokyo: Bungei Shunjū, 1980.

(The Budget Bureau of the Finance Ministry), by Kuribayashi Yoshi-mitsu;[21] *"Sengo umare" erīto kanryō no sugao* (The Real Faces of Elite Bureaucrats Who Were "Born After the War"), by Koitabashi Jirō;[22] and *Nihon kanryō hakusho* (White Paper on Japanese Bureaucrats), by Sataka Makoto.[23]

Tahara's book guides the reader through the inner workings of fifteen central-government ministries and agencies. Not only does it provide much insight into the idiosyncrasies of each organization but it also helps to dispel the myth of bureaucratic dominance, showing the myriad constraints under which bureaucrats must operate.

Unlike Tahara, Kuribayashi focuses on a single bureaucratic organization, the legendary Budget Bureau of the Finance Ministry, drawing on long years of observation, interviews with seventeen persons who have headed the Budget Bureau in the postwar period (only three decreased former bureau chiefs were excluded), and factual and statistical information on the Bureau's structure and personnel. One learns fascinating details about the people who help shape Japan's national budget, their background, values, and modes of operation. One also gains insight into the dynamics of the Budget Bureau as a living organization. Kuribayashi has also published a twin volume on the Tax Bureau (Shuzei-kyoku) of the Finance Ministry.[24]

Koitabashi's book provides us with still another view of Japan's administrative elite: the backgrounds, perspectives, and experiences of twenty section chiefs, all of whom were born in 1945. Intrigued by the news that a total of thirty-three bureaucrats born in that watershed year became section chiefs in the national-government ministries and agencies in 1985, Koitabashi sought them out, managing to interview twenty of them. What emerges from his interviews is a portrait of elite bureaucrats who are bright, dedicated, and hardworking. Their single most important trait is a strong sense of mission—not only to serve their country but also to bridge the gap between those who have experienced war and those who haven't.

Sataka's professed goal is to delineate bureaucrats' modus operandi as well as true intentions (*honne*) through concrete examples and illustrations. What he actually does is to provide a guided tour of the

21. Tokyo: Kōdansha, 1986.
22. Ibid.
23. Ibid.
24. *Ōkurashō shuzei-kyoku* [The Tax Bureau of the Finance Ministry] (Tokyo: Kōdansha, 1987).

literature on Japanese bureaucracy. He makes up for the lack of depth with a breadth of coverage. Not only are all the key issues mentioned, but an impressive number of works by a wide range of authors are cited and summarized.

Among magazines the most useful is *Kankai* (The Bureaucratic World), which typically carries an up-to-date profile of a central-government ministry or agency in every issue. Over the years it has published serialized articles on such topics as administrative vice ministers, "noncareer" (that is, nonelite) civil servants, former bureaucrats who have become members of the Diet, and the phenomenon of *zoku giin* (the so-called tribal Dietmen whose specialization and expertise in specific policy areas have helped to undercut the power of bureaucrats). Another magazine worthy of special mention is *Bungei shunjū* (Spring and Autumn in Literature and Arts), whose monthly column, "Kasumigaseki konhidensharu" (Confidential Report from Kasumigaseki), albeit gossipy, helps the reader to keep abreast of the latest developments in Japan's bureaucratic circles.

As sources of authoritative facts and, especially, statistics pertaining to the structure and operations of the Japanese civil service, nothing can match government publications. The latter, indeed, are indispensable to a study of Japan's administrative elite. Particularly useful are the annual reports and monthly bulletins of the National Personnel Authority (NPA) [Jinji-in]. The former can be found in various sources, notably *Kanpō* (Official Gazette), *Nenji hōkokusho* (Annual Report), and *Kōmuin hakusho* (White Paper on Civil Servants). Of these the most accessible is *Kōmuin hakusho,* which began to appear in the mid-1970s. Prepared by the NPA for submission to the Diet and the Cabinet, the annual reports contain both narrative accounts of and comprehensive statistics on such topics as civil-service examinations, appointments and resignations of civil servants, compensation, disciplinary actions against civil servants, training programs, and the handling of appeals by civil servants on adverse personnel actions.

The NPA's monthly bulletin, known as *Jinji-in geppō,* serves as an important supplement to the annual reports. The bulletin provides not only much information and insight that are not found in the annual reports but also more details on items that receive only a passing mention in the latter. Texts of roundtable discussions on various issues confronting the civil service, in which both civil servants and outside observers take part, are frequently illuminating, as are essays and reminiscences by those who have had firsthand experience in events relating to the civil service. The bulletin frequently carries full texts of key reports on such topics as a reappraisal of training programs, the NPA's annual recommendation on civil-servants' compensation, and the NPA's recommendation on reducing the civil-servants' work week (with the aim of eventually introducing a five-day week). By contrast, the annual reports typically carry only summaries or excerpts.

In short, if conducted with diligence and discrimination, a scrutiny of Japanese-language sources that are publicly available can go a long way toward yielding a credible picture of the key dimensions of Japanese-government bureaucracy, including the salient attributes of its administrative elite.

As the preceding discussion makes plain, anyone who ventures into the realm of Japanese bureaucracy is entering not a terra incognita but a well-mapped terrain. What, then, does this study propose to contribute? For one thing, it is designed to fill the void in the literature: an up-to-date overview of several key dimensions of Japan's administrative elite. More important, it proposes to explore the question of whether and to what extent the salient patterns of Japanese government bureaucracy as manifested by its administrative elite are idiosyncratic. This would necessitate a quasi-comparative perspective. Although a full-fledged, cross-national comparison is highly desirable, it is beyond the capability of a lone researcher with limited resources.

As an alternative to a full-scale comparative analysis, I propose to introduce a crude comparative backdrop from time to time. The backdrop will necessarily be sketchy, eclectic, and unbalanced; occasionally, it will substitute conceptual models for specific details. Four advanced industrial democracies will be used to provide the comparative frame of reference: the United States, Great Britain, France, and West Germany. Although a plausible argument for choosing other countries can no doubt be made—for example, Asian countries such as China and Korea, which have a common cultural heritage with Japan[25]—the four Western democracies were chosen for two reasons: First, the political criterion of democracy and the economic criterion of advanced industrialization seem to outweigh other considerations. Second, in a practical sense, these Western countries have had more influence on Japanese bureaucracy than have China or other non-Western countries. In fact, the Japanese themselves frequently use these four countries as referents for comparison.

25. See, for example, Albert M. Craig, ed., *Japan: A Comparative View* (Princeton: Princeton University Press, 1979).

Another thing this study attempts to present is a diachronic analysis of sorts. What are the principal elements of continuity and change between the prewar and postwar periods? Can we identify any significant signs of change during the postwar period? Relevant statistical evidence will be scrutinized with the aim of finding tentative answers to these questions.

In conclusion, the study will attempt to assess the strengths and weaknesses of Japan's administrative elite and to speculate on the practical and theoretical implications of the Japanese experience.

We shall begin by sketching in broad strokes the historical back-drop—namely, the salient characteristics of Japanese bureaucracy in the prewar period. Next, we shall discuss the first serious attempt in Japanese history to reform the legal and structural framework of its bureaucracy during the first and only foreign occupation that Japan has ever experienced, the American occupation following Japanese defeat in World War II.

Against this broad background, we proceed to analyze several major dimensions of Japan's administrative elite—recruitment, promotion, socialization, modes of interaction, and rewards. For each of these dimensions we shall examine a wide array of information—pertinent statistical data, impressionistic evidence, scholarly opinions, journalistic interpretations, and reports of participant-observers. All but a handful of the sources utilized in the study are in the public domain; the few exceptions consist of unpublished government documents and insights gained from informal conversations and interviews with government officials.

In brief, the following pages will (1) delineate the major attributes of Japan's administrative elite, managers of the Japanese developmental state, (2) assess "the universality and the particularity of the Japanese experience,"[26] (3) ascertain the patterns of continuity and change in the structure and functioning of the administrative elite, and (4) explore the implications of the Japanese model.

26. The phrase is borrowed from Albert M. Craig, "Introduction," ibid., p. 8.

CHAPTER TWO

Japanese Bureaucracy During the Prewar Era

To a striking degree, the characteristics of Japanese government bureaucracy were formed in the prewar period. A brief survey of its historical background will, therefore, enable us to appreciate the extent of continuity and change between the prewar and postwar patterns of Japanese bureaucracy. We shall dwell upon the circumstances surrounding the emergence of modern bureaucracy in the Meiji era, its power and prestige, and the outstanding aspects of its structure and behavior, notably, stratification, elitism, legalism, security of tenure, and retirement practices.

EMERGENCE

If by bureaucracy we mean a pattern of organizing and managing human affairs on the basis, inter alia, of expertise demonstrated by education or experience, bureaucracy did not emerge in Japan until after the Meiji Restoration in the latter half of the nineteenth century.[1] To be

---

1. Mori Hiroshi and Yazawa Shūjirō, *Kanryōsei no shihai* [Rule by Bureaucracy] (Tokyo: Yūhikaku, 1981), p. 162; Ōe Shinobu, "Nihon ni okeru kanryōsei no kiseki" [The Locus of the Bureaucratic System in Japan], *Hōgaku seminaà zōkan, sōgō tokushu shirizu, 9: Naikaku to kanryō* [Legal Studies Seminar Extra Issue, Comprehensive Special Series, 9: The Cabinet and Bureaucrats], Mar. 1979, p. 105.

sure, Japan did borrow the idea of civil-service examinations from T'ang China in the seventh century, but, unlike the situation in China, where it flourished, the idea was never fully implemented.[2]

During the Tokugawa period (1603–1868), structural arrangements for administration that existed both in the central government and in the fiefs were patrimonial rather than bureaucratic. The criterion of recruitment to key offices was primarily ascriptive, such as membership in the shogun's immediate vassalage in Edo and the possession of a specified feudal family rank in the fiefs. In its waning days, however, the Tokugawa shogunate was compelled by the crisis precipitated by the arrival of Commodore Matthew C. Perry's four "black ships" to recruit officials on the basis of "demonstrable merit." This was done, it should be stressed, only within the elitist boundaries. Nonetheless, the recruitment of "men of relatively low social status" to important positions in Edo and, particularly, the "appointment of subjects of individual fiefs to offices in the shogunal government" signaled the beginning of the end of the traditional feudal hierarchy.[3]

If the Meiji Restoration opened the way for a fundamental restructuring of Japan's political system, it did not usher in a modern bureaucratic system immediately. On the contrary, the first two decades of the Meiji era saw the implementation of a spoils system: key government positions were doled out to those who played the leading role in the Restoration—the lower samurai from the fiefs of Satsuma, Choshu, Tosa, and Hizen as well as court nobles who had collaborated. An interesting aspect of the spoils system pertained to its use as a device for coopting the opponents of the new regime. Some leaders of the

2. Spaulding, *Imperial Japan's Higher Civil Service Examinations*, pp. 9–19. For a study that underscores the early development of bureaucracy in Japan, arguing that Japanese bureaucracy had reached maturity as early as the late seventh and early eighth centuries, see Nomura Tadao, *Nihon kanryō no genzō* [The Original Portrait of Japanese Bureaucrats] (Tokyo: PHP Kenkyūjo, 1983). T. J. Pempel writes: "Bureaucratic strands wind through Japan's history from at least the Nara Period (710–84), but the establishment of a modern bureaucracy dates from the opening of Japan by the West in the middle of the nineteenth century." See his "Organizing for Efficiency," p. 78.

3. Masamichi Inoki, "The Civil Bureaucracy" in Robert E. Ward and Dankwart A. Rustow, eds., *Political Modernization in Japan and Turkey* (Princeton: Princeton University Press, 1964), pp. 283–87. See also Bernard S. Silverman, "The Bureaucracy and Economic Development in Japan," *Asian Survey* 5, no. 11(Nov. 1965), pp. 529–37. Even Nomura's study shows that ascriptive criteria eclipsed those of achievement in the recruitment and promotion of officials in the eighth and ninth centuries. Nomura, *Nihon kanryō no genzō*, esp. pp. 63–91.

opposition clamoring for "freedom and civil rights" (*jiyū minken*) were coopted into the government.[4]

As the forces of democracy grew in strength, however, the Meiji oligarchs were compelled to make concessions, including a commitment to establish a parliament by the year 1890. The need to cope with opposition politicians and to guard against the possibility of the abuse of "free appointment" privileges by party politicians upon winning power provided the oligarchs with a strong incentive to institutionalize the merit principle in the recruitment of officials. The most compelling pressure of all, however, emanated from the outside. The revision of the humiliating unequal treaties with Western powers embodying the principle of extraterritoriality necessitated the establishment of a modern judicial system. This in turn called for the enactment of a constitution as well as administrative, civil, and criminal laws along Western lines. All this would also require the adoption of a credible system of recruiting officials to man the judicial apparatus.[5]

To fashion a modern system of government equipped to handle all these problems, the Meiji oligarchs not only invited Western experts to Japan but also dispatched delegations to Europe on extended learning tours. Those who went abroad on such missions, of whom Itō Hirobumi was the most prominent, appear to have been deeply impressed by what they saw and heard in Berlin and Vienna. From such Prussian and Austrian mentors as Rudolf von Gneist, Albert Mosse, and Lorenz von Stein they learned the rudimentary principles of limited constitutionalism, parliamentary government, and a civil-service system. Regarding the latter, two things struck the Japanese most: the principle of imperial prerogative in appointment and the principle of recruitment based on educational attainments. Those with the proper

---

4. Wada Zen'ichi, "Bunkan nin'yō seido no rekishi" [The History of the Appointment System for Civil Officials], I, *Jinji-in geppō* [Monthly Bulletin of the National Personnel Authority] 95(Jan. 1959): 10. According to data compiled by proponents of *jiyū minken* in 1874, 65.7 percent of *chokunin* officials (bureau chiefs and above) and 37.6 percent of *sōnin* officials came from the fiefs of Satsuma, Chōshu, Tosa, and Hizen. Satsuma and Chōshu together accounted for 44.8 percent of the *chokunin* and 27.8 percent of the *sōnin* officials. Fukumoto Kunio, *Kanryō* [Bureaucrats] (Tokyo: Kōbundo, 1959), pp. 81–82. For definitions of *chokunin* and *sōnin* officials, see table 1 and the accompanying text later in this chapter.

5. Spaulding, *Imperial Japan's Higher Civil Service Examinations,* esp. pp. 4–5, 34. For a Marxian analysis of the relationship between the *jiyū minken* movement and bureaucracy, see Yamanaka Einosuke, *Nihon kindai kokka no keisei to kanryōsei* [The Bureaucracy and the Formation of the Modern Japanese State] (Tokyo: Kōbundo, 1974).

educational credentials, the Japanese were told, must first pass appropriate examinations before being appointed.[6]

The trials, tribulations, and politics that accompanied the adoption of coherent civil-service examinations for administrative, judicial, and diplomatic personnel need not detain us here, for they have already been analyzed in Spaulding's definitive study. What needs to be stressed, however, is that although the German model clearly exerted major influence on the thinking of Japanese leaders, the system they ultimately adopted was far from a carbon copy of the Prussian prototype. In terms of the sequence of the key steps involved, the first significant step was the establishment of law schools in the 1870s—the French law course in the Justice Ministry and the Anglo-American law course in the Education Ministry. Next came the establishment of the bar examination in 1876, followed by the adoption of the Judicial Appointment Rule in 1884.[7]

Then, in July 1887, the first general-examination ordinance was promulgated, extending examinations from the judiciary to all parts of the government. The new system set up two levels of civil-service examinations: higher examinations for *sonin* officials and ordinary ones for *hannin* officials. It retained, however, the privileged status of Tokyo Imperial University (*Tōdai*) graduates. Just as they were exempt from the bar and judicial examinations, so they would continue to be exempt from the higher civil-service examinations. Although the exemption under the 1887 ordinance would be extended to Tōdai graduates in law and letters only, that in no way diminished the privileged status of all Tōdai graduates. Tōdai men in the other fields, such as agriculture, engineering, and medicine, would be eligible for appointment to technical posts in government without taking examinations along with all other technical personnel. The requirement of a three-year training period following initial appointment was an echo of the German model. In the revamping of the examination system in 1893, however, the Tōdai exemption was abolished in the administrative examinations, though it was retained in the judicial. In the same year, separate examinations for diplomatic and consular personnel were established. Then, during the first two decades of the twentieth century a struggle was waged to ensure legal equality among all

6. Spaulding, *Imperial Japan*, pp. 46–50.
7. Ibid., pp. 33–72.

examination candidates, culminating in the abolition of exemptions in toto; a unification of examination systems was also accomplished, bringing under the single umbrella of higher examinations the three disparate fields of law, administration, and diplomacy.[8]

POWER AND PRESTIGE

According to the distinguished Japanese political scientist Rōyama Masamichi, the Meiji Restoration helped to transform Japan from a "feudal police state" (*hōkenteki keisatsu kokka*) into a "centralized bureaucratic state" (*chūō shūkenteki kanryō kokka*). Although the Meiji government enshrined the doctrine of imperial sovereignty, he writes, it was in reality controlled by a coalition of *hanbatsu* (domain cliques) and court nobles. More important, it replaced the feudal warrior system with its twin functional equivalents, the military and the bureaucracy.[9]

Bureaucracy, in other words, was part of the ruling elite in prewar Japan. Its power and prestige were greatly augmented by the explicit linking of bureaucratic authority and imperial prerogatives. Article 10 of the Meiji constitution of 1889 stipulated that "the Emperor determines the organization of the different branches of the administration and salaries of all civil and military officers, and appoints and dismisses the same."[10] This implied that officials were appointed by and accountable to the Emperor only; hence they were the Emperor's officials (*tennō no kanri*) rather than civil servants. So long as the prestige of the Emperor remained supreme and the myth of imperial rule was kept alive, therefore, his officials could exercise virtually unfettered authority in his name.

The position of the bureaucracy vis-à-vis political parties and the Imperial Diet was bolstered by the constitution and practice alike. Pursuant to the advice of their Prussian and Austrian mentors, the Meiji oligarchs had taken pains to establish the framework of the bureaucratic

---

8. Ibid., pp. 73–178; Watanabe Yasuo, "Nihon no kōmuinsei" [The Civil Service System of Japan] in Tsuji Kiyoaki, ed., *Gyōseigaku kōza, dai 2-kan: Gyōsei no rekishi* [Lectures on Public Administration, vol. 2: The History of Public Administration] (Tokyo: Tōkyō Daigaku Shuppankai, 1978), pp. 114–16.

9. Rōyama Masamichi, "Kindai kanri seido no hattatsu" [The Development of a Modern Bureaucratic System] in Rōyama Masamichi, *Gyōseigaku kenkyū ronbunshū* [Collection of Research Papers on Public Administration] (Tokyo: Keisō Shobō, 1965), p. 229.

10. Spaulding, *Imperial Japan*, p. 83; Wada, "Bunkan nin'yo seido no rekishi," I, p. 13.

system prior to the formation of the Diet. This meant that all the rules regarding the structure and functioning of the bureaucracy were embodied in imperial ordinances rather than in statutes. This practice was continued even after the Diet came into being.[11]

Although the Diet did emerge as a significant political force, particularly during the Taisho era (1912–26), it never attained sufficient power to control the executive branch. As the instrument and embodiment of executive power, the bureaucracy was thus assured a dominant role in the political system. Further enhancing bureaucratic power was the entry of bureaucrats into political parties, eventually constituting one of the two key groups in ruling parties, together with the so-called "pure politicians."[12] As Spaulding suggests, the bureaucracy was never a pliant tool of the cabinet, its putative master. Virtually all cabinets, including military cabinets "at the zenith of their power," found it necessary to govern the country "by informal coalitions or working agreements with career civilian bureaucrats, chiefly examination men."[13] A striking index of the power of the bureaucracy is that, of the thirty men who served as prime ministers in prewar Japan, only two lacked a bureaucratic background, either civil or military. The exceptions were Prince Saionji Kinmochi (1906–08 and 1911–12) and Prince Konoe Fumimaro (1937 and 1940–41).[14]

Generally speaking, power and prestige go hand in hand; hence, despite the absence of survey data, one may surmise that bureaucrats in prewar Japan, symbols as well as wielders of awesome power, enjoyed high prestige. One indication of their prestige was the consistently keen competition for the higher civil-service examinations, the gateway to the upper ranks of the bureaucracy. In the period 1928–43, the failure rate of applicants for the administrative section of the higher civil-service examinations averaged 90 percent. Moreover, the overwhelming proportion of the successful candidates came from Tokyo Imperial Univer-

11. Inoki, "The Civil Bureaucracy," pp. 291–92.

12. Robert A. Scalapino, "Elections and Political Modernization in Prewar Japan" in Robert E. Ward, ed., *Political Development in Modern Japan* (Princeton: Princeton University Press, 1968), pp. 249–91; Robert A. Scalapino, *Democracy and the Party Movement in Prewar Japan* (Berkeley: University of California Press, 1962).

13. Robert M. Spaulding, Jr., "The Bureaucracy as a Political Force, 1920–45" in James W. Morley, ed., *Dilemmas of Growth in Prewar Japan* (Princeton: Princeton University Press, 1971), p. 76.

14. Inoki, "The Civil Bureaucracy," p. 293; *Bessatsu kokkai benran: Shiryō sōshūhen* [Separate-Volume Supplement to the National Diet Handbook: Complete Collection of Materials] (Tokyo: Nihon Seikei Shinbun Shuppanbu, 1975), pp. 6–7.

sity, the most prestigious of all institutions of higher learning in prewar Japan.[15]

It is worth noting that bureaucrats may have been more feared than respected. Their arrogance was legendary, and tales of the abuse of bureaucratic power were legion.[16] The well-known phrase, *kanson minpi* (officials revered, citizens despised), not only summed up a major theme in the political culture of prewar Japan; it also epitomized the reality of bureaucratic dominance in Japanese society.

STRUCTURE AND BEHAVIOR

STRATIFICATION

The prewar Japanese bureaucracy was a veritable caste system. It embraced distinct classes of persons, and the status differences and social distances between the classes were wide. The most basic distinction was between officials (*kanri*) and nonofficials (*hikanri*). The officials, who were appointed either by the Emperor or by the government to which authority had been delegated, owed an unlimited loyalty to the Emperor and were regulated by public law. The nonofficials, on the other hand, lay outside the scope of the Emperor's appointment authority and were subject to the rules of employment contract in private law.[17]

The officials were divided into four distinct classes: (1) *shinninkan*, (2) *chokuninkan*, (3) *sōninkan*, and (4) *hanninkan*. The main criterion of this classification was the distance from the Emperor or, alternatively, the mode of appointment. *Shinnin* officials were awarded their letters of appointment, signed by the Emperor and countersigned by the prime minister, in a palace ceremony called the *shinnin shiki* and attended by the Emperor. *Chokunin* officials, too, received letters of appointment bearing the signatures of both the Emperor and the prime minister but without a palace ceremony. *Sōnin* officials, on the other hand, were appointed by the prime minister acting on behalf of the cabinet and on

---

15. Spaulding, *Imperial Japan*, pp. 265, 268–69. Some relevant statistics will be presented later in this chapter (see table 2).

16. See, for example, Fukumoto, *Kanryō*, pp. 80–95; Mori and Yazawa, *Kanryōsei no shihai*, pp. 162–65 and passim.

17. Watanabe, "Nihon no kōmuinsei," pp. 112; Miyake Tarō, *Gyōseigaku to gyōsei kanri* [Public Administration and Public Management] (Tokyo: Sakai Shoten, 1974), pp. 78–88.

TABLE 1   *Classification of Higher Officials in Prewar Japan*

Class	Grade	Illustrative Positions
shinninkan		cabinet minister
chokuninkan	1	vice-minister
		senior bureau chief
	2	bureau chief
		senior section chief
sōninkan	3	section chief
	4	senior *jimukan* (assistant section chief)
	5	*jimukan*
	6	*jimukan*; chief of a tax office
	7	chief, tax office
	8	chief, police station
	9	chief, security guards

SOURCE: Hata Ikuhiko, *Kanryō no kenkyū: Fumetsu no pawa, 1868–1983* (Tokyo: Kōdansha, 1983), p. 75.

authority delegated by the Emperor. Finally, *hannin* officials were appointed by the individual ministers exercising delegated authority. The first three classes of officials were collectively known as *kōtōkan* (higher officials). There were nine grades among the *kōtōkan* and four among the *hanninkan*.[18] Table 1 displays the ranks and grades of the higher officials, together with their corresponding positions. The barrier between the higher and ordinary officials was so great as to be all but insurmountable; they could be compared with commissioned and noncommissioned officers in the armed forces.[19]

Because they were outside the realm of public law, the nonofficials (*hikanri*) were subject to the vagaries of the changing needs and budgetary resources of individual ministries. Neither their qualifications nor their duties were precisely defined. Nonetheless, there were generally three types of nonofficials: (1) *koin*, (2) *yōnin*, and (3) *shokutaku*. The *koin* performed routine clerical tasks, but many of them aspired for promotion to the *hannin* rank eventually. The *yōnin* engaged in manual

18. Watanabe, "Nihon no kōmuinsei," pp. 112–13; Miyake, *Gyōseigaku to gyōsei kanri*, pp. 79–82; Murobushi Tetsurō, *Kōkyū kanryō* [Higher Civil Servants] (Tokyo: Sekai Shoin, 1983), pp. 28–29.

19. For a comparison of the *kōtōkan-hanninkan* dichotomy to the distinction between commissioned and noncommissioned officers in the military, see Spaulding, "The Bureaucracy as a Political Force," pp. 37–38 and Johnson, *MITI and the Japanese Miracle*, pp. 57–58. For an inside account of the privileges of *kōtōkan*, see Hayashi, *Nihon kanryō kenkoku ron*, pp. 5–10.

labor. Finally, the *shokutaku* typically had special ties with a cabinet
minister or a parliamentary vice-minister, serving him for the duration
of their terms of office. Many *shokutaku* were retired officials and
persons engaged in specialized research activities for the government.[20]

We have already seen that civil-service examinations were the
principal means by which civil officials were recruited. Those who
passed the higher civil-service examinations were eligible for appointment as *sōninkan* trainee (*shihō*), whereas those who passed the
ordinary civil-service examinations could become *hanninkan* apprentice
(*minarai*). In neither case was appointment automatic. Passing these
examinations simply certified that the successful candidates were
qualified for government service. The actual hiring was done by each
government ministry or agency, typically following an interview. In
most cases the candidates themselves had to take the initiative. From
1887 to 1893, graduates of Tokyo Imperial University were exempt
from the higher civil-service examinations. In a sense, graduation from
Tōdai could be viewed as the chief means of recruitment into the higher
civil service, whereas passing the examination was the auxiliary means.
For Tōdai was intended from the outset to serve as a training school for
the core members of the bureaucracy.[21]

Another important mode of civil-service recruitment was *senkō*
(evaluation), which was applied to teachers, engineers, physicians, and
other technical personnel. Until 1899, moreover, all *chokunin* officials,
which included not only section chiefs, bureau chiefs, and vice-ministers
but also the chief of the cabinet secretariat, the chief of the cabinet
legislation bureau, and prefectural governors, were subject to "free
appointment." The scope of discretionary appointment, however,
steadily dwindled in subsequent years. Finally, the significance of the
ordinary civil-service examinations was considerably diluted in 1913,
when all graduates of middle schools were granted exemption; previously, only public-middle-school graduates had been exempt. In addition, all *koin* with five years or more of experience became eligible for
hannin positions.[22]

Behind the veil of seeming complexity stood one simple fact: the
prewar Japanese bureaucracy contained distinctly unequal strata. At the
bottom of the pecking order were "nonofficials." Then came ordinary

20. Watanabe, "Nihon no kanryōsei," pp. 113–14.
21. Ibid., pp. 114–15; Wada, "Bunkan nin'yō seido no rekishi," I, pp. 11–13.
22. Watanabe, "Nihon no kōmuinsei," pp. 115–16; Wada, "Bunkan nin'yō seido no
rekishi," II, *Jinji-in geppō* 96(Feb. 1959): 13–15.

or *hannin* officials. Above them all reigned higher officials or *kōtōkan*. Although the wall separating the ordinary and higher officials was by no means impenetrable, it was nonetheless high. After the abolition of the "imperial university privilege" (*teidai tokken*) in 1893, nearly all aspirants for elite administrative positions had to scale the heights of the higher civil-service examinations.

ELITISM

Another striking characteristic of the prewar Japanese bureaucracy was its domination by graduates of Tokyo Imperial University. Of the ninety-seven men who were appointed as higher-civil-service trainees (administrative) in the 1888–91 period, all but nine were Tōdai graduates. More important, in two of the four years involved, not a single examination candidate was appointed. In fact, administrative examinations were not even held in 1891, a situation that was repeated in the following year. Inasmuch as "the function of the examinations was simply to fill positions not claimed by Tōdai graduates," no examinations were necessary in those years, because of the availability of a sufficient number of Tōdai men. The government's decision in 1893 to abolish the Imperial University exemption stemmed not simply from its desire to accommodate the critics of the privilege but also from the practical need to cope with growing numbers of Tōdai graduates.[23]

However, the preponderance of Tōdai men in the upper echelons of the bureaucracy continued unabated. The principal reason for this was that Tōdai men dominated the administrative section of the higher civil-service examinations in both absolute and proportionate terms. Whereas the overall success rates (ratios of successful to total candidates) were 25 percent in 1906, 7 percent in 1941, 14 percent in 1942, and 15 percent in 1943, those for Tōdai men were 50 percent, 16 percent, 29 percent, and 25 percent in those years. About 47 percent of all successful candidates in the 1941–43 period came from Tōdai, whereas about 10 percent was supplied by Kyoto Imperial University.[24] If we look at longer time periods, as we do in table 2, the preponderance of Tōdai men in the examinations becomes even more pronounced. Roughly six out of ten successes came from Tōdai. The two top

23. Spaulding, *Imperial Japan*, pp. 90–99. The quotation is from p. 91.
24. These statistics were either adapted or estimated from ibid., pp. 268–69 and 277 (tables 48, 49, and 54).

TABLE 2   *Successful Candidates in the Administrative*
Section of the Higher Civil-Service Examination, by
Year and University Background

	Year							
	1894–1917		*1918–1931*		*1932–1947*		*1894–1947*	
University	N	%	N	%	N	%	N	%
Tokyo	1,566	76.3	2,033	57.8	2,370	59.3	5,969	62.4
Kyoto	101	4.9	379	10.8	315	7.9	799	8.4
Other	385	18.8	1,107	31.4	1,309	32.8	2,797	29.2
TOTAL	2,052	100.0	3,519	100.0	3,994	100.0	9,565	100.0

SOURCE: Hata Ikuhiko, *Kanryō no kenkyū: Fumetsu no pawa, 1868–1983* (Tokyo: Kōdansha, 1983), p. 18.

universities, Tōdai and Kyōdai, together accounted for seven out of every ten successes.

Inoki Masamichi's analysis of the academic background of 1,377 higher civil servants (excluding judicial officials) whose biographical sketches appeared in the 1937 edition of *Jinji kōshinroku* (Who's Who) revealed that 73.1 percent were Tōdai graduates and 9.0 percent were Kyōdai graduates.[25] This is consistent with the data on the successful candidates in the higher examinations discussed above. In comparative terms, the only other country that can match this record is the United Kingdom. According to R. K. Kelsall, the academic background of British senior civil servants (those above the rank of assistant secretary) in 1939 was as follows: of those who entered the civil service through open competition, 51.3 percent had graduated from Oxford and 25.7 percent from Cambridge. When those who entered the civil service through other routes are added, the overall proportion of Oxford men becomes 41.3 percent, and that of Cambridge men 20.1 percent. Significantly, 19 percent of the 1939 senior civil servants included in Kelsall's analysis lacked university education altogether.[26]

If, as suggested above, the predominance of Tōdai men in the upper ranks of the bureaucracy was a function of their preponderance among the successful candidates in the higher civil-service examinations, then

25. Inoki, "The Civil Bureaucracy," p. 296.
26. R. K. Kelsall, *Higher Civil Servants in Britain* (London: Routledge and Kegan Paul, 1955), p. 138. table 22. The size of Kelsall's sample was 179.

what accounted for this latter phenomenon? A simplistic explanation might be that, assuming that the examinations were valid and reliable, Tōdai men were better prepared for them by virtue of their superior intellectual ability and academic training. Given its high prestige, Tōdai attracted both high-caliber students and distinguished faculty. It is also widely believed that Tōdai men enjoyed an edge in competition thanks to the near monopoly of the posts of higher examiners by Tōdai professors.[27]

According to Spaulding, the proportion of Tōdai professors among administrative examiners in four different time periods was as follows: 1894–1905: 46.0 percent; 1906–17: 66.0 percent; 1918–28: 44.6 percent; and 1929–41: 41.2 percent.[28] With the exception of 1906–17, Tōdai professors were in the minority among the administrative high examiners. In terms of the university background of all administrative high examiners during the four periods, however, the picture changes substantially, with Tōdai graduates accounting for 72.5 percent, 95.9 percent, 85.7 percent, and 67.5 percent, respectively.[29] Although Spaulding interprets these data as disproving the view that the performance of Tōdai men in the higher examinations was related to the control of the latter by the professors and alumni of Tōdai, it seems nonetheless clear that Tōdai men did enjoy advantages in more ways than one. Their previous exposure to lectures and examinations by such a high proportion of the examiners was bound to be beneficial not only in the written but also in the oral phase of the higher examinations.

The preponderance of Tōdai graduates in the higher civil service also bespoke its elitist character in terms of social origins. Although admission to Tōdai was open to all on the basis of merit, in practice only a very small number of students from poor families could attend it on "scholarships provided by former feudal lords and other rich people." Because "one had to be able to afford six years of schooling— three of higher, or preparatory, school and three of university work," most students at Tōdai were in fact "the sons of upper and upper-middle-class families (of civil bureaucrats, military officers, landlords, rich farmers, businessmen, and industrialists)."[30] Of the 1,377 higher civil servants in 1937 analyzed by Inoki, "358 (26.4 percent) were of

27. Satō Tomoyuki et al., *Tōdaibatsu* [University of Tokyo Clique] (Tokyo: Ēru Shuppansha, 1972), p. 196.
28. Spaulding, *Imperial Japan,* p. 249.
29. Ibid., p. 251.
30. Inoki, "The Civil Bureaucracy," pp. 295–96.

TABLE 3   *Occupation of Fathers of Prewar Bureaucrats*

Occupation	N	%	Cumulative %
Government officials:			
Higher officials	49	8.7	
Ordinary officials	31	5.5	14.2
Judges or prosecutors	17	3.0	17.2
Professors	25	4.5	21.7
Other	28	5.0	26.7
Military	25	4.4	31.1
Members of Diet	20	3.6	34.7
Attorneys	6	1.1	35.8
Physicians	30	5.3	41.1
Nobility (*kazoku*)	12	2.1	43.2
Businessmen	26	4.6	47.9
Teachers	18	3.2	51.0
Company employees	14	2.5	53.5
Shinto or Buddhist priests	10	1.8	55.3
Agriculture and forestry	134	23.8	79.1
Brewing	16	2.8	81.9
Merchants	55	9.8	91.7
Skilled and unskilled workers	15	2.7	94.4
Unknown	31	5.5	99.9
TOTAL	562	99.9	

SOURCE: Hata Ikuhiko, *Kanryō no kenkyū: Fumetsu no pawa, 1868–1983* (Tokyo: Kōdansha, 1983). p. 14. Although Hata does not provide any dates (years) for which these data are applicable, he indicates that all of the persons included in the table were born after 1871.

samurai (*shizoku*) origin and 17 (1.2 percent) were of noble (*kazoku*) origin." This means that "72.4 percent of the civil servants were commoners (*heimin*)."[31]

Table 3 provides us with a few more details regarding the social origins of prewar Japanese bureaucrats. A major drawback of the data displayed in the table, however, is that they do not specify the time period to which they pertain. The table nonetheless reveals that the single largest category of fathers' occupation is government officials, indicating a high degree of occupational succession. If we discount ordinary officials, however, the proportion of government officials drops to 21.2 percent, which is below that of "agriculture and forestry" (*nōringyō*). This broad category probably subsumes landlords and rich

31. Ibid., p. 296.

farmers. No matter how one defines elitist occupations, they appear to be disproportionately represented.

LEGALISM

Closely related to the phenomenon of Tōdai dominance in the higher civil service was its markedly legalistic orientation. This was manifested in two related ways: the preponderance of law graduates among the higher civil servants and their preoccupation with formal rules. The popular or journalistic term for this phenonomenon was *hōka banno* (the omnipotence of law). The emergence of *hōka banno* was due to a number of circumstances. First and foremost, the decision of the Meiji leaders to emulate the Prussian model and to require legal training as the principal qualification for civil-service appointment was a key contributing factor. The preferential treatment given to Tōdai law graduates in the early days of the civil service was another. In fact, within Tōdai itself, the faculty of law (*hōgakubu*) enjoyed the status of primus inter pares: in the 1880s its dean served concurrently as the president of Tōdai. He was also empowered to supervise all other law schools that had come into being in Tokyo, of which there were five.[32]

The subjects in which candidates were tested in the higher civil-service examinations were predominantly law-related. The administrative examinations from 1894 to 1928 had six required subjects: constitutional law, administrative law, criminal law, civil law, international law, and economics. In addition, candidates were required to select one subject from a set of four electives: criminal procedure, civil procedure, commercial law, and finance.[33] From 1929 to 1941, criminal law and international law were dropped from the list of compulsory subjects; instead, they were added to the greatly expanded list of elective subjects. The other subjects that were newly added were political science, political history, Japanese history, economic history, agricultural policy, industrial policy, social policy, ethics, logic, sociology, psychology, philosophy, and Japanese and Chinese literature. Candidates were required to choose three subjects from the preceding

32. "Tōkyō Daigaku no hyakunen" Henshū Iinkai, *Tōkyō Daigaku no hyakunen, 1877–1977* [Hundred Years of the University of Tokyo, 1877–1977] (Tokyo: Tōkyō Daigaku Shuppankai, 1977), pp. 85–93. From 1886 to 1919 the Faculty of Law was called the College of Law (*Hōka Daigaku*).

33. Spaulding, *Imperial Japan*, p. 210.

list.[34] The 1929 reorganization, then, made it possible for administrative candidates to take only three law-related subjects, instead of five.

The 1937 data examined by Inoki indicate that about 47 percent of the higher civil servants were graduates of Tōdai's law faculty. If graduates of other law faculties were added, such as those of Kyoto, Tohoku, Kyushu, and Chūō universities, the proportion of law graduates would increase markedly. Of the Tōdai men in the sample, over 63 percent were products of its law faculty.[35] Another study, by Hata Ikuhiko, found that a total of 5,969 Tōdai men passed the administrative higher examinations between 1894 and 1947 and that 94.7 percent of them ($N = 5,653$) were graduates of its law faculty.[36]

The legalistic approach to administration spawned and perpetuated by the predominance of law graduates in Japanese bureaucracy was exemplified by extreme stress upon rules and precedents: nearly all important matters of administration, and sometimes even trivial ones, needed to be grounded in law—statutes, ordinances, regulations, or precedents. In the words of Milton J. Esman:

> Regardless of the emergency nature of specific situations or social necessity, [the official] construes the absence of specific legal authority as full justification for failure to act; and regardless of common sense, he follows regulations to the letter. This dependence on legality resolves all new operating problems into legal problems which can be met only by the issuance or amendment of regulations. The code of regulations thus increases in bulk and complexity. To those trained to understand them, the provisions of the code become surrounded with an inviolability which frequently overrides in importance the situation they are designed to settle.[37]

Esman argues that an explanation of the prevalence of legalism and other aspects of prewar Japanese administration in terms of German and Prussian origins is inadequate. For "while many features of German administration were successfully transplanted, others never took root." As examples of the procedures the Japanese failed to emulate, Esman cites the "in-service training of young officials" and "Germany's highly integrated budget system and its flexible central departmental staff organization."[38] It should be pointed out, however, that the Japanese

34. Ibid., p. 213.
35. Inoki, "The Civil Bureaucracy," pp. 296–97.
36. Hata, *Kanryō no kenkyū*, p. 17.
37. Milton J. Esman, "Japanese Administration—A Comparative View," *Public Administration Review* 7, no. 2 (Spring 1947): 101.
38. Ibid., p. 109.

did embrace the idea of postentry training, even though it was never fully implemented.

In any event, Esman believes that cultural and societal variables offer better clues to Japanese practices. Whereas, in the United States, the tradition of individual rights, equality, limited government, and utilitarianism helped to foster a distinctly pragmatic approach to administration, such a tradition was conspicuously absent in Japan. On the contrary, Japanese society valued the collectivity above the individual, hierarchy above equality, loyalty to the emperor and the state, and reverence for established authority and traditional ways of doing things. Furthermore, legalism served the interests of the ruling elite in the Meiji period and beyond. According to Esman:

> The concept of *Rechtsstaat* . . . was adopted [from Prussia] primarily to convince the western world that because all acts of Japanese officials were regulated by a strict rule of law, extraterritoriality could safely be withdrawn. Legalism, however, had other important uses for Japanese officialdom. It provided them a detailed and intricate mystery which only initiates into the legal priesthood could properly understand. By making government a complex web of administrative regulations, by thus establishing the indispensability of legal learning, the Samurai and their successors have protected their monopoly of higher administrative positions and preserved the power of the bureaucracy against possible assault by the military, the nobility, the financial clique, or the political parties.[39]

Although quite plausible, these ideas are necessarily speculative; credible evidence with which to test their validity is not readily available. Nonetheless, the salience of legalism in the prewar Japanese bureaucracy is beyond challenge, and its deleterious effects are widely recognized.

JIMUKAN VS. GIKAN

A corollary of the ascendancy of legalism was the subordination of technical specialists (*gikan*) to administrative generalists (*jimukan*).[40] We have previously noted that the *gikan* were recruited without

39. Ibid., pp. 109–11. The quotation is from p. 111. It should be stressed that the "successors" to the samurai mentioned by Esman were predominantly commoners (72.4 percent in Inoki's 1937 sample). Only 26.4 percent of the 1937 sample was of samurai (*shizoku*) origin. see n. 30, above.

40. In prewar Japan, the term *jimukan* was used in two distinctly different senses. First, it referred to all non-*gikan*. Second, it encompassed *sōninkan* with grades 4 through 6. See table 1.

TABLE 4   *Speed of Promotion, by Field (Administrative vs. Technical Officials) and Ministry*

| | Ministry & Field | | | | | |
| | Home Affairs | | Posts and Telecom. | | All Ministries[a] | |
Step	Admin.	Tech.	Admin.	Tech.	Admin.	Tech.
From entry to grade 7	1.6	2.2	2.2	1.4	2.1	2.10
From grade 7 to grade 6	2.1	2.8	2.2	2.1	2.0	2.3
From grade 6 to grade 5	2.3	2.5	2.5	2.5	2.2	2.6
From grade 5 to grade 4	2.7	2.10	2.7	2.8	2.4	2.8
From grade 4 to grade 3	2.9	2.10	2.10	2.11	2.7	2.11
From grade 3 to grade 2	6.1	11.7	5.0	9.5	5.7	9.5
From grade 2 to grade 1	2.11	7.0	2.1	4.8	3.1	4.5
From entry to grade 1	20.2	31.6	19.3	25.6	19.10	27.0
N	46	25	30	24	151	186

SOURCE: Jinji-in, Kyūyokyoku, "Kyū kanri seidoka ni okeru kōtōkan no keireki chōsa no kekka gaiyō," *Kikan jinji gyōsei* 25 (Aug. 1983): 95 and 99–100.
NOTE: The numbers with periods refer to years and months. Hence 1.6 means 1 year and 6 months.
   [a]Six ministries are included in this total: Home Affairs, Finance, Posts and Telecommunications, Railroads, Agriculture, and Commerce and Industry.

examination through screening (*senkō*). Although they acquired *sonin* rank and therefore were classified as higher officials (*kōtōkan*), only a small fraction of them was given managerial or supervisory positions. Chiefs of sections, divisions, and bureaus dealing with complex technical matters were typically *jimukan* trained in law but totally lacking in substantive expertise.

Moreover, as table 4 shows, there was a sizable gap between the two types of officials in the speed of promotion. In the Ministry of Home Affairs, *gikan* trailed behind *jimukan* every step of the way. It took *gikan* eleven more years than *jimukan* to reach grade 1. Those who made it, however, were the lucky ones, for the vast majority did not. In the technically oriented Ministry of Posts and Communications, *gikan* had an edge over *jimukan* in the early years of their career and then began to lose ground. The overall disadvantage of six years and three months, nonetheless, was considerably better than the lag of eleven years and four months in the Home Affairs Ministry. When all six ministries are considered, *jimukan* enjoy an edge in all stages of promotion, accumulating a net advantage of over seven years.

This anomalous situation bred inefficiency and conflict and had demoralizing effects on technical personnel, many of whom were graduates of Tōdai and other prestigious universities. Because there were more *gikan* than *jimukan* in the prewar higher civil service (about 53 percent to 47 percent), the situation in effect amounted to minority rule—the triumph of dilettantism over expertise.[41]

SECTIONALISM

Nakane Chie has coined the term *tate shakai* (vertical society) to underscore the precedence of vertical over horizontal relationships—or *ba* (frame) over *shikaku* (attribute)—in Japan.[42] In organizational terms, this idea implies the development of a strong sense of identification with the organization and intense feelings of solidarity among all members of the organization. Two personnel practices helped to bolster such a tendency: decentralized recruitment and lifetime employment. The former meant that although the civil-service examinations were centrally administered, the actual recruitment and appointment of qualified candidates was the responsibility of each ministry. Hence one became an official, not of the Japanese imperial government as such, but of the Home Ministry, the Finance Ministry, and so on. The custom of lifetime employment meant that one was expected to stay in the same organization until retirement. Temporary assignments outside one's own ministry were more frequent than interministerial transfers on a permanent basis. Within the same ministry, however, officials were rotated between the headquarters and the field as well as between different bureaus, divisions, and sections.[43]

41. Lt. Col. Hugh H. MacDonald and Lt. Milton J. Esman, "The Japanese Civil Service," *Public Personnel Review* 7. no. 4 (Oct. 1946): 218–19; Watanabe, "Nihon no komuinsei," p. 130. Of the 186 *gikan* covered by table 4, 145 (78 percent) were Tōdai graduates and 20 (10.8 percent) were graduates of Kyōdai. All of the remainder had gone to either Kyushu or Tohoku University. On the other hand, 142 of the 152 *jimukan* (94 percent) were Tōdai men. The remainder were all Kyōdai graduates. See Jinji-in, Kyūyokyoku, "Kyū kanri seidoka ni okeru kōtōkan no keireki chōsa no kekka gaiyō" [A Summary of the Results of an Investigation into the Background of Higher Officials Under the Old Bureaucratic System], *Kikan jinji gyōsei* [Public Personnel Administration Quarterly] 25 (Aug. 1983): 96.

42. Nakane Chie, *Tate shakai no ningen kankei: Tan'itsu shakai no riron* [Human Relations in a Vertical Society: The Theory of a Homogeneous Society] (Tokyo: Kōdansha, 1967), pp. 26–67 and passim.

43. The administrative officials in Jinji-in's study, on which table 4 was based, experienced between eleven and thirteen changes of assignment; the average duration of each assignment was less than two years. Jinji-in, Kyūyokyoku, "Kyū kanri seidoka ni okeru kōtōkan no keireki chōsa no kekka gaiyō," p. 108.

Takahashi Hideki's analysis of the career patterns of 145 officials who entered the Finance Ministry after passing the higher civil-service examinations during the Taishō era (1912–26) shows that those who eventually achieved the positions of bureau chief or administrative vice-minister typically served as financial clerks (_zaimu shoki_) in overseas diplomatic or consular missions within the first year or two of appointment and then as heads of local tax offices (_zeimushochō_) before being assigned to the headquarters. After serving in a number of posts, they would reach the post of section chief in their fourteenth year of service.[44]

Such practices, reinforced by the cultural norms of _tate shakai_, bred jurisdictional rivalries between ministries that were dysfunctional for the government as a whole. Jealous guarding of turfs even occurred within the same ministry in some cases.[45]

SECURITY OF TENURE

Civil servants in prewar Japan enjoyed security of tenure, a sine qua non of rational-legal bureaucracy as stipulated by Max Weber.[46] As was true in the Weberian model, this was a relative kind of security rather than an absolute one. In Weber's words, "where legal guarantees against arbitrary dismissal or transfer are developed, they merely serve to guarantee a strictly objective discharge or specific duties free from all personal considerations."[47]

An imperial ordinance on the status of civil officials (_Bunkan Bungenrei_) promulgated in 1899 enumerated three grounds on which civil officials might be discharged: (1) inability to perform duties due to injury, illness, or enfeeblement of mind and body; (2) request by an official invoking illness or other personal circumstances; and (3)

44. Takahashi Hideki, "Kōbun seidoka no shōshin jittai no bunseki" [Analysis of Promotion Patterns Under the (Prewar) Higher Examination System] I, _Jinji-in geppō_ 342(Aug. 1979): 23–24.

45. For an elaboration of this point, see Albert M. Craig, "Functional and Dysfunctional Aspects of Government Bureaucracy" in Vogel, ed., _Modern Japanese Organization and Decision-Making_, pp. 15–17. See also Spaulding, "The Bureaucracy as a Political Force," pp. 56–60. Spaulding points out that the adverse effects of sectionalism were somewhat mitigated by "informal collaboration among bureaucrats of different ministries," which "appears to have been very common." Ibid., p. 58.

46. Hans Gerth and C. Wright Mills, trans. and eds., _From Max Weber: Essays in Sociology_ (New York: Oxford University Press, 1946), pp. 202–3; Max Weber, _The Theory of Social and Economic Organization_, trans. A. M. Henderson and Talcott Parsons (New York: Oxford University Press, 1947), pp. 333–34.

47. Gerth and Mills, _From Max Weber_, p. 202.

reduction in force occasioned by reorganization. The same ordinance specified that officials might be furloughed for any of the following reasons: (1) recommendation of disciplinary action by the disciplinary committee; (2) being charged with a crime; (3) reduction in force occasioned by reorganization; and (4) administrative necessity in the ministry or agency concerned. Because this last-mentioned ground lent itself to abuse by party politicians, it was tightened up in 1932 by requiring review of any proposed furlough on grounds of administrative necessity by the committee on the status of officials. The second ground for furlough was also revised to read "being indicted in a criminal case."[48]

EARLY RETIREMENT

Although civil servants enjoyed a relatively high degree of job security and were in effect guaranteed lifetime employment, their actual careers were fairly short. According to MacDonald and Esman, most higher officials were expected to retire in their late forties. In as much as the pension scheme allowed civil officials "to retire after 17 years of service on one third of their base pay," those who retired in their late forties or even in their early fifties found it necessary to supplement their income somehow.[49] Some found their "second careers" in private business, and others "received Imperial nominations to the old House of Peers."[50]

48. Wada, "Bunkan nin'yō seido no rekishi," II, pp. 10–11; ibid., III, *Jinji-in geppō* 97 (Mar. 1959): 8–9.
49. MacDonald and Esman, "The Japanese Civil Service," pp. 222–23. The quotation is from p. 222. Chalmers Johnson writes, however, that the "prewar civilian bureaucracy did not retire as early as contemporary officials do." See his article "The Reemployment of Retired Government Bureaucrats in Japanese Big Business," *Asian Survey* 14, no. 11 (Nov. 1974): 958. In the absence of any statistical evidence, it is difficult to reconcile the conflicting views.
50. Johnson, ibid., p. 958. Kusayanagi Daizō writes that prewar pensions were generally sufficient to support retired civil officials. See his book, *Kanryō ōkoku ron* [On the Kingdom of Bureaucrats] (Tokyo: Bungei Shunjū, 1975), p. 78. Strictly speaking, whether pensions were adequate or not is a relative matter. From 1931 to 1945, for example, the basic salary of administrative vice-minister was 5,796 yen, and that of bureau chief was 4,572 yen. The amount of annual pension for a former vice-minister, therefore, would be 1,932 yen, and that for a former bureau chief 1,524 yen. This would mean that the retired vice-minister would still receive more than the highest-paid *hannin* official in his midcareer. The pension for a retired bureau chief, on the other hand, would be on a par with the salary of the second-highest-paid *hannin* official (1,540 yen) and a *sonin* official with four or five years of service. See the salary schedule for 1931 officials in Watanabe, "Nihon no komuinsei," p. 129. Between 1894 and 1935, a total of 146 retired bureaucrats served as cabinet ministers, 152 as members of the House of Peers, 295 as members of the House of Representatives, and 24 as elected prefectural governors. Fifteen others served as advisers to the Privy Council. See Hata, *Kanryō no kenkyū*, p. 25.

A key factor that helps to explain the phenomenon of early retirement was the unwritten rule within the bureaucracy decreeing that all members of the same entering class in a given ministry should resign as soon as one of them attained the position of administrative vice-minister. This custom served the dual function of sparing the vice-minister the embarrassment of having to issue orders to members of his peer group and of clearing the way for advancement of younger officials to senior posts. The former is an important consideration in Japanese culture, where a strong sense of hierarchy is counterbalanced by an equally strong sense of equality among the cohort. Having passed the higher civil-service examination and entered the ministry in the same year, the cohort typically forged extremely close personal ties throughout their government careers.

CONCLUSION

In sum, the emergence of a modern government bureaucracy in prewar Japan resulted from both internal and external factors. The decision of the Meiji oligarchs to adopt the trappings of modern government, including a constitution, a parliament, a cabinet, and a merit bureaucracy, reflected their desire not only to appease the internal forces championing the cause of democracy but also to convince foreign powers that Japan merited respect and, above all, equal treatment.

Both the constitutional framework and the structure and principles of bureaucracy that the Japanese ultimately adopted were patterned after the German model. Enshrining the myth of imperial supremacy, the new system, in effect, bestowed awesome powers on those who presumed to act as the emperor's agents, which included the bureaucrats. The single most important feature of the bureaucracy was the institutionalization of the merit principle: civil-service examinations became firmly established as the principal means of selecting the most qualified candidates for the exercise of bureaucratic authority.

The Japanese also borrowed from their German model a system of rigid stratification, which separated officials from nonofficials and divided officials into two distinctly unequal status groups, *kōtōkan* and *hanninkan*. The former was in turn divided into three classes and nine grades. The veritable caste system all this spawned necessarily entailed a pronounced degree of elitism. Such elitism, it should be stressed, was based not on ascription but on achievement. A major factor contributing to and sustaining this tendency was the domination of the higher civil service, both in number and in influence, by graduates of Tokyo Imperial University, an institution designed originally as a training school for government officials.

Another notable feature of the prewar Japanese bureaucracy was legalism, which manifested itself in two ways: the preponderance of law graduates in the higher civil service and the preeminence of laws, rules, regulations, and precedents in public administration. A corollary of these twin phenomena was the ascendancy of administrative officials trained in law over technical specialists. Although a numerical minority, the former controlled most of the levers of power, outperforming the latter in promotion by a substantial margin.

The propensity of bureaucratic organizations to guard their bailiwicks against encroachment by their rivals is a universal phenomenon. However, it was reinforced in Japan by the cultural norms of a "vertical society" and by institutional practices; the latter included the decentralized hiring of civil servants, the custom of lifetime employment, and the infrequency of interministerial transfers. Like their counterparts elsewhere, Japanese civil servants enjoyed a high degree of job security. However, its benefits were somewhat diluted by the practice of early retirement; "lifetime" employment meant considerably less than what it implied, for, according to MacDonald and Esman, retirement typically occurred in the late forties, the prime of the bureaucrat's life. This, too, was a function, in part, of cultural norms, notably a strong sense of equality among the cohort and the resultant difficulty of maintaining hierarchical relationships among them. No less important was the function the practice performed for the organization as a whole: facilitating frequent turnovers at its upper echelons, where, because of the structural imperative of a hierarchical organization, positions become progressively scarce.

The Japanese experience demonstrated the inherent limits of foreign institutional models. Although they perform the indispensable function of guiding the uninitiated groping in the dark, their actual impact in the adopted country is contingent upon the dynamics of politics and, above all, their interaction with cultural norms.

CHAPTER THREE

Civil-Service Reform Under the American Occupation

After its unconditional surrender in World War II, Japan entered a new phase: the first foreign occupation in its history. Nominally an Allied occupation, it was in reality an American show. The seven-year occupation proved to be an epochal turning point in Japanese history, for it helped to lay the groundwork for the democratization of Japanese society and polity alike.

As part of the multifaceted program of political democratization, the Supreme Commander for the Allied Powers (SCAP) carried out a comprehensive reform of Japan's civil-service system. What were the objectives of the reform? How was it implemented? What problems and difficulties did it encounter? What did it actually accomplish? This chapter will explore these questions, with special attention to the differing perceptions of SCAP and Japanese participants in what Robert E. Ward has called "an experiment in planned political change."[1]

THE BACKDROP

THE LEGACY OF ABORTIVE REFORMS

The prewar Japanese bureaucracy, which struck American observers as archaic, even abominable, had its share of domestic critics as well. There

---

1. Robert E. Ward, "Reflections on the Allied Occupation and Planned Political Change in Japan" in Ward, ed., *Political Development in Modern Japan*, pp. 477–535.

were a series of proposals for reform, some emanating from the government itself. The first serious proposal for reform came from the Hirota Koki government (March 1936–February 1937), which had been formed in the aftermath of the attempted coup d'état known as the 26 February incident. Widely viewed as originating in the military, the proposal called for the establishment of a central personnel agency under the direct control of the prime minister and for the expansion of the scope of discretionary appointment. The former was aimed at increasing government efficiency by combating "sectionalism"—the endemic interministerial rivalries—whereas the latter must be viewed against the backdrop of the emasculation of political parties. In as much as the possibility that party politicians might abuse the power of discretionary appointment had been eliminated, there was no longer any compelling reason to restrict the appointment powers of the government.[2]

The first Konoe government (June 1937–January 1939) revived the idea of civil-service reform. In January 1938 it circulated a proposal, drafted by the cabinet legislation bureau, to establish a central personnel agency, increase the scope of discretionary appointment, revise the higher civil-service examination, initiate a program for retraining officials, and abolish security of tenure for officials. Among other things, these measures were aimed at undercutting sectionalism, enabling the government to recruit capable people from a broader base, combating *hōka bannō* (the omnipotence of law graduates), and rejuvenating the bureaucracy. However, the proposal ran into stiff resistance by bureaucrats, particularly those in the powerful Home Ministry. It was eventually watered down to two components: utilizing the existing mechanism of periodic administrative vice-ministers' conferences in lieu of a new personnel agency and setting up a cabinet personnel committee designed to foster personnel exchanges among the various ministries.[3]

The year 1941 saw a proliferation of proposals for civil-service reform: they emanated from such diverse sources as the Imperial Rule Assistance Association (Taisei Yokusankai), the newly created government party that replaced all other political parties; the Japan Chamber of Commerce and Industry (Nihon Shōkō Kaigisho); and the Associa-

2. Ide Yoshinori, *Nihon kanryōsei to gyōsei bunka* [Japanese Bureaucracy and Administrative Culture] (Tokyo: Tōkyō Daigaku Shuppankai, 1982), pp. 151–52; Watanabe, "Nihon no kōmuinsei, p. 131."
3. Watanabe, "Nihon no kōmuinsei," p. 131; Ide, *Nihon kanryōsei*, pp. 152–55; Miyake, Gyōseigaku to gyōsei kanri, pp. 88–97.

tion for the Study of National Policy (Kokusaku Kenkyūkai). The proposal put forth by the Taisei Yokusankai is particularly noteworthy, for it was based on comments elicited from thirty-five leading scholars, journalists, and former officials. Among other things, it advocated (1) the establishment of a cabinet personnel agency (Naikaku Jinji-chō) empowered to unify, coordinate, and control personnel administration in all ministries and agencies; (2) the reclassification and refinement of all government positions along functional lines; (3) the elimination of *hōka bannō,* coupled with the recruitment of promising persons solely on the basis of character and ability; (4) the introduction of an administrative audit system and the clarification of responsibility on the part of officials; (5) the curtailment of frequent reassignments among officials; (6) the replacement of lethargy (*koto nakare shugi*) with an active and responsible posture; (7) the training and retraining of officials; (8) the replacement of sectionalism with communication and cooperation among the various ministries and agencies; and (9) the promotion of scientific procedures, efficiency, and speed in public administration.[4]

The Kokusaku Kenkyūkai echoed most of the preceding ideas and added a few new ones: the preferential treatment of persons possessing special skills, improved treatment of lower-level officials, and the exchange of personnel between the public and private sectors, the central government and localities, and the center and the periphery (*kanmin, chūō-chihō, nai-gaichi no kōryū jinji*). Endorsing all of these ideas, the Japan Chamber of Commerce and Industry particularly stressed the importance of reforming the civil-service examinations and expanding the scope of discretionary appointment. The reform of the examinations, in its view, should focus on the elimination of both *hōka bannō* and what it saw as as an overemphasis on knowledge. In sum, there emerged a broad consensus on three key points: (1) the need for change in the basic posture of officials and for the establishment of a new code of behavior for officials, (2) the need for the reform or introduction of various institutional and technical devices, and (3) the importance of setting up a central personnel agency.[5]

These sweeping suggestions, however, produced but meager results. The only thing the second Konoe cabinet (July 1940–July 1941) succeeded in implementing was a limited reform of the higher examina-

4. Ide, *Nihon kanryōsei,* pp. 147–49; Miyake, *Gyōseigaku,* pp. 98–99.
5. Ide, *Nihon kanryōsei,* pp. 149–50.

tions.[6] Whether what happened can be described as reform is debatable. As analyzed by Spaulding, there were three changes in the examination system, of which the "first two were obviously political: Japanese history was to become a compulsory subject in all three career fields [administrative, judicial, and diplomatic], and there was to be a compulsory oral in constitutional law which would include a 'character' examination." The third change had to do with the abolition of diplomatic examinations as a separate, independent category. This, according to Spaulding, was an "essentially punitive" move against the diplomatic service, which "had long annoyed other ministries with its air of exclusiveness and had antagonized the army by resisting its policies in China."[7]

Instead of being abolished altogether, however, the diplomatic examinations were absorbed into the administrative examinations; moreover, because candidates for the diplomatic service continued to be differentiated from other candidates, what had changed was form, not substance. The effects of the Konoe revisions were further diluted by the suspension of all examinations after 1943, a development that was necessitated by the conscription of university students into military or other war-related services.[8] The compromise solution of the proposal for a cabinet personnel agency, namely, the setting up of an interministerial liaison committee within the Home Ministry, fizzled amidst the confusion of a wartime government in its final throes.[9]

PRELUDE TO REFORM IN OCCUPIED JAPAN

The Occupation took the form of indirect rule, hence the Japanese government nominally retained authority to initiate some policy measures. More important, the Japanese government was primarily responsible for implementing all policy directives emanating from SCAP. As it became clear that SCAP's top priority was the democratization of Japan, the leaders of the Japanese government realized that reform of the bureaucracy would be a matter of time. As a self-defensive measure, they tried to anticipate and forestall any SCAP-initiated reform: as early as September 1945 the cabinet legislation bureau was instructed

6. For details of the reform, see Wada, "Bunkan nin'yō seido no rekishi," III, pp. 10–11.
7. Spaulding, *Imperial Japan's Higher Civil Service Examinations,* p. 175.
8. Ibid., p. 176.
9. Ide, *Nihon kanryōsei,* p. 156.

to mobilize all of its resources to study the matter and submit a draft plan.[10]

On 13 November, the Shidehara cabinet approved a plan containing the following features:

First, official nomenclature (*kanmei*) shall be streamlined and unified. All the titles bearing the expression *kan* (literally "official") shall be replaced by one or another of the two titles, *jimukan* (administrative official) and *gikan* (technical official).

Second, the distinction between higher officials (*kōtōkan*) and ordinary officials (*hanninkan*) shall be abolished. The ranks of *chokuninkan, sōninkan,* and *hanninkan* shall be replaced by grades 1 through 3 (*ikkyū, nikyū,* and *sankyū*).

Third, there shall be established a unified compensation system that distributes rewards according to length of service and merit, regardless of rank or grade.

Fourth, the frequency of reassignments shall be curtailed. Means of implementing the principle whereby each official serves in one position for a fixed period of time shall be studied.

Fifth, while maintaining the system of appointing officials from among those who have passed competitive examinations, the government shall explore ways of increasing the scope of appointments based on evaluation (*senkō nin'yō*) and of improving the examination system in the following way: (1) reappraise the subjects in which candidates are examined with a view to identifying the best-qualified candidates for all openings; (2) appoint a substantial number of practitioners from both the public and private sectors as examiners so as to achieve a balance between theory and practice in the examinations; (3) study the possibility of instituting a trainee (or probationary) system in conjunction with the higher examinations.

Sixth, the possibility of providing all new appointees with several months of training both within the government and in the private sector shall be studied. For in-service training, either an institute shall be established or existing academic institutions such as universities shall be utilized.

10. Ibid., pp. 157–58.

Seventh, the possibility of placing an inspector (*kansatsukan*) both in the cabinet and in each ministry shall be studied. It will be his responsibility to monitor performance and study ways of improving employee welfare with a view to increasing efficiency and equity.

Eighth, the possibility of establishing a performance-evaluation system both within the cabinet and in each ministry shall be studied. All officials in grade 2 or below shall be subject to such a system insofar as their promotion, salary increase, and other rewards are concerned.[11]

What was striking about the preceding plan was that the proposed changes were more cosmetic than substantive. The substitution of "grades 1, 2, and 3" for *chokuninkan, sōninkan,* and *hanninkan,* for example, did not really address the fundamental issue of status hierarchy in the bureaucracy. Nor did the plan contain many ideas that were really new. Nearly all of the ideas had been proposed before. Moreover, most of the items in the plan called for further study rather than immediate action. Finally, there was a conspicuous omission in the plan: nowhere did it mention the idea of setting up a central personnel agency, notwithstanding its prominent place in the wartime proposals for reform. In a word, this episode demonstrated that the Japanese government was either unable or unwilling to initiate meaningful change in the bureaucracy on its own.

DRAWING UP THE BLUEPRINT FOR REFORM

THE ESMAN MEMORANDUM

It was against this backdrop that the first significant step in the direction of civil-service reform was taken by SCAP. On 30 January, 1946, First Lieutenant Milton J. Esman of the Public Administration Division, Government Section, SCAP General Headquarters, wrote a memorandum for Brigadier General Courtney Whitney, chief of the Government Section. Esman, who had served on the staff of the United States Civil Service Commission before entering military service, began by noting the power and pivotal position of the bureaucracy in Japanese society.

---

11. Ibid., pp. 158–60; Miyake, *Gyōseigaku,* pp. 110–11.

"Of all the major bulwarks of feudal and totalitarian Japan," he wrote, "only the bureaucracy remains unimpaired. The bureaucracy will definitely outlast the occupation and will play a decisive role of moulding the future of Japan."[12]

What disturbed Esman most was the absence of any sign that the bureaucracy was likely to change its ways "without constant pressure and guidance from this Headquarters." He saw a direct linkage between democracy and bureaucracy: "Modern democratic government requires a democratic and efficient public service. Merely to reform obvious abuses—which has not yet been accomplished—will not provide the minimum level of efficiency necessary to democratic administration now that the police are no longer available to perform the operating function of government." Hence, Esman concluded, only "a thorough-going democratization and modernization of the civil service" would ensure the survival of a democratic political system in the post-Occupation period. Such a step would necessitate "relentless pressure from this Headquarters" as well as "guidance on the proper techniques to employ."[13]

In addition to the concerns noted above, there was a compelling practical consideration: SCAP feared the possibility that "ideologically hostile bureaucrats would by administrative sabotage nullify Occupation policies or the programs of Japanese political leaders evolved pursuant thereto." SCAP sought to reduce the risk not only by "constant vigilance and surveillance" but also by "the removal of identifiable militarists and ultranationalists from public life." Another countermeasure was the strengthening of countervailing institutions, notably the Diet.[14] Yet SCAP was under no illusion that these measures could effectively curb the entrenched powers of the bureaucrats. In fact, SCAP's purge program that was implemented between 1946 and 1948 hardly touched the bureaucracy. According to Hans H. Baerwald, only "145 members of the senior civil service" were actually removed. All

12. See the text of Esman's memorandum in the Supreme Commander for the Allied Powers (SCAP), Government Section, *Political Reorientation of Japan* (Grosse Pointe, Mich.: Scholarly Press, 1968), vol. 2: Appendixes, p. 578. This is a reproduction of a report originally published in 1949 by the U.S. Government Printing Office.

13. Ibid., In prewar and wartime Japan, the police performed multiple functions: in addition to maintaining law and order, they exercised "thought control," mobilized the populace for various purposes, and served as the bulwark of state power. This is what Esman was referring to when he used the phrase, "now that the police are no longer available to perform the operating functions of government."

14. Ibid., I, pp. 246–47.

told, 830 out of 42,251 bureaucrats (1.9 percent) who were screened were purged.[15] In short, it was plain that a basic restructuring of Japanese bureaucracy was prerequisite to both the short-term needs and the long-term goals of the Occupation.

Recognizing the need for reform, however, was one thing; undertaking effective measures to fill that need was quite another. As T. J. Pempel shows, there was a considerable gap between American rhetoric and behavior. Not only did civil-service reform receive a relatively low priority from SCAP; both its conception and its implementation were flawed by the "unquestioned search for rationality and efficiency" and by "organizational politics."[16] Let us nonetheless examine the sequence of key events pertaining to civil-service reform in occupied Japan.

JAPANESE REQUEST FOR ASSISTANCE

Consistent with the tone of the Esman memorandum, which strongly advocated the need for pressure and guidance, SCAP first considered the option of issuing a formal memorandum "directing the Japanese Government to appoint a special commission of experts to draft proposals for basic reform of civil-service system under SCAP guidance pursuant to standards to be set up by SCAP." However, it decided that a more prudent course of action would be to try to induce the Japanese to initiate the necessary action in the direction desired by SCAP. In February 1946 the cabinet legislation bureau submitted to the government section a plan for limited reform of the civil service based on the cabinet decision of November 1945. Included in the proposed plan were a simplification of official nomenclature; the abolition of the ranks of *chokuninkan, sōninkan,* and *hanninkan* in favor of three numbered grades; a simplification of pay and allowance scales; and some changes in the content of the higher civil-service examination. Acknowledging that the plan would not entail any fundamental changes, the bureau nonetheless "claimed that it represented an initial break in the traditional system and was a forerunner of more basic changes." The government section cleared the plan with reservations: it called the plan

15. Hans H. Baerwald, *The Purge of Japanese Leaders Under the Occupation* (Berkeley: University of California Press, 1959), p. 82.
16. T. J. Pempel, "The Tar Baby Target: 'Reform' of the Japanese Bureaucracy," in Robert E. Ward and Sakamoto Yoshikazu, eds., *Democratizing Japan: The Allied Occupation* (Honolulu: University of Hawaii Press, 1987), pp. 157–87. The quotations are from p. 181.

"a step in the right direction" but insisted that "fundamental reforms" must still occur.[17]

As it became increasingly plain that the strategy of inducing the Japanese government to initiate basic structural reform of its bureaucracy was ineffective, the idea of a more forceful approach was resuscitated. In April 1946, the government section reconsidered the option of issuing a formal SCAP directive on civil-service reform to the Japanese government. There was support for the idea from five other sections of the General Headquarters. The main obstacle to such action was that it would be inconsistent with the "technique of leadership as opposed to direction employed by the Government Section beginning about March 1946." Had an unexpected break not come, however, such a directive would most probably have been issued. On 3 May, a letter signed by Finance Minister Shibusawa Keizō was delivered to the finance division of the economic and scientific section of the SCAP General Headquarters. It requested assistance in the revision of the salary and allowance system of Japanese government personnel in accordance with a position-classification plan and suggested that SCAP invite some experts from the United States to "give advice and make a draft plan for the revision now under consideration."[18]

The immediate response of the finance division was to forward the letter to the government section for appropriate action. The latter's counterpart in the Japanese government was the cabinet legislation bureau, which also had jurisdiction over matters affecting the civil service as a whole. However, in keeping with the tradition of "sectionalism," the Finance Ministry had neither consulted nor notified the bureau of what it was doing. The two government agencies, in short, were on a collision course. A potentially serious conflict was averted, however, when the Japanese cabinet on 14 May reached a compromise: in return for an apology from the finance minister, the director general (*chōkan*) of the legislation bureau accepted the idea of requesting the visit of an American advisory mission. Accordingly, the cabinet approved and forwarded to SCAP a formal request to that effect in its

17. SCAP, *Political Reorientation*, pp. 247–48. The quotation is from p. 247. See also Ide, *Nihon kanryōsei*, pp. 161–62 and 169–70.

18. SCAP, *Political Reorientation*, pp. 248 and 259. Although the narrative says on p. 248 that the letter was "personally submitted" by the Finance Minister on 3 May 1946, the text of the letter on p. 579 bears the date 25 Apr. 1946. It is probable that the letter was written and signed on 25 Apr. but not delivered to the SCAP General Headquarters until 3 May.

name. The stage was thus set for the entry of American experts onto the scene.[19]

It should be stressed that there was a considerable gap between Japanese and American perceptions of these moves. The Japanese left no doubt that what was being requested was technical assistance on a specialized subject—a restructuring of their salary and allowance system based on a position-classification plan. The Americans, on the other hand, interpreted the Japanese request as envisaging a comprehensive review of the entire civil-service system. The official history of the Occupation prepared by the government section states: "The Japanese Government was now officially on record as requesting, with complete cabinet accord, the assistance of a mission of American experts to study and draft plans for a *fundamental reform of its civil service system.*"[20] This is not to suggest that the reform-minded Americans were not aware of the perception gap. In fact, the official SCAP history goes on to note that whereas "the Japanese request was motivated by a desire for higher efficiency and morale, . . . the Occupation's basic aim was democratization."[21]

THE HOOVER MISSION

In November 1946, the United States Personnel Advisory Mission to Japan arrived in Tokyo. It was headed by Blaine Hoover, president of the Civil Service Assembly of the United States and Canada, and included three other members: Manlio F. DeAngelis, Chief, Program Planning Staff, the United States Civil Service Commission (USCSC); Robert S. Hare, Chief, Field Classification, USCSC; and W. Pierce MacCoy, Director of Personnel, the United States Department of State. Prior to the arrival of the Hoover mission, the Japanese government had set up the Administrative Research Bureau (Gyōsei Chōsabu) under the jurisdiction of the prime minister, with the understanding that the Bureau would serve as the counterpart to the mission.[22]

19. Ibid., pp. 248 and 580.
20. Ibid., p. 248. Emphasis added. For a discussion of Japanese perceptions, see Asai Kiyoshi, *Shinpan kokka kōmuinhō seigi* [Detailed Commentaries on the National Public Service Law, New Edition] (Tokyo: Gakuyō Shobō, 1970), pp. 1–3; Ide, *Nihon kanryōsei*, pp. 174–75.
21. SCAP, *Political Reorientation*, pp. 248–49. For an informative discussion of the perception gap and other problems during the Occupation, see Kusayanagi Daizō, *Nihon kaitai* [The Dissolution of Japan] (Tokyo: Gyōsei, 1985), pp. 241–53 and passim. The focus of this book is on the SCAP-ordered dissolution of the Home Ministry.
22. SCAP, *Political Reorientation*, pp. 249–50; Asai, *Shinpan kokka kōmuinhō seigi*, p. 2.

How the two worked together or failed to work together is another interesting story that illustrates the inherent asymmetry of victor and vanquished in an occupied territory. Whereas the official history of the Occupation gives the impression that the two worked closely and harmoniously, a Japanese participant in the process paints a strikingly different picture. According to SCAP's version:

> Organized conferences between the Mission and the President and Division Directors of Staff of the Administrative Research Bureau were instituted [on] December 24, 1946. The work of the Mission and the Bureau was integrated and for technical purposes decentralized. Committees under the advisorship of the Mission members and including Division Directors of the Administrative Research Bureau were set up to conduct investigation in designated areas of personnel administration within the Japanese Government. These committees immediately launched their programs.[23]

Asai Kiyoshi, who served as the director of the Public Servants' Division (Kōmuinbuchō) in the bureau at the time, writes, however, that the "organized conferences between the Mission and . . . the Bureau" consisted of two get-togethers during which only idle remarks (*zatsudan*) were exchanged, that the nature of collaboration between the two sides was confined to technical matters only, and that no one from the Japanese side had been asked to provide any input into the drafting of a new public-service law then under way.[24] In short, what the Japanese did was not to work with but to work for the Americans.

An important step in the Hoover mission's work was to supervise the Administrative Research Bureau in conducting a "pilot" position-classification survey with multiple aims: to generate data on the relationship between pay and the actual work performed by the various types of government employees, "to develop effective methods of making position classification surveys in the Japanese Government and to try them out," and to train Japanese experts in position classification.[25]

What the pilot survey yielded was not only the first position-classification plan in the history of Japanese public administration but also a wealth of information about the structure and functioning of the Japanese bureaucracy. In general, the new data served to confirm the old impressions about Japanese administration and to reinforce the ethnocentric biases of Western observers: Japanese bureaucracy was found to

23. SCAP, *Political Reorientation,* p. 250.
24. Asai, *Shinpan kokka kōmuinhō seigi,* p. 2.
25. SCAP, *Political Reorientation,* p. 250.

be "weak" in virtually all areas—recruitment, examination, compensation, employee utilization and evaluation, recreation, retirement, equitable treatment of employees, and even discipline. The only areas in which "Japanese administrators had gained some experience . . . [that] could be utilized in building a modern personnel program" were those of "personal [sic] training, health and welfare." What concerned the American experts was that, apart from its premodern nature, the Japanese bureaucracy was still dominated by "old-line officials of the predemocratic" era who might impede, even sabotage, programs and policies aimed at the democratization of Japan. The mission concluded that "the legislative enactment of a national public service law" embodying high "standards of merit and equitable treatment in public personnel administration" would help "force out" such people, while simultaneously allowing "the selection and appointment of objectively qualified replacements."[26]

In drafting a national public-service law, the mission sought to be guided by four key criteria: (1) adequacy, (2) simplicity of standards, (3) recognition of the individuality of Japan, and (4) practicality.[27] Whether the actual performance matched the professed goals, however, is open to question. Total exclusion of the Japanese in the drafting process, for example, seriously undercut the mission's ability to implement the last two criteria. Even the first two lost much meaning, because their contents were unilaterally determined by the Americans without a sufficient understanding of Japanese perceptions of what was adequate and simple.

On 24 April 1947, five months after its members set foot in Japan, the mission completed a draft of the proposed law and submitted an interim report to SCAP. The speed with which this was done reflected the mission's sense of urgency in replacing "the feudalistic bureaucracy" with a "modern system of civil service." The report contained three key recommendations:

first, the creation within the Japanese Government of a powerful central personnel agency;

second, action to secure enactment of the proposed national public service law, providing service-wide standards of personnel administration under

---

26. Ibid., pp. 250–51. The Americans were not alone in perceiving the threat to democratic reforms posed by the entrenched bureaucrats. For an expression of similar views, see Tsuji, *Shinpan Nihon kanryōsei no kenkyū*, pp. 242–81.

27. SCAP, *Political Reorientation*, p. 251.

which a democratically oriented merit service could be established and the efficiency of the service promoted; and

third, the establishment of civil service division in the Government Section to advise the Supreme Commander for the Allied Powers on programs, policies, and procedures relative to the reform of the personnel system of the Japanese Government.[28]

The civil-service division was established on 1 June 1947, and took over the work of the mission, which was officially terminated on 16 June 1947. The chairman of the mission, Blaine Hoover, however, was appointed as head of the new division, thus ensuring continuity of outlook and a smooth transition. Hoover was concurrently appointed special assistant to the chief of the government section.[29] Meanwhile, on 11 June 1947, the Japanese government learned for the first time of the existence and contents of the draft legislation. Its leaders, including those who had supposedly collaborated in the work of the Hoover mission, were dumbfounded. Some of them used the expression "Yabu o tsutsuite hebi o dashita" ('One pokes at a bush and causes a snake to come out'). That is to say, what the Japanese did was to ask for technical assistance in reforming their pay and allowance system but received instead a comprehensive plan for a fundamental reform of the entire civil-service system. What is more, the plan was in reality a command. Hoover is said to have told Katayama Tetsu, the newly elected Socialist prime minister of Japan, that the draft must be enacted into law "without any revision within a few weeks."[30]

ENACTING THE NATIONAL PUBLIC-SERVICE LAW

JAPANESE HANDLING OF THE HOOVER DRAFT

So long as the Occupation adhered to the policy of indirect rule, it was the responsibility of the Japanese to turn the draft into a law. Furthermore, if the goal of effecting fundamental reform that would outlast the Occupation was to be attained, it was imperative that the Japanese be persuaded of the intrinsic merits of the draft. Viewed from this perspective, the apparently high-handed manner in which the

28. Ibid., p. 252.
29. Ibid., p. 253.
30. Ide, *Nihon kanryōsei,* pp. 183–90; Asai, *Shinpan kokka kōmuinho seigi,* pp. 2–3; Ward, "Reflections on the Allied Occupation," p. 509.

Hoover mission behaved was bound to be counterproductive in the long run. The personality of Blaine Hoover appears to have been a source of difficulty, for he was perceived by the Japanese as arrogant, arbitrary, and insensitive to Japanese needs.

The cabinet legislation bureau and the administrative research bureau worked jointly on the translation of the draft into Japanese, completing the task within a week. The Japanese version laid bare numerous problem areas. For one thing the articles were overly long. In many cases, what would normally require twenty separate articles in a Japanese statute was jammed into a single article. As for its substance, the Japanese were particularly struck by the extensive powers and special status of the proposed National Personnel Authority, the prohibition of strikes by government employees, and the position of the Emperor. After dividing the national public service into the regular government service (*ippan shoku*) and the special government service (*tokubetsu shoku*), the American draft had listed the Emperor under the latter.[31]

Even though the new constitution of Japan that had just entered into force formally downgraded the Emperor to a mere "symbol of the state and of the unity of the people" (art. 1), the Japanese found it hard to swallow the notion that the Emperor was a *tokubetsu shoku* employee of the Japanese government, along with the prime minister, ministers of state, vice-ministers, ambassadors, judges, and other high-ranking officials.[32]

The Japanese version of the draft was circulated among all government ministries and agencies, and their views and comments were solicited. On the basis of the latter, the administrative research bureau, in collaboration with the cabinet legislation bureau, prepared a memorandum on "Opinions on the Draft National Public-Service Law." The memorandum, dated 24 June 1947, acknowledged the need for a "fundamental reform of our country's bureaucratic system" so as to enable "national public servants" to become the "servants of the people in a true sense," noted that the draft was designed to fill that need, and stated that the document, on the whole, was an acceptable one. However, it added, there were a number of problems from a technical standpoint as well as from the perspective of the new constitution and

31. Ide, *Nihon kanryōsei*, pp. 190–91.
32. The constitution was promulgated on 3 Nov. 1946, and entered into force on 3 May 1947. It replaced the Meiji constitution of 1889. See SCAP, *Political Reorientation*, pp. 82–118.

other related laws that needed to be ironed out before the draft could be fully accepted. It then enumerated ten points:

1. It is not clear whether the National Personnel Authority will be independent of or subject to the supervision of the prime minister; it will be necessary to make the status of the authority consistent with the constitution that enshrines the basic principles of a parliamentary cabinet system (*gi'in naikakusei*).

2. The draft lacks any provisions regarding the status of officials, such as a guarantee against arbitrary dismissal. Even though the gap may be filled by regulations of the authority, the basic principles on this issue should be embodied in the proposed law.

3. The draft states that regulations issued by the authority (*Jinji-in kisoku*) shall have the same effect as laws and that its decisions shall be final and not subject to judicial review. This raises questions about the authority's relationship with the Diet and the Supreme Court and ought to be changed.

4. The scope of this law ought to be limited so as to exclude the Emperor, court employees who are not judges, employees of the public prosecutor's office (Kensatsuchō), and teachers.

5. The organization and finances of the National Personnel Authority are questionable. It may be advisable to delete the provisions that confer special status on its president and commissioners as well as those dealing with its finances.

6. The significance of promotion examinations remains unclear; it seems unwise to base all promotions on the results of examinations.

7. There is a need to clarify the meaning of the provisions regarding strikes by employees.

8. The provisions dealing with punishments need to be streamlined and made more explicit in accordance with the principle that all crimes and punishments ought to be determined by law (*zaikei hōtei shugi*).

9. The format of this law should be changed to conform to that of other Japanese laws.

10. There is a view that the draft should be so revised as to make it applicable to local-government employees as well.[33]

---

33. Ide, *Nihon kanryōsei,* pp. 191–92.

The preceding views were conveyed to the American authorities on 26 June in a document that had been especially drawn up for that purpose. The Japanese argued that stylistic changes were necessary to dispel the impression that the law was of foreign origin. Substantive changes were justified on the ground that, without them, the Japanese government would lack the confidence to submit the draft to the Diet as its own and to argue convincingly and responsibly for its passage. Stressing that it had no objections whatever to the purposes and general principles of the proposed law, the Katayama government appealed for American cooperation in adapting the draft to the realities of Japan.[34]

These were indeed compelling arguments vis-à-vis the Occupation, which officially adhered to the policy of government by leadership rather than by direction and had reiterated the view that the Japanese must be allowed to develop institutions suited to their own needs if the democratic experiment was to succeed. Nonetheless, Hoover told Prime Minister Katayama that since the charge given to him by General MacArthur was to ascertain whether the Japanese government accepted or rejected the draft in its entirety, he lacked the authority to forward a conditional answer. He did, however, intend to report to General MacArthur that the Japanese authorities concurred in the aims and basic ideas of the draft and predicted that discussions with the Japanese would soon begin. Incidentally, Hoover reportedly insisted on dealing only with the prime minister. On 3 July, Hoover asked the Japanese government to submit proposed changes in the form of draft legislation by 7 July. Katayama sought and received an extension of this deadline to 31 July.[35]

On 10 July, Hoover left Japan for the United States on an extended leave, entrusting the task of overseeing the passage of the proposed law to C. P. Marcum, his deputy in the civil-service division. The Japanese, recalling the maxim "oni no inai aida no sentaku" (doing laundry while the devil is away), worked feverishly to produce their own draft legislation incorporating all desired changes, both stylistic and substantive. In a covering letter accompanying the new draft sent to the government section on 31 July, Prime Minister Katayama minimized the importance of proposed changes, saying that they were either stylistic or minor. "Although [the revised draft] may appear to be considerably different from your original draft," he said, "it is not substantially

34. Ibid., pp. 192–94.
35. Ibid., p. 194.

different from [your draft] in terms of basic principles." The key changes cited in his letter, nonetheless, were revealing. The power of the National Personnel Authority would be reduced by, inter alia, omitting the provisions dealing with its finances that would have given it a measure of independence in budgetary matters; the authority's power to enact regulations having the effect of law would be reduced; and key provisions dealing with the prohibition of strikes by public servants would be deleted.[36]

Significantly, all of the preceding points remained intact in the final version approved by the government section on 26 August 1947. What is more, when the Japanese authorities failed to resolve a dispute pertaining to a key concept in position classification with Marcum, it resorted to the devious tactic of leaving it in the English version but deleting it in the Japanese version. Needless to say, it was the latter that was submitted to the Diet for approval. The subsequent discovery of this ploy by Hoover led to the temporary abolition of the cabinet legislation bureau.[37]

Up to this point, at the request of SCAP, all the information regarding civil-service reform had been withheld from the public, including members of the Diet. The publication of the draft by the Katayama government on 27 August, three days prior to its formal submission to the Diet, therefore marked its entrance into the public arena. Press reaction was generally favorable. Major dailies endorsed the proposed legislation; they noted that the establishment of the National Personnel Authority and the proposal to use examinations not only for recruitment but also for promotion would help bolster the merit principle, place personnel administration on a scientific basis, and improve efficiency, equity, and objectivity.[38]

The reaction of other groups, on the other hand, was far from favorable. Even the Japan Socialist party, the senior partner in the coalition government of Katayama, voiced reservations in the Diet. The Socialists were concerned that the draft's emphasis on preserving the independence and political neutrality of civil servants and on promoting

---

36. Ibid., pp. 194–96.
37. Ibid., pp. 196–97; Asai, *Shinpan kokka kōmuinhō seigi*, p. 3. The disputed concept was "class" in English and *shokkyū* in Japanese. The two sides could not agree on its precise meaning or importance in position classification. The Cabinet Legislation Bureau was abolished on 15 Feb. 1948, and reestablished on 1 Aug. 1952. Naikaku Seido Hyakunen-shi Hensan Iinkai, ed., *Naikaku hyakunen no ayumi* [The Path of One Hundred Years of the Cabinet] (Tokyo: K. K. Ōkyō, 1985), pp. 129 and 137.
38. Ide, *Nihon kanryōsei*, p. 198.

technical efficiency entailed the risk that the supreme goal of democratization might be compromised. The greatest danger, in their view, was not the patronage system but the feudalistic, faction-ridden, and privilege-conscious nature of Japanese bureaucrats. They favored the replacement of the National Personnel Authority with a five-member personnel committee (Jinji Iinkai) and the introduction of a free appointment system (*jiyū nin'yō seido*) for officials above a certain level that would rely on the evaluation of candidates by the personnel committee. Such a system would, among other things, open the way for the appointment (that is, lateral entry) of experts from outside the government.[39]

The view that the goal of democratization should take precedence over all others was echoed by the Association for the Study of Public Law (Kōhō Kenkyūkai). The association called for the introduction of an impeachment system for corrupt officials, for further limitation of the authority's rule-making power, for the adjustment of official nomenclature to eliminate undemocratic connotations (for example, the deletion of the suffix *kan* from titles of public servants), and for the protection of the rights of lower-grade employees to guard against discrimination.[40]

The Coordination Council for Public Service Unions (Zen Kankō Rōdō Kumiai Kyōgikai or Zenkankō) also found the draft to be weak, even retrogressive, from the standpoint of democratizing the bureaucracy. It was particularly disturbed by what it saw as the denial of fundamental rights of public servants, notably labor-related rights, arguing that such matters as their status, separation, and compensation should not be covered by the proposed law but be subject to labor legislation and contracts. The Zenkankō also favored replacing the National Personnel Authority with a personnel committee, restricting its rule-making power, and expanding the scope of free appointments. It further called for the abolition of educational requirements in civil-service examinations, the guarantee of the freedom of political activity by public servants, and the substitution of a social-security system for a pension system.[41]

39. Ibid., pp. 199–200.
40. Ibid., pp. 200–201.
41. Ibid., pp. 201–2. The phrase "educational requirements" needs to be clarified. Theoretically, "graduates of a middle school or recognized equivalent" could take the higher civil-service examination under the old system by first passing the preliminary examination. "Graduates of a higher school or recognized equivalent," however, were allowed to skip the prelim. In reality, most of the successful candidates had some college education. Spaulding, *Imperial Japan*, p. 262.

A surprisingly large proportion of these ideas found their way into the national public-service law that was approved by the House of Representatives of the Diet on 15 October and by the House of Councillors the following day. The National Personnel Authority thus gave way to the National Personnel Commission; the term of office for its three members was reduced from six years (renewable up to eighteen years) to four years (renewable up to twelve years); its rule-making powers were further reduced; impeachment was added to the causes for dismissal of public servants; and their political rights, such as the right to stand for an elective office, were recognized.[42]

In sum, it is plain that, from the American standpoint, what was enacted into law by the Japanese Diet in October 1947 was a watered-down version of the original draft. However, it would be too simplistic to view the revisions in the hands of the Japanese as the product of the bureaucracy's scheme to perpetuate its power. The notion of a powerful central personnel agency, although by no means alien to the Japanese, evoked fear and resistance from the Left and the Right alike. The entrenched bureaucrats justifiably saw the danger of the erosion of their power, whereas proponents of democracy feared that the proposed agency might help perpetuate the privileged position of senior bureaucrats. The near-unanimous support for the guarantee of labor and political rights for public servants, moreover, stemmed primarily from the widespread desire for democratization.

THE FIRST REVISION OF THE LAW

So long as the Occupation continued and Hoover remained as chief of the civil-service division, however, the Japanese had but a slim chance of getting away with what they had done. Upon returning to his post in November 1947, Hoover was infuriated to learn of the fate of his draft and assigned a top priority to the revision of the law. Simultaneously, he initiated the process of organizing and staffing the Temporary National Personnel Commission and collecting information on the structure, functions, and key personnel of the various ministries and agencies.[43]

A detailed schedule of operations prepared by the civil-service division reflected Hoover's determination to guide the Japanese every

42. Ide, *Nihon kanryōsei*, pp. 202–03.
43. Asai, *Shinpan kokka komuinhō seigi*, p. 4; "Zadankai: Jinji-in no omoide arekore" [Roundtable Discussion: Recollecting Aspects of the National Personnel Authority], *Jinji-in geppō* 100 (June 1969): 11; SCAP, *Political Reorientation*, pp. 253–55.

step of the way toward the goal of implanting a new civil-service system on their soil. However, practical difficulties hampered his task. The official history of the Occupation dealing with civil-service reform, prepared under Hoover's supervision, noted that the need to rely on "remote control," the language barrier, and cabinet reshuffles had contributed to unforeseen delays.[44]

The language barrier appears to have been a major source of difficulty, for the Japanese complained of the low caliber of translators in the SCAP General Headquarters. Most of the translators were nisei (second-generation Japanese born in the United States) who did not understand the legal terminology so prevalent in the vocabulary of Japanese government.[45] Indeed, the ease with which the Japanese succeeded in circumventing the intentions of SCAP with regard to the initial enactment of the national public-service law probably had a great deal to do with the language barrier, which had been turned into an advantage by the Japanese.[46]

These problems notwithstanding, the civil-service division took complete charge of recruiting the staff for the Temporary National Personnel Commission. In January 1948 it devised an open competitive examination, had it translated into Japanese, and supervised its administration. A quarter of about one thousand persons who took the examination were selected and given the first basic-training course, also devised by the civil-service division. Not only was the training material prepared by the Americans, but lectures were delivered by American instructors in English and then translated into Japanese. Members of the first class of this training program, which lasted for five months, were utilized as discussion leaders in the next session, which was shortened to two months. Thereafter, Japanese instructors took over the classes.[47]

44. SCAP, *Political Reorientation,* pp. 255–56. The schedule of operations is reproduced on p. 255.

45. Ashitate Chūzō, "Kōhei shinsa no omoide" [Recollections of the Equity Process (i.e., evaluation of complaints concerning adverse action against civil servants)], *Jinji-in geppō* 274 (Dec. 1973): 18–19.

46. This episode exemplified the general tendency of Japanese bureaucrats and politicians to engage in subtle subversion of SCAP policy whenever the latter was perceived as threatening. In the words of a perceptive Japanese observer: "Although [Japanese politicians and bureaucrats] permitted themselves no display of open opposition, they attained their ends by undercover resistance of various kinds. Agreeing to the *principle* of a given reform, they very often succeeded in subtly changing its *nature* in the course of carrying it out." Masataka Kosaka, *100 Million Japanese: The Postwar Experience* (Tokyo: Kodansha International, 1972), p. 50.

47. "Zadankai: Jinji-in no omoide arekore," p. 11; Nagahashi Susumu, "Kaisōbun: Jinji-in sōsetsu no koro" [Reminiscences: the Early Days of the National Personnel Authority], *Jinji-in geppō* 274(Dec. 1973): 16–17; SCAP, *Political Reorientation,* p. 257.

Meanwhile, work on the revision of the national public-service law proceeded, and a series of proposed amendments was completed in May 1948. Continuing labor unrest, particularly "strikes and other dispute tactics on the part of organized government employees" underscored the urgency of prompt legislative action. However, "serious differences of opinion . . . developed between the Government Section's Civil Service Division and the Economic and Scientific Section's Labor Division on such questions as scope of coverage of the National Public Service Law, the meaning of collective bargaining as applied to government workers, and the use of strikes or dispute tactics against the government." The impasse was broken by General MacArthur on 6 July; on 22 July he sent a letter to the prime minister of Japan suggesting that the law be revised in accordance with his recommendations.[48]

Given the realities of the Occupation, the MacArthur letter had the force of a command, leaving the prime minister no option but to comply. Addressing the various weaknesses in the existing law, MacArthur laid a special emphasis on the prohibition of strikes by government employees. "No person holding a position by appointment or employment in the public service of Japan or in any instrumentality thereof should resort to strike or engage in delaying or other dispute tactics which tend to impair the efficiency of government operations," he wrote. In his view, "any person, holding such a position, who resorts to such action against the public of Japan thereby betrays the public trust reposed in him and forfeits all rights and privileges accruing to him by virtue of his employment." Recalling that the aim of civil-service reform was to ensure the democratization of Japan, he declared that the "success of this reform is accordingly no less a primary objective of the Occupation than it is a prerequisite to the future well-being of the people of Japan." Finally, he urged the prime minister to undertake "immediately" "a comprehensive revision of the National Public Service Law" along the lines suggested by him, promising all necessary assistance by the SCAP headquarters.[49]

The government of Prime Minister Ashida Hitoshi acted with dispatch. Within nine days of receipt of the letter, it promulgated a government ordinance (*seirei*) temporarily prohibiting public servants from engaging in collective bargaining, strikes, or delaying or other dispute tactics. The ordinance specifically cited the letter from the

48. SCAP, *Political Reorientation*, pp. 258–59.
49. See the text of the letter in *ibid.*, vol. II, Appendixes, pp. 581–83.

Supreme Commander for the Allied Powers as the basis for the prohibition.[50]

Three days earlier, on 28 July, the Japanese government had received from Hoover SCAP's proposed amendments in both English and Japanese. Determined not to repeat the same mistake, Hoover had instructed the Temporary National Personnel Commission to prepare the Japanese translation in utmost secrecy. His apparent calculation that the commission, which would become a major beneficiary of the proposed revisions, would keep the vow of secrecy was off the mark. Asai Kiyoshi, then chairman of the commission, decided that, given the importance of the matter, he was duty-bound to apprise his government of the situation. Prime Minister Ashida, the chief and deputy chief of his secretariat, and a few other cabinet members thus became aware of what was happening. Hoover was reported to have been asked by the Japanese whether his proposals left any room for amendments and to have replied in the negative.[51]

The proposals sent a shock wave through both the Japanese government and, particularly, labor circles. The Ashida government therefore tried very hard to persuade SCAP to accept some amendments. In the end, only minor ones were allowed. On 9 November, a bill to revise the national public-service law was submitted to the Diet, convened especially for that purpose, by the newly formed second Yoshida government. Although the special Diet session proved to be turbulent, with the opposition parties trying to inject other issues, it nonetheless approved the bill in three weeks. Whereas the House of Representatives added a few minor amendments, the House of Councillors failed to do so because of the lack of time. The revised law was promulgated on 3 December 1948 and entered into force on the same day.[52]

Of the 125 articles in the original law, 32 had been extensively revised and 77 partially revised. Fourteen new articles had been added. Hence this represented a major overhaul of the law. Nonetheless, the key changes could be summed up under three headings:

First, the scope of the law was expanded. This was accomplished by shifting certain types of positions from the special government service to the regular government service. Examples of positions so affected

50. Jinji-in, *Jinji gyōsei nijūnen no ayumi* [The Path of Twenty Years of Public Personnel Administration] (Tokyo: Ōkurashō, Insatsukyoku, 1968), p. 37.

51. Asai, *Shinpan kokka komuinhō seigi*, pp. 5–6.

52. Jinji-in, *Jinji gyōsei nijūnen*, pp. 37–38; Ide, *Nihon kanryōsei*, pp. 219–23.

were the director general of the cabinet legislation bureau, the vice-minister of each ministry, the counselor of each ministry, manual laborers, employees of the National Diet, court investigators, and certain personnel of government enterprises. All of these positions came within the purview of the national public-service law.

Second, the powers of the central personnel agency were strengthened. Not only was the name that SCAP had originally recommended, the National Personnel Authority (Jinji-in), restored, but its status was upgraded from that of an external agency (*gaikyoku*) of the prime minister's office to a component agency of the cabinet. Its rule-making powers were enhanced: it now monopolized the power to make rules aimed at implementing the standards set in the national public-service law; the erstwhile requirement that all rules must be approved by the prime minister was jettisoned. The authority's financial position was bolstered by the acquisition of the privilege of "double budget": should the cabinet decide to revise the authority's proposed expenditures, it must submit to the Diet both the revision and the original request.

Third, measures to tighten discipline in the public service were introduced. This meant, primarily, that public servants were stripped of the right to strike and to employ delaying and other dispute tactics, were forbidden to run for elective offices or become officers in a political party or any other political organization, and were barred from all political activities other than voting. As a result, the gap between public servants and private-sector employees widened considerably.[53]

THE AFTERMATH

S-1 EXAMINATION

The passage of the national public-service law in 1947 and its substantial revision in 1948 helped to establish the basic legal and institutional framework for the modernization and democratization of the Japanese-government bureaucracy. However, SCAP knew all along that a comprehensive civil-service law and a strong central personnel agency would be powerless to overcome the inertia, or, worse yet, the resistance of the old-line bureaucrats. What was needed, therefore, was

---

53. Jinji-in, *Jinji gyōsei nijūnen,* pp. 37–39; Asai, *Shinpan kokka kōmuinhō seigi,* pp. 6–11.

a mechanism through which to identify and weed out the most unfit and to infuse the bureaucracy with fresh blood. To accomplish this goal, article 9 of the supplementary provisions of the national public-service law required the holding of an examination to fill all administrative positions at the level of section chief and above.[54]

In the course of preparing for the examination, SCAP's Civil Service Division decided that "the examination should have none of the aspects of a purge," even though that "would probably make it difficult to attain the objectives of the examination in full measure." Underlying this decision were two considerations: first, "many of the more recalcitrant and unadaptable officials had [already] been eased out under pressure of the various SCAP sections"; second, it was deemed most important "to preserve the integrity and objectivity of the examination." The civil-service division also decided to make the examination "open and competitive," rather than qualifying. In other words, all incumbents of designated positions would be required to compete with other candidates if they wished to be reappointed. Insofar as designating positions subject to examination was concerned, the key criterion was whether or not their duties were primarily administrative. The positions of administrative vice-minister, bureau chief, division chief, and section chief in the regular administrative agencies were included, in accordance with the law. A total of 2,621 positions were designated as subject to examination, and they were in turn grouped into 60 occupational areas ranging from general administration to police.[55]

Each designated position was not only allocated to an occupational group but also placed in one of four administrative levels. Level 1 encompassed administrative vice-ministers and comparable positions (such as directors general of agencies) and level 4 encompassed section chiefs and their equivalents. The examination was designed to measure four essential characteristics: "(a) administrative aptitude, (b) technical competence, (c) satisfactory character, and (d) physical fitness." Administrative knowledge and aptitude were tested through two procedures. First, each candidate was required to take a written examination

54. Maynard N. Shirven and Joseph L. Speicher, "Examination of Japan's Upper Bureaucracy," *Personnel Administration* 14, no, 4 (July 1951): 48–50. When they wrote this article, the authors were on the staff of the SCAP General Headquarters. Shirven was Chief of the Civil Service Division, the Government Section, and Speicher was Chief of the Examinations Branch of the same Division.

55. Ibid., pp. 50–52.

consisting of "90 multiple-choice items relating to organization, personnel administration, financial management, principles of supervision, interpretation of data, and other facets of the practical work of public administrators." Second, in addition to the written test, a candidate was required to meet "a qualifying standard of practical experience." A candidate for the position of administrative vice-minister, for example, "was required to have served at least one year as a bureau chief or in a position of similar responsibility."[56]

The decision to include a test of technical competence was based on SCAP's perception that "one of the principal weaknesses of the Japanese civil-service system was the preponderance of officials with only legal training and background in positions where technical knowledge was essential." Candidates for positions in 45 of the 60 occupational groups were required to take tests consisting of "80 multiple-choice items constructed from basic reference material and from experience in the occupation." These tests were said to have been "rather elementary in nature." In addition, the candidates had to meet the experience requirement in the occupational area of their choice.[57]

Determination of "satisfactory character" was the responsibility of the National Personnel Authority's bureau of investigation. First, the candidate's own statements relating to his experience, education, and personal history contained in his application were verified. Second, an attempt was made to evaluate his personality traits by obtaining ratings on such qualities as "ability to train subordinates, originality, and planning ability" from at least three persons familiar with the candidate's previous experience. On the basis of these data, each candidate was given an overall score of either pass or fail. The final component of the examination was designed "to eliminate those candidates who were physically unfit for the performance of the duties of the designated positions." Inasmuch as incumbent employees of the national and local governments and other public bodies were subjected to periodic medical examinations, only candidates from outside the government were required to take the physical examination.[58]

Unhappy about the imposed nature of the examination and uncertain about its results, the bureaucrats tried to force its cancellation by postponing the submission of applications until the last minute. The

56. Ibid., pp. 52–53.
57. Ibid., p. 53.
58. Ibid., pp. 54–55.

"war of nerves," however, was won by SCAP, and before the deadline was past "a total of 12,000 applications from 8,076 individuals had been filed for the 2,621 designated positions." After preliminary screening, 7,815 candidates were allowed to take the examination. The administrative aptitude test was given on 15 January 1950, and the technical tests for various occupational groups were given from 20 to 22 January. Because no time limit was imposed and candidates were permitted to smoke and were served hot tea, the examination was dubbed a "paradise examination." It was also called S-1, signifying that it was the first examination for supervisory personnel in postwar Japan.[59]

Did the examination accomplish its purpose? Directly, it helped to eliminate about 21 percent of incumbents. At level 1 (administrative vice-minister), however, the attrition rate was only 12 percent. "Indirectly, it is estimated that an additional 10–20 percent may have been eliminated. For example, when the examination was announced, a number of incumbents either resigned or did not apply for the examination, while others secured transfers to non-designated positions." One reason for the remarkably high rate of retention of incumbents was that they were given preferential treatment: once they passed the examination, they "were likely to be reappointed regardless of their position on the eligibility list"—that is, regardless of their actual scores in the examination.[60]

Unbeknownst to SCAP, the Japanese bureaucrats also resorted to the "self-defensive measure" of asking other qualified candidates to withdraw their names from the eligibility list.[61] So widespread and effective was this practice, in fact, that of the 175 persons who were appointed to levels 1 and 2 positions following the examination, only one was a "civilian"—that is, a person who had not previously served as a government official.[62] Not surprisingly, the examination served to tarnish the image of SCAP even among those who survived the ordeal. The administrative-aptitude test, for example, was perceived as being too simplistic and of questionable validity. Recalling his experience two decades later, one Japanese participant wrote that senior civil servants

59. Ibid., p. 55; Jinji-in, *Jinji gyōsei nijūnen*, p. 119. For a detailed analysis of the S-1 examination, see Miyake, *Gyōseigaku*, pp. 112–28. He provides examples of questions along with correct answers.
60. Shirven and Speicher, "Examination of Japan's Upper Bureaucracy," pp. 56–57.
61. Kaneji Hiroshi, "Jinji-in no omoide" [Recollections on the National Personnel Authority] in Jinji-in, *Jinji gyōsei nijūnen*, p. 53.
62. Hata, *Kanryō no kenkyū*, p. 106.

taking the test had been appalled by SCAP's low opinion of their ability reflected in the "simpleminded and mechanical" questions in the test.[63]

POST-OCCUPATION DEVELOPMENTS, 1952–87

Notwithstanding the lofty goals pursued by the Occupation, its methods of operation were autocratic and frequently high-handed, generating resentments on the part of the Japanese people, particularly those in the bureaucracy and in the Diet. The formal termination of the Occupation in April 1952, therefore, paved the way for a reappraisal of the various reform measures implemented under American tutelage. The sentiment for revision of the national public-service law was quite strong, because it was perceived as an alien imposition not suited to Japanese needs. The National Personnel Authority had become an object of intense resentment, not only because of its unprecedented powers but also because it had served as a tool of SCAP's civil-service division. Proposals for reform, even abolition, of the authority were justified on various grounds.[64]

The government and the ruling party argued that the authority's independence and powers undermined the cabinet-responsible system on which the Japanese government was based. They further pointed to what they described as deleterious effects of the authority's annual recommendations on compensation: the latter allegedly provided fuel for organized labor's spring offensive for wage increases and influenced wage levels in the private sector. The opposition parties and labor organizations, on the other hand, advocated reform of the authority on the ground that it was not fulfilling its original goal of safeguarding the interests of public servants. The main function of the annual recommendations on compensation, they argued, was to legitimize the government's policy of holding wages and salaries to a minimum.

Another consideration that underscored the need for revision of the law was its incompatibility with Convention Number 87 of the International Labor Organization (ILO), which the Japanese government was interested in ratifying. The ILO treaty called for a guarantee by its contracting parties of their citizens' right to establish and join

---

63. Hayashi Shūzō, "Shiken jigoku iroiro" [Aspects of an Examination Hell], *Jinji-in geppō* 236 (Oct. 1970): 4. See also "Zadankai: Jinji-in no omoide arekore," p. 13.

64. Asai, *Shinpan kokka kōmuinhō seigi*, pp. 15–16. For an account of the resentment the authority faced and how it overcame attempts to emasculate it in the waning days of the Occupation, see Tomioka Shōzō, "'Hoittoni keikoku shokan' o sukūpu" [Getting a Scoop on the "Whitney Warning Letter"], *Kankai* [The Official World], July 1986, pp. 188–93.

labor unions, the unions' autonomy, their right to establish and join federations and international organizations, and other labor-related rights.[65]

None of the nine formal proposals for the revision of the national public service law submitted to the Diet between May 1952 and December 1963, however, succeeded in mustering sufficient support. By the time a bill for revision of the law was submitted to the Diet for the tenth time in January 1965 by the first Satō government, a sense of urgency had been added: the powerful labor federation Sōhyō (Nihon Rōdō Kumiai Sōhyōgikai, or the General Council of Japan Labor Unions) and a union representing locomotive engineers of the national railroads had filed a complaint against the Japanese government with the ILO, and there were signs that other labor unions might follow suit. The ILO had already initiated an investigation into the complaint. Against such a backdrop the Sato government cited the need to amend the provisions in the national public-service law pertaining to the rights of public servants to organize so that Japan might ratify ILO Convention Number 87.

Additionally, the government stressed the need to establish a system of responsibility in public-personnel administration, proposing to set up a new personnel agency within the office of the prime minister. Instead of replacing the National Personnel Authority, however, the new agency, to be called the Bureau of Personnel (Jinji-kyoku), would simply take over some of the functions previously performed by the authority and by the Finance Ministry. Specifically, the bureau would be given jurisdiction over the efficiency, welfare, and service of public servants, their retirement allowances, the compensation of special-service public servants, the coordination of personnel management among the various ministries and agencies, and the collection and analysis of statistical data regarding personnel administration. The bill embodying the preceding proposals was approved by both houses of the Diet on 17 May 1965. On the same day the Diet also passed a bill empowering the government to ratify ILO Convention Number 87.

In sum, the period of "trial" for the National Personnel Authority came to an end in 1965 with its powers only marginally altered.[66] The

---

65. Asai, *Shinpan kōmuinhō seigi*, p. 16; Jinji-in, *Jinji gyōsei nijūnen*, pp. 39–40.

66. Tsuji Kiyoaki, a distinguished student of Japanese public administration, characterized the thirteen years following the end of the American Occupation as the "period of trial for the National Personnel Authority" (*Jinji-in no kurō no jidal*). See "Zadankai: Korekara no jinji gyōsei" [Roundtable Discussion: Public Personnel Administration in the Days Ahead], *Jinji-in geppō* 274(Dec. 1973): 4.

civil-service reform spearheaded by the Occupation thus overcame the first significant challenge to its viability. Although numerous changes were introduced in subsequent years, none can be characterized as major. The more noteworthy changes pertained to (1) civil-service examinations, (2) the expansion of postentry training programs, (3) the introduction of a mandatory retirement system, and (4) reorganization of government agencies.

The civil-service-examination system has undergone change three times in the postoccupation period. Until 1956, higher civil servants were recruited through the examination to recruit sixth-grade national civil servants (6-*kyū shoku kokka kōmuin saiyō shiken*). But in 1957, in conjunction with the revision of the grade system from a fifteen-grade to an eight-grade system, the sixth-grade civil-service examination was renamed the higher civil-service examination (*kokka kōmuin saiyō jōkyū shiken*). The erstwhile fifth-grade civil-service examination became the intermediate civil-service examination (*kokka kōmuin saiyō jūkyū shiken*). Along with the lower civil-service examination (*kokka kōmuin saiyō shokyū shiken*), the civil-service-examination system now consisted of three distinct levels.[67]

Then in 1960, the higher civil-service examination was subdivided into types A and B (*kōshu* and *otsushu*). Officially, however, this change was characterized as the renaming of the previous higher civil-service examination (HCSE) as the type-B HCSE, accompanied by the introduction of an entirely new examination, the type-A HCSE. The stated rationale for the change was that the new type-A examination would make the civil service more competitive with the private sector, for it would upgrade the initial rank of new employees (from grade 7 to grade 6) and improve their prospects for promotion to managerial positions.[68] As we shall see shortly, however, what really happened was the creation of two distinct classes of higher civil servants: those in the elite track (type-A-examination graduates) and those in the quasi-elite track (type-B-examination graduates).

The latest change in the examination system occurred in 1985, when the type-A HCSE was renamed the type-I civil-service examination (*isshu shiken*), the type-B HCSE was abolished, the intermediate examination was, in effect, replaced by the type-II civil-service examination (*nishu shiken*), and the lower examination was renamed the

67. Jinji-in, *Jinji gyōsei nijūnen*, p. 136.
68. Ibid., p. 137.

type-III civil-service examination (*sanshu shiken*). Officially, however, the type-II examination was described as an entirely new examination rather than a successor to the intermediate examination. It was, in fact, characterized as an upgraded version of the intermediate examination, which in the preceding years had become a vehicle for recruiting not high-school graduates but primarily university graduates. This reflected in part the increase in the number of university graduates in the general population and in part the competitiveness of the higher civil-service examinations. Whether the change will lead to the recruitment of candidates for middle-level management who are better qualified than before, however, remains to be seen.

On the other hand, the educational level of the applicants for the type-II examination in the first two years of its existence was slightly higher than that of applicants for the intermediate examination. Whereas in 1984, the last year in which the intermediate examination was given, only 1 percent of applicants had done some graduate work, the proportion increased to 1.6 in 1985 and to 1.8 in 1986. Among the successful candidates, the increase was more substantial: from 1.8 percent in 1984 to 4.2 percent in 1985 and to 3.8 percent in 1986. So far as university graduates were concerned, however, the picture changed very little. Although the proportion of university graduates increased slightly among all applicants (80.5 percent in 1984, 82.1 percent in 1985, and 81.5 percent in 1986), it remained all but identical among the successful candidates (91.3 percent in 1984, 91.5 percent in 1985, and 91.3 percent in 1986). Overall, the proportion of the applicants with at least some university education increased from 81.5 percent in 1984 to 83.3 percent in 1986, and that of the successful applicants with the same level of educational attainments increased from 93.1 percent in 1984 to 95.1 percent in 1986. There was also notable change in the type of universities attended by successful applicants. The proportion of those who had attended national universities increased from 31.8 percent in 1984 to 38.7 percent in 1986, whereas that of those who had attended private universities decreased from 57.2 percent to 52.2 percent in the same period.[69] Although this may be viewed as an indirect indicator of the greater competitiveness of the type-II examination as compared with that of its predecessor, it also suggests a step backward from the standpoint of making the civil service more democratic.

69. Jinji-in, *Kōmuin hakusho* [White Paper on Civil Servants], 1987 (Tokyo: Ōkurashō, Insatsukyoku, 1987), p. 36.

Another development related to the civil-service examinations is the gradual lifting of restrictions on women, a development that is plainly conducive to democratization. In 1979 women were allowed for the first time to take entrance examinations to state-run schools that train air-traffic controllers, maritime-security officers, and meteorologists. There were 479 women applicants, of whom 36 were successful.[70] In the following year, women were allowed to take civil-service examinations for "national tax specialists" (*kokuzei senmonkan*) and guards in the imperial palace. There were 573 women applicants for the former, of whom 32 were successful, and 91 women applicants for the latter, of whom 2 were successful.[71] Restrictions were further relaxed in 1981, allowing women to become border guards (*nyūkoku keibikan*) and prison guards (*keimukan*). Three women (out of 163 female applicants) passed the examination for the former, and 54 women (out of 466 female applicants) passed the examination for the latter.[72]

Another noteworthy trend is a phenomenal increase in the number and variety of training programs for civil servants. Inasmuch as we shall examine the civil-servants' postentry training at length in chapter 6, it will suffice here to note a few statistics. Whereas in the late 1940s there existed only a dozen or so training programs, in which less than 1 percent of the civil servants participated, by the late 1960s the number of training programs had exceeded 4,100 and nearly 17 percent of the civil servants participated in them. By the late 1970s, nearly one out of every four civil servants was participating in some 6,700 programs. Finally, in the mid-1980s nearly four of every ten civil servants were participating in 9,200 programs. These programs encompassed a wide array of organizations, the entire spectrum of civil servants up to the section-chief level, and the whole gamut of subjects.[73]

In 1985, a mandatory retirement system for civil servants went into effect. With a few exceptions, the retirement age was set at sixty. Civil servants whose duties and responsibilities are deemed to be "special" or who cannot be easily replaced, however, would be allowed to extend their retirement age up to five years. Physicians and dentists were prime examples of such persons.[74] The new system, however, was not

---

70. Ibid., 1980, p. 25.
71. Ibid., 1981, p. 25.
72. Ibid., 1982, p. 26.
73. Jinji-in, *Nenji hōkokusho* [Annual Report], 1948–49 through 1986 (Tokyo: Ōkurashō, Insatsukyoku, 1950–87).
74. Jinji-in, *Kōmuin hakusho*, 1982, pp. 44–47; ibid., 1986, pp. 51–52.

expected to affect the retirement practices of higher civil servants, who retire in their fifties. We shall examine this issue in detail in chapter 8.

Finally, we shall note briefly salient changes in the structure of the executive branch of the Japanese government. To list the most noteworthy of them, we must mention the establishment of the Economic Planning Agency in 1955, the Science and Technology Agency in 1956, the Ministry of Home Affairs (Jichishō, initially translated as the Ministry of Autonomy) in 1960, the Environment Agency in 1971, the Okinawa Development Agency in 1972, the National Land Agency in 1974, and the Management and Coordination Agency in 1984. In most of these cases, existing organizations were renamed, upgraded, or restructured. To cite two examples, in 1960 the Autonomy Agency (Jichichō) was upgraded to the Ministry of Home Affairs, and in 1984 the Administrative Management Agency was in effect replaced by the Management and Coordination Agency (Sōmuchō), which also assumed some of the functions that had previously been performed by the prime minister's office.[75]

Even though the goal of "administrative reform" (gyōsei kaikaku) has received much attention in the postoccupation period, actual results attained have been meagre. The number of "regular service" national civil servants (ippan shoku kokka kōmuin) has ranged from 643,057 in 1955 to 867,172 in 1981. In 1986, it declined to 847,004.[76] Although a significant streamlining of the government structure would require a thoroughgoing reappraisal and a substantial reduction of the powers of the central-government ministries and agencies, the entrenched powers of the bureaucracy have thus far forestalled such an approach, necessitating the adoption of a "uniform reduction method" whereby all ministries and agencies are required to eliminate the same number of bureaus, sections, or other units.[77] A recent example of such an approach is Prime Minister Takeshita Noboru's plan to seek a transfer

75. Gyōsei Kanrichō, Gyōsei kanri no genjō: Gyōsei kaikaku no dōkō [The Present Condition of Administrative Management: Trends in Administrative Reform] (Tokyo: Ōkurashō, Insatsukyoku, 1984), pp. 56–57.

76. For these and related statistics, see Jinji-in, Jinji gyōsei sanjūnen no ayumi [The Path of Thirty Years of Public Personnel Administration] (Tokyo: Ōkurashō, Insatsukyoku, 1978), p. 544; idem, Kōmuin hakusho, 1978 through 1987.

77. For a critical assessment of this issue, see Yoshinori Ide, "Administrative Reform and Innovation: the Japanese Case," International Social Science Journal 21, no. 1 (1969): 56–67; Naka Mamoru, "Kongetsu no shōten: Nakasone gyōkaku no sannenban o sōkatsu suru" [Focus of the Month: Summarizing Three and a Half Years of Nakasone's Administrative Reform], Kankai, Aug. 1986, pp. 82–93.

of one unit from each national-government ministry or agency to the local level.[78]

The poor record of the Japanese government in administrative reform should caution against minimizing the results of the Occupation reforms. Let us attempt to assess the latter in an impressionistic way.

AN ASSESSMENT OF
THE OCCUPATION REFORM

SCAP's program of civil-service reform in Japan was part of its larger program of democratization. Convinced that the democratization of the political system as a whole would be incomplete or even jeopardized without a corresponding change in the government bureaucracy, SCAP pursued the twin goals of modernizing and democratizing the Japanese civil-service system.

The principal instrument of the reform was a comprehensive civil-service law, of which the centerpiece was to be a powerful central personnel agency. Armed with quasi-legislative powers as well as a measure of independence, such an agency would function as the principal guardian of merit principles in the recruitment, promotion, and remuneration of civil servants. The civil-service law would also pave the way for the introduction of a position-classification system for the first time in Japanese history; additionally, by prohibiting strikes and other dispute behavior by civil servants, the law would help ensure both the integrity of government operations and the political neutrality of its personnel.

Paradoxically, however, the lofty objective of democratization was pursued in a patently undemocratic fashion. As the Japanese appeared to be incapable of initiating and implementing any significant reform on their own, SCAP simply imposed its will on them, behaving in a "highly dogmatic and inflexible" manner.[79] Although the relationship between the conqueror and the conquered was bound to be asymmetrical, it nonetheless allowed the Japanese some room for maneuver. This was facilitated by SCAP's policy of indirect rule and the language barrier. The unauthorized revision of the American draft of the national

78. *Asahi shinbun,* 5 Dec. 1987. Prime Minister Takeshita did, however, indicate some flexibility, which would allow certain agencies exemption from the proposed reduction.

79. Ward, "Reflections on the Allied Occupation," p. 509.

public-service law in the legislative stage was a case in point, although it proved to be short-lived.

In the short run, SCAP attained all of its major goals: the enactment of a comprehensive civil-service law, the establishment of a central personnel agency, and the introduction of modern concepts and procedures of public-personnel management. Nonetheless, whether all this would materially change Japan's bureaucratic landscape hinged on how the Japanese themselves would respond to the innovations.

As things turned out, some of the ideas, although enshrined in law, were never implemented, notably position classification and the use of examination in promotions. Nor have the power and influence of the National Personnel Authority turned out to be nearly as great as its American architects had hoped. As will be shown in the following pages, moreover, the old patterns of Japanese bureaucracy—stratification, elitism, legalism, retirement practices, and the like—have proved to be singularly resilient.

Our tentative assessment of this unique experiment—an externally imposed reform inspired by democratic ideals but implemented in an authoritarian fashion—is, then, a mixed one. It was neither a rousing success nor a dismal failure. At a minimum, it accomplished something the Japanese had never been able to do: the establishment of a central personnel agency endowed with a modicum of independence and modest amounts of authority to safeguard the ideals of democracy, equity, and efficiency in public administration.

In comparative terms, what the Americans did in occupied Japan was not actually unique. Efforts to reform the civil-service system were also made in occupied Germany. Even though the two occupations occurred contemporaneously, they differed in a major way: whereas the Allied occupation of Japan was in fact an American show, that of Germany was a joint or, more accurately, a disjointed operation. That may help account for the meagre results of the American and British attempts at civil-service reform in their occupation zones. The reform implemented by the government of the Federal Republic of Germany bore little relationship to the objectives embodied in Military Government Law No. 15, jointly proclaimed by the American and British occupation authorities on 19 February 1949.[80]

---

80. For an informative analysis by a former participant in the U.S. occupation of Germany, see Arnold Brecht, "Personnel Management" in Edward H. Litchfield et al., *Governing Postwar Germany* (Ithaca: Cornell University Press, 1953), pp. 263–93.

Before we leap to the conclusion that all externally guided reforms of civil-service systems have but slim chances of success, however, we need to note that some of the SCAP-initiated reforms were more successful than others. The modest outcome of the civil-service reform, for example, stands in stark contrast to SCAP's record in other areas, notably the revision of the Japanese constitution, the expansion of the franchise, and land reform. As Ward has demonstrated, the Occupation was most successful when it was able to implement the strategy of creating "new vested interests" by finding a clientele group, activating it, and enacting reform legislation that created new vested interests for the clientele. SCAP's "failure to establish and cultivate a clientele group of adequate size and influence," in his view, may have been "a basic reason" for the "failure" of the civil-service reform.[81]

In other words, it is theoretically possible that SCAP could have attained better results had it made determined efforts to create a structure of vested interests among the Japanese bureaucrats. To be sure, the constraints were formidable indeed: the Japanese bureaucrats' instinct for self-preservation, the perception gap between the Americans and the Japanese, the language barrier, and the myopia and ethnocentrism of some of the key American participants.

Most important, perhaps, was the gap between American rhetoric and behavior. Although SCAP extolled the importance of bureaucratic reform and underscored its pivotal role in Japan's democratization, what it actually sought was not a fundamental reduction of bureaucratic power nor a measurable increase in the external constraints on bureaucrats but the more modest goal of making the bureaucracy efficient and modern. As T. J. Pempel argues, this was perhaps a logical concomitant of dominant traditions in "American administrative practice during the mid-twentieth century," which also included functional fragmentation and "the dominance and penetration of particular government agencies by special interests."[82] Pempel shows that jurisdictional rivalries among not only Japanese government ministries but also their counterpart units in the SCAP General Headquarters, particularly cross-national alliances that resulted therefrom, played a significant role in impeding reform.[83] In sum, even though SCAP accomplished what no Japanese government had managed to do, the accomplishment nonetheless left something to be desired.

81. Ward, "Reflections on the Allied Occupation," pp. 528–31.
82. Pempel, "The Tar Baby Target," p. 161.
83. Ibid., pp. 173–79.

CHAPTER FOUR

Recruitment

Of all the variables affecting the performance of a government bureaucracy, none is as universally important as the caliber of its personnel. No matter how well endowed it may be in terms of funds, legislative mandate, and constituency support, a bureaucracy's operating effectiveness is likely to be severely curtailed unless it is staffed by competent and dedicated people. How to recruit and retain such people, then, becomes a task of the highest priority for nearly all bureaucracies.

In the case of the Japanese-government bureaucracy, however, a number of factors magnify further the importance of recruitment. First, the custom of lifetime employment underscores the imperative necessity of selecting the right persons initially. Second, the persistence of decentralized recruitment despite the creation of a central personnel agency, coupled with an extremely low degree of lateral mobility—that is, interagency transfers—helps to foster both competition and caution in the recruitment process. Third, the multiple-track system of recruitment, under which the future leaders of government ministries and agencies must be identified and selected at the outset, raises the stakes of initial recruitment. Moreover, the virtual absence of probationary appointment further enhances the importance of selectivity in recruitment.

In this chapter we shall first note a few general attributes of the Japanese civil service that may help us to understand its system of recruitment. We shall then scrutinize the modes of recruitment, with particular attention to the higher civil-service examination. Next, we shall examine the patterns of recruitment. That is, what are the actual results obtained during the postwar period? Statistical data will be analyzed with the aim of ascertaining continuity and change in key areas. Finally, we shall compare the Japanese experience with those of four industrialized democracies in the West.

AN OVERVIEW OF
THE JAPANESE CIVIL SERVICE

To place the discussion of recruitment in perspective, it is necessary to note a few outstanding aspects of the Japanese civil service. The preceding chapter has already delineated its basic legal and institutional framework. The national public-service law spells out its basic standards, principles, and procedures. The law sets up the National Personnel Authority as one of the two "central personnel administrative organs" (*chūō jinji gyōsei kikan*).[1] Until 1984, the Bureau of Personnel in the prime minister's office was the other organ. In July of that year, however, the Bureau of Personnel was transferred to the newly created Management and Coordination Agency (Sōmuchō).[2] In practice, the authority functions as the principal personnel agency in the Japanese government.

At the policy making level, the authority consists of three commissioners (*jinjikan*) who are appointed by the Cabinet for four years with the approval of both houses of the Diet. No two commissioners may belong to the same political party or be graduates of the same faculty of the same university. They may be reappointed but their maximum term of office is twelve years. One of the commissioners is designated by the cabinet as president (*sōsai*) of the authority. The commissioners may not be removed from office except through impeachment. The daily operations of the authority are in the hands of a staff of about seven hundred persons headed by the secretary general (*jimu sōchō*).[3]

---

1. Chapter 2, articles 3 through 25 of the national public-service law in Jinji-in, *Ninmen kankei hōreishū* [Collection of Laws and Ordinances Concerning Appointments and Dismissals], 1984 ed. (Tokyo: Ōkurashō, Insatusukyoku, 1984), pp. 14–19.

2. Gyōsei Kanrichō, *Gyōsei kanri no genjō: Gyōsei kaikaku no dōkō*, pp. 26–28. In the 1984 reorganization the Administrative Management Agency (Gyōsei Kanrichō) was abolished and most of its functions were taken over by the newly created Management and Coordination Agency.

3. For details regarding the organization and functions of the National Personnel Authority, see Katō Hisabumi, *Jinji-in: Nihon no shihai kiko* [The National Personnel

In 1987, the president of the authority was Utsumi Hitoshi. Born in 1917, Utsumi graduated from the law faculty of the University of Tokyo in 1941 and entered the Home Ministry in the same year. He retired from the civil service after serving as the administrative vice-minister of the Defense Agency. He was appointed to his current position in 1984 by his former classmate in both Tōdai and the Home Ministry, Prime Minister Nakasone Yasuhiro. The other two commissioners were Sano Hiroyoshi (b. 1916) and Ishizaka Seiichi (b. 1922). A 1937 graduate of Aoyama Gakuin University who majored in English literature, Sano had worked as a journalist for *Asahi shinbun* and NHK and as a political commentator before being appointed to his present position in 1985. Ishizaka graduated from Tōdai's engineering faculty in 1944, where he also did graduate work, and served in the Ministry of International Trade and Industry (MITI) for twenty-five years. He was appointed a commissioner in 1986. Traditionally, one of the three commissioners has always been a former journalist and another has had a scientific or engineering background.[4]

The basic principles guiding the Japanese civil service may be summed up in two words: democracy and efficiency. Democracy implies that unlike the Emperor's officials in prewar Japan, the public servants in postwar Japan must be true to their name: as article 15 of the 1946 constitution puts it, "all public officials are servants of the whole community and not of any group thereof."[5]

To help attain this goal, the public service must be opened up to the entire people: the principle of open and equal access to civil-service appointments needs to be implemented. This does not mean that all citizens are guaranteed government jobs, which no government can afford to do, but that they are assured of an equal opportunity to compete for such jobs. This is where the other principle comes into play:

Authority: An Organization That Controls Japan] (Tokyo: Rōdō Junpōsha, 1966); Kyōikusha, ed., *Kaikei Kensa-in, Jinji-in, Naikaku Hōseikyoku* [The Board of Audit, the National Personnel Authority, and the Cabinet Legislation Bureau] (Tokyo: Kyōikusha, 1979), pp. 69–116; and Satō Tatsuo, *Kokka kōmuin seido* [The National Public-Service System] (Tokyo: Gakuyō Shobō, 1975), pp. 13–16. See also the text of the National Public Service Law (*kokka kōmuinhō*) in Jinji-in, *Ninmen kankei hōreishū*, 1984 ed., pp. 12–45.

4. Taniai Kenzō, "Kankai jinmyaku chiri: Chūō shōchōhen: Jinji-in no maki" [Who's Who in Central-Government Ministries and Agencies: The National Personnel Authority], *Kankai*, Aug. 1987, pp. 39–41.

5. For the English text of the Japanese constitution, see Suekawa Hiroshi, ed., *Iwanami kihon roppō, Shōwa 49-nenban* [Iwanami Six Fundamental Laws, 1974 Edition] (Tokyo: Iwanami Shoten, 1973), pp. 110–16.

that of efficiency. In other words, the guiding criterion of civil-service appointments shall be merit—the objective qualifications of candidates as demonstrated in their educational attainments, experience, and performance in examinations. The mechanism through which and the degree to which these twin principles are translated into reality will be the focus of our inquiry in this chapter.

Let us now attempt to clarify the bewildering array of categories in the Japanese civil service. As of 1 July 1987, there were a total of 4,506,725 public employees (*kōmuin*) in Japan, of whom 1,172,797 belonged to the national government and the remainder to the various local governmental units. As figure 1 shows, the national public employees are divided into two broad categories: the general service (*ippan shoku*) and the special service (*tokubetsu shoku*). The latter, which comprised 328,507 employees in July 1987, encompasses such diverse positions as the prime minister, ministers of state, commissioners of the National Personnel Authority, deputy director general of the cabinet secretariat, director general of the cabinet legislation bureau, parliamentary vice-ministers, judges and other employees of the courts, members of the Diet and their secretaries, and employees of the Defense Agency.[6]

The *ippan shoku* public employees are in turn divided into (1) those governed by the regular compensation law (*kyūyohō shokuin*), (2) those governed by the special compensation law (*kyūyo tokureihō shokuin*), and (3) public prosecutors. In July 1987 there were 505,791, 336,332, and 2,167 persons respectively in the three categories. Nearly 90 percent of public employees who are subject to the special compensation law are postal employees; the remainder are engaged in such specialized occupations as forestry, printing, and engraving.[7]

Finally, the *ippan shoku* public employees who are subject to the regular compensation law are subdivided into seventeen categories, each of which carries its own salary schedule. They are (1) the Administrative Service I, (2) the Administrative Service II, (3) the Specialized Administrative Service (*senmon gyōsei shoku*), (4) the Taxation Service, (5) the Public Security Service I, (6) the Public Security Service II, (7) the Marine Service I, (8) the Marine Service II, (9) the Educational

6. See art. 2 of the national public-service law in Jinji-in, *Ninmen kankei hōreishū*, 1984 ed., p. 13. All the statistics cited here are taken from Jinji-in, *Kōmuin hakusho*, 1988, esp. p. 251.
7. Ibid., pp. 39 and 168.

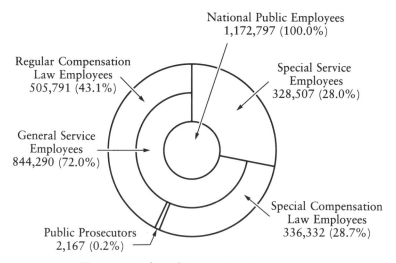

Fig. 1.   Number of National Public Employees
SOURCE: Jinji-in, *Kōmuin hakusho, 1988* (Tokyo: Ōkurashō, Insatsukyoku, 1988), p. 251.

Service I, (10) the Educational Service II, (11) the Educational Service III, (12) the Educational Service IV, (13) the Research Service, (14) the Medical Service I, (15) the Medical Service II, (16) the Medical Service III, and (17) the Designated Service (*shitei shoku*).[8]

By far the single most important of these categories in terms of both size and relevance for this study is the Administrative Service I. In 1987 it consisted of 227,725 or 46.8 percent of all persons covered by the seventeen salary schedules. It includes most people whom one ordinarily associates with civil service. The Administrative Service II salary schedule, on the other hand, covers drivers of automobiles, operators of all mechanized equipment, guards, and other people who are engaged in similar activities. The Specialized Administrative Service, which was newly established in 1985, encompasses inspectors and judges of the Patent Agency, inspectors of ships, those who work in the air-traffic-control field, and others whose duties require specialized knowledge and skills. The Educational Service I schedule covers the faculty and staff of colleges and universities. With 52,619 persons under its rubric, it was the second-largest category in 1987. The schedule for the Designated Service, on the other hand, is one of the smallest, subsuming under its rubric such positions as administrative vice-minister, head of

8. Ibid., p. 168.

an external bureau (*gaikyoku*)—an entity that is affiliated with but not an integral part of a ministry or an agency—bureau chief, dean of a college, head of a laboratory or a research institute, and director of a hospital or a sanatorium. In 1987 these positions numbered 1,357.[9]

MODES OF RECRUITMENT

Among the continuities between the prewar and postwar civil-service systems is the reliance on both competitive examinations and evaluation (*senkō*) in recruiting government officials. The national public-service law makes the use of competitive examinations the rule and permits the use of evaluation only in those cases where the National Personnel Authority has certified that the use of competitive examination would be inappropriate (article 36). Competitive examinations are administered by the National Personnel Authority. There are four general categories of exceptions: (1) top-level executive positions such as administrative vice-minister that call for managerial and supervisory abilities and competence to deal with external groups; (2) positions requiring licenses or certificates issued by the state, such as physicians, dentists, and nurses; (3) positions for which the candidates have already demonstrated their suitability by performing satisfactorily either in equivalent positions or in those requiring a greater degree of expertise and responsibility; and (4) special positions for which there is a scarcity of qualified candidates.[10] It should be noted that evaluation does not preclude but frequently entails some kind of written examination.

Although the first civil-service examination for the recruitment of national public employees under the national public-service law was not held until January 1949, there were other examinations both prior to and following that date. In 1946 and 1947 a modified version of the higher examination (*kōtō shiken*) was given three times.[11] As noted in the preceding chapter, competitive examinations were also held in 1948 to recruit staff members of the temporary National Personnel Authority. Then in 1950 there were "S-1 examinations," which was a unique experiment designed to further the Occupation's policy of democratiza-

9. Ibid.; "Sankō shiryō (kyūyo kankei)" [Reference Material (Related to Salary)], *Jinji-in geppō* 440 (Sept. 1987): 30.
10. "Jinji yōgo haya wakari: senkō" [A Quick Guide to Personnel Terms: Evaluation], *Jinji-in geppō* 87(May 1958): 17. For a more technically oriented explanation, see "Senkō ni yoru shokuin no saiyō" [Selection of Public Employees by Evaluation], ibid. 94 (Dec. 1958), 20–23.
11. Wada, "Bunkan nin'yō seido no rekishi," III, p. 13.

tion. Meanwhile, the regular civil-service examinations under the new law have been held every year since 1949. Although they have undergone many changes over the years, their principal characteristics are nonetheless worth noting.

First, there are three distinct levels. The highest level (*jōkyu* until 1984, *isshu* since 1985) is aimed at graduates of four-year colleges; the intermediate level (*chūkyū* until 1984, *nishu* since 1985) at graduates of junior colleges; and the lower level (*shokyū* until 1984; *sanshu* since 1985) at high-school graduates. From 1960 to 1984 the *jōkyu* examinations were divided into two types: A (*kōshu*) and B (*otsushu*).[12] During this period, then, there were in effect four levels of examinations, each of which led to appointment at a different grade. Of the four levels, the type-A higher examination was equivalent to the prewar higher civil-service examination, and the lower examination approximated the ordinary civil-service examination. The remaining two—the type-B higher exam and the intermediate exam—must be viewed as postwar innovations.

It is noteworthy that none of these examinations has ever had a formal educational requirement. The type-A higher civil-service examination, for example, was open to anyone between the ages of twenty-one and thirty-three regardless of educational attainments. In practice, however, the educational level of candidates taking the civil-service examinations has been quite high, reflecting the rising level of educational attainments in the general population. Between 15 and 16 percent of applicants for the type-A (or I) higher civil-service examination in recent years have had postgraduate education. The proportion increases to about 40 percent among the successful candidates. Moreover, the success rates of candidates with graduate education seem much higher than those of university graduates. For graduates of junior colleges and high schools, the probability of passing the higher examination seems negligible. Most striking of all, perhaps, are the statistics pertaining to the intermediate examination. Although geared to junior-college graduates, it has attracted growing numbers of applicants with four years of university education and more. By the 1980s, the latter accounted for

12. The type-B higher civil-service examination was originally designed to serve as a supplemental means of recruiting scientists and engineers into the higher civil service. So far as administrative personnel were concerned, it was intended to be a gateway for future midlevel managers. However, until 1966 nearly all of those who passed the type-B examination in the administrative fields were those who had failed the type-A higher civil-service examination, which applicants were allowed to take in tandem. In 1967 this privilege was rescinded. Jinji-in, *Jinji gyōsei nijūnen no ayumi*, p. 123.

more than 90 percent of the successes in the examination. Even the lower examination has attracted a sizable number of university and junior-college graduates. These two groups together have accounted for about 17 percent of the successes in the lower examination in recent years.[13]

It was partly in response to the changing character of the intermediate examination that the examination system was reorganized in 1985. The intermediate examination having effectively been turned into a vehicle for recruiting university graduates, there was a need to come to grips with that reality. Specifically, its prestige needed to be upgraded in order that the national government might compete successfully with local governments and private firms in the recruitment arena. Moreover, the demand for graduates of the type-B higher civil-service examination had steadily decreased over the years. On the other hand, the implementation of a mandatory retirement system beginning in 1985 would pave the way for generational change in the middle echelons of the national-government bureaucracy, making it necessary to increase the supply of capable middle-level administrators. Given these considerations, the National Personnel Authority decided to abolish the type-B higher examination, upgrade the intermediate examination, and rename all three examinations. The type-A higher examination became simply type I, the intermediate became type II, and the lower examination became type III.[14]

A second noteworthy feature of the civil-service examinations pertains to specialization, for all candidates are required to choose a specific field of specialization. In the higher (type I) examination, candidates must choose one of the following twenty-eight fields: public administration, law, economics, psychology, education, sociology, mathematics, physics, geology, information engineering, electrical engineering, electronics and communications, mechanical engineering, civil engineering, architecture, chemistry, metallurgy, energy engineering, pharmacy, agriculture, agricultural economics, agricultural chemistry, agricultural engineering, animal husbandry, forestry, fishery science, erosion control (*sabō*), and landscape design (*zōen*).[15]

---

13. For relevant statistics, see Jinji-in, *Kōmuin hakusho*, 1985, p. 28; ibid., 1986, pp. 29–31; ibid., 1987, pp. 35–36.

14. "Saiyō shiken taikei no saihen seibi ni tsuite" [On the Reorganization and Adjustment of the Recruitment Examination System], *Jinji-in geppō* 411(Apr. 1985): 10–17.

15. Jinji-in, *Kōmuin hakusho*, 1987, p. 29.

From 1949 to 1954, candidates for the higher examination opting for the field of public administration were allowed to choose an additional field of specialization. Now candidates for the type-II examination are given a choice of twelve fields: public administration, library science, physics, electrical engineering and electronics, mechanical engineering, civil engineering, architecture, chemistry, energy engineering, agriculture, agricultural civil engineering (*nōgyō doboku*), and forestry. All but three of these fields are also available for type-III-examination candidates. The exceptions are library science, physics, and energy engineering. Two fields that are unique to the type-III examination are postal affairs (*yūsei jimu*) and taxation.[16]

Table 5 presents some statistics regarding the fields of specialization represented in the hiring of those who have passed the higher civil-service examination (HCSE) in the 1960–86 period. Note that this table pertains not to the successful applicants but to those who were actually hired by the various ministries and agencies. As we shall see below, only about half of the successful applicants receive appointments. The table shows that those choosing law and the social sciences as their fields of specialization in the HCSE, most of whom become administrative officials (*jimukan*), have always been a minority. In fact, until 1972 they were eclipsed by those choosing engineering and the natural sciences. In subsequent years, although "law and the social sciences" has become the largest of the three categories, it has nonetheless remained well below the 50-percent mark, hovering around 40 percent.

A third feature of the examination system is that all examinations have multiple stages. The first stage in the higher examination consists of two sets of multiple-choice tests. The first set, known as *kyōyō shiken* (general-culture test), is made up of sixty questions designed to test general knowledge, aptitude, and intelligence; it lasts three hours. The second set, called *senmon shiken* (specialized test), contains the same number of questions and is designed to measure the level of expertise in the candidate's chosen field of specialization and lasts three and a half hours. Between 90 and 95 percent of candidates are eliminated in this initial phase.[17]

---

16. For the type-III examination, public administration is subdivided into administrative affairs (*gyōsei jimu*) A and B. See ibid., pp. 30–31 and "Saiyō shiken taikei no saihen," pp. 14–15.

17. Juken Shinpō Henshūbu, *Kōmuin shiken mondai to taisaku: Jōkyū shiken, '85-nenban* [Questions and Strategies for Civil-Service Examinations: The Higher Examination, 1985 Edition] (Tokyo: Hōgaku Shoin, 1984), pp. 2–206.

TABLE 5   Recruitment of Higher Civil Servants,
by Field of Specialization

Field

Year[a]	Law and Social Sciences[b]		Engineering and Natural Sciences		Agriculture and Related Fields		All Fields	
	N	%	N	%	N	%	N	%
1960	246	37.0	286	43.1	132	19.9	664	100.0
1962	308	35.9	429	50.0	121	14.1	858	100.0
1964	349	35.5	454	46.2	179	18.2	982	99.9
1966	289	35.4	351	43.0	177	21.7	817	100.1
1970[c]	277	38.0	304	41.7	148	20.3	729	100.0
1972	235	37.2	260	41.1	137	21.7	632	100.0
1974	266	40.2	255	38.6	140	21.2	661	100.0
1976	238	42.0	193	34.0	136	24.0	567	100.0
1978	263	40.8	229	35.5	153	23.7	645	100.0
1980	254	41.4	189	30.8	171	27.8	614	100.0
1982	250	40.4	202	32.7	166	26.9	618	100.0
1984	272	39.5	233	33.9	183	26.6	688	100.0
1985	308	42.7	243	33.7	170	23.6	721	100.0
1986	292	41.3	254	36.0	160	22.7	706	100.0

SOURCES: *Jinji-in geppō,* 196 (June 1967): 10; Jinji-in, *Nenji hōkokusho,* 1971–1987 (Tokyo, 1972–88).
    [a]The year refers not to the year in which civil servants were hired but the year in which they passed the higher civil-service examination.
    [b]Until 1971 this category included four fields: public administration, law, economics, and psychology. In 1972 education, psychology, and sociology were added to the list.
    [c]The data from 1970 to 1984 pertain to those who passed the type-A higher civil-service examination only. The 1985 data refer to those who passed the type I-higher civil-service examination.

In the second phase, candidates are again subjected to two sets of tests, one specialized and the other general. But unlike the previous tests, these consist of essay-type or problem-solving-type questions. Those opting for the field of public administration, for example, must choose three subjects out of five (constitutional law, political science, social policy, public administration, and principles of economics) and answer one essay question in each subject. They are given three hours in which to compose three essays. To give some examples of questions: "discuss equality and discrimination in democracy" (political science), "discuss the similarities and differences between public administration and private management" (public administration), "discuss measures for dealing with the aging of the work force" (social policy), and "discuss the microeconomic foundations of the Keynesian macroeconomics" (economics).[18]

The general test (sōgō shiken) in this phase typically requires the applicant to answer two questions in two and a half hours. Its aim is to test the candidate's ability to synthesize ideas and his judgment, analytic ability, and ability to think. A frequently used device is to present long excerpts from an article, often in English, and then ask the candidate to summarize and evaluate the main arguments.[19] There is then a brief oral examination (jinbutsu shiken) during which the candidate is questioned about his motives for choosing government service, his interests and hobbies, and other matters. About half of the candidates surviving the first round are eliminated in the second round of competition.[20]

A fourth and final feature of the examination system that needs to be explained is the decentralization of hiring. Officially, recruitment activities should not commence until early October after the final results of the higher examination have been announced. The National Personnel Authority compiles rosters of successful candidates (saiyō kōhosha meibo) for each field of specialization; names are listed in the order of the scores earned. Upon receipt of requests from the ministries and agencies, the authority forwards lists of eligible candidates, whose numbers typically exceed the number of vacancies by a ratio of five to one. Actual hiring is supposed to begin in early November.[21]

Unofficially, however, the process begins in early August immediately after the completion of the second phase of the higher examination. Even though half of them will be eliminated in the competition, the candidates nonetheless begin to pound the pavement in Kasumigaseki—a section of Tokyo's Chiyoda district where government offices are located—in a ritual known as kanchō hōmon (visits to government

18. Kōmuin Shiken Jōhō Kenkyūkai, ed. 88 nendo-han kōmuin saiyō shiken shirizu: Isshu kokka kōmuin shiken [1988 Edition, Civil-Service-Examination Series: Type-I National Public-Employee Examination] (Tokyo: Hitotsubashi Shoten, 1986), p. 46. All of these questions are from the tests intended for applicants taking the public-administration option.

19. For examples of questions in the general test, which are too long to be translated here, see ibid., pp. 382–99.

20. Tashiro Kū, "Nihon gyōseikan kenkyū, III: gyōseikan no kyaria keisei katei (1)" [A Study of Japanese Public Administrators, Part III: The Making of Administrator's Career (1)], Kankai, Dec. 1981, pp. 69–71; Juken Shinpō Henshūbu, ed., Watashi no totta kokka jōkyū shiken toppahō, 86-nenban [How I Passed the National Higher (Civil-Service) Examination, 1986 Edition] (Tokyo: Hōgaku Shoin, 1984). The last-mentioned source is a collection of essays by nineteen persons who passed the higher examination in 1984.

21. "Kōmuin shiken gōkaku kara saiyō made" [From Passing the Civil-Service Examination to Being Hired], Jinji-in geppō 103 (Sept. 1959): 14–15.

agencies). It is widely believed that candidates from top-rated universities enjoy an edge, particularly if they have strong academic records and are likely to receive high scores in the examination. A participant-observer notes that grades received at Tōdai's Law Faculty carry more weight than scores in the higher examination, for, in his view, the former is a more reliable gauge of the candidate's intellectual ability than the latter. Inasmuch as the level of difficulty is about the same in both the higher examination and examinations taken in Tōdai's Law Faculty, he states, how one has performed over a two-and-a-half-year period ought to mean more than one's score in a single examination.[22] Another observer notes, however, that one's rank in the higher examination is far more important than one's grades in college. He speculates that to have a good chance of being selected by the Ministry of Finance, which hires only twenty-five or so elite-track civil servants a year, one must rank among the top fifty successful candidates in HCSE.[23]

Government ministries and agencies are known to seek out outstanding candidates from time to time, utilizing their *kone* (connections). *Senpai* (seniors) from the same university, especially from athletic or other clubs, and professors can play the role of match-maker. A candidate who had earned the third highest scores in the higher examination in the mid-1960s, for example, received a telephone call from a *senpai,* a former member of Tōdai's English Speaking Society. Over lunch, the *senpai* made a pitch for the Finance Ministry, which the candidate eventually chose over the Ministry of International Trade and Industry.[24]

During the unofficial visits to government ministries and agencies, some candidates receive signals about possible appointment. Typically, a candidate visits a number of ministries and agencies and then narrows his choice to a few. After repeated visits to a ministry or agency, he may even receive a signal about a possible offer of appointment. Some candidates report having received an informal decision (*nainaitei*) as early as late August—a full month before the final results of the HCSE are published and formal ministerial examinations (oral) begin.[25]

As we shall see later in the chapter, there are signs that the gap

22. Katō, *Kanryō desu, yoroshiku,* pp. 39–40.
23. Kuribayashi, *Ōkurashō shukeikyoku,* p. 30. Katō served in the Home Ministry, whereas Kuribayashi is referring to the Finance Ministry.
24. Ibid., pp. 19–22. In this case the recruitment activity took place after the final results of the higher civil-service examination were announced.
25. Juken Shinpō Henshūbu, ed., *Watashi no totta kokka jōkyū shiken,* pp. 120–21.

between Tōdai and the other universities is slowly being narrowed and that the disadvantages of private-university graduates are becoming increasingly less severe.

Table 6 presents some statistics about the higher civil-service examinations. It is plain that they are keenly competitive. As column D shows, only a small proportion of the applicants pass the examinations. What needs to be stressed is that the number of applicants is invariably greater than the number of those who actually take the examinations. During the years for which relevant statistics are available, about 18 percent of those who submitted their applications failed to show up. This means that the numbers in column D overstate the extent of competition during the years 1967 and 1973–1988. Nonetheless, during most years, over 95 percent of those who took the examinations failed. The number of applicants peaked in 1979 and leveled off in subsequent years, whereas the number passing increased steadily during the same period. This led to a notable increase in the proportion of successful candidates (column D), although it still remains well below 10 percent even after allowance is made for the discrepancy between the number of applicants and the number of those taking the examinations.

The table also demonstrates that passing the highly competitive examinations by no means ensures an appointment to a civil-service position. As column E shows, only about half of the successful candidates are actually hired. This does not mean, however, that the remainder are simply bypassed. In the 1976–84 period, three out of ten candidates who had passed the type-A higher examination and four out of ten candidates who had passed the type-B higher examination either withdrew their names from the rosters of eligibles or failed to respond to further communication from the government. In the 1981–86 period, the withdrawal rate of type-A candidates increased sharply, to about 37 percent. The proportion of type-B candidates withdrawing from the roster also increased, from 33 percent in 1981 to 52 percent in 1984.[26]

The higher withdrawal rate of type-B candidates reflected their somewhat limited career prospects as compared with those of type-A candidates. Not only did the former have relatively limited choice in terms of potential employers, but they were not expected to rise to the apex of the bureaucratic pyramid. Type-A candidates, on the other hand, faced a wider range of options as well as fairly rapid advancement in the civil service. Although all graduates of the HCSE theoretically

26. The rates of withdrawal or nonresponse were calculated from the data in Jinji-in, *Kōmuin hakusho*, 1978–1986.

TABLE 6 *Results of Higher Civil-Service Examinations, in Selected Years*

Year	(A) Number of Applicants	(B) Number Passing	(C) Number Hired	(D) $\frac{B}{A}$ %	(E) $\frac{C}{B}$ %
1949[a]	21,438*[b]	2,355[c]	833		35.4
1952	24,392*	2,142	961	8.8	44.9
1955	23,053*	1,314	635	5.7	48.3
1958	20,228*	1,751	761	8.7	43.5
1961					
A[d]	9,152*	1,133	642	12.4	56.7
B	693*	397	183	57.3	46.1
1964					
A	12,420*	1,434	814	11.5	56.8
B	1,449*	373	146	25.7	39.1
1967					
A	21,567	1,364	667	6.3	48.9
B	3,659	148	68	4.0	45.9
1970					
A	14,550*	1,353	729	9.2	53.9
B	2,069*	143	91	6.9	63.6
1973					
A	30,129	1,410	639	4.7	45.3
B	4,855	134	58	2.8	43.3
1976					
A	44,518	1,136	567	1.3	49.9
B	5,417	100	55	1.0	55.0
1979					
A	51,896	1,265	615	2.4	48.6
B	4,814	90	54	1.9	60.0
1982					
A	36,856	1,383	618	3.8	44.7
B	3,646	95	53	2.6	58.8
1985	36,072	1,655	721	4.6	43.6
1988	28,833	1,814		6.3	

SOURCE: Jinji-in, *Nenji hōkokusho,* 1948–49 through 1986 (Tokyo: Ōkurashō, Insatsukyoku, 1950–87); *Asahi shinbun,* 7 Sept. 1988 (evening ed.).

NOTE: The numbers in column A with asterisks refer to those applicants who actually took the examinations. During those years, between 10.5 and 22.6 percent of the applicants failed to show up for the exams. The mean no-show rate is 18.3 percent. The relevant statistics are not available for the remaining years.

[a]There were two examinations in 1949. The data reported here pertain to the one given in Nov. of that year.

[b]This number includes candidates for both grade-6 (higher-level) and grade-5 (intermediate-level) positions.

[c]Those who passed the grade-6 exam only.

[d]From 1960 to 1984 the higher civil-service examination consisted of two types: A (*kōshu*) and B (*otsushu*). In 1985, type B was abolished, and type A renamed type I.

qualified as *kyaria* (career civil servants), in practice the prestige and upward mobility implied by the term *kyaria* were not equally shared by all of them. In Japan, *kyaria* refers to elite-track bureaucrats, and *nonkyaria* (noncareer) refers to all the remainder.[27]

Since 1971, the largest proportion of type-B graduates was hired by the National Tax Administration Agency (Kokuzeichō). In that year the proportion was 51.6 percent, and by 1975 it had risen to 59.0 percent. In 1985, the last year for which type-B graduates were eligible for civil-service appointment, the proportion stood at 77.8 percent.[28] In the Finance Ministry, of which the NTAA is an external bureau (*gaikyoku*), informal distinctions are maintained among *honshō kyaria* ("career" civil servants hired by the ministry proper), *kokuzei kyaria* ("career" civil servants hired by the NTAA), *zaimu kyaria* ("career" civil servants hired by the Financial Bureau [Zaimukyoku], and *zeikan kyaria* ("career" civil servants hired by the customs). Journalists who cover the Finance Ministry sum up the differential speeds of promotion among the various groups of civil servants as follows: "The *honshō kyaria* rides the jet airplane, the *kokuzei kyaria* the bullet train (*shinkansen*), the *zaimu kyaria* the special express (*tokkyū*), the *zeikan kyaria* the express (*kyūkō*), and the *nonkyaria* the slow train (*donkō*)."[29]

The successful applicants who either voluntarily withdraw their names or fail to fill out forms required for further consideration do so because they have other options. Some have offers from private firms. Others may choose to pursue graduate studies. Still others may have passed the judicial examination and opted for entry into the Judicial Training Institute. If we add up those who are hired and those who withdraw, then we are left with only 20 to 25 percent of the successful applicants who fail to receive offers of appointment from government ministries and agencies. No data are available regarding what happens to those people.[30]

27. Tashiro Kū, "Nihon gyōseikan kenkyū, VII: kyaria to nonkyaria" [A Study of Japanese Public Administrators, Part VII: Career and Noncareer], *Kankai*, Apr. 1982, pp. 68–79.

28. The National Tax Administration Agency (NTAA) began to hire type-B graduates in 1968; however, the number remained small (17 in 1968, 16 in 1969, and 26 in 1970) until 1971, when 197 were hired. Jinji-in, *Nenji hōkokusho*, 1961–1986 (Tokyo: 1962–87).

29. Kuribayashi, *Ōkurashō shukeikyoku*, p. 43.

30. The proportion of the successful candidates who neither withdrew nor were hired in selected years is as follows: 1960, (type A) 15.4 percent, (type B) 26.0 percent; 1965, (A) 26.1 percent, (B) 27.3 percent; 1970, (A) 20.9 percent, (B) 18.2 percent; 1975, (A) 25.0 percent, (B) 7.1 percent; 1980, (A) 23.2 percent, (B) 10.0 percent; 1985, (type I) 19.6 percent. Jinji-in, *Nenji hōkokusho*, 1961, 1966, 1971, 1976, 1981, and 1986 (Tokyo, 1962–1987).

TABLE 7   *Modes of Recruitment of Civil Servants in Japan*

Year	Examination[a]	Evaluation	Both Modes	% by Examination
		All Positions		
1957	3,397	11,845	15,242	22.3
1961	8,712	27,853	36,565	23.8
1965	14,079	28,611	42,690	33.0
1969	12,198	16,100	38,298	31.9
1973	11,169	22,993	34,162	32.7
1977	10,886	18,883	29,769	36.6
1981	15,383	19,618	35,001	44.0
1985	16,105	19,730	35,958[b]	44.8
		Administrative Service I Positions Only		
1957	2,200	1,015	3,215	68.4
1961	6,673	3,865	10,538	63.3
1965	8,991	2,522	11,513	78.1
1969	8,003	2,120	10,123	79.1
1973	7,794	2,635	10,429	74.7
1977	6,523	2,180	8,703	75.0
1981	8,665	2,076	10,741	80.7
1985	9,976	2,114	12,186[b]	81.9

SOURCE: Jinji-in, *Nenji hōkokusho*, 1958–1986 (Tokyo: Ōkurasho, Insatsukyoka, 1959–87).

[a]"Examination" refers to all levels of civil-service examinations.

[b]The totals for 1985 are larger than the sums of examination and evaluation, because they include persons whose mode of recruitment is classified as "reappointment."

PATTERNS OF RECRUITMENT

EXAMINATION VS. EVALUATION

The available statistics suggest a number of noteworthy patterns in the recruitment of civil servants during the postwar period. In the first place, although competitive examination was intended to be the principal mode of recruitment, evaluation (*senkō*) has played and continues to play a very imporant role. As table 7 shows, if we look at the civil service as a whole, it is evaluation, not competitive examination, that has served as the primary mode of recruitment. Until the early 1960s, fewer than one in four new appointees had taken civil-service examinations. Although the proportion has increased steadily since then, it has yet to reach the 50-percent mark.

The overall picture, however, is misleading, for it is affected, to a large extent, by the recruitment patterns of specialized personnel, such as educators and health-care specialists. When such personnel are excluded, that is to say, when we focus on civil servants in the Administrative Service I only, the picture changes appreciably.[31] In 1957, almost seven of every ten Administrative Service I bureaucrats were recruited through competitive examinations, and by 1965 the proportion rose to 78 percent. In the 1980s, eight of every ten civil servants who were appointed to Administrative Service I positions each year were examination-certified.

Because these numbers pertain to new hirings only, however, we need to take note of the situation concerning the incumbent civil servants. So far as the total population of the Administrative Service I was concerned, those who had been recruited through the various competitive examinations constituted 60.7 percent of the total in March 1986, a substantially lower proportion than that for the new appointees in recent years.[32] It should also be stressed that only a very small proportion of the examination-qualified appointees had passed the higher civil-service examinations. When both types A and B are considered, the proportion has averaged about 9 percent. The average drops to about 6 percent when type A alone is taken into account.

Another glimpse of the patterns of recruitment is provided by table 8. It must be borne in mind that whereas table 7 pertained to new appointees only, this table presents data on *incumbent* civil servants covered by the Administrative Service I salary schedule. To make our task manageable, however, only the occupants of grades 1 through 3 will be analyzed.[33] Focusing on grade 1 first, we see a clear trend toward institutionalization, in which the higher civil-service examination has emerged as the dominant mode of entry into the elite positions. Whereas in 1970 only one-quarter of the grade 1 occupants had passed the higher civil-service examination, by 1972 over one-third of them had done so. By 1974, higher-examination-qualified incumbents were in the major-

31. As mentioned previously, the Administrative Service (I) accounts for nearly half of general-service civil servants and includes most people who perform clerical, administrative, and managerial functions. The other categories of civil servants encompass revenue and custom agents, crews of state-owned vessels; teachers, professors, researchers, and educational administrators; and health-care personnel.

32. Jinji-in, *Kōmuin hakusho,* 1987, p. 46.

33. These grades refer to the system that was in use until 20 Dec. 1985. On 21. Dec. 1985, a new system went into effect. See "Kyūyoho no kaisei ni tsuite" [On the Revision of the Compensation Law], *Jinji-in geppō* 421 (Feb. 1986): 6–47.

TABLE 8   *Civil Servants in Administrative Service I Positions, by Mode of Recruitment and Current Grade*

Mode of Recruitment (%)

Year	Grade[a]	Examination			Evaluation	Both Modes	N
		Higher	Middle	Lower			
1970	1	25.8	—	—	74.2	100.0	1,070
	2	28.5	0.1	—	71.4	100.0	3,824
	3	21.2	0.6	—	78.2	100.0	7,031
1972	1	34.5	—	—	65.5	100.0	1,105
	2	35.2	0.2	—	64.6	100.0	4,086
	3	21.4	1.8	0.1	76.7	100.0	8,755
1974	1	53.8	0.3	—	45.9	100.0	1,109
	2	39.4	0.8	—	59.8	100.0	4,386
	3	20.2	3.2	0.5	76.1	100.0	10,553
1976[b]	1	68.2	0.2	—	31.6	100.0	1,219
	2	40.0	1.6	0.0[c]	58.4	100.0	4,621
	3	18.5	4.7	0.9	75.9	100.0	12,464
1978	1	76.0	0.2	—	23.7	100.0	1,344
	2	40.3	2.1	0.1	57.5	100.0	4,846
	3	17.1	5.4	1.5	76.1	100.0	15,454
1980	1	79.0	0.5	—	20.5	100.0	1,418
	2	40.4	4.3	0.8	54.5	100.0	5,041
	3	17.7	6.9	2.4	73.0	100.0	15,959
1981	1	80.3	0.5	0.1	19.1	100.0	1,450
	2	40.4	4.8	1.0	53.8	100.0	5,071
	3	18.2	7.7	3.0	71.1	100.0	16,512
1982	1	81.4 (81.2)[d]	1.2	0.1	17.3	100.0	1,447
	2	39.8 (39.2)	6.1	1.5	52.6	100.0	5,180
	3	18.4 (16.4)	8.6	3.8	69.2	100.0	17,024
1983	1	81.5 (79.4)	1.9	0.3	18.2	100.0	1,458
	2	40.1 (39.2)	6.8	2.3	50.9	100.1	5,258
	3	19.2 (16.8)	9.5	4.9	66.5	100.0	17,480
1984	1	80.2 (79.7)	1.9	1.2	16.7	100.0	1,445
	2	40.6 (39.6)	7.0	2.7	49.7	100.0	5,370
	3	18.6 (16.3)	10.0	6.3	65.1	100.0	17,906

SOURCES: Jinji-in, *Nenji hōkokusho*, 1971–1985 (Tokyo: Ōkurashō, Insatsukyoku, 1972–86).

[a]Although a new system of grades went into effect on 21 Dec. 1985, this table is based on the old system. Grade 1 encompasses assistant bureau chief (*kyoku jichō*), division chief (*buchō*), and senior-level section chief (*kachō*) in the central-government ministries; grade 2 encompasses junior-level section chief; and grade 3 encompasses senior-level assistant section chief (*kachō hosa*).

[b]The data for 1976–84 pertain to the situation at the end of the year.

[c]N = 2.

[d]The figures in parentheses refer to type-A higher examination only. The breakdown between types A and B is available for 1982–84 only.

ity, and by the early 1980s the higher civil-service examination had become the source of 80 percent of grade-1 officials.

Note also that since 1974 those who had passed the intermediate civil-service examination began to appear in grade 1. Although their actual number is quite small—3 each in 1974, 1976, and 1978, 7 each in 1980 and 1981, 16 in 1982, and 27 each in 1983 and 1984—it is nonetheless significant that products of the intermediate-level examination can and do rise to such high positions. What is more, in 1981 an alumnus of the lower civil-service examination reached grade 1 for the first time in the postwar period. The number has steadily increased in the ensuing years: 2 in 1982, 5 in 1983, and 18 in 1984.

Turning to grade 2, we see the same general trend: a steady increase in the proportion of examination-qualified incumbents over the fifteen-year span. Unlike the situation in grade 1, however, it was not until the end of 1983 that examination had produced a bare majority of incumbents. While the proportion of those who passed the higher civil-service examination appears to have stabilized at the 40-percent mark since 1974, that of the intermediate-examination graduates has shown a marked growth throughout the period. We also find a steady increase in the number of lower civil-service-examination graduates: 2 in 1976, 3 in 1978, 40 in 1980, 53 in 1981, 80 in 1982, 120 in 1983, and 143 in 1984.

As for grade 3, the situation is notably different. Not only has evaluation eclipsed examination by a ratio of seven to three, but the rate of change has been rather low. Alumni of both the intermediate and lower examinations have nonetheless made steady progress. In sum, table 8 demonstrates several distinct trends: (1) access to the positions of assistant bureau chief, division chief, senior-level section chief, and their equivalents is gradually becoming limited to those who have passed the higher civil-service examinations; (2) a tiny fraction of those who entered the civil service by way of the intermediate examination can attain these high-level positions; and (3) that goal is within the reach of even alumni of the lower examination. Realistically, however, the highest position level that the latter can aspire to appears to be that of junior-level section chief or its equivalent.

A statistical breakdown among the higher-examination-certified civil servants is available for the years 1982 through 1984 only. It shows that graduates of the type-B higher examination are concentrated in lower grades: whereas 51 (1982) to 53 percent (1984) of the type-A higher-examination graduates occupied the top three grades, only 12 (1982) to

14 percent (1984) of the type-B higher-examination graduates did so. The actual number of type-B graduates in grade 1 was negligible: 3 each in 1982 and 1983 and 7 in 1984. This means that there were more lower-examination graduates in the top grade than there were type-B graduates (18 compared with 7 in 1984). In grade-2 positions, lower-examination graduates outnumbered type-B graduates by 80 to 30 in 1982, 120 to 46 in 1983, and 143 to 56 in 1984.[34]

UNIVERSITY BACKGROUND OF
SUCCESSFUL CANDIDATES

In chapter 2 we saw that the prewar Japanese bureaucracy was dominated by graduates of Tokyo Imperial University in its higher echelons and that the phenomenon was a function of the preponderance of Tōdai men among the successful candidates in the higher civil-service examinations. Table 9 presents statistics that suggest the continuation of that age-old pattern. At first glance, the phenomenon of Tōdai dominance in the higher civil-service examinations appears to be less pronounced in the postwar period than it was during the earlier era. Even though Tōdai has never ceased to be the single largest supplier of successful candidates in the higher examinations, its share of the pot has declined somewhat. The precipitate decline in 1972, however, (41-percent decline in absolute numbers and 45-percent decline in proportional terms) is an aberration triggered by an unusual circumstance: because of disruptions caused by campus unrest, no students were admitted to the University of Tokyo in 1968, which in turn led to a sharp decline in the number of its graduates in 1972. In the succeeding years, Tōdai has supplied between three and four out of every ten successful candidates.

Kyoto University (Kyōdai) has retained its position as the number-two supplier of senior bureaucrats in the postwar period. Although its share has generally remained well below one-half of Tōdai's share, there has consistently been an unbridgeable gap between Kyōdai and all other universities. In the 1966–84 period, the number-three position alternated among three schools—Hokkaido University, Tohoku University, and Tokyo Institute of Technology (Tōkyō Kōgyō Daigaku). Hokkaido

34. These statistics are not displayed in table 8; they were taken from Jinji-in, *Kōmuin hakusho*, 1984, p. 36; ibid., 1985, p. 44, and 1986, p. 44.

TABLE 9   Successful Candidates in Higher Civil-Service
Examinations, by University Background

Year	Tokyo University N	%	Kyoto University N	%	Other[a] N	%	Total N	%
1936	138	71.1	4	2.1	52	26.8	194	100.0
1941–43	547	46.7	112	9.6	512	43.7	1,171	100.0
1947[b]	154	81.5	10	5.3	25	13.2	189	100.0
1966[c]	318	21.1	142	9.4	1,047	69.5	1,507	100.0
1967	350	25.7	174	12.7	840	61.6	1,364	100.0
1970	335	24.8	129	9.5	889	65.7	1,353	100.0
1971	453	32.3	174	12.4	774	55.3	1,401	100.0
1972[d]	266	17.9	146	9.8	1,078	72.3	1,490	100.0
1973	499	35.4	204	14.5	707	50.1	1,410	100.0
1974	435	29.1	191	12.8	870	58.1	1,496	100.0
1975	459	35.2	172	13.2	674	51.6	1,305	100.0
1976	461	37.3	193	15.6	582	47.1	1,236	100.0
1977	488	38.0	211	16.4	585	45.6	1,284	100.0
1978	535	38.2	211	15.1	655	46.7	1,401	100.0
1979	541	39.9	206	15.2	608	44.9	1,355	100.0
1980	519	38.6	216	16.1	609	45.3	1,344	100.0
1981	545	37.6	210	14.5	696	47.9	1,451	100.0
1982	563	38.1	191	12.9	724	49.0	1,478	100.0
1983	547	34.9	203	12.9	818	52.2	1,568	100.0
1984	527	31.8	216	13.0	915	55.2	1,658	100.0
1985	541	32.7	219	13.2	895	54.1	1,655	100.0
1986	548	31.9	231	13.4	939	54.7	1,718	100.0
1987	525	30.9	220	13.0	951	56.1	1,696	100.0
1988	583	32.1	207	11.4	1,024	56.5	1,814	100.0

SOURCES: The 1936 and 1947 figures were calculated from Hata Ikuhiko, *Senzenki Nihon kanryōsei no seido, soshiki, jinji* (Tokyo: Tōkyō Daigaku Shuppankai, 1981), pp. 597–602 and 646–50; the 1941–43 figures were calculated from Robert M. Spaulding, Jr., *Imperial Japan's Higher Civil Service Examinations* (Princeton: Princeton University Press, 1967), pp. 269 and 277; the 1966 and 1967 figures are from *Jinji-in geppō* 197(July 1967): 15, and 209 (July 1968): 15; the 1970–71 figures are from Satō Tomoyuki et al, *Tōdaibatsu* (Tokyo: Eru Shuppansha, 1972), p. 176; the remaining data are from *Asahi shinbun*, 22 Aug. 1972, 9 Sept. 1974 (evening ed.), 1 Nov. 1975 (evening ed.), 26 Oct. 1976, 25 Oct. 1978, 15 Oct. 1983, 1 Oct. 1984 (evening ed.), 1 Oct. 1985 (evening ed.), 1 Oct. 1986 (evening ed.), and 7 Sept. 1988 (evening ed.) *Mainichi shinbun*, 11 Sept. 1985 (evening ed.), 15 Oct. 1979, 15 Oct. 1980, 15 Oct. 1981, and 15 Oct. 1982; *Nihon keizai shinbun*, 15 Sept. 1987.

[a]This category includes not only those who attended the other colleges and universities but also those without college education.

[b]The data presented in this row pertain only to the examination given in Dec. 1947. A similar examination was given in Apr. of the same year, producing a total of 173 successes.

[c]The data for 1966–71 pertain to type A only.

[d]The data for 1972–84 represent the combined totals of both types A and B. The type-B exam was abolished in 1985.

University retained the third spot continuously from 1977 to 1984.[35] Even in its best years, Hokkaido University, which is clearly the strongest of the three contenders for the number-three position, did not come close to matching Kyōdai's performance, even though it did break through the 100 barrier in 1979 for the first time, repeating the feat in 1984.

Significantly, all of these universities are national universities (*kokuritsu daigaku*). In 1985, however, Waseda University, a private institution of higher learning, captured the number-three position for the first time: it produced eighty successful candidates in the higher examination, accounting for 4.8 percent of all successes. Even though Waseda's total was identical to its 1984 total, it turned out to be one more than Hokkaido's, which had suffered a nearly 20-percent decline in the number of successful candidates.[36] In 1986 Waseda, which had increased its total to eighty-two, was overtaken by Tokyo Institute of Technology, which produced eighty-nine successes.[37] In 1987 Tohoku University had ninety-two successful applicants, and in 1988 it had ninety-five. Waseda had eighty-five successful applicants in 1987 and ninety-one in 1988.[38]

As table 10 shows unmistakably, national universities have consistently outperformed the other two types of universities, public (*kōritsu daigaku*) and private (*shiritsu daigaku*). In all five years for which data are available, we see substantially higher success rates (ratio of successful to all applicants) for national-university graduates than for those of the other two types of universities. In those years, national-university graduates were between 2 and 4.5 times more likely to pass the type-A higher examination than those of public universities and between 7 and 20 times more likely to pass the examination than those of private universities. Graduates of public universities were better off than those of private universities by a substantial margin: the former's chances of passing the examination were between 1.7 and 7.7 times greater than the latter's. If we look beyond the aggregate figures, we find

35. *Jinji-in geppō* 197 (July 1967): 15, and 209 (July 1968): 15; Satō Tomoyuki et al., *Tōdaibatsu*, p. 15; *Asahi shinbun*, 22 Aug. 1972, 9 Sept. 1974 (evening ed.), 1 Nov. 1975 (evening ed.), 26 Oct. 1976 (evening ed.), 25 Oct. 1978, 15 Oct. 1983, and 1 Oct. 1984 (evening ed.); *Mainichi shinbun*, 11 Sept. 1973, 15 Oct. 1979, 15 Oct. 1980, 15 Oct. 1981, and 15 Oct. 1982.
36. *Asahi shinbun*, 1 Oct. 1985 (evening ed.).
37. Ibid., 1 Oct. 1986 (evening ed.). In 1987, undergraduate enrollments at selected universities were as follows: Tokyo, 14,379; Kyoto, 11,553, Hokkaido, 10,167; Tōhoku, 10,075; Kyushu, 9,978; Tokyo Institute of Technology, 3,578; Waseda, 40,532; Keiō, 22,839; and Chūō, 30,745. Association of International Education, Japan, ed., *Japanese Colleges and Universities 1987* (Tokyo: Maruzen, 1987).
38. *Nihon keizai shinbun*, 15 Sept. 1987; *Asahi shinbun*, 7 Sept 1988 (evening ed.).

TABLE 10   *Proportion of Successes Among All
Candidates in Type-A Higher Civil-Service
Examination, by Type of University*

Type of university	Year				
	1967	*1975*	*1980*	*1983*	*1985*
National					
Number Applying	9,767	18,389	24,232	18,510	17,573
Number passing	1,138	1,116	1,154	1,332	1,369
% passing	11.7[a]	6.1	4.8	7.2	7.8
Public					
Number applying	1,082	1,423	1,516	1,065	1,068
Number passing	64	34	18	17	20
% passing	5.9[b]	2.3	1.2	1.6	1.9
Private					
Number applying	9,133	16,821	18,678	14,621	14,797
Number passing	134	52	81	126	167
% passing	1.5[c]	0.3	0.4	0.9	1.1
All[d]					
Number applying	21,567	37,825	45,131	34,854	34,089
Number passing	1,364	1,206	1,254	1,478	1,562
% passing	6.3	3.2	2.8	4.2	4.6

SOURCES: The data for 1967, including those in notes a, b, and c, were calculated from tables 4 and 6 in "Showa 40-nendo jokyu shiken to saiyo jokyo," *Jinji-in geppō*, 209 (July 1968): 13 and 15. The remaining data were obtained from the National Personnel Authority during the author's visit to that agency in June 1985. No breakdown by university is available for the years 1975, 1980, 1983, and 1984. Total numbers of applicants and successes are based on Jinji-in, *Nenji hōkokusho*, 1967–1984 (Tokyo: Okurasho, Insatsuyoku, 1968–1985).

[a]Top performers in this group were University of Tokyo: 33.3 percent ($N = 350$), Kyoto University: 25.7 percent ($N = 174$); Tokyo Institute of Technology: 24.2 percent ($N = 17$); Osaka University: 19.3 percent ($N = 36$); Nagoya University: 16.3 percent ($N = 40$); Kyushu University: 13.1 percent ($N = 53$); Yokohama National University: 13.1 percent ($N = 23$); Tohoku University: 12.1 percent ($N = 56$). In terms of the number of successful candidates, Hokkaido University ($N = 56$), Tokyo University of Education ($N = 28$), Nagoya Institute of Technology ($N = 26$), and Tokyo University of Agriculture and Engineering ($N = 22$) also performed well, even though their success rates fell below the mean for the group as a whole.

[b]The top two in this group were Osaka City University (7.3 percent, $N = 13$) and Tokyo Metropolitan University (6.8 percent, $N = 17$).

[c]The top two in this group were Keiō University (7.0 percent, $N = 16$) and Waseda University (6.7 percent, $N = 43$).

[d]Because the total number of applicants and successes include nonuniversity graduates, it is greater than the sum of the three types of university.

wide variations among individual universities within each type. Unfortunately, a breakdown by university is available for 1967 only. As the notes in table 10 show, the success rate of Tōdai graduates was the highest (33.3 percent) and that of Kyōdai trailed not too far behind (25.7 percent). The top performers among public and private universities were virtually indistinguishable in terms of their success rates: Osaka City University and Tokyo Metropolitan University in the former group, with 7.3 and 6.8 percent, respectively, were only a fraction of a percentage point ahead of Keiō (7.0 percent) and Waseda (6.7 percent) in the latter group.

As we have seen previously, however, those who have passed the higher civil-service examinations do not ipso facto become civil servants. To get a more meaningful picture, therefore, we need to ascertain whether the pattern of dominance by graduates of national universities and, particularly, by a few elite universities continues in the hiring stage. Table 11 gives us a breakdown by type of universities for recent years. It reveals that the advantages of national-university graduates have begun to diminish at the hiring stage. Only in 1975 did they enjoy a substantial edge over graduates of public and private universities. In 1980, the latter registered higher rates of appointment than the former, and the same pattern was repeated in 1983, 1984, 1985, and 1986.

What is especially noteworthy is the performance of private-university graduates: their hiring rates in the 1980s have eclipsed those of national-university graduates by a substantial margin. When this is viewed in conjunction with a steady increase of private-university graduates in the proportion of successful candidates in the higher examination (for example, 8.5 percent in 1982, 10.1 percent in 1983, 12.8 percent in 1984, 11.1 percent in 1985, 12.6 percent in 1986, 13.1 percent in 1987, and 13.4 percent in 1988),[39] we can anticipate the dawning of the day when attending a private university is no longer perceived as a handicap in civil-service employment. The slight decline in the share of private-university graduates in 1985 was offset by an increase in absolute numbers from 167 in 1984 to 184 in 1985. In 1986, their share nearly returned to the 1984 level in proportional terms and reached a new high (N = 217) in absolute numbers. The year 1987 saw the best record in twenty-one years for private universities in absolute (N = 221) and proportional (13 percent) terms alike. In 1988 the record improved further: 243 private university graduates passed the

---

39. *Yomiuri shinbun*, 16 Oct. 1983, and 15 Sept. 1987; *Mainichi shinbun*, 1 Oct. 1984 (evening ed.); *Asahi shinbun*, 1 Oct. 1985 (evening ed.), 1 Oct. 1986 (evening ed.), and 7 Sept. 1988 (evening ed.).

TABLE 11   *Proportion of Successful Type-A Higher Civil-Service Examination Candidates Who Were Hired by Ministries and Agencies, by Type of University*

	Year					
Type of University	*1975*	*1980*	*1983*	*1984*	*1985ᵃ*	*1986*
National						
Number passing	1,116	1,154	1,332	1,369	1,435	1,462
Number hired	642	642	568	578	680	595
% hired	57.5	55.6	42.6	42.2	47.4	40.7
Public						
Number passing	34	18	17	20	26	24
Number hired	13	13	10	10	12	6
% hired	38.2	72.2	58.8	50.0	46.2	25.0
Otherᵇ						
Number passing	4	1	3	5	10	15
Number hired	2	0	1	3	6	3
% hired	50.0	0	33.3	60.0	60.0	20.0
Total						
Number passing	1,206	1,254	1,478	1,562	1,655	1,718
Number hired	678	701	655	688	795	706
% hired	56.2	55.9	44.3	44.0	48.0	41.1

SOURCE: Jinji-in, *Kōmuin hakusho*, 1985–88 (Tokyo: Ōkurashō, Insatsukyoku, 1985–88).

ᵃIn 1985, the type-A higher civil-service examination was renamed the type-I higher civil-service examination.

ᵇThis category includes those who did not go to college.

higher examination, accounting for 13.4 percent of all successes. A look at absolute numbers, on the other hand, helps us to appreciate a key fact: notwithstanding the increase in the *rates* of hiring, the *number* of private- and public-university graduates entering the higher civil service remains low. Between eight and nine out of every ten new appointees in the six years covered by table 11 came from national universities.

The continued dominance of national universities becomes plain when we turn from aggregate statistics to more specific data, of which only fragments are available. First, we have the testimony of Tashiro Kū, a former bureau chief in the National Personnel Authority, who writes that between 110 and 115 of the 160 candidates hired from the 1980 roster of type-A eligibles in the field of law were graduates of Tōdai's law faculty. That accounted for 69 to 72 percent of the total. Tashiro reports that this was not an atypical year.[40]

40. Tashiro, "Nihon gyōseikan kenkyū, VII: kyaria to nonkyaria," pp. 89–90.

Second, we have data regarding the university background of the new hiring by the Ministries of Finance and Home Affairs. Looking at the Finance Ministry in selected years first, we find the predominance of Tōdai graduates; they constituted 77.3 percent (17 out of 22) of the 1970 entering class, 76.9 percent (20 out of 26) of the 1975 class, 82.6 percent (19 out of 23) of the 1980 class, and 84.6 percent (22 out of 26) of the 1985 class. About 75 percent of Tōdai men hired by the Finance Ministry during these years were graduates of its law faculty. Non-Tōdai graduates came principally from Kyōdai and Hitotsubashi University. In 1970, 1975, and 1980, these three universities were the exclusive sources of Finance Ministry recruits. In the twenty-three-year period from 1960 to 1982, only 8 graduates of private universities were hired by the Finance Ministry on the career track: 4 from Keiō, 3 from Waseda, and 1 from Chūō.[41]

Turning to the Home Ministry, we find a similar situation. The proportion of Tōdai graduates among all new appointees in selected years was as follows: 1950: 100.0 percent (3 out of 3); 1955: 62.5 percent (5 out of 8); 1960: 75.0 percent (9 out of 12); 1965: 76.9 percent (10 out of 13); 1970: 80.0 percent (12 out of 15); 1975: 81.3 percent (13 out of 16); 1980: 88.2 percent (15 out of 17); and 1985: 93.7 percent (14 out of 15). All but 3 of the 81 Tōdai graduates hired by the Home Ministry in these years came from its law faculty. Of the 18 non-Tōdai men, 10 were Kyōdai graduates, all of them in law, and 3 were graduates of Tokyo Institute of Technology. Only 2 came from private universities.[42]

How may one account for the slow increase in the number of private-university graduates in the higher civil service? If one may hazard a speculation, a number of factors may be cited. One is the changing perception of the higher civil service: the view that it is the exclusive preserve of graduates of a few elite national universities is being increasingly rejected by students of private universities. And the success of the latter in scaling the wall of the higher civil service will undoubtedly help reinforce this trend. Another factor may be the

41. The data for 1960 through 1982 are from Jin Ikkō, *Ōkura kanryō: Cho-erīto shūdan no jinmyaku to yabō* [Finance Ministry Bureaucrats: the Personal Connections and Ambitions of a Super-Elite Group] (Tokyo: Kōdansha, 1982), appendix: "Ōkurashō zen kyaria ichiran" [Complete List of Career Civil Servants in the Finance Ministry], unpaged. The 1985 data are from *Shūkan Yomiuri* [Weekly Yomiuri], 16 Dec. 1984, p. 171.

42. Jin Ikkō, *Jichi kanryō* [Home Ministry Bureaucrats] (Tokyo: Kōdansha, 1986), pp. 232–57. These pages list all new appointees from 1947 to 1985.

narrowing of the gap between national and private universities in terms of the caliber of students. That is to say, the gap between those who enter the top-rated national universities and those who enter the top-rated private universities may not be as great as is generally believed.[43] A third, and probably the most important, factor is the apparent change in the attitudes of the hiring agencies. Many of them appear to be making a conscious effort to diversify the background of new elite-track appointees.

Another dimension of the educational background of new recruits into the higher civil service is their level of education. As we have already noted, the educational level of applicants for all types of civil-service examinations has increased appreciably over the past two decades, and this is bound to affect the situation at the hiring stage as well. Nearly four out of ten persons who were hired as higher civil servants in 1975, 1980, and 1983, for example, had done graduate work. Scientists and engineers show the highest level of educational attainments, whereas "law and the humanities" graduates display the lowest. Indeed, it is striking that between 65 and 76 percent of scientists and engineers hired during the three years mentioned above had done graduate work.[44]

All this is clearly linked to the rapid increase in the graduate population. Whereas the number of university students increased 2.9 times between 1960 and 1980, that of graduate students increased 3.4 times during the same period. What is more, the number of graduate students in the natural sciences and engineering grew 6.7 times in the twenty-year period, as compared with a mere two-fold increase in the number of graduate students in the humanities and social sciences.[45] It

43. Of the applicants who take entrance examinations to both Tōdai and a top-rated private university, a sizable proportion is known to pass the former but fail the latter. In 1984, for example, 30 (or 24 percent) of the 127 graduates of Yoyogi Seminar, a leading preparatory school in Tokyo, who passed the entrance examination to Tōdai's Law Faculty failed the entrance examination to Waseda University's Faculty of Politics and Economics. Overall, 32 percent of the 275 Yoyogi graduates who were admitted to Tōdai's humanities faculties (*bunka kei*) were rejected by Waseda's Faculty of Politics and Economics. Of the Yoyogi graduates who passed the entrance examination to Tōdai's Faculty of Medicine, reputed to be the most competitive in Japan, about 20 percent failed the entrance examination to Keiō University's Faculty of Medicine. "Juken sensen de kigyō kyōsō de ima 'Tōdai shinwa' no hōkai ga hajimatta!" ["The Myth of the University of Tokyo" Has Begun to Crumble on the (University) Entrance Examination Front and in the Competition Among Business Enterprises], *Shūkan gendai*, 2 Mar. 1985, pp. 22–27.

44. These statistics were obtained from the National Personnel Authority during the author's visit to that agency in June 1985.

45. Monbushō, ed., *Waga kuni no kyōiku suijun* [The Educational Level of Our Country], 1980 (Tokyo: Okurashō, Insatsukyoku, 1981), appendixes 66 and 67.

Theodore Lownik Library
Illinois Benedictine College
Lisle, Illinois 60532

is noteworthy that the door to the higher civil service is not totally closed to those lacking university diplomas: a total of 15 such persons were hired in 1975, 1980, 1983, 1984, 1985, and 1986 (see table 11).

On balance, however, the picture that emerges from the preceding survey is the continuing dominance of a few elite universities, particularly Tōdai, in both the examination and hiring stages of higher civil servants. On the other hand, the steady increase in the proportion of private-university graduates, both among the successful candidates in the higher examination and among those who are actually hired by government ministries and agencies, suggests that the process of incremental change may have already begun.[46]

HŌKA BANNŌ

Let us now turn to another age-old pattern in Japanese bureaucracy: the dominance of law graduates (hōka bannō). Table 12 displays some data suggestive of how law has fared as a field of specialization in the higher civil-service examination in the postwar period. In a word, it has become the single most important field, accounting for between 14 and 27 percent of the successful candidates during the 1955–87 period. The total number of fields during the period has ranged from twenty-four to twenty-seven. The number and proportion of successful candidates in the next four fields (type A or type I only) in selected years are as follows:

1955: economics, 142 (10.8 percent); public administration, 111 (8.4 percent); civil engineering, 100 (7.6 percent); mechanical engineering, 93 (7.1 percent).

1965: mechanical engineering, 165 (10.2 percent); civil engineering, 160 (9.9 percent); physics, 149 (9.2 percent); chemistry, 100 (6.2 percent).

1975: civil engineering, 150 (12.4 percent); chemistry, 84 (7.9 percent); economics, 83 (6.9 percent); physics, 80 (6.6 percent).

46. Another sign of change worth mentioning is that in 1986 the Ministry of Trade and Industry (MITI) hired a graduate of a foreign university as a career civil servant for the first time in its history: a 24-year-old Japanese who had graduated from Brown University with a major in econometrics. MITI's chief of the Minister's Secretariat said that the appointment reflected MITI's goal of securing "persons with rich international experience" in view of the growing internationalization. See "Kasumigaseki konhidensharu" [Confidential Report from Kasumigaseki], Bungei shunjū, Jan. 1986, p. 171.

TABLE 12   *Law Compared with Other Fields in Higher Civil-Service Examination*

Year	(A) Law Candidates Passing N	(B) All Candidates Passing N	(C) Law Candidates Hired N	(D) All Candidates Hired N	(E) $\frac{A}{B}$ %	(F) $\frac{C}{D}$ %	(G) $\frac{C}{A}$ %	(H) $\frac{D}{B}$ %
1955	311	1,314			23.7			
1957	345	1,801			19.2			
1959	352	1,596			19.6			
1961[a]	308	1,133			27.2			
1964	298	1,434			20.8			
1965	299	1,624			18.4			
1969	251	1,306			19.2			
1970	252	1,353	183	729	18.6	25.1	72.6	53.9
1971	261	1,401	170	676	18.6	25.1	65.1	48.3
1972	242	1,410	145	632	17.2	22.9	59.9	44.8
1973	262	1,410	157	639	18.6	24.6	59.9	45.3
1974	249	1,375	168	661	18.1	25.4	67.5	48.1
1975	237	1,206	158	619	19.7	25.5	66.7	51.3
1976	235	1,136	154	567	20.7	27.2	65.5	49.9
1977	240	1,206	159	592	19.9	26.9	66.3	49.1
1978	245	1,311	153	645	18.7	23.7	62.4	49.2
1979	229	1,265	144	615	18.1	23.4	62.9	48.6
1980	229	1,254	160	614	18.3	26.1	69.9	49.0
1981	226	1,361	153	648	16.6	23.6	67.6	47.6
1982	237	1,383	148	618	17.1	23.9	62.4	44.7
1983	221	1,478	147	655	15.0	22.4	66.5	44.3
1984	220	1,562	146	688	14.1	21.2	66.4	44.0
1985	242	1,655	180	721	14.6	25.0	74.4	43.6
1986	251	1,718	176	706	14.6	24.9	70.1	41.1
1987	250	1,696			14.7			

SOURCES: Jinji-in, *Nenji hōkokusho,* 1970–1987 (Tokyo: Ōkurashō, Insatsukyoku, 1971–88); *Jinji-in geppō* 134 (Apr. 1962): 12, 170 (Apr. 1965): 18, 183 (May 1966): 13, and 423 (Apr. 1986): 31.

[a]The data for 1961–81 pertain to the type-A higher civil-service examination only.

1985: civil engineering, 212 (12.8 percent); economics, 110 (6.6 percent); physics, 110 (6.6 percent); electronics, 110 (6.6 percent).[47]

The preceding data indicate that the gap between law and the other top fields is fairly wide: only in the 1980s has the next field begun to

47. Jinji-in, *Nenji hōkokusho,* 1955, 1965, 1975, and 1985 (Tokyo, 1956, 1966, 1976, and 1986).

challenge law in number and proportion. In 1983, civil engineering surpassed law for the first time, with 228 successful candidates, 7 more than law. In 1985, however, law recaptured its paramount position, and the situation remained unchanged in 1986 and 1987.

More important, about a quarter of the successful candidates who are actually hired have law as their field of specialization. Comparison of columns G and H in table 12 shows that the proportion of successful candidates in law who are actually hired has consistently surpassed that of all candidates by 15 to 20 percent, reaching an all-time high of 29 percent in 1986. Moreover, law offers the widest range of options to the successful candidate in terms of government employment, for virtually every agency recruits law specialists every year. The other fields that offer relatively abundant options to the candidates are economics and public administration, but neither can match law.

It should also be noted that the hiring rates for successful candidates in engineering and the natural sciences are relatively low. Because of attractive alternatives in the private sector, a large proportion of these candidates withdraw, and this has in turn prompted the government to pass a larger number of candidates in the technical fields than would be the case otherwise. The hiring rates for candidates who passed the 1986 higher examination in selected scientific and engineering fields were as follows: physics, 23.6 percent; chemistry, 26.8 percent; information engineering, 18.7 percent; electrical engineering, 25.8 percent; electronics, 25.9 percent; mechanical engineering, 25.0 percent; civil engineering, 25.9 percent; and metallurgy, 15.0 percent. Among the technical fields, those related to agriculture have the highest hiring rates, which reflects the relative scarcity of private-sector alternatives in them.[48]

The preponderance of law as a field of specialization in the higher civil-service examination tends to accentuate the influence of elite universities. As table 13 shows, Tōdai supplies about seven out of ten successes in the field of law. Comparison of this table with table 9 indicates that Tōdai's share of successful candidates in law is about twice its share of all successful candidates. When law, economics, and public administration are combined—the three fields have traditionally supplied a disproportionate share of top administrators in Japanese bureaucracy—Tōdai's share declines slightly.

48. These rates were calculated from the data in Jinji-in, *Kōmuin hakusho,* 1986, p. 25, and 1987, pp. 40–41. The hiring rates for agriculture-related fields in 1986 were as follows: agriculture, 56.0 percent; agricultural economics, 38.7 percent; agricultural chemistry, 42.2 percent; agricultural engineering, 50.0 percent; animal husbandry, 48.0 percent; and forestry, 62.9 percent.

TABLE 13 *Successful Candidates in Type-A Higher
Civil-Service Examination, by Field of Specialization
and University Background*

Field and University	1975		1980		1983		1984	
	N	%	N	%	N	%	N	%
Law:								
Tokyo	159	67.1	157	68.6	169	76.5	143	65.0
Kyoto	45	19.0	32	14.0	17	7.7	23	10.5
Other	33	13.9	40	17.4	35	15.8	54	24.5
Subtotal	237	100.0	229	100.0	221	100.0	220	100.0
Economics:								
Tokyo	43	51.8	53	58.2	55	57.9	42	44.7
Kyoto[a]	9	10.8	6	6.6	11	11.6	8	8.5
Other	31	37.4	32	35.2	29	30.5	44	45.8
Subtotal	83	100.0	91	100.0	95	100.0	94	100.0
Law, Economics and Public Administration								
Tokyo	211	61.2	217	62.0	234	65.7	193	54.5
Kyoto	58	16.8	42	12.0	32	9.0	33	9.3
Other	76	22.0	91	26.0	90	25.3	128	36.2
Subtotal	345	100.0	350	100.0	356	100.0	354	100.0

SOURCE: Unpublished data obtained from the National Personnel Authority during the author's visit to that agency in June 1985.
[a]Hitotsubashi University outperformed Kyoto University during all four years covered by this table. Hitotsubashi's share of the successful candidates in the field of economics was as follows: 1975, 12; 1980, 18; 1983, 10; and 1984, 9.

As we shall see in the following chapter, the importance of law increases further when promotion patterns are examined. The nature of the educational experience that candidates in law undergo, therefore, will be a major component of our inquiry into the socialization of Japanese higher civil servants. At this point, however, it is necessary to explain briefly what specialization in law signifies in the Japanese context. The most important thing to bear in mind is that being a law graduate (that is, a graduate of a faculty of law in a university) is not the same thing as being a lawyer. All faculties of law in Japan are undergraduate institutions. Although their graduates receive a substantial amount of legal training as well as law degrees (*hōgakushi* [bachelor of law]), only a small proportion of them take the judicial examination, and still a smaller proportion pass it.

In 1986, for example, only 1 in 49 applicants passed the examination. Of the 486 successful candidates, 97 (20.0 percent) came from Tōdai, 85 (17.5 percent) each from Waseda and Chūō universities, 32 (6.6 percent) from Kyōdai, and 25 (5.1 percent) from Keiō University. Interestingly, three of the top five universities are private—Waseda, Chūō, and Keiō. The judicial examination is said to be so difficult that only a handful of those who pass it do so on their first try. The average age of the successful candidates in recent years has hovered around twenty-eight, about five years higher than the average age of graduation from a law faculty. In 1986, a record number of women (59 or 12.1 percent of all successes) passed the judicial examination.[49]

Those who pass the judicial examination must undergo two years of postgraduate training at the state-run Judicial Training Institute (Shihō Kenshūjo). At the end of the two years they must take another examination, consisting of both written and oral tests. Those who pass the second examination are officially certified to enter the legal profession, as judges, public prosecutors, and attorneys. Of the 450 persons who successfully completed their training in April 1986, 70 became judge trainees (hanjiho), 34 became public prosecutors, and the remainder opted for careers as attorneys.[50] In a sense, the Judicial Institute can be equated with a law school in the United States. Given that only five hundred or fewer qualified lawyers are produced in this fashion each year, it is not surprising that the number of lawyers in Japan is exceedingly small. In 1983 there were an estimated 12,500 attorneys in private practice, approximately 1 per 10,000 population. This contrasts sharply with the situation in the United States, where the ratio was about 1 lawyer per 400 population (about 600,000 attorneys).[51]

For all but a handful of the people involved, then, graduation from a faculty of law does not foreshadow a career in the legal profession; it simply signifies completion of what amounts to general education. Law graduates, in other words, are generalists, not specialists. As such they

49. *Asahi shinbun*, 1 Nov. 1986, and 21 May 1987. For a description of the Judicial Examination, see *Tōkyō Daigaku shinbun* (weekly), 5 July, 1976, p. 3.

50. Although nearly all trainees of the Judicial Training Institute pass the second examination, it is by no means automatic. In 1986, eight trainees were accused of cheating in the examination and failed to graduate with their classmates. *Asahi shinbun*, 27 Mar., 3 Apr. (evening ed.), 4 Apr. and 5 Apr. 1986.

51. "Land Without Lawyers," *Time*, 1 Aug. 1983, pp. 64–65. "Although the Japanese have a highly developed sense of individual rights, social harmony, not personal justice, is the basis of their law. Litigation, never common, has actually decreased over the past 15 years." Ibid., p. 64.

enjoy a wide range of options. A study of some 24,000 graduates of Tōdai's law faculty about whom information was available in 1958 showed that the largest proportion, 44 percent, were either in banking or in private enterprises. The second-largest group, 23 percent, was in the civil service. Next, about 13 percent were in the legal profession (7 percent as judges or prosecutors and 6 percent as attorneys). The remainder were scattered in such fields as education, journalism, and politics.[52] Data on the destinations of Tōdai law graduates in the 1970s and 1980s confirm that the preceding trend continues without any notable modifications.[53]

MALE DOMINANCE

Prewar Japan was a male-dominated society. Politically, this was symbolized by the lack of franchise for women. It was natural that the government bureaucracy should mirror the inferiority of women in the larger society. Legally, however, women were placed on an equal footing with men in the competition for civil-service appointments as early as 1909, when they became eligible for the higher civil-service examination. However, they did not actually end male monopoly until 1928, when three women passed the judicial section of the higher civil-service examination. In 1931, a women passed its administrative section for the first time but was never offered an appointment to the higher civil service. Although more women passed the judicial section, no other women passed the administrative section before it was abolished after the Japanese defeat in World War II.[54] As two American observers wrote in 1946: "The status system shows little scope for female service. The only women who have invaded the higher civil service are a few physicians and one labor executive in the Welfare Ministry. Even among ordinary officials, there are very few women; generally the exclusion is quite complete."[55] To what extent has the situation changed since 1946?

The earliest available information regarding the sexual composition of the civil service pertains to 1958. A government survey of general-service employees covered by the regular compensation law revealed

52. Shimizu Hideo, *Tōkyō Daigaku Hōgakubu: Nihon erīto no manmosu kichi* [The University of Tokyo Faculty of Law: A Mammoth Base of Japan's Elite] (Tokyo: Kōdansha, 1965), p. 48.
53. See *Tōkyō Daigaku shinbun*, 28 June 1976, and Hata, *Kanryō no kenkyū*, p. 189.
54. Hata, *Kanryō no Kenkyū*, pp. 103–4.
55. MacDonald and Esman, "The Japanese Civil Service," p. 215.

that 62,128 (17.2 percent) of the 360,328 civil servants were women. However, only 802 of the women civil servants had college degrees. In other words, only 1.6 percent of all civil servants with college degrees were women. The proportion increased sharply—to 14.7 percent—when graduates of junior colleges were examined.[56]

In terms of average monthly salaries, female college graduates in the civil service earned 41.9 percent less than their male counterparts, and female graduates of junior colleges earned 30.5 percent less than their male colleagues with the same amount of education. When the length of service is held constant, the gender gap in compensation narrows somewhat. Women college graduates with less than one year of service earned 5.6 percent less than men with the identical background, but the disparity nearly quadrupled for women with fifteen to twenty years of service.[57]

By 1976, some progress had been registered in the overall picture. The proportion of women in the civil service increased slightly, to 19.5 percent, and the proportion of women among college graduates in the civil service increased fourfold, to 6.8 percent. Meanwhile, the gender gap in compensation became markedly narrower. This was especially true when comparison was made between men and women with the same level of education and the identical length of service; in fact, women with less than two years of service earned slightly more than their male counterparts. However, the gap for those with longer experience remained, although it had been substantially reduced.[58]

Table 14 shows that women have by no means been shut out of the higher civil-service examination. On the contrary, between 4 and 8

56. Jinji-in, *Nenji hōkokusho*, 1958, p. 50. To a large extent, the scarcity of college-educated women in the Japanese civil service reflected the scarcity of college-educated women in Japanese society as a whole. Of 1,858 persons who graduated from four-year colleges in 1950, only 31 (1.7 percent) were women. The situation had improved markedly by 1955: 13,544 (14.3%) of the 94,735 university graduates that year were women. The proportion of women among university graduates increased steadily thereafter: 16.2 percent in 1965, 21.6 percent in 1975, and 24.7 percent in 1980. Among graduates of junior colleges, women began to surpass men in 1953, and by the late 1960s, eight of every ten junior-college graduates were women. In 1980, 155,200 (91.3 percent) of the 169,930 persons who graduated from junior colleges were women. Monbushō, ed., *Waga kuni no kyōiku suijun*, 1980, appendixes 137 and 138.

57. Jinji-in, *Nenji hōkokusho*, 1958, pp. 48–49.

58. The gap for women with 15 to 20 years of service had been reduced from 19 percent in 1958 to 8.3 percent in 1976. See Jinji-in, kyūyokyoku, *Kokka kōmuin kyūyotō jittai chōsa hōkokusho* [Report on an Investigation into the Actual Conditions of National Civil Servants' Compensation and Related Matters], 15 Jan. 1976 (Tokyo: Ōkurashō, Insatsukyoku, 1976), pp. 4–5 and 38–39. Chap. 8 discusses further the question of the gender gap in compensation.

TABLE 14   *Women Passing Higher Civil-Service*
Examinations, in Selected Years

Year	(A) Type A	(B) Type B	(C) Total	(D) C as % of All Successful Candidates
1963	125	35	160	8.7
1964	119	24	143	7.9
1965	77	25	102	5.1
1966	51	17	78	4.5
1967	52	7	59	3.9
1969	—	—	69	4.6
1972	48	22	70	4.7
1973	32	12	44	2.8
1974	—	—	59	3.9
1975	—	—	45	3.4
1976	—	—	61	4.9
1977	—	—	42	3.3
1978	43	11	54	3.9
1979	41	9	50	3.7
1980	40	11	51	3.8
1981	56	15	71	4.9
1982	49	11	60	4.1
1983	73	19	92	5.9
1984	86	8	94	5.7
1985	105[a]	—	105	6.3
1986	128	—	128	7.5
1987	116	—	116	6.8
1988	150	—	150	8.3

SOURCES: *Jinji-in geppō* 170 (Apr. 1965): 21 and 197 (July 1967): 11–12; *Asahi shinbun*, 5 Sept. 1967 (evening ed.), 1 Nov. 1975 (evening ed.), 26 Oct. 1976, 25 Oct. 1978, 15 Oct. 1983, 1 Oct. 1984 (evening ed.), 1 Oct. 1985 (evening ed.), 1 Oct. 1986 (evening ed.), 7 Sept. 1988 (evening ed.); *Mainichi shinbun*, 19 Aug. 1969, 11 Sept. 1973, 15 Oct. 1979, 15 Oct. 1980, 15 Oct. 1981, 15 Oct. 1982, 1 Oct. 1984 (evening ed.); *Yomiuri shinbun*, 16 Oct. 1983, 15 Sept. 1987.

[a]In 1985 the type-A examination was replaced by the type-I examination, and the type-B examination was abolished.

percent of the successful candidates in recent years have been women. The peak for women was reached in the early 1960s, when they constituted 8 to 9 percent of the successful candidates. From 1966 to 1982, the number of successful women candidates remained well below 100—in fact, close to half that number—and their proportion consistently fell short of the 5 percent mark. In 1983, however, women registered a substantial gain in both absolute and proportional terms. In

1984 not only did women sustain the same rate of gain as the previous year's, but, for the first time in the history of the higher civil-service examination, they received the highest grade in four fields: sociology, pharmacy, agriculture, and agricultural economics.[59] In 1985 women broke the 100 barrier for the first time in twenty years, and their proportion among all the successful candidates, too, was the highest since 1964. Women were top-scorers in two fields, chemistry and pharmacy.[60] In 1986 women continued their upward trend, gaining twenty-three in absolute numbers and 1.2 percentage points in their share of the successes over the previous year.[61] In 1987 although women registered a slight decline both in absolute numbers and in proportional terms, they produced top scorers in four fields for the second time in three years: sociology, psychology, education, and pharmacy. In 1988 women had their best performance in twenty-five years: 150 successes (8.3 percent of all successes). They also produced top scorers in three fields: public administration, psychology, and animal husbandry.[62]

Another notable pattern has to do with the ratios of types A and B. As we saw in table 6, since the 1970s successful type-A candidates have outnumbered successful type-B candidates by the ratios of between ten and fifteen to one. Among women, however, the ratios until 1984 hovered around four to one. In fact, when women's share of successful type-A candidates alone is examined, there is a slight deterioration in the picture. Except for 1963, 1964, and 1984, women's share of the total type-A successes is about a half percentage point below that of type-B successes. To sum up, in the category that really counts in terms of upward mobility, women still have a long way to go.

How do women compare with men in terms of their rates of success in the higher civil-service examination? Table 15 presents the relevant statistics for 1983 and 1984. It shows that although women lag behind men in their success rates in all major categories of specialization, the gap is the narrowest in "law and the humanities," where the difference is only a half percentage point. The widest gap is found in "science and engineering," where men's success rates were 2.6 to 2.7 percentage points higher than women's. Although women's success rates improved

59. *Mainichi shinbun*, 1 Oct. 1984 (evening ed.).
60. *Asahi shinbun*, 1 Oct. 1985 (evening ed.).
61. Ibid., 1 Oct. 1986 (evening ed.).
62. *Yomiuri shinbun*, 15 Sept. 1987; *Asahi shinbun*, 7 Sept. 1988 (evening ed.).

TABLE 15   *Distribution of Applicants for Higher Civil-Service Examination (Type A), by Field of Specialization and Sex, 1983 and 1984*

Field and sex	Number Applying		Number Passing		Percentage Passing	
	1983	*1984*	*1983*	*1984*	*1983*	*1984*
Law and humanities						
Men	14,947	14,731	372	372	2.5	2.5
Women	1,743	1,824	34	37	2.0	2.0
Science and engineering						
Men	11,117	10,898	759	801	6.8	7.3
Women	602	593	25	27	4.2	4.6
Agriculture						
Men	6,445	6,043	288	325	4.5	5.4
Women	491	541	14	22	2.9	4.1
All fields						
Men	32,509	31,672	1,419	1,498	4.4	4.7
Women	2,836	2,958	73	86	2.6	2.9

SOURCE: Unpublished data obtained from the National Personnel Authority during the author's visit to that agency in June 1985.

somewhat in 1984 compared with 1983, so did men's, thus leaving the overall gender gap intact.

One bright spot in table 15, so far as women are concerned, is that nearly half of women's successes are found in "law and the humanities," compared with only about a quarter of men's successes. This is good news for women, primarily because candidates in "law and the humanities" enjoy an edge in upward mobility. In terms of specific fields, as opposed to groups of fields, the top five for women in 1983 were pharmacy (13), law (11), education (6), sociology (6), and agricultural chemistry (6). These five fields together accounted for 57.5 percent of all successful women candidates. In 1984, three fields tied for the fifth position. The top fields were law (12), agricultural chemistry (11), pharmacy (9), chemistry (7), psychology (5), education (5), and sociology (5). These seven fields together accounted for 62.8 percent of all successful women candidates.[63]

63. These statistics were obtained from the National Personnel Authority during the author's visit to that agency in June 1985.

As noted, success in the higher civil-service examination does not automatically translate into an appointment to the higher civil service. Hence we need to know how many women actually are appointed to the higher civil service. Table 16 presents two kinds of data pertinent to the question. First, column B displays the number of new women appointees to Administrative Service I positions who have passed either the type-A or type-B higher civil-service examination. Second, column A displays the number of all higher-examination-qualified women civil servants who occupy Administrative Service I positions in the years indicated. Looking at column B first, we see that the number of new women appointees is quite small. Column D indicates, moreover, that their proportion is equally small. Only in 1985 and 1986 did women in the type-A category exceed 4 percent of the total new appointees. So far as the less prestigious type B is concerned, women's proportion surpassed the 10-percent mark three times, in 1976, 1982, and 1985. In fact, in all of the twelve years covered in the table, type-B women surpassed type-A women in proportional terms, though the record is mixed in terms of absolute numbers.

Turning to column A, we find that with the notable exception of 1977, the total number of higher-examination-certified women in Administrative Service I positions increased steadily until 1984. Although 1977 registered a 23-percent decline, the following year saw an 18-percent increase, and by 1979 the 1976 level was all but restored. In subsequent years we see a steady increase until 1985, when the number declined by 12 percent over the previous year. In proportional terms the picture has remained relatively stable: at no time did the combined totals of types A and B exceed 4 percent. When we focus on type A only, we find that women's share is below the 3-percent mark; even though a breakdown by types A and B is not available for the years 1975 through 1981, we can surmise that the same general pattern holds. It should be stressed that table 16 displays data for women in Administrative Service I positions only. If we were to examine all women who are in the higher civil service, the picture would improve somewhat. The number of women who are graduates of the type-A (or type-I) higher examination, for example, doubles, and their proportion increases by 1 to 2 percent.

If we focus on the administrative elite in the narrow sense, that is, those civil servants who have attained at least the position of section chief or its equivalent, we find that women are even more underrepresented than the preceding statistics suggest. In 1987, one could count

TABLE 16 *Women in Administrative Service I Positions in the Higher Civil Service*

Year	(A) All Incumbents	(B) New Appointees	(C) A as % of Total (Men + Women)	(D) B as % of All New Appointees
1975				
A	461[a]	16	3.6	3.0
B		22		8.8
1976				
A	478	12	3.5	2.3
B		22		11.8
1977				
A	366	12	2.8	2.5
B		5		3.9
1978				
A	433	14	3.1	2.7
B		6		5.0
1979				
A	473	19	3.3	3.7
B		9		6.8
1980				
A	482	17	3.4	3.4
B		10		8.5
1981				
A	494	20	3.4	4.0
B		8		5.6
1982				
A	307	20	2.6	3.8
B	220	18	7.1	12.8
1983				
A	331	16	2.8	3.2
B	226	12	6.9	7.3
1984				
A	328	17	2.8	3.3
B	238	17	7.1	9.9
1985				
A	253	24	2.4	4.4
B	248	14	7.1	10.4
1986				
A	266	24	2.5	4.4
B	255	—	6.9	—

SOURCE: Jinji-in, *Nenji Hōkokusho*, 1976–1987 (Tokyo: Ōkurasho, Insatsukyoku, 1977–88).

NOTE: A refers to persons who have passed the type-A higher civil-service examination or its equivalent; B refers to persons who have passed the type-B higher civil-service examination or its equivalent.

only twelve such women serving in the headquarters (*honshō*) of the twelve main ministries. In fact, only six ministries had women in elite positions: Labor (4), Health and Welfare (3), MITI (2), Agriculture (1), Justice (1), and Education (1). By including those serving in the "field" (*gaikyoku*), we could increase the total to seventeen and the number of ministries represented to seven (with the Finance Ministry being added). Inclusion of the other government agencies would add eight more: four from the National Personnel Authority and two each from the prime minister's office and the Economic Planning Agency. Actually, one of the two women in the prime minister's office had been temporarily detached from the Labor Ministry.[64]

Of the twenty-five women, two were bureau chiefs, one was chief of a prefectural bureau, ten were section chiefs, three were chiefs of offices (*shitsu chō*), two were counselors (*sanjikan*), two others were directors of research institutes, and the rest held miscellaneous titles that were equivalent to section chiefs. Their age ranged from 41 to 59, the median age being 47. In terms of educational background, twelve were graduates of Tōdai, three were from International Christian University, and the remainder had gone to Tōhoku, Keiō, Waseda, Ochanomizu, and other universities. Two, both nurses, had not attended college. In terms of field of study, the largest number (five) had studied general education (*kyōyō*). Law and the humanities tied for second place with four each. Economics and pharmacy followed with two each. The remaining women had majored in various fields ranging from mathematics to nursing.

The two highest-ranking women were employed in the Ministries of Labor and Health and Welfare, respectively. Satō Ginko, a 1958 graduate of Tōdai's general-education faculty, was chief of the Labor Ministry's Women's Bureau. Since 1947, when the bureau was first created, it has always been headed by a woman.[65] The other senior woman, Nagao Ritsuko, was promoted to her position as chief of the Children's and Families' Bureau of the Health and Welfare Ministry in September 1987. She thus became not only the first woman bureau chief in her ministry but also the first woman to attain a bureau-chief rank

64. These data are based on a review of all the higher civil servants listed in *Seikai kanchō jinji roku, 1988-nenban* [Who's Who in Politics and Government, 1988 Edition] (Tokyo: Tōyō Keizai Shinpōsha, 1987).
65. Sano Mitsuko, *Josei kanryō: Sono ishiki to kōdō* [Women Bureaucrats: Their Consciousness and Behavior] (Tokyo: Jihyōsha 1983), p. 397.

outside the Labor Ministry. She is a 1958 graduate of Tōdai's literature faculty and a twenty-nine-year veteran in her ministry.[66]

The third-highest-ranking woman in 1987 was Matsumoto Yasuko, chief of the Labor Ministry's Bureau of Labor Standards in Saga prefecture. A 1959 graduate of Waseda University (politics and economics), she had previously served as a section chief in her ministry and as chief of a women's-affairs office in the prime minister's office.[67]

Another woman who merits brief mention is Sakamoto Harumi. A 1962 graduate of Tōdai's law faculty, she became, in the same year, the first woman ever hired by the Ministry of International Trade and Industry (MITI) on its elite track. After compiling a distinguished record in MITI, she was appointed chief of the Sapporo Bureau of International Trade and Industry in June 1986 and subsequently drew much attention and praise for her handling of her new job. In June 1987, however, she abruptly resigned her position. Shortly thereafter she became an adviser to the Daiichi Kangyō Bank, Japan's largest bank.[68]

Most of the women who opt for careers in the higher civil service do so in the belief that in so doing they are likely to encounter markedly less discrimination than they would in the private sector. For many women, there is no other viable choice. According to a 1976 Tōdai graduate who entered the Finance Ministry in the same year, even graduates of Tōdai's economics faculty are not in much demand in the private sector if they happen to be women; she chose public employment "by the process of elimination."[69] In the case of Sakamoto Harumi, however, an explicit commitment of equal treatment was said to have been obtained prior to her entry into MITI.[70]

Nearly all women, nonetheless, do run into difficulties. Some discover that they are expected by their male superiors to perform such traditionally feminine tasks as serving tea, cleaning up the office, and answering telephones for other people. One woman, Matsumoto

66. *Asahi shinbun*, 26 Sept. 1987. For a profile of Nagao, see Sano, *Josei kanryō*, pp. 193–218.
67. For a profile of Matsumoto, see Yoshihara Atsuko, *Sukāto o haita kōkyū kanryō* [Higher Civil Servants Who Wear Skirts] (Tokyo: K. K. Kanki Shuppan, 1986), pp. 107–33.
68. *Asahi shinbun*, 19 June 1987; "Kasumigaseki konhidensharu," *Bungei shunjū*, Feb. 1986, p. 192, and Oct. 1987, p. 180. For a profile of Sakamoto, see Sano, *Josei kanryō*, pp. 277–302 and Yoshihara, *Sukāto o haita kōkyū kanryō*, pp. 35–106.
69. Sano, *Josei kanryō*, p. 122.
70. Yoshihara, *Sukāto o haita kōkyū kanryō*, pp. 23 and 67. Sakamoto had another offer from a major private firm, which gave her some bargaining power.

Yasuko, upon being asked to do such chores at a prefectural office of the Labor Ministry in her second year, flatly refused to take turns as a telephone operator, even though she did serve tea. When her superior tried to persuade her in front of all other women civil servants, none of whom was on the career track, she countered by proposing that in return for women's serving tea, men should clean up the office. Her proposal was tacitly accepted.[71] Her intransigence apparently did not hurt her career, for, as we have seen, she later served as a section chief and chief of a prefectural bureau.

A number of women also report incidents in which, when they answer telephones or greet visitors, the callers or visitors ask to talk with the "person in charge," refusing to believe that they are talking to such persons. The most difficult of all, however, is the challenge posed by children. Since most do not get home until 9 or 10 P.M. on most days and, during the budget-preparation period, the working hours are extended further, they need to find housekeepers and baby-sitters. Many end up enlisting the aid of their mothers.

Women in the elite track try very hard not to deviate from the unwritten social norms of Japanese bureaucracy. These entail having drinks with colleagues and, especially, subordinates after work and playing mah-jongg, a favorite pastime of Japanese bureaucrats, with them.

In sum, although Japanese bureaucracy is no longer the bastion of male supremacy that it once was, it still has a long way to go before women achieve a semblance of equality or, at least, reasonably fair representation, in its high echelons. The handful of women who have either attained or are on their way toward attaining senior ranks appear to have educational and other credentials that either equal or surpass those of their male counterparts.

RECRUITMENT OF DIPLOMATS

Recruitment of foreign-affairs personnel merits brief discussion, because it is handled separately in Japan, as is true in most other countries. It was not until Japan regained its sovereignty in 1952 that the Ministry of Foreign Affairs formally took over the responsibility of conducting examinations, of which there were two until 1962: the examination to select diplomats and consuls and the examination to

71. Ibid., pp. 107–33.

select foreign-affairs clerks. The former was equivalent to the higher civil-service examination. From 1963 to 1976, there were three types of examinations: the higher-level examination to select foreign-affairs civil servants, the intermediate examination to select foreign-affairs civil servants, and the examination to select language trainees for the Ministry of Foreign Affairs. The last-named examination was also an intermediate one aimed at recruiting graduates of junior colleges. In 1977 the two intermediate examinations were consolidated into the examination to select specialist employees of the Ministry of Foreign Affairs. And in 1985 the higher-level examination was renamed the type-I examination to select foreign-affairs civil servants, in conjunction with the revision of the civil-service examinations in other fields.[72]

Table 17 displays some data about the higher-level (or type-I) foreign-service examination. Although the data are incomplete, it is nonetheless striking that an extraordinary number of applicants fail either to show up for or complete the first stage of the examination. Their proportion is twice as high as that for the higher civil-service examination. This appears to be a function of the difficulty of the examination; many applicants are so intimidated by it that they either have second thoughts about taking the examination or give up after sampling the first few subjects.

What does the examination actually consist of? Open to Japanese citizens between the ages of twenty and twenty-eight regardless of their educational background, the examination has two stages. In the first stage, applicants are tested in (1) general education (*ippan kyōyō*), (2) a foreign language, (3) constitutional law, (4) international law, (5) principles of economics, (6) diplomatic history, and (7) two elective subjects, to be chosen from administrative law, civil law, public finance, and economic policy. The general-education test consists of sixty multiple-choice questions, which must be answered in three hours. This is a key test, for all applicants who do not pass it are automatically disqualified no matter how well they may do in the other subjects. Aimed at testing the applicant's general knowledge and analytic ability, the questions in this test encompass the humanities and the social and natural sciences; they also include problems in mathematical reasoning and quantitative data analysis. In 1986, for example, the general-education test contained questions on Western philosophy, existential-

---

72. Jinji-in, *Nenji hōkokusho,* 1948–49 through 1952, 1963, and 1964; Jinji-in, *Kōmuin hakusho,* 1978 and 1986.

TABLE 17   *Results of Higher-Level Foreign-Service Examination*

Year	(A) Number Applying	(B) Number Taking Exam	(C) Number Passing	(D) Number Hired	(E) $\frac{C}{A}$ %	(F) $\frac{C}{B}$ %
1949[a]	683		14	12	2.0	
1950	625	378	20	20	3.2	5.3
1951	934	526	19	18	2.0	3.6
1963[b]	421	243	21		5.0	8.6
1964	415	228	23		5.5	10.1
1965	409	210	24		5.9	11.4
1966	432	295	24		5.6	8.1
1967	483	245	25		5.2	10.2
1968	603	354	20		3.3	5.6
1969	492	298	25		5.1	8.4
1970	458	306	25		5.5	8.2
1971	522		25		4.8	
1972	504		23		4.6	
1973	487		28		5.7	
1974	589		26		4.4	
1975	595		24	24	4.0	
1976	907		24	23	2.6	
1977	1,074		27	26	2.5	
1978	1,157	426	27	27	2.3	6.3
1979	1,193		29	29	2.4	
1980	1,213		27	27	2.2	
1981	1,201		25	24	2.1	
1982	1,230		26	26	2.1	
1983	1,173		25	25	2.1	
1984	1,274		30	29	2.4	
1985[c]	1,148		29	28	2.5	
1986	1,128	519	28	28	2.5	5.3
1987	1,039	510	26		2.5	5.1
1988	844	397	25		3.0	6.3

SOURCES: Jinji-in, *Nenji hōkokusho*, 1948–49 through 1986 (Tokyo: Ōkurasho, Insatsukyoku, 1950–87); *Mainichi shinbun*, 28 Oct. 1978; *Asahi shinbun*, 22 Oct. 1983, 8 Oct. 1984 (evening ed.), 7 Sept. 1988 (evening ed.); *Nihon keizai shinbun*, 6 Oct. 1986, 15 Sept. 1987.

[a]The examination was called the examination to select diplomats and consuls (*gaikōkan ryōjikan saiyō shiken*).

[b]The name was changed to the higher-level examination to select foreign-affairs civil servants (*gaikō kōmuin saiyō jōkyū shiken*).

[c]The name was changed to the type-I examination to select foreign-affairs civil servants (*gaimu kōmuin saiyō isshu shiken*).

ism, famous battles in world history, modern Korean history, Japanese poetry, world geography, logic, analysis of trade statistics, and interpretation of economic graphs.[73]

For the foreign-language test, the applicant must choose one of the following: English, French, German, Russian, Spanish, Chinese, and Arabic. He is then asked to translate texts in the language of his choice into Japanese and vice versa. The tests for the remaining subjects typically consist of two essay questions (or topics) that must be answered in two hours. To give some examples from the 1985 examination:

[International Law]

1. If the fundamental human rights of a private individual who resides in a foreign country are violated, what are the internationally recognized remedies at his disposal?

2. Discuss the immunities of consuls and other consular personnel from the judicial and police jurisdictions of their receiving state.

[Principles of Economics]

1. Discuss the role of public enterprises in a free-market economy from the standpoint of economic theory.

2. Discuss the theoretical advantages and disadvantages of the gold-standard system in comparison with the floating-exchange-rate system.

[Diplomatic History]

1. World War II and the relations among Japan, the United States, and the Soviet Union (1939–45).

2. The movement toward the integration of Europe in the wake of World War II (1945–58).[74]

Those who pass the first stage of the examination must take the second round of tests, which comprise (1) a physical examination; (2) oral tests in constitutional law, international law, and principles of economics; (3) a foreign-language test (composition and conversation); (4) a comprehensive written test; and (5) a character test (*jinbutsu shiken*). The comprehensive test (*sōgō shiken*) consists of writing an essay on a given topic, such as "Japan and the security and prosperity of Asia," "on security" (*anzenhoshō o ronzu*), and "Japan and Southeast Asia." The candidate is expected to demonstrate his mastery of essential information, analytic acumen, and ability to think independently. The

---

73. Juken Shinpō Henshūbu, *Gaikōkan shiken mondaishū* [Collection of Questions in the Foreign-Service Examination] (Tokyo: Hōgaku Shoin, 1987), pp. 9–28 and 61–62.
74. Ibid., p. 327.

character test has two components: an interview and a group discussion. In the latter, eight to ten applicants are assembled in a room, given a problem (usually a diplomatic one), and asked first to state their individual views and then to engage in discussion among themselves. Successful candidates stress the importance of striking a balance between being able to articulate one's own views clearly and showing respect for the views of other participants.[75]

To return to table 17, we see in column C that only about two dozen or so of the applicants pass the examination each year; hence the competition rate is quite high (see column E). What is more, unlike the situation in the higher civil-service examination, nearly all successful candidates are hired. In fact, all of the handful of the successful candidates who were not hired in the period covered by the table had voluntarily withdrawn from further consideration.

What of the university background of successful candidates? In the period from 1945 to 1955, 78.1 percent of the successful candidates (100 out of 128) came from Tōdai. The remainder came from Tokyo University of Foreign Languages ($N = 6$, 4.7 percent), Kyōdai ($N = 5$, 3.9 percent), Tokyo College of Commerce [the predecessor of Hitotsubashi University] ($N = 4$, 3.1 percent), Harbin University ($N = 4$, 3.1 percent), and a handful of other institutions.[76] If we look at a later period, 1965–74, we find a marked decline in the share of Tōdai graduates—49.4 percent (121 out of 245)—and an increase in the share of the other universities—Hitotsubashi: 15.5 percent ($N = 38$); Kyōdai: 11.8 percent ($N = 29$); Keiō: 8.2 percent ($N = 20$); and Tokyo University of Foreign Languages: 4.5 percent ($N = 1$).[77]

In 1978, Tōdai maintained its top position with 44.4 percent (12), followed by Hitotsubashi, 14 percent (4). Kyōdai tied for third place with Tokyo University of Foreign Languages with 11.1 percent each (3 each).[78] In 1982 Tōdai remained at the top with 53.8 percent (14), and Hitotsubashi and Kyōdai retained their traditional second and third spots, with 15.4 percent (4) and 11.5 percent (3), respectively.[79] In 1986 Tōdai produced 71.4 percent (20) of the successes, and Waseda and

75. Ibid., pp. 63, 75–90, 194–97.
76. Nagano Nobutoshi, *Nihon gaikō no subete* [All About Japanese Diplomacy] (Tokyo: Gyōsei Mondai Kenkyūjo Shuppankyoku, 1986), p. 328.
77. Nagano Nobutoshi, *Gaimushō kenkyū* [A Study of the Ministry of Foreign Affairs] (Tokyo: Saimaru Shuppankai, 1975), p. 42.
78. *Mainichi shinbun*, 28 Oct. 1978.
79. Ibid., 23 Oct. 1982.

Kyōdai tied for second place with two successes each. Four other universities supplied one successful candidate each: Hitotsubashi, Keiō, Aoyama Gakuin, and Harvard.[80] In 1987 only four universities supplied all 26 successful candidates—Tōdai: 19 (73.1 percent); Kyōdai: 3; Hitotsubashi: 3; and Waseda: 1. In 1988 the number of universities supplying successful candidates remained the same—Tōdai: 17 (68.0 percent); Hitotsubashi: 4; Kyōdai: 2; and Keiō: 2.[81] In the eleven-year period 1978–88, Tōdai produced 60.3 percent (179) of all successful candidates, and Hitotsubashi produced 11.4 percent (34). Kyōdai placed third with 9.4 percent (28) of the total successes.[82]

In sum, not only is the phenomenon of Tōdai dominance replicated in the recruitment of diplomats, but its degree is somewhat accentuated. Hitotsubashi, previously known as Tokyo College of Commerce (1920–44) and Tokyo College of Industry (1944–49), is a prestigious national university with a tradition of excellence in business and economics.[83] All in all, the pattern of dominance by national universities continues in the foreign-service field as well.

How have women fared in this exclusive domain? Until the mid-1970s, only two women had passed the higher-level foreign-service examination, but beginning in the latter half of the 1970s, there were one or two women in each year's career-track entering class in the Foreign Ministry. In the nine-year period 1978–87, a total of sixteen women passed the higher-level foreign-service examination. The grand total of all women who have passed the examination in the postwar period (1949–88), however, is a mere twenty. In 1980 and 1986, there were three women among the successful candidates in the examination. In 1983, however, there were none. In 1987 one of the twenty-six successful candidates was a woman. The twenty-five successful candidates in 1988 also included a woman. Of the sixteen women who passed the examination in the 1978–87 period, five were graduates of Tōdai and two others had done graduate work there. Five were graduates of Hitotsubashi. The remaining four had studied abroad—two at Colum-

80. *Nihon keizai shinbun,* 6 Oct. 1986 (evening ed.).
81. Ibid., 15 Sept. 1987; *Asahi shinbun,* 7 Sept. 1988 (evening ed.).
82. Nagano Nobutoshi, "Za Kasumigaseki (9): Gaimushō: Nihon gaikō o ugokasu pawa" [Kasumigaseki Series (9): The Ministry of Foreign Affairs: The Power That Moves Japanese Diplomacy], *Kankai* (Mar. 1986): 39; *Yomiuri shinbun,* 7 Oct. 1985 (evening ed.); *Nihon keizai shinbun,* 6 Oct. 1986 (evening ed.), 15 Sept. 1987, and *Asahi shinbun,* 7 Sept. 1988 (evening ed.).
83. Sōgō Gakusei Mondai Kenkyūjo, ed., *Nihon daigaku taikan* [An Overview of Japanese Universities] (Tokyo: Nihon Gakujutsu Tsūshinsha, 1973), p. 117.

bia University, one at Harvard University, and one at Oxford University in England.[84]

In the entire postwar period, no woman in the career foreign service has ever achieved ambassadorial rank; the highest rank attained by a woman was that of minister. Although two women have served as ambassadors, neither was a career diplomat.[85] Given the need for extended service abroad at periodic intervals, careers in the foreign service would be even more difficult to combine with the burdens of a family life than those in the civil service in general. Hence the long-term prognosis for women in the foreign service does not appear to be good.

INTERNATIONAL COMPARISONS

How does Japan's record in the recruitment of its higher civil servants compare with those of other industrialized democracies, specifically, the United States, Great Britain, France, and West Germany? Each country has a different procedure for recruiting its higher civil servants.

Although the picture in the United States is somewhat complicated by the existence of multiple channels of recruitment, including political appointment, the inauguration in 1977 of the Presidential Management Intern Program (PMIP) has spawned a method that comes closest to those employed by the other industrialized democracies in selecting their respective elite-track civil servants.

Presidential Management Interns (PMI) are selected through a four-stage process. In the first stage, deans and directors of graduate programs in "general management with a public focus" nominate a limited number of their top students. Next, the U.S. Office of Personnel Management (OPM), the successor to the U.S. Civil Service Commission, "reviews each nominated application to determine if the nominee meets the basic eligibility requirements." Then follows the regional screening process, during which eligible nominees participate in "group and individual problem-solving exercises, through which they will be evaluated on their leadership, oral communication and interpersonal

84. Nagano, "Za Kasumigaseki (9): Gaimushō," p. 99; *Nihon keizai shinbun*, 6 Oct. 1986 (evening ed.); *Yomiuri shinbun*, 15 Sept. 1987. The Harvard graduate was pursuing her second bachelor's degree at Tōdai's Law Faculty when she passed the examination in October 1986.
85. *Shūkan Yomiuri*, 19 June 1985, p. 165; *Asahi shinbun*, 13 Nov. 1985 and 2 Feb. 1986; Nagano Nobutoshi, "Kankai jinmyaku chiri—chūō shōchōhen: Gaimushō no maki" [Who's Who in Government: Central Ministries and Agencies: The Ministry of Foreign Affairs], *Kankai*, Apr. 1987, pp. 40–54.

skills, and their organizing, planning, problem-solving and decision-making abilities." In addition, nominees must complete a writing sample. They are divided into panels of not more than eight students, each of which is rated by a panel of two to four public managers. These panels are convened at approximately thirty-five sites across the country. In the final stage of the competition, all nominees who have received qualifying ratings in the third stage have their writing sample and credentials evaluated by the OPM, and about 250 finalists are selected for the PMIP each year.[86]

The responsibility of obtaining an actual appointment falls on the shoulders of the finalists. Although all of them find jobs, competition for certain agencies and locations is intense. PMIs start at the grade-9 level and can expect to be promoted to grade 11 after completing one year. After completion of the two-year program, the interns are eligible to advance to grade 12 with career or career-conditional status.[87]

In Great Britain, until the late 1960s, induction into the administrative class was required of aspiring higher civil servants, and this was done by two different methods of competitive examination. Following the publication of the report of the Fulton committee in 1968, however, the administrative class was abolished. Under the new system, higher civil servants are recruited as administrative trainees (AT). Applicants must undergo a three-stage screening process. First, they must take the qualifying test, which "consists of a series of written papers. Typically, a candidate must: reduce an article of 1,500 words to a summary of 300 to 350; give advice on an imaginary government problem . . . ; analyse some tables of social statistics; and answer tests on verbal intelligence, comprehension and data sufficiency."[88]

About three-quarters of the candidates are eliminated in this initial stage. Those who survive then face two and a half days of grueling examination by the Civil Service Selection Board, popularly known as the Cizbee. Candidates are divided into groups of five or six candidates, each of which is evaluated by a panel of three judges—"a chairman, who is usually a retired permanent secretary; a psychologist; and an observer, who is a youngish civil servant who passed Cizbee a few years ago." The tasks the candidates are required to perform include writing

86. U.S. Office of Personnel Management, *The Presidential Management Intern Program, 1980–1981* (Washington: Government Printing Office, 1981), pp. 10–11.
87. Ibid., pp. 12 and 2.
88. Peter Kellner and Lord Crowther-Hunt, *The Civil Servants; An Inquiry into Britain's Ruling Class* (London: MacDonald Futura Publishers, 1980), p. 120.

essays and position papers, participating in group discussion, engaging in "committee exercises," undergoing personal interviews, and taking intelligence and general-knowledge tests. Approximately half of the candidates pass the Cizbee, and then must go to "a short formal interview with the Final Selection Board (FSB). Almost 80 percent of the candidates who reach the FSB are offered jobs as ATs or equivalent posts in the Diplomatic Service or in the Inland Revenue Service.[89] Between 250 and 300 ATs are appointed each year, of whom a substantial number (about 100) are "internal candidates," that is, incumbent civil servants in executive-level positions who want to speed up their promotion process.[90]

The gateway to the French higher civil service is admission to the Ecole Nationale d'Administration (ENA). There are two types of entrance examination to ENA, one for external candidates and another for internal candidates. External candidates must be twenty-five years of age or less and graduates of a university or a *grande école*. Internal candidates (those who are already in the civil service) must be aged 30 or less, graduates of a university or a *grande école,* and have at least five years of experience in a public-sector job. Between 20 and 30 percent of the successful candidates come from the internal competition. In addition, one or two students are admitted without examination from the Ecole Polytechnique.[91] From 1982 to 1985, ten places were set aside for "union leaders and local elected officials, such as small-town mayors, who took different—and, some said, easier—examinations from those required of other applicants." This method of admission, called the "third way," was abolished in 1986.[92]

There are two main stages in the entrance examination to ENA. In the first stage, candidates must take a series of written examinations, each lasting from three to five hours. Depending on whether one

89. Ibid., pp. 124–36.
90. Ōki Yū, "Igirisu seifu shokuin no nin'yō seido" [The Appointment System of Government Employees in England], II, *Jinji-in geppo* 292(June 1975): 29; Tashiro, "Nihon gyōseikan kenkyū, VII," p. 77. In the British civil service the term "executive" does not carry the same exalted connotation as it does in other countries. Executive positions refer to middle-level positions occupied primarily by nonuniversity graduates.
91. Nomura Nario, "Furansu kanri no nin'yō seido" [The Appointment System of French Officials], II, *Jinji-in geppō* 220(June 1969): 14 and 24; Henry Parris, "Twenty Years of l'Ecole Nationale d'Administration," *Public Administration* (London) 43 (Winter 1965): 395–411. The proportion of external candidates has steadily declined over the years. It was 52 percent at its peak (1953). The age limit of external candidates is not strictly enforced.
92. *New York Times,* 24 Aug. 1986.

chooses law or economics as the field of specialization, the subjects of the examination may vary. Applicants in law, for example, are tested in public law; analysis of legal material; social problems involving the application of law, social policy, or international problems; and economics. They must also take an essay test in a subject chosen from business law, economic geography, modern history, linguistics, sociology, psychology, mathematics, statistics, and other fields. There is then a common five-hour-long essay test for both law and economics candidates covering contemporary political, economic, social, or international problems. Only those who pass the written examinations are allowed to proceed to the second stage, which consists primarily of oral examinations. In addition to the subjects covered in the first stage, they include foreign-language examinations. In addition, there is a physical-fitness test consisting of a short-distance dash, a long jump, a discus throw, chin-ups, and swimming. Although 160 candidates succeeded in clearing all these hurdles and were admitted to the prestigious ENA in 1985, the number was scheduled to be reduced by 50 percent by 1987.[93]

In West Germany, aspirants for a career in the higher civil service must undergo even more stringent processes of selection and training. First, they must pass a state examination that is equivalent to a university graduation examination. Those who pass may then begin two and a half years of preparatory service in a government agency. During this period the trainees do not receive a salary but modest stipends for living expenses. Upon completion of such service, they are allowed to take the second state examination. Successful candidates are certified as full-fledged jurists (*Volljurist*) and earn the title of assessor. An "Assessor can apply to a public authority of his choice for an administrative post in the higher grade." If accepted, he becomes a trainee. Only after a probationary period, which may last three years, will he be appointed as a permanent official.[94] In other words, a university graduate must pass two separate state examinations and two

93. Nomura, "Furansu kanri no nin'yō seido," II, p. 19; Suzuki Kazuo, "ENA (Furansu Kokuritsu Gyōsei Gakuin) no kyōiku seido" [The Educational System of ENA (the French National School of Administration)], II, *Jinji-in geppō* 321(Nov. 1977): 23–24; *Asahi shinbun,* Aug. 1986; *New York Times,* 24 Aug. 1986.

94. Nevil Johnson, *State and Government in the Federal Republic of Germany: The Executive at Work* (Oxford: Pergamon Press, 1983), p. 183; Sumitomo Tadashi, "Nishi Dōitsu ni okeru kanri nin'yō seido" [The Appointment System of Officials in West Germany], *Jinji-in geppō* 131(Jan. 1962): 7.

probationary periods spanning five and a half years to gain entry into the higher civil service on a permanent basis.[95]

What these methods of recruiting higher civil servants have in common are their selectivity and reliance on extended training periods. In both absolute and relative terms, the number of people selected is substantially fewer in these countries than is the case in Japan. As we shall see later, moreover, the length and content of training received by graduates of the type-I (or type-A) higher civil-service examination cannot even begin to compare with those of their counterparts in the Western democracies. In one sense, the Japanese system appears to be more open than those of America and Western Europe. For there is no formal educational requirement in Japan. The practical significance of this formal flexibility evaporates quickly, however, when the actual track record is examined.

Moreover, the rigor with which the track system is adhered to in Japan has no parallel elsewhere. Internal candidates in both Britain and France, are allowed to compete with external candidates for admission to the elite corps. In France, in particular, between a quarter and a third of successful candidates in the entrance examination to ENA are internal candidates. As for the United States, the apparent rigidity of the PMIP's admission requirements is diluted by a number of considerations. First, there is an abundance of opportunities, in terms of the sheer number of programs and their flexibility, for obtaining the necessary credentials even for incumbent government officials. Second, the manner in which the selection process operates is calculated to ensure equality of opportunity to a very high degree. Third, there is a great deal of mobility, both vertical and lateral, in the American federal bureaucracy. On the other hand, West Germany seems to come close to matching Japan's rigid stratification, for it provides relatively little opportunity for those who have not undergone the arduous process of state examinations and probationary periods to attain the upper rungs of its bureaucratic ladder. However, the rigidity of the West German

95. For descriptions of the West German system, see, in addition to the work cited above, David Southern, "Germany" in F. F. Ridley, ed., *Government and Administration in Western Europe* (New York: St. Martin's Press, 1979), pp. 137–43; Klaus von Beyme, *The Political System of the Federal Republic of Germany* (New York: St. Martin's Press, 1983), pp. 149–54; Hans Joachim von Oertzen, "Republic Personnel Management in the Federal Republic of Germany," *International Review of Administrative Sciences* 49, no. 2 (1983): 210–17; Sumitomo Tadashi, "Nishi Dōitsu renpō kanri no nin'yō seido" [The Appointment System of West German Federal Officials], 2 parts, *Jinji-in geppō* 215(Jan. 1969): 6–9, and 217(Mar. 1969): 12–15.

system is tempered by an extensive use of political appointment in the top echelons of its bureaucracy.[96]

What of the phenomenon of domination by elite universities? Both Britain and France manifest a similar phenomenon. From 1948 to 1963, Oxford and Cambridge Universities provided 81 percent of successful candidates in methods I and II competition for direct entrants to the administrative class. But unlike the situation in Japan, the two top universities split the successes fairly evenly, Cambridge trailing behind Oxford by the ratio of four to six.[97] After the reforms of the late 1960s, the Oxbridge dominance seemed to slacken slightly. In the mid-1970s, about 65 percent of external candidates for administrative trainees who passed the Final Selection Board came from the two universities. Oxbridge's share decreased in the late 1970s to slightly over 50 percent.[98]

With regard to France, between 70 and 90 percent of successful external candidates in the entrance examination to ENA are products of Instituts d'Etudes Politiques (IEP), of which the institute situated in Paris supplies over 90 percent. When successful internal candidates are added, the share of the IEPs drops to about 60 percent. The IEPs, which are state institutions, in effect serve as preparatory schools for ENA entrance examinations; as such they attract students and graduates of both universities and *grandes écoles*.[99]

Turning to the United States, we find nothing that can match the elitism of Japan, Britain, and France. A 1959 survey found that of the 7,640 career civil servants holding the rank of GS 14 or higher, no more than 3 percent came from any single university. In fact, it was not an Ivy League university but George Washington University and the City College of New York that shared the top positions, with 3 percent each. The top ten universities together supplied only 21 percent of the career civilian executives, and the top thirty universities brought the proportion to a mere 42 percent. Only in the Foreign Service did Ivy League universities appear at the top. But Harvard, Yale, and Princeton together were the source of only 14 percent of senior Foreign Service

96. Southern, "Germany," p. 142.
97. Geoffrey K. Fry, *Statesmen in Disguise: The Changing Role of the Administrative Class of the British Home Civil Service, 1853–1966* (London: Macmillan, 1969), p. 435. The statistics were calculated from table 5.
98. Kellner and Crowther-Hunt, *The Civil Servants*, pp. 120–23 and 137.
99. Suzuki, "ENA no kyōiku seido," III, *Jinji-in geppō* 322(Dec. 1977): 19; Ezra N. Suleiman, *Politics, Power, and Bureaucracy in France: The Administrative Elite* (Princeton: Princeton University Press, 1974), p. 54; *New York Times*, 24 Aug. 1986.

officers.[100] The PMIP became even more egalitarian: 250 finalists chosen in 1978 were spread among 127 different graduate schools, and the same pattern was repeated in subsequent years.[101] In West Germany the problem does not arise at all, because students are allowed to take courses in any of the state universities and many of them attend several universities during their academic careers. There is no one university that is dominant in terms of reputation.[102]

Is the predominance of law graduates replicated outside of Japan? Here West Germany resembles Japan closely, which is not surprising in view of the German influence on the prewar Japanese bureaucracy. Although hard data are not available, the legalistic bias in German administration is well known. In the words of Herbert Jacob: "German administration . . . went much further in its obeisance to legal formulas than most administrative organizations, for its officials were specifically trained in the law. . . . The university training received by German administrators concentrated heavily in law."[103] Speaking of the post-war period, Lewis J. Edinger writes that "a civil servant, who wants to rise above a medium-grade position, no matter what his task will be, must usually have a degree in law."[104] Finally, Nevil Johnson estimated in 1983 that about two-thirds of West German higher civil servants might be lawyers.[105]

It is worth noting that, as is true in Japan, a law degree in and of itself has no professional significance in West Germany. In order to enter the legal profession, the candidate must undergo the same procedure as the candidate for the higher civil service: two state examinations and two prolonged periods of postgraduate training. What sets West German law graduates apart from their Japanese counterparts, however, is that the former must, in effect, qualify for a professional career in law before they can become full-fledged members

100. Lloyd W. Warner et al., *The American Federal Executive* (New Haven: Yale University Press, 1963), p. 372, table 51B.

101. U.S. Office of Personnel Management, *The Presidential Management Intern Program: Anniversary Report, 1978–1980* (Washington: Government Printing Office), pp. 3 and 21–23.

102. Tashiro Kū, "Nihon gyōseikan kenkyū, IV: Gyōseikan no kyaria keisei katei, 2," *Kankai,* Jan. 1982, p. 92.

103. Herbert Jacob, *German Administration Since Bismarck: Central Authority Versus Autonomy* (New Haven: Yale University Press, 1963), p. 203.

104. Lewis J. Edinger, *Politics in Germany: Attitudes and Processes* (Boston: Little, Brown, 1968), p. 46.

105. Johnson, *State and Government in the Federal Republic of Germany*, p. 183. Another scholar writes that depending on how one defines a "lawyer," the proportion can range from 46 to 85 percent. See Southern, "Germany," p. 139.

of the higher civil service. Interestingly, there is even a German phrase that is comparable to *hōka bannō*, namely, *Juristenmonopol* (monopoly by lawyers). The Japanese attempt to alleviate the problem has also been duplicated in West Germany; there are laws and regulations that are designed to place those who have majored in economics, finance, and sociology on a par with law graduates in their competition for the higher civil service.[106]

As already noted, candidates for admission to the French ENA must choose between two fields: law and economics. About 70 percent of them opt for law.[107] In the United States, where a law degree is all but synonymous with a license to practice law, it is not a significant factor in the higher civil service. The study by Warner and his associates cited earlier found that less than 8 percent of the senior career civil servants had law degrees. Overall, only 12 percent of all federal executives, both civilian and military, in the sample (1,582 out of 12,929) had law degrees. So far as the sources of the law degrees were concerned, only three law schools had produced more than 5 percent: George Washington (18.6 percent), Georgetown (6.9 percent), and Harvard (6.6 percent). The fact that two of these law schools are situated in Washington, D.C., suggests that many Federal executives may have earned their law degrees after entering the government service.[108]

The PMIP, the most recent vehicle of elite recruitment in the U.S. federal government, is aimed explicitly at attracting candidates with graduate training in management. Sixty-eight percent of the 250 interns selected in 1978, for example, had graduate degrees in public administration. The remainder were spread among business administration (8 percent), urban studies (6 percent), international studies (3.2 percent), public policy (2.8 percent), planning/resource management (2.8 percent), and other related fields (such as general management, criminal justice, social work, and political science).[109]

The British administrative class was traditionally dominated by those who had majored in history and classics. Fifty-eight percent of direct entrants to the class in the 1948–56 period (methods I and II combined) and 51 percent of them in the 1957–63 period had taken their degrees in these two subjects. The proportion of those who had taken their degrees

106. Sumitomo, "Nishi Dōitsu renpō kanri no nin'yō seido," I, p. 9.
107. Nomura, "Furansu kanri no nin'yō seido," II, p. 25.
108. Warner et al. *The American Federal Executive*, p. 369, table 48B.
109. U.S. Office of Personnel Management, *The Presidential Management Intern Program: Anniversary Report*, p. 3.

in law during the two periods were 3 and 5 percent, respectively.[110] The post-Fulton reforms have not produced any substantial change; although the proportion of graduates in history and classics has declined, the majority of successful candidates for administrative-trainee positions have nonetheless continued to be "arts" (that is, humanities) graduates.[111]

The underrepresentation of women in the higher echelons of government bureaucracy is a universal phenomenon. In none of the Western industrialized democracies have women achieved parity with men in the higher civil service. However, the degree to which women are underrepresented varies widely. In general, women have been making notable progress in the United States. Warner and his colleagues found in their 1959 survey that only 145 of the 10,851 civilian federal executives who responded to their questionnaires were women, "about one in seventy-five of the civilian federal executives."[112] Two decades later the first class of the PMIs contained 116 women, accounting for 46 percent of the total. Twenty-one percent of them were nonwhites.[113]

In France, the proportion of women among those who are admitted to the ENA has steadily increased. It was about 13 percent in the late 1970s and 25 percent in the mid-1980s.[114] In Britain, women first gained entry into the administrative class during World War I on a temporary basis and then became eligible to compete for AC positions in the mid-1920s. From 1925 to 1945, however, the proportion of women among successful candidates for the administrative class remained at or below 7 percent. During the postwar period, the proportion increased to about 10 percent, a situation that has remained unchanged in the post-Fulton era.[115]

With respect to the other aspects of recruitment, there are certain parallels and contrasts between Japan and the other countries. The 20-percent no-show rate in Japan's higher civil-service examinations,

110. Fry, *Statesmen in Disguise,* p. 436. Percentages were calculated from table 6.
111. Kellner and Crowther-Hunt, *The Civil Servants,* pp. 120–23; Ōki Yū, "Igirisu seifu shokuin no nin'yō seido," I, p. 18.
112. Warner et al., *The American Federal Executive,* p. 177.
113. U.S. Office of Personnel Management, *The Presidential Management Intern Program: Anniversary Report,* p. 3.
114. Suzuki, "ENA no kyōku seido," I, p. 25; *New York Times,* 24 Aug. 1986.
115. Kelsall, *Higher Civil Servants in Britain,* pp. 169–77; Kellner and Crowther-Hunt, *The Civil Servants,* p. 12. Regarding West Germany, the proportion of women in the federal civil service as a whole is said to be about 21 percent. However, their percentage in the higher civil service is unknown. Oertzen, "Public Personnel Management in the Federal Republic of Germany," p. 212.

for example, is replicated in England and France. The effective rate of competition also appears to be equally high in all three countries, although the Japanese rate, particularly in recent years, remains unsurpassed. When it comes to the rate of appointment, however, the picture changes markedly. In general, the rate is much higher in the other countries than it is in Japan. Nearly all successful candidates receive civil-service appointments in the Western democracies, whereas only half of them do so in Japan.

In sum, international comparisons suggest that most of the phenomena that characterize Japanese patterns of recruiting higher civil servants are not confined to that country. Nonetheless, the variations among the five countries in terms of the salience, pervasiveness, and intensity of some of the phenomena should not be overlooked. In general, the Japanese system emerges as somewhat more closed and less egalitarian than its Western counterparts. Before we can make an overall comparative assessment, however, we need to examine the other dimensions of the Japanese higher civil service.

CHAPTER FIVE

Promotion

The process by which a bureaucracy promotes its members to higher positions has tremendous practical implications. If we accept the notion that, in general, the higher one's position in the bureaucratic pyramid, the greater one's influence and impact, then it becomes plain that the promotion process determines who shall exert power and influence in the bureaucracy. The character and caliber of the bureaucracy's outputs, be they goods, services, decisions, or policies, will hinge, to an important extent, on who is promoted to the higher positions and how.

No less important are the effects of the promotion process and outcomes on the morale of bureaucrats. Unless it is handled with strict impartiality, without fear or favor, on the basis of generally accepted and objectively verifiable criteria, the promotion process has the potential of demoralizing a large proportion of bureaucrats. The structural imperative of bureaucratic organization makes it inevitable that the number of people who can be promoted decreases steadily as they climb the ladder. In other words, the number of potential beneficiaries of the promotion process will vary inversely with the proximity of each echelon to the summit. Can the process be managed in such a way as to placate those who are left behind? How can one ensure that only the most qualified will reach each higher stage in the climb?

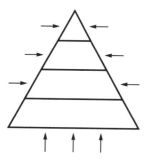 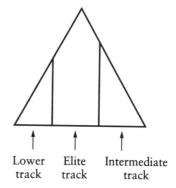

Lower   Elite   Intermediate
track   track   track

Fig. 2   Two Models of Promotion

Open Competitive Model

1. Promotion open to all regardless of mode of entry.

2. Lateral entry permitted at all levels.

3. The principal criterion of promotion is demonstrated merit rather than length of service.

Closed Multitrack Model

1. Initial mode of entry determines the track each civil servant will follow.

2. No lateral entry permitted.

3. Within each track, length of service plays a key role in promotion up to a certain point.

In general, two polar models of promotion in a government bureaucracy can be postulated. The distinguishing attributes of the two models are displayed in figure 2. In the first model, which we shall call the open competitive model, all members of the bureaucracy, in theory, embark on their careers with equal chances of being promoted. The particular manner in which one has entered the organization has no bearing on one's prospect of upward mobility. Nor does the level of entrance examination one has taken predetermine the course, speed, and limits of one's promotion in future years. Such openness and flexibility also imply permeability. The organization permits and even encourages a steady inflow of fresh talent at all levels. It follows logically from the foregoing that the principal criterion of promotion shall be merit rather than seniority. This, of course, does not mean that length of service will not matter; rather it means that top priority will be given to demonstrated merit. Given the difficulty of measuring merit, however, length of service will play a major role insofar as the promotion of those with more or less equal track records is concerned.

In the second model, which we shall label the closed multitrack model, the single most important factor that impinges on the promotion process is the mode of initial entry. Depending on the type and level of examination and evaluation one has undergone, one enters a distinctly demarcated track—an elite track that leads to the top, an intermediate track that allows one to advance only to a position of moderate authority, or a lower track that all but bars promotion to a managerial position. Such a multitrack system is maintained with a high degree of rigidity; very few persons are allowed to enter any of the tracks at points other than the starting line, and even fewer are permitted to cross the demarcation lines of each track at midpoint. Lateral entry into intermediate and higher levels of the hierarchy from the outside is virtually unheard of. Then, too, although merit does play an important role in promotion within each track, length of service is far more controlling here than is the case in the other model. With very few exceptions, members of each entering class within each track tend to ascend the ladder in lockstep up to a certain point.

It should be stressed that these two models neither conform precisely to the ongoing reality nor exhaust all the possibilities. In practice, some systems may represent modified versions of one or the other. Nonetheless, the United States comes closest to approximating the open competitive model, whereas Japan exemplifies the closed multitrack model better than any other country. The West German system resembles, although it does not duplicate, the Japanese system. The situation in Britain and France can perhaps be characterized as a mixture of both models; we may call it the open multitrack model. The chief distinguishing mark of this model is that those who have entered a lower track or an intermediate one are allowed to cross over to the elite track in the midstream provided that they can clear certain hurdles. Thus both the British and French systems set aside a large proportion of places in their administrative trainee program and in the Ecole Nationale d'Administration, respectively, for internal candidates—that is, those who are already in the civil service.

In the remainder of this chapter, we shall probe the chief aspects of the promotion process in the Japanese civil service. The bulk of our discussion will be based on a combination of descriptive statistics and impressionistic evidence.

SALIENT ASPECTS OF
THE PROMOTION PROCESS

THE MULTITRACK SYSTEM

We have already seen that the Japanese civil service employs a closed multitrack system. There are four readily identifiable tracks based on the level and type of the entrance examination taken by the civil servant. Track 1, which can be equated with the elite track, is open to those who have passed the type-A higher civil examination (type I since 1985) or its equivalent. Track 2 is open to those who have passed the type-B higher civil-service examination (abolished in 1985) or its equivalent; we shall label it the quasi-elite track. Those who have passed the intermediate civil-service examination (type II since 1985) are launched on track 3, which can lead to middle-level positions in the Japanese bureaucracy. Track 4 is reserved for those who have passed the lower civil-service examination (type III since 1985); these are the men and women who will perform the routine tasks of the Japanese government at lower levels.

As noted in the preceding chapter, however, the most meaningful distinction may be found between the elite track on one hand and all the others on the other. Although civil servants on the quasi-elite track are regarded as part of *kyaria* (career civil servants), along with those on the elite track, their status is not equal. The vast majority of the civil servants who are known as *nonkyaria* (noncareer) actually remain in the civil service longer than the elite bureaucrats.

It should also be recalled that it is by no means impossible for *nonkyaria* civil servants to rise to the level of section chief and even beyond. In fact, most ministries seem to have a few section-chief positions reserved for their exceptionally capable *nonkyaria* employees.[1]

Table 18 presents some data on the relative size of each track. Note that the data pertain only to administrative service I positions. Inasmuch as the breakdown between types A and B of the higher civil-service examination is available for new appointees only, the table is based on the latter. As we can see, both the number and proportion of track 1

---

1. For profiles of *nonkyaria* civil servants who have attained the position of section chief or higher in selected ministries and agencies, see the series on "Nonkyaria no sekai" [The World of Noncareer (Civil Servants)], *Kankai,* Apr. 1983–Feb. 1984.

TABLE 18   *New Appointees to Administrative Service I*
Positions, by Mode of Entry

	Examination					
Year	*Higher A*	*Higher B*	*Intermediate*	*Lower*	Evaluation	Total
1961						
N	339	99	771	5,464	3,865	10,538
%	3.2	0.9	7.3	51.9	36.7	100.0
1966						
N	511	140	849	7,546	1,741	10,787
%	4.7	1.3	7.9	70.0	16.1	100.0
1971						
N	521	128	831	7,078	2,408	10,966
%	4.8	1.2	7.6	64.5	21.9	100.0
1976						
N	528	187	987	4,759	1,666	8,127
%	6.5	2.3	12.1	58.6	20.5	100.0
1981						
N	497	143	1,544	6,481	2,076	10,741
%	4.6	1.3	14.4	60.4	19.3	100.0
1986						
N	549[a]	0[b]	1,916	6,711	2,677	12,096[c]
%	4.5	0	15.8	55.5	22.1	100.0

SOURCE: Jinji-in, *Nenji hōkokusho*, 1962–87 (Tokyo: Ōkurashō, Insatsukyoku, 1963–88).

[a]The number refers to those who have passed the type-I higher civil-service examination (HCSE).

[b]The type-B HCSE was abolished in 1985.

[c]This number is greater than the sum of all the preceding numbers in this row because it includes 96 civil servants who were rehired and 149 civil servants who were recruited through special examinations.

(higher A) appointees have remained rather small. On the average, only about one in twenty new appointees in any given year is launched on the elite track. The smallest category, both in absolute and relative terms, however, is track 2 (higher B). Whereas the type-A (or type I) higher examination, the gateway to track 1, encompasses the whole gamut of specialties, numbering twenty-eight, the type-B higher examination, until it was abolished in 1985, covered only four fields of specialization: law, economics, civil engineering, and library science. The last-named field was available only in the type-B examination.[2] Track 3 (intermedi-

2. Jinji-in, *Kōmuin hakusho*, 1985, p. 23.

ate) has steadily increased in size over the years, accounting, as of 1986, for 1 out of 6.3 new civil servants in administrative-service I positions. Not surprisingly, the largest category is track 4 (lower), which has absorbed about 60 percent of the new civil servants throughout the period.

The category of "evaluation" needs to be discussed briefly. Strictly speaking, this is not a separate track, for it encompasses civil servants who are equivalent in status to those in all four tracks. In 1985, for example, the National Personnel Authority certified 88 new appointees who had not taken any examination as "equivalent" to type-I graduates and 10 others as "equivalent" to type-II graduates. The former consisted of 47 doctorate holders, 17 holders of master's degrees, and 24 physicians, and all of the latter were holders of master's degrees.[3]

On the other hand, a small number of the civil servants who are hired through "evaluation" do take examinations that are described as "equivalent to the regular [civil service] examinations." In 1985 a total of 304 candidates took such examinations at the type-I level in such fields as shipbuilding, nuclear engineering, biology, forestry, textiles (*sen'igaku*), design (*ishōgaku*), archaeology, and history of architecture. Twenty-nine of the candidates passed their respective examinations and were hired by eleven different agencies and ministries. In 1985 also, 77 out of 613 applicants were hired as intermediate-level civil servants in the same manner.[4] Although all of these civil servants are legally entitled to the same treatment as graduates of the civil-service examinations at their "equivalent" levels, it is doubtful that the legal stipulations are faithfully implemented. With rare exceptions, only those who pass the type-I civil-service examination have the privilege of launching their careers on the elite track.[5]

3. Ibid., 1987, p. 45. It should be noted that, strictly speaking, physicians in Japan do not hold doctorates; their medical degree is officially called "Bachelor of Medicine" (*igakushi*). Some physicians, however, earn postgraduate degrees—e.g., Doctor of Science in Medicine (*igaku hakase*).

4. Ibid., pp. 42–44.

5. For a story of one such exception, see "Kanryō shusshin seijika genzan: Fujin no chi'i kōjō kakeru" [Interview with Bureaucrats-Turned-Politicians: Gambling on the Improvement of the Position of Women], *Kankai*, Nov. 1985, pp. 88–96. The subject of this interview article is Kubota Manae, a Socialist member of the House of Councillors. She was hired by the Ministry of Labor in 1951, a year after her graduation from Keiō University's Law Faculty. Although she had not taken any civil-service examination, she was treated as an elite-track civil servant; she retired as a division chief in 1982 and was elected to the upper house of the Diet in the following year. However, she lost her bid for reelection in 1986. See *Asahi shinbun*, 8 July 1986. In her interview with the *Kankai* magazine, she attributed her successful career in the bureaucracy to "luck."

SALIENCE OF SENIORITY

Another striking characteristic of the promotion process in Japanese bureaucracy is the role played by the year of entry of civil servants (*nenji*). Typically, recruitment occurs once a year, hence those who enter in the same year on the same track in effect become members of the same class. In a few instances, however, recruitment has occurred twice a year, thus giving birth to two separate classes in the same year. In all cases, however, the year of entry is believed to be all but controlling insofar as advancement on the career ladder is concerned. That is to say, members of the same *nenji* in a given ministry are promoted to the next higher level at roughly the same time until they reach that of assistant section chief (*kachō hosa*).[6]

From then on, further advancement is contingent upon a combination of factors, of which seniority is but one. Those who are left behind usually resign. Finally, when one of the lucky survivors who have climbed nearly to the top reaches the peak of his civil-service career, namely, the position of administrative vice-minister (*jimu jikan*), all of his remaining colleagues in the same entering class resign. In so doing, not only do they spare both themselves and the new vice-minister the awkwardness of substituting hierarchical relationships for erstwhile ties of equality, but they also clear the path for the advancement of their *kōhai* (juniors or members of the succeeding entering classes).

The general pattern sketched above, however, needs to be qualified. First, because not all positions at the same level are equal in importance, differentiation is bound to occur from the early stage. As we shall see shortly, service in certain key positions early in one's career enhances the probability of one's outdistancing the other members of one's cohort in the race toward the coveted title of administrative vice-minister. Second, the unwritten rule that one shall resign when one's classmate reaches the final destination is far from sacrosanct. In the 1945–83 period, the rule was violated at least once in all the twelve ministries. In the Ministry of Agriculture, Forestry, and Fisheries, deviations from the rule occurred seven times, and both the Finance and Foreign Ministries witnessed five exceptions to the rule. In many cases, however, classmates of the newly promoted administrative vice-minister who did not

6. Tashiro Kū, "Nihon gyōseikan kenkyū, VIII: Gyōseikan no shōshin kanri, i" [A Study of Japanese Public Administrators, Part VIII: Management of Their Promotion, 1], *Kankai*, May 1982, p. 73.

resign were either assigned to or had already been occupying positions as chiefs of "external bureaus" (*gaikyoku chōkan*). That is to say, they were outside the regular chain of command of the ministries concerned and hence were not subject to direct supervision by the administrative vice-minister. In the case of the Foreign Ministry, this took the form of service as an ambassador abroad. In fact, it is a well-established pattern in the Japanese diplomatic service for an outgoing vice-minister to be appointed to a major ambassadorial post. This ensures that several senior ambassadors at any given time shall serve under their *kōhai*.[7]

In the Ministry of International Trade and Industry, the top two civil-service positions—the administrative vice-minister and the vice-minister for international affairs (*tsūshō sangyō shingikan*)—are usually occupied by members of the same class, and both resign simultaneously.[8] In the Ministry of Justice, the administrative vice-ministership is not the terminal career position but a stepping stone to other, more prestigious positions. Although the ministry hires graduates of both the higher civil-service examination and the judicial examination, it is the latter who control the levers of power. Differentiated by the year of graduation from the Judicial Training Institute, nearly all of them are public prosecutors. Known as *ateken,* their supremacy in the Justice Ministry is sometimes described as "prosecutor's imperialism" (*kenji teikoku shugi*). The highest position attainable by them is that of prosecutor general (*kenji sōchō*), and the administrative vice-minister is several rungs below that position. Given all this, the appointment of a

---

7. For data on the administrative vice-ministers of the twelve ministries and other agencies during the postwar period, see the series on "Jimu jikan kenkyū" [A Study of Administrative Vice-Ministers], *Kankai,* Jan. 1982–June 1983. For additional data on the Foreign Ministry, see Nagano, *Gaimushō kenkyū,* pp. 92–96, Nagano, *Nihon gaikō no subete,* pp. 297–300, and Nagano, "Kankai jinmyaku chiri: Gaimushō no maki," pp. 40–54. A particularly notable example of deviation from the general rule is the case of Sunobe Ryōzō, who succeeded his *kōhai* (a member of the 1941 entering class) as administrative vice-minister in the Foreign Ministry. A member of the 1940 class, Sunobe had previously served as ambassador to the Republic of Korea; his tenure as vice-minister lasted from July 1981 to January 1983.

8. Nawa Tarō, "Jimu jikan kenkyū: Tsūsanshō" [A Study of Administrative Vice-Ministers: The Ministry of International Trade and Industry], *Kankai,* Mar. 1982, p. 130. In 1987 the two top positions were occupied by members of the 1955 class: Fukukawa Shinji (AVM) and Kurota Makoto (vice-minister for international affairs). Both were born in 1932 and graduated from Tōdai's Law Faculty in 1955. *Shōwa 62-nenban Tsūshō Sangyōsho meikan* [Directory of the Ministry of International Trade and Industry, 1987 Edition] (Tokyo: Jihyōsha, 1987), pp. 3–4; *Seikai kanchō jinji roku 1987-nenban,* p. 452.

new administrative vice-minister does not precipitate a wave of resignations by his classmates.[9]

THE "ELITE COURSE"

As noted, the basic pattern of progression for elite-track civil servants remains the same until they reach the level of assistant section chief, that is, for the first ten years or so. Most ministries try to give their future leaders on-the-job training through the policy of rotation. In the Ministry of Finance, for example, the first six or seven years are set aside for such training (*minarai kikan*). Although experience varies from individual to individual, most first-year trainees are assigned to a particular section where they are initiated into the mores of the "Ōkura [Finance Ministry] family."[10] They are expected to run errands for superiors and perform all sorts of routine, even menial, tasks.

During the second year, the trainees are likely to be assigned to one of the local tax offices to learn about the practical side of internal revenue and finance as "inspectors" (*chōsakan*). Third-year trainees turn their attention to more theoretical matters, devoting their full time to study either in Japan or abroad. Next, they are exposed to substantive work of the ministry in Tokyo, eventually being promoted to subsection chiefs (*kakarichō*). In the fifth or sixth year comes the capstone of the trainee's career—appointment as chief of a local tax office (*zeimushochō*). Besides entailing a fair amount of prestige and power, this provides the trainees with the first real opportunity to test their mettle. How they handle themselves in this leadership position will be closely monitored by their superiors in Tokyo.[11]

9. Setō Shūzō, "Jimu jikan kenkyū: Hōmushō" [A Study of Administrative Vice-Ministers: the Ministry of Justice], *Kankai*, Nov. 1982, pp. 66–75; Ikeda Toyoharu, "Kankai jinmyaku chiri: Hōmushō Kensatsuchō no maki" [Who's Who in Government: The Ministry of Justice and the Public Prosecutor's Office], ibid., Mar. 1981, pp. 30–41. In 1986, whereas a 1951 graduate of the Judicial Training Institute (JTI) served as the administrative vice-minister of the Justice Ministry, a 1947 JTI graduate occupied the post of prosecutor general. Three other persons in the Supreme Public Prosecutor's Office and all the chief prosecutors in the eight Higher Prosecutor's Offices had more seniority than the vice-minister. The preceding information was culled from *Seikai kanchō jinji roku 1987-nenban*, pp. 311–22.

10. Sakakibara, *Nihon o enshutsu suru shin kanryō-zō*, pp. 39–41. This book is based on Sakakibara's participant observations. I shall present more details on the on-the-job training of Finance Ministry bureaucrats in the next chapter.

11. Takamoto Mitsuo, *Ōkura kanryō no keifu* [The Genealogy of Finance Ministry Bureaucrats] (Tokyo: Nihon Shoseki Kabushiki Kaisha, 1979), pp. 49–51. Fragmentary evidence suggests that appointment as local tax chief can occur as early as the trainee's fifth year and as late as his seventh year. Some trainees are not given this opportunity at all, whereas others are given the privilege twice in a row. See *Shōwa 62-nenban Ōkurashō meikan* [Directory of the Finance Ministry, 1987 Edition] (Tokyo: Jihyosha, 1986).

The second hurdle awaits the bureaucrat at the level of assistant section chief (*kachō hosa*). Some bureaucrats are elevated to this level immediately upon completion of their training period. Others must undergo a few more years of apprenticeship. An assistant section chief must display competence in a wide range of activities: research, negotiation, and drafting bills and policy proposals. Those who receive high marks during their days as assistant section chiefs are given choice assignments when they are sent either abroad or to the field in the next round. Such "desirable" locations as embassies and consulates in industrialized democracies in America and Western Europe as well as major cities in Japan are said to be reserved for them.[12]

The bureaucrat encounters the third hurdle when he reaches the level of section chief after about ten years of service as assistant section chief or its equivalent in a number of different sections and units. In addition to demonstrating skills in research, negotiation, and legislative draftsmanship, as mentioned earlier, a section chief is called upon to engage in coordination, provide leadership, deal with personnel matters, and be knowledgeable about a wide range of matters. The manner in which one meets such a multiplicity of challenges will help determine one's chances of advancement in subsequent years. The verdict will come when a handful of classmates are picked as chiefs of the three core sections in the minister's secretariat (*kanbō sanka*)—the secretarial section, the documents section, and the research and planning section—and as chiefs of the principal section in each bureau, usually called the general affairs section (*sōmuka*). For those who are passed over, the prospect of promotion to the position of bureau chief in the ministry proper becomes rather dim, which in turn implies that they may no longer be in the race to become administrative vice-minister.[13]

A review of the career patterns of fifty persons who have served as administrative vice-ministers in ten ministries reveals that forty-one (82 percent) had previously served as chief of either core sections in the secretariat or the principal section of a bureau. The pivotal role of *kanbō* sections is suggested by the fact that thirty-two persons (62 percent) had served as their chiefs. Of these, twenty-two had eventually become chiefs of the secretariat (*kanbōchō*). Twelve others in the sample had

12. Takamoto, *Ōkura kanryō no keifu*, pp. 52–54.
13. Ibid., pp. 54–63. All eight persons who held the position of bureau chief (including chief of the minister's secretariat) in the Finance Ministry in late 1986 had served as chiefs of either "core" sections in the minister's secretariat or principal sections in bureaus. All but one had also served as assistant chiefs of such sections. *Shōwa 62-nenban Ōkurashō meikan*, pp. 11, 40, 55, 61, 68, 81, 87, and 97.

Theodore Lownik Library
Illinois Benedictine College
Lisle, Illinois 60532

also served as *kanbōchō,* bringing the total number of former administrative vice-ministers with *kanbocho* experience to thirty-four (68 percent). All told, only six had not served in any of three key posts—*kanbō* section chief, chief of the principal section of a bureau, and *kanbōchō.*[14]

It should be stressed that the relative position of the secretariat in the internal structural hierarchy of a ministry or an agency is not uniformly high. It is only in those ministries and agencies that have adopted the system of a "grand secretariat" (*dai kanbōchō sei*) that its chief outranks the chiefs of all bureaus (*kyokuchō*). Examples include the Ministries of Foreign Affairs, Transport, and Construction. As will be explained shortly, however, the Ministry of Construction has a dual hierarchy, one pertaining to administrative officials (*jimukan*) and another to specialists (*gikan*), hence the chief of its secretariat does not necessarily outrank chiefs of technical bureaus. In other ministries the secretariat is on a par with a middle-level bureau. In a few ministries, notably the Ministry of Posts and Telecommunications, the secretariat is at the bottom of the pecking order.[15]

Regardless of its position in the hierarchy, however, the work of the secretariat is intrinsically important. The well-known phenomenon of "sectionalism" tends to foster rivalry among bureaus within most ministries, as is suggested by such phrases as "there are bureaus but no ministry" (*Kyoku atte shō nashi*)[16] and "the bureaus that resemble 'independent kingdoms'" (*"dokuritsu ōkoku" no yō na kakukyoku*).[17] This underscores the importance of coordination; the parochial interests and perceptions of the various bureaus must be adjusted and harmonized to further the goals of the ministry as a whole. Externally, the task of representing the ministry vis-à-vis politicians, the Diet, and interest groups must also be performed by a unit with a broad, ministry-wide perspective.

14. These statistics were culled from the biographical sketches of fifty former administrative vice-ministers in Watanabe Yasuo, "Kōmuin no kyaria" [The Career Patterns of Civil Servants] in Tsuji Kiyoaki, ed., *Gyōseigaku kōza, dai 4-kan: Gyōsei to soshiki* [Lectures on Public Administration, vol. 4: Public Administration and Organization] (Tokyo: Tōkyō Daigaku Shuppankai, 1976), pp. 193–98.
15. Kyōikusha, *Kanryō* [Bureaucrats] (Tokyo: Kyōikusha, 1980), p. 76. An assessment of the relative rank of the secretariat can be obtained by reviewing the year of entry of incumbent officials as well as the career patterns of administrative vice-ministers. See the long-running series on "Kankai jinmyaku chiri" [Who's Who in Government] in *Kankai,* Jan. 1981–, as well as the series on administrative vice-ministers cited earlier.
16. Ishii Masashi, "Kankai jinmyaku chiri: Ōkurashō no maki" [Who's Who in Government: The Ministry of Finance], *Kankai,* Oct. 1981, p. 45.
17. Hashimoto Gorō, "Kankai jinmyaku chiri: Kōseishō no maki" [Who's Who in Government: The Ministry of Health and Welfare], *Kankai,* Dec. 1981, p. 39.

These pivotal roles are performed by the secretariat. Consequently, chiefs of its key sections dealing with general affairs, personnel, and budget need to be exceptionally well-qualified. Their duties expose them to the whole gamut of problems and issues confronting their ministry, challenging them to exercise and develop skills in compromise, negotiation, and a judicious balancing of diverse interests. In a word, a stint as a core section chief in the secretariat both broadens and tests the civil servant. Those who emerge from such experience with their reputation either intact or enhanced are marked for still weightier challenges thereafter.[18]

In short, the preceding discussion suggests that the promotion patterns of Japanese higher civil servants are affected by a number of factors: (1) *nenji*, or the year of entry; (2) the preentry record, notably grades received during university days and in the higher civil-service examination; and (3) the postentry record. The latter two are related, for an initial assignment to a core unit hinges to a large extent on the preentry record; such an assignment in turn affords the civil servant opportunities and challenges that are a cut above those provided by routine assignments. Creditable or outstanding performance in preferred posts has a snowball effect, allowing the civil servant progressively to build up his credentials. Being assigned to an important project also enables the civil servant to come into contact with senior persons in strategic places; getting to know them and, better yet, making favorable impressions on them will be definite assets in his future advancement.[19]

JIMUKEI VS. GIJUTSUKEI

Elite-track bureaucrats can be broadly divided into two groups: *jimukei* (administrative group) and *gijutsukei* (technical group). Those belonging to the former are known as *jimukan* (administrative officials), and

18. It is extremely rare for a civil servant without previous experience as a section chief to be appointed as chief of one of the key sections in the secretariat. A random review of the career patterns of those who have served as chiefs of core sections in the secretariats of the various ministries suggests that they typically have behind them six to nine years of experience as "ordinary section chiefs" (*hira kachō*). See *Nihon kankai meikan* [Who's Who in Japanese Government], vol. 33 (Tokyo: Nihon Kankai Jōhōsha, 1981), and *Seikai kanchō jinji roku 1988-nenban*.

19. On the importance of being given challenging assignments, consult Ōno Mitsuru, "Jimu jikan kenkyū: Kensetsushō" [A Study of Administrative Vice-ministers: The Ministry of Construction], *Kankai*, Dec. 1982, pp. 81–82. Criteria of good performance vary from ministry to ministry. In MITI they are said to include (1) ability to generate new policy proposals, (2) skill in translating the above into the language of legislation or regulations, (3) ability to do the necessary *nemawashi* ["root-binding" or preparatory work], (4) leadership ability, and (5) ability to promote intraministerial harmony. Nawa, "Jimu jikan kenkyū: Tsusansho," p. 132.

those affiliated with the latter as *gikan* (technical officials). Although this dichotomy is largely a function of one's academic background, strictly speaking, it is the field of specialization chosen in the higher civil-service examination that places an official in one of the two groups.

Those who choose—that is, are tested in—public administration, law, economics, psychology, education, and sociology are generally headed for careers as *jimukan,* and those who opt for any of the remaining fields are expected to become *gikan.* There being no formal educational requirements in the civil-service examinations, in terms of either the level of educational attainments or fields of study, it is theoretically possible for a candidate with technical background, such as agriculture, engineering, or the natural sciences, to choose public administration, law, or economics as his field of specialization. Given the highly competitive nature of the higher civil-service examination, however, such a candidate would need an extraordinary amount of preparation in order to succeed.

If we examine the distribution of higher civil servants at the entry level by their fields of specialization, we find that *gikan* outnumber *jimukan* by considerable margins. Whereas the proportion of *jimukan* has remained relatively stable at or near the 40-percent mark, there has been some notable change in the internal composition of *gikan.* The proportion of engineers and natural scientists declined from 50 percent in 1962 to 31 percent in 1980, but that of specialists in agriculture doubled during the same period, from 14 to 28 percent.[20] That such change occurred at a time when the relative importance of agriculture in the Japanese economy was steadily declining may seem odd. On the other hand, the number of people involved is quite small. More important, if agriculture has declined in importance as measured by its share of gross domestic product and by the proportion of people engaged in it, its political significance, albeit on the wane, has by no means diminished.[21]

20. For relevant statistics, see "Shōwa 41-nendo kokka kōmuin saiyō jōkyū (kōshu, otsushu) shiken gōkakusha no saiyō jōkyō" [The Situation Regarding the Hiring of Those Who Passed the National Higher Civil Service Examination (Types A and B) in 1966], *Jinji-in geppō,* 196 (June 1967): 10–16; Jinji-in, *Nenji hōkokusho,* 1971–1986 (Tokyo, 1972–87).

21. The contribution of agriculture, forestry, and fishing to Japan's gross domestic product declined from 6 percent in 1970 to 3.2 percent in 1985. More dramatic is the decline in the proportion of the total labor force engaged in agriculture and forestry from 24.3 percent in 1965 to 9.6 percent in 1980. Prime Minister's Office, Statistics Bureau, *Statistical Handbook of Japan, 1981* (Tokyo: Prime Minister's Office, Statistics Bureau, 1981), pp. 27 and 105; Management and Coordination Agency, Statistics

TABLE 19   *Higher Civil Servants, by Year and Field of Academic Specialization (Percentages)*

	Year		
Field	*1949–59*	*1972–73*	*1986*
Law	68.5	64.0	59.2
Humanities and social sciences	6.2	12.1	18.3
Engineering, natural sciences, and others	25.3	23.9	22.5
TOTAL	100.0	100.0	100.0
N	810	1,622	1,015

SOURCES: The 1949–59 data are from Akira Kubota, *Higher Civil Servants in Postwar Japan* (Princeton: Princeton University Press, 1969), p. 79; the 1972–73 data are based on analysis of a random sample of higher civil servants listed in *Nihon kankai meikan*, vols. 24 and 25 (Tokyo: Nihon Kankai Jōhōsha, 1972 and 1974); the 1986 data are based on analysis of a random sample of higher civil servants listed in *Seikai kanchō jinji roku, 1987-nenban* (Tokyo: Tōyō Keizai Shinpōsha, 1986).

What is of primary interest to us, however, is the phenomenon of unequal promotional opportunities for *jimukan* and *gikan*. Inasmuch as direct statistical evidence is not available, we shall examine data— provided in table 19—pertaining to the fields of academic specialization of the civil servants who have already attained the position of section chief or above. It is safe to equate those whose fields of academic specialization were law, the humanities, or the social sciences with *jimukan* and the remainder with *gikan*. Whereas only about four in ten elite-track bureaucrats at the entry level are *jimukan*, seven or eight in ten senior bureaucrats (section chiefs or above) turn out to be *jimukan*. To put it differently, the roles of the majority and the minority are reversed as the upper rungs of the promotional ladders are reached, with *gikan* turning into the minority. Table 19 also shows that the proportion of *gikan* among senior bureaucrats has not changed much during the past three decades, hovering around 23 to 25 percent. Among *jimukan*, on the other hand, the proportion of those who have studied law has

Bureau, *Statistical Handbook of Japan, 1987* (Tokyo: Japan Statistical Association, 1987), p. 26. The agricultural lobby demonstrated its political clout in 1986 when it successfully blocked the government's attempt to reduce the official purchase price of rice by 3.8 percent. In 1987, however, the government succeeded for the first time since 1956 in adopting a plan to reduce the official purchase price of rice by 5.95 percent. *Asahi shinbun*, 6 Aug. 1986; 2 and 4 July 1987.

TABLE 20   *Administrative Vice-Ministers, by Field of Specialization, 1981–87*

Field[c]	Core[a]		Periphery[b]		All	
	N	%	N	%	N	%
Law	42	80.8	26	54.2	68	68.0
Economics	6	11.5	8	16.7	14	14.0
Engineering	3	5.8	10	20.8	13	13.0
Agriculture	1	1.9	3	6.2	4	4.0
Other	0	0	1	2.1	1	1.0
TOTAL	52	100.0	48	100.0	100	100.0

SOURCES: *Kankai*, June 1981–Oct. 1987; *Asahi shinbun*, May 1986–Sept. 1987; *Seikai kanchō jinji roku 1987-nenban* (Tokyo: Tōyō Keizai Shinpōsha, 1986) and ibid., *1988-nenban* (Tokyo: Tōyō Keizai Shinpōsha, 1987).

[a]"Core" refers to the twelve ministries (*shō*) of the Japanese national government.

[b]"Periphery" refers to the agencies (*chō*) where the highest career official carries the title of administrative vice-minister (*jimu jikan*).

[c]"Field refers to the faculty (*gakubu*) from which the administrative vice-ministers graduated.

declined slightly, although they still constitute an overwhelming majority, whereas the proportion of those who have majored in the humanities and social sciences has increased appreciably.

A study by Tashiro Kū of 139 civil servants who were occupying the position of bureau chief in 1981 revealed that only 26 (18.7 percent) of them had majored in technical subjects in college. Fifteen had studied engineering, 6 medicine, and 5 agriculture.[22] Table 20 examines the situation at the summit of the bureaucratic pyramid. If we look at the core ministries only, we find a virtual monopoly of the top career post by *jimukan*. Of the four exceptions, one is not really an exception, because the person in question is a *jimukan* in terms of his bureaucratic career notwithstanding his graduation from Tōdai's faculty of agriculture. Hence there are only 3 *gikan* among the 52 persons who served as administrative vice-ministers in the core ministries during the seven-year period. All three are, in fact, beneficiaries of a unique system based on a custom that decrees the alternation of the top bureaucratic post in the Ministry of Construction between *jimukan* and *gikan*. This unwrit-

22. Tashiro Kū, "Nihon gyōseikan kenkyū, V: Gyōseikan no kyaria keisei katei, 3," p. 73.

ten rule has been scrupulously observed throughout the postwar period.[23]

In the periphery—that is, such agencies as the Science and Technology Agency, the National Land Agency, the Environment Agency, and the Economic Planning Agency—the proportion of *gikan* rises to 29 percent. However, with a few exceptions, these agencies tend to be overshadowed by the core ministries in terms of both prestige and power.

In sum, although it is no longer as blatant as it used to be, the prewar bias against technical officials in Japanese bureaucracy has by no means vanished. It is plain that so far as promotional opportunities are concerned, administrative officials continue to enjoy a distinct edge over their technical counterparts.

TŌDAIBATSU?

In the preceding chapter we noted that the University of Tokyo is the single largest source of both successful candidates in the higher civil-service examination and those who are actually hired by the various ministries and agencies each year. Given this, one should not be astonished to learn that the numerical preponderance of Tōdai graduates continues in the higher echelons of Japanese bureaucracy. But because the progressive diminution of the number of positions in the bureaucratic pyramid dictates an unequal distribution of rewards in the promotion process, the real question is whether graduation from Tōdai makes any difference in the process.

Table 21 provides some statistics that bear on the question. First, the overall proportion of Tōdai graduates among higher civil servants has remained quite high throughout the postwar period. It has ranged from a low of 58 percent (1986) to a high of 73 percent (1954). The proportion of Tōdai men among the higher civil servants in 1937 was 73 percent.[24] Second, although the proportion remained relatively stable until the early 1970s, it declined appreciably by the mid-1980s. Third, with a few exceptions, the proportion of Tōdai graduates is correlated

23. Ōno, "Jimu jikan kenkyū: Kensetsushō," pp. 76–78; Kobayashi Ken'ichi, "Kankai jinmyaku chiri: Kensetsushō no maki" [Who's Who in Government: The Ministry of Construction], *Kankai,* Sept. 1982, pp. 32–41; Kawana Hideyuki, "Kankai jinmyaku chiri: Kensetsushō no maki," ibid., Mar. 1987, pp. 42–56.
24. Inoki, "The Civil Bureaucracy," p. 296. Inoki analyzed the biographical entries of 1,377 higher civil servants in the 1937 edition of *Jinji kōshin roku* [Who's Who].

TABLE 21   *Proportion of Higher Civil Servants Who
Attended University of Tokyo, by Year and Level*

Year	Level				Total	N[a]
	1	2	3	4		
1949	58.7	80.7	67.8	64.0	65.8	(386)[b]
1954	89.7	80.5	82.6	69.8	72.7	(339)[b]
1959	95.0	85.8	72.7	63.1	68.5	(365)[b]
1972–73[c]	93.0	83.1	—	66.8	70.9	960
1986	86.7	76.0[d]	50.9	52.0[e]	57.7	1,036

SOURCES: The 1949–59 data are from Akira Kubota, *Higher Civil Servants in Postwar Japan* (Princeton: Princeton University Press, 1969), p. 74; the 1972–73 data are from B. C. Koh and Jae-On Kim, "Paths to Advancement in Japanese Bureaucracy," *Comparative Political Studies* 15, no. 3 (Oct. 1982): 294; the 1986 data are based on analysis of a random sample of higher civil servants listed in *Seikai kanchō jinji roku, 1987-nenban* (Tokyo: Tōyō Keizai Shinpōsha, 1986).
NOTE: Level 1 includes administrative vice-ministers (*jimu jikan*) and directors-general (*chōkan*). Level 2 includes chiefs of secretariat (*kanbō chō*), bureau chiefs (*kyokuchō*), and assistant bureau chiefs (*kyoku jichō*). Level 3 includes division chiefs (*buchō*) and assistant division chiefs (*bu jichō*). Level 4 includes section chiefs (*kachō*) and equivalents.
[a]N refers to the total number of cases in the sample, not the number of Tōdai graduates.
[b]Because Kubota provides only the number of cases for all three years (N = 1092), the yearly subtotals were estimated from the distribution of his total sample by year.
[c]Level-3 civil servants were not included in this subsample.
[d]When assistant bureau chiefs are excluded, the percentage increases to 83.4.
[e]When senior section chiefs are examined separately, the percentage jumps to 68.1.

with position level. That is to say, the higher the position level, the greater the proportion of Tōdai graduates.

There are three exceptions to this pattern: level 1 in 1949, level 2 in 1954, and level 2 in 1986. The 1949 data reflect the combined effects of the purge of higher civil servants under the Occupation and the Occupation's policy of encouraging the recruitment and promotion of non-Tōdai graduates.[25] The reversal of order between levels 2 and 3 in 1954 and between levels 3 and 4 in 1986 needs to be understood in the context of what level 3 really signifies. The positions of division chief (*buchō*) and assistant division chief (*bu jichō*) encompassed by this level do not fit neatly into the hierarchical ordering of ranks. Although divisions are technically below the level of bureaus, the former exist only in exceptional cases. Moreover, in terms of the seniority and grade level of incumbents, division chiefs are in some cases on a par with

25. Kubota, *Higher Civil Servants in Postwar Japan*, pp. 74–77.

TABLE 22   *Higher Civil Servants (Core and Periphery),
by University Background and Rank, 1986*

University and faculty	Admin. Vice-Minister		Bureau Chief		Section Chief		Total	
	N	%	N	%	N	%	N	%
Tokyo law	16	72.7	95	65.5	256	38.8	367	44.4
Tokyo other	3	13.6	26	17.9	94	14.3	123	14.9
Kyoto law	1	4.6	6	4.1	40	6.1	47	5.7
Kyoto other	1	4.6	2	1.4	35	5.3	38	4.6
Other law	1	4.6	6	4.1	71	10.8	78	9.4
Other other	0	0	10	6.9	163	24.7	173	20.9
TOTAL	22	100.1	145	99.9	659	100.0	826	99.9

SOURCE: Based on analysis of higher civil servants listed in *Seikai kanchō jinji roku 1987-nenban* (Tokyo: Tōyō Keizai Shinpōsha, 1986). The table encompasses all persons holding the position of administrative vice-minister and bureau chief and a random sample of those holding the position of section chief in twenty-three government agencies, including all twelve ministries, in late 1986.

senior-level section chiefs or junior-level assistant bureau chiefs. Hence it is not unreasonable to ignore level 3 altogether in ascertaining general patterns of progression between levels.

As we saw in chapter 4, the number-two position in terms of university background is occupied by Kyoto University. In 1937, Kyōdai provided 9 percent of higher civil servants.[26] Kyōdai's share, during the postwar period, was as follows: 1949–59: 5.5 percent; 1972–73: 7.2 percent; and 1986: 10.5 percent.[27] Table 22 further illustrates the dominance of the two top universities in the upper rungs of Japanese bureaucracy. Note that, unlike the preceding table, this one pertains only to those civil servants who occupied positions of administrative vice-minister (*jimu jikan*), bureau chief (*kyokuchō*), and section chief (*kachō*) in twenty-three government ministries and agencies in 1986. It excludes others who occupied equivalent positions but did not carry the titles mentioned above. Nor does it include those who held the title of division chief (*buchō*).

26. Inoki, "The Civil Bureaucracy," p. 296.
27. For the sources of these statistics, see table 20.

Aside from confirming the general patterns discussed above, the table shows that the elitist complexion of Japan's higher civil service is accentuated when Kyōdai is added to the picture. The two universities together account for seven in ten higher civil servants overall, and their share of the pot increases to 89 percent at the bureau-chief level and to 95 percent at the vice-ministerial level. If we add up all law graduates in the table, we find that they account for 60 percent of the total, which is about the same as Tōdai's overall share. In other words, this table confirms the reality of the twin phenomena—dominance of both elite-university graduates and law graduates (*hōka bannō*).

To conclude from the preceding discussion that the top reaches of Japanese bureaucracy remain the exclusive club of alumni of the top two universities, however, would be a mistake. As table 23 shows, graduates of other universities do manage to reach the summit from time to time. Two of the three exceptions in the core are graduates of Kyushu University, one of the former imperial universities. The third, a graduate

TABLE 23   *Administrative Vice-Ministers, by University Background, 1981–87*

University and Faculty	Core		Periphery		All	
	N	%	N	%	N	%
Tokyo law	38	73.1	23	47.9	61	61.0
Tokyo other	7[a]	13.5	15[b]	31.2	22	22.0
Kyoto law	2	3.8	2	4.2	4	4.0
Kyoto other	2[c]	3.8	4[d]	8.3	6	6.0
Other law	2[e]	3.8	1[f]	4.2	3	3.0
Other other	1[g]	1.9	3[h]	6.2	4	4.0
TOTAL	52	99.9	48	100.0	100	100.0

SOURCES: *Kankai*, June 1981–Oct. 1987; *Asahi shinbun*, May 1986–Sept. 1987; *Sekai kanchō jinji roku 1987-nenban* (Tokyo: Tōyō Keizai Shinpōsha, 1986), and ibid., *1988-nenban* (Tokyo: Tōyō Keizai Shinpōsha, 1987).
NOTE: For definitions of "core" and "periphery," see table 20.
   [a]Economics: 6, agriculture: 1.
   [b]Engineering: 7, economics: 6, agriculture: 2.
   [c]Engineering: 2.
   [d]Engineering: 2, one each from agriculture and economics.
   [e]Kyushu University and Okayama University.
   [f]Tohoku University.
   [g]Kyushu University (engineering).
   [h]Keiō University (economics), Kyushu University (engineering), Tokyo University of Arts and Sciences (*Tōkyō Bunri Daigaku*).

of Okayama University, served as the administrative vice-minister of MITI from June 1984 to June 1986. The four universities represented in the periphery are Tohoku, Kyushu, Keiō, and Tōkyō Bunri Daigaku. Like Kyushu, Tohoku is a former imperial university, whereas Keiō is a top-rated private institution of higher learning. In sum, five of the seven exceptions are graduates of universities that are "first-rate" (*ichiryū*) by Japanese standards. If reaching the top is one's objective, then having proper academic credentials appears to be a necessary condition, albeit by no means a sufficient one.

The domination of the highest civil-service positions by graduates of the two top universities constitutes one of the striking continuities between the prewar and postwar periods. In the 1949–59 period, Tōdai provided 83.7 percent of the administrative vice-ministers, and Kyōdai provided the remainder.[28] Table 23 shows that the picture has changed but marginally: Tōdai's share of administrative vice-ministerial positions in both the core and the periphery during the 1981–87 period was 83 percent—all but identical with the situation two or three decades earlier. What has changed is that, because of inroads by other universities, Kyōdai's share has declined from 16.3 percent to 10 percent. In a word, although the elitist trend continues, the duopoly of Tōdai and Kyōdai has begun to crumble slowly but surely.

A COMPARATIVE PERSPECTIVE

Because of the paucity of hard statistical data on the promotion patterns of the Western industrialized democracies, we can make only broad, impressionistic generalizations by way of comparison. We have noted that systems of promotion can be differentiated along such dimensions as equality of promotional opportunities, permeability, and principal criteria of promotion. Such an approach allows us to posit two polar models of promotion: (1) the open competitive model and (2) the closed multitrack model.

These two models are exemplified by the United States and Japan, respectively. Although there are multiple modes of entry into the American federal bureaucracy—the presidential management-intern program serving as the functional equivalent of Japan's higher civil-service examination—mode of entry per se does not necessarily predetermine either the probability or the speed of the civil servant's

28. Kubota, *Higher Civil Servants*, p. 77.

advancement in the United States. This is clearly shown by the frequency of lateral entry, a practice that not only allows what the Japanese would call *yokosuberi* (side slip) but gives the lateral entrant an equal opportunity of promotion. Whether merit always eclipses seniority in promotion decisions is hard to document. Nonetheless, the primacy of merit is underscored by such devices as the regularized system of performance appraisal, the Merit System Protection Board, and the Senior Executive Service.[29] An extensive use of political appointment, on the other hand, dilutes the role of merit to an appreciable degree.

In what specific ways does Japan approximate the closed multitrack model? And where do the three European democracies fit? That the initial mode of entry all but predetermines whether one will follow the elite track in Japan is beyond doubt. Only in the early years of the postwar period did exceptions to this rule occur. In recent years, it has become next to impossible for someone who has not entered the civil service via the type-A (or type-I) higher examination to become a "career" civil servant in the sense in which the Japanese use the term. An extreme manifestation of this trend is the emergence of what is known as *beppyō-gumi* (separate-list group) in the Ministry of Transport, to which those civil servants who have passed the type-A (or type-I) higher examination after entering the government service through other means are relegated. Also assigned to the group in the ministry are graduates of the type-B higher examination. For all practical purposes these people are not treated as full-fledged "career" civil servants.[30] In other words, it is not simply *whether* but also *when* one has passed the type-A (or type-I) examination that becomes a decisive factor in one's advancement.

To say that the initial mode of entry practically determines whether one will be launched on the elite track is not to imply that those who fail to get on the track will ipso facto forfeit an opportunity ever to attain an elite status, namely, section chief or above. Although their chances of being promoted to such high positions are patently slim, some of them will nonetheless make it. In a word, the Japanese system is not a completely closed one.

29. David T. Stanley, "Civil Service Reform in the United States Government (1)," *International Review of Administrative Sciences* 48, nos. 3–4 (1982): 305–14.

30. Uemoto Ryōhei, "Nonkyaria no sekai: Un'yūshō no maki" [The World of Noncareer (Civil Servants): The Ministry of Transport], *Kankai*, Sept. 1983, p. 154. It should be stressed that *beppyō-gumi* is not an official term.

In another sense, however, the Japanese system does resemble an exclusive club more closely than any of its counterparts in the Western democracies: its impermeability to lateral entry. To be sure, political appointees do exist in the Japanese-government bureaucracy, notably cabinet ministers, parliamentary vice-ministers (*seimu jikan*), and, occasionally, an ambassador or a minister in the diplomatic service. The exceptions in the diplomatic service, of whom there have been but a handful in the entire postwar period, have consisted for the most part of women who had already risen to high positions in other parts of the government bureaucracy.[31]

What is the relative weight of merit and seniority in the promotion process in the Japanese civil service? For those who enter the elite track at the outset, promotion to the position of assistant section chief and perhaps to that of section chief or its equivalent as well may hinge primarily on length of service. On the other hand, merit does influence their upward mobility in a number of ways: first, their preentry record affects their chances of obtaining preferred assignments at the outset; second, their performance thereafter is closely monitored by their superiors, thus becoming a major factor in the latter's personnel decisions; third, because promotion of members of the same entering class does not always occur simultaneously with clocklike precision, nor are all positions at the same level equal in prestige, subtle but nonetheless real differentiation is bound to occur. In a word, it is possible for a select few to build up a better track record than the other members of their cohort. Cumulatively, all this may add up not only to a differential speed of advancement but also to an unequal distribution of its probability. In sum, although seniority is strongly correlated with advancement, the role of merit becomes increasingly salient as the higher rungs of the promotional ladders are reached.

Among the three West European countries with which we are concerned, only West Germany presents the possibility of approximating Japan in meeting the key criteria of the closed multitrack model. Like Japan, West Germany has distinctly unequal classes of civil

---

31. The most recent "political" appointee is Akamatsu Ryōko, a career bureaucrat in the Ministry of Labor. She was chief of the ministry's Women's Bureau when she was appointed as Japan's ambassador to Uruguay in November 1985. That was actually her second stint in the diplomatic service, for she had previously served as a minister in the Japanese Mission to the United Nations. The first woman ever to serve as an ambassador in Japan's diplomatic service was also a political appointee recruited from the Ministry of Labor. Takahashi Hiroko, who became Japan's ambassador to Denmark in 1980, had been a career civil servant in the Labor Ministry. *Asahi shinbun*, 13 Nov. 1985.

servants, differentiated by their respective modes of entry, of which the Higher Service (*hoherer Dienst*) stands at the apex. However, promotion from the Executive Service (*gehobener Dienst*) to the Higher Service does occur, as does promotion from the Clerical Service (*mittlerer Dienst*) to the Executive Service and from the Basic Service (*einfacher Dienst*) to the Clerical Service. In fact, members of the Executive Service who are promoted to the Higher Service need not even be university graduates. They must, however, meet the following requirements: (1) provide demonstration of merit, (2) have had fifteen years of service, (3) be between the ages of forty and fifty-eight, (4) have attained the highest grade in the Executive Service, and (5) have completed a three-year preparatory period, which may be shortened but not dispensed with altogether.[32]

Because all this is not too different from lateral entry, the German system can be described as somewhat more permeable than the Japanese one. In fact, lateral entry in its unadulterated form—namely, entry from outside the government bureaucracy—is known to occur in the West German higher civil service. In theory, the positions of Division Head (*Ministerialdirektor*) or above are to be filled by political appointment; in practice, many of those who ostensibly belong to such a "political class" are "non-political career officials."[33] Promotion within the Higher Service is said to be based primarily on "an overall assessment of ability, achievements, and attitudes," a process that entails the use of two assessors and assessment conferences.[34] In short, although West Germany appears to approximate the closed multitrack model, it displays a somewhat greater degree of permeability and flexibility than does Japan.

So far as Britain and France are concerned, both are considerably more open, in terms of promotional opportunities for their respective civil servants, than either Japan or West Germany. As already noted, not only do both explicitly provide for the entry of internal candidates into their respective elite tracks, but a sizable proportion of the latter do in fact enter the Ecole Nationale d'Administration and the administrative-

32. Sumitomo, "Nishi Dōitsu renpō kanri no nin'yō seido," II, pp. 13–14; Ulrich Becker and Berend Kruger, "Personnel Administration and Personnel Management" in Klaus Konig et al., ed., *Public Administration in the Federal Republic of Germany* (Antwerp: Kluwer-Deventer, 1983), p. 260; and Oertzen, "Public Personnel Management in the Federal Republic of Germany," p. 214.

33. Johnson, *State and Government in the Federal Republic of Germany*, p. 190; Becker and Kruger, "Personnel Administration," p. 260.

34. Ibid., pp. 260–61.

trainee program respectively. Moreover, promotion of nonelite-track civil servants to elite-level positions occurs on a much larger scale in Britain than is the case in Japan and West Germany.[35] Although lateral entry appears to be relatively rare in both Britain and France, their higher civil servants are quite mobile across departmental boundaries. Members of the French *grands corps,* in particular, may even move temporarily into the political arena or into the public or private sectors of industry.[36] In this connection, the higher civil servants in West Germany, too, are considerably more mobile than their counterparts in Japan. Mobility takes the form not only of interdepartmental transfers but also of movements between the Federal government and the Lander.[37]

The low frequency of lateral entry in Britain and France means that neither fits the open competitive model neatly. Because they are substantially more open than Japan, however, they do not seem to approximate the closed multitrack model, either. Hence the rationale for a new model: the open multitrack model. In a strict sense, all of these differences are matters of degree rather than of substance; no system is as open as it purports to be or as closed as it is theoretically capable of being. Nonetheless, marginal differences in the relative degree of openness should not be minimized. With these caveats in mind, we reach the inescapable conclusion that Japan does indeed lag behind the four Western nations in openness and flexibility.

35. G. K. Fry, *"The Administrative Revolution" in Whitehall: A Study of the Politics of Administrative Change in British Central Government since the 1950s* (London: Croom Helm Ltd., 1981), p. 151; D. R. Steel, "Britain" in Ridley, ed., *Government and Administration in Western Europe,* p. 40.

36. Howard Machin, "France" in Ridley, ed., *Government and Administration,* p. 92.

37. Johnson, *State and Government in the Federal Republic of Germany,* p. 184. A West German scholar writes, however, that such personnel movements should be regarded as exceptions rather than the norm. See Oertzen, "Public Personnel Management in the Federal Republic of Germany," p. 215.

CHAPTER SIX

Socialization

A CONCEPTUAL FRAMEWORK

A major dimension of government bureaucracy is its outputs. In what ways do its members perform their official functions? How do they behave from the standpoint of substance and style? Do they exhibit the requisite level of expertise, effectiveness, and efficiency? Are they responsive to the needs and demands of their ultimate constituency, namely, the citizenry as a whole? Do they display a judicious balance of impartiality and empathy? Whose interests are uppermost in their minds—their own personal interests, those of their bureau, those of their ministry, or those of their nation?

Although the constraints of data and other resources do not allow us to explore these key questions in our study, we can nonetheless dwell on some of the factors that may help shape the outputs of Japan's administrative elite. Of the many variables that can yield some clues, three are particularly noteworthy: (1) substantive expertise, (2) role perceptions, and (3) expediency. The linkage between expertise and performance is quite plain: for operations requiring specialized knowledge and skills, expertise is a necessary, albeit not a sufficient, condition. Role perceptions are a repertoire of learned responses to external stimuli. Finally, bureaucratic behavior may reflect "rational calculations of the individual's chances for advancement."[1] The process by

---

1. John A. Armstrong, *The European Administrative Elite* (Princeton: Princeton University Press, 1973), p. 7.

which the first two are acquired can be described as socialization, broadly defined. In a narrow sense, socialization refers to the process by which societal expectations and norms help shape administrators' role perceptions. In the words of Orville Brim, the "behavior required of a person in a given position or status is considered to be his prescribed role, and the requirements themselves can be called role prescription. . . . If socialization is role learning, it follows that socialization occurs throughout an individual's life."[2]

Although socialization is a lifelong process, childhood, particularly early childhood, is believed to be the most critical period. Adult socialization or "resocialization" is said to be "inordinately difficult if not impossible." To facilitate the determination of the kinds of socialization that are relevant for administrative elites, John A. Armstrong proposes three abstract models of administrative-elite recruitment: (1) the maximum-deferred-achievement model, (2) the maximum-ascriptive model, and (3) the progressive-equal-attrition model.[3]

The first model "assumes that no selection is made among the male cohort until its members reach the appropriate age level for high administrative posts."[4] When the choice is finally made, it is based on universalistic criteria, thus giving all equal access. If this model is operative, the relevant socialization processes would be "the mass socialization prevailing in the society during the four to five decades when the cohort was attaining the age required for selection for top administrative posts" and "socialization after attainment of top posts."[5]

At the polar opposite of the first model stands the second model, which posits that "at an early age a very small portion of the male cohort is selected to occupy the top administrative posts when the individuals attain the required age." Inasmuch as "the group chosen in infancy is segregated for socialization purposes throughout its life span," the relevant socialization process becomes exclusively that of the special elite.[6]

The third model "assumes that at each of several equal time intervals the same proportion of the male cohort is eliminated from eligibility for top administrative parts, until just the requisite number to fill available

---

2. As quoted by Armstrong, ibid., p. 15.
3. Ibid., pp. 17–23.
4. Ibid., p. 17.
5. Ibid., p. 18.
6. Ibid., pp. 18–19.

posts remains when the appropriate age level is attained." Under this model, the relevant socialization processes would be "(1) the mass socialization characteristic of the population" insofar as early childhood is concerned, (2) the adolescent and early-adult socialization of the groups chosen at successive stages, and (3) socialization after induction into administrative organizations as well as after attainment of elite status.[7]

On the basis of our inquiry into the recruitment and promotion patterns of Japan's administrative elite in the preceding chapters, how shall we characterize the Japanese case? Although none of the three models captures the idiosyncrasies of the Japanese situation perfectly, one comes closer to approximating the Japanese reality than the other two. If we define "top administrative posts" as those of section chiefs or their equivalents and above, then the maximum-deferred-achievement model is inappropriate for Japan, for the probability of attaining such posts is significantly affected by the mode of initial entry into the civil service. At the age of twenty-two or twenty-three, when a "career" civil servant typically enters the Japanese government, initial selection actually occurs. Of the 35,958 persons who became civil servants in 1985, for example, fewer than 1,500 and most probably about 800 can realistically entertain the hope of rising to the position of section chief or above in the national government after two decades or so of continuous service. These are the men and women who have passed the higher civil-service examination or its equivalent.[8]

Nor does Japan fit the maximum ascriptive model, for, theoretically, no one is excluded from competition until he or she has taken the higher civil-service examination. There is no preselection of a small proportion of infants or children for elitist roles in the bureaucracy at a later stage.[9] In this connection the absence of formal educational requirements for civil-service examinations is particularly noteworthy.

On the other hand, the progressive-equal-attrition model does seem to encapsulate the most salient aspects of Japan's administrative elite.

7. Ibid., pp. 20–22.

8. These statistics are taken from Jinji-in, *Kōmuin hakusho*, 1987, p. 46. Note that the numbers cited here refer not to the Administrative Service I but to the entire civil service. Of the 1985 appointees, 823 had passed the type-I (formerly type-A) higher civil-service examination (HCSE) and an additional 659 had passed the type-B HCSE. For statistics on the Administrative Service I only, see table 18 in the preceding chapter.

9. According to Armstrong, though "no complex European society in recent centuries has approached [the Maximum Ascriptive Model] very closely, . . . most of the systems we examine [those of Britain, France, Germany, and Russia during the various historical periods] *do tend toward this model.*" Armstrong, *European Administrative Elite*, p. 19; emphasis added. For an elaboration of this point, see chap. 11 of his book.

At successive levels of the educational pyramid the probability of passing the higher civil-service examination becomes negligible for a large number of people. Entrance into top-rated middle schools enhances one's chances of entering top-rated high schools. Attendance of the latter in turn increases one's probability of entering top-rated universities. And students of the latter have an edge over the others in the higher civil-service examination. As we saw in chapter 4, there is a strong relationship between the type of university one attends and the probability of passing the higher civil-service examination. Table 10 showed us that national universities have consistently outperformed both public and private universities not only in absolute terms but also in the ratios of successful to all candidates. All this suggests that progressive attrition does indeed occur.

Nor does the process stop at the induction stage. As the preceding chapter has shown, attrition occurs after the civil servants have attained the rank of section chief or its equivalent. Only about a third of section chiefs belonging to the same entering class advance to the level of bureau chief. Beyond that, competition becomes even keener. Eventually, only one member of the class or, in some cases, none at all, reaches the summit—the coveted post of administrative vice-minister.

Notwithstanding the above, the Japanese reality does not conform to the criteria of the progressive-equal-attrition model in two important respects: first, at successive stages attrition occurs in a relative, not an absolute, sense. What happens is not the elimination of potential candidates from competition for elite administrative posts but a significant decline in their probability of success. To take the extreme case of those who fail to enter a four-year college altogether, the door to the elite track in the civil service is not totally closed for them. In 1984, for example, 41 of the 2,958 persons who passed the type-A higher civil-service examination lacked university education. Eleven of them had not gone beyond high school, and the remainder were products of either junior colleges or higher professional and technical schools (*kōtō senmon gakkō*). In terms of success rates alone—that is, the ratio of successful to total candidates—the nonuniversity group did not lag very far behind the university group: 6.4 percent as against 8.7 percent. On the other hand, it is obvious that most people without university education took themselves out of the competition altogether.[10]

---

10. The statistics cited above were obtained from the National Personnel Authority during my visit to that agency in June 1985.

Second, to the extent that attrition occurs, it is not "equal" in the sense in which Armstrong defines it: "At each of several equal time intervals the same proportion of the male cohort is eliminated from eligibility for top administrative posts."[11] Neither the time intervals at which attrition occurs nor the proportion of the male cohort that is virtually eliminated are equal in the Japanese case.

In sum, although all three conceptual models present problems for analysis of Japanese data, the third model seems the least objectionable of the three. Hence one need not follow rigidly the guidelines for investigating socialization processes that the progressive-equal-attrition model prescribes. Given the limits of available data, we shall first delineate briefly some general characteristics of precollegiate socialization in Japan. Next, we shall examine the socialization experiences of students in the law faculty of the University of Tokyo, the premier training ground of Japan's administrative elite. Finally, we shall discuss postentry socialization of the higher civil servants.

SOCIALIZATION OF JAPANESE YOUTH: AN OVERVIEW

TWO VIEWS

In most societies the principal agents of preadult socialization are the family, schools, and peer groups. Although all three are important in Japan, schools appear to play the pivotal role. According to William K. Cummings:

> Education occupies a much more central place in the lives of Japanese than American youth. Japanese children believe their performance has great personal consequences; they go to school more hours out of each year; they have fewer alternate ways to spend their time. Moreover, their parents encourage them to work hard in school. It might be said that the Japanese student's relation to his school approaches that of a patient or criminal to a total institution.[12]

What, then, are the principal values that pupils learn in Japanese primary and secondary schools? As part of the democratization program, the American Occupation authorities made a major effort to

11. Armstrong, *European Administrative Elite*, p. 20. Emphasis added.
12. William K. Cummings, *Education and Equality in Japan* (Princeton: Princeton University Press, 1980), p. 145.

reform the educational system. Among other things, the power of the central government to control teachers and curriculum was curtailed, locally elected educational commissions were given the power of supervision over schools, teachers were encouraged to form professional associations, and the contents as well as the methods of teaching were democratized.[13]

The extent to which the goals of the Occupation were actually attained is debatable. That of decentralization, for example, proved to be elusive. With the restoration of full sovereignty to Japan in 1952 came a gradual revival of old ways. The national government, through the Ministry of Education, has regained much of its erstwhile authority over educational policy. Although teachers have emerged as a powerful counterweight to the government under the leadership of the radical Japan Teachers Union (JTU, or Nikkyōsō), they have had only limited success in blunting the power of the increasingly conservative Ministry of Education. Nonetheless, some scholars credit JTU with having helped to diffuse democratic values among Japanese school children.[14]

Taken as a whole, the various components of Japanese schools add up to an effective tool for creating "new values," which Cummings sums up as the "egalitarian sentiment." In his view, this sentiment consists of three parts:

1. *An egalitarian orientation to jobs.* This orientation stresses the ways in which all jobs contribute to the greater good and hence are deserving of respect. Grading of jobs in terms of their importance or prestige is deemphasized.

2. *An orientation toward individualism.* This orientation encourages the nurturance of personally conceived goals and evaluates highly striving to realize these personal goals instead of merely following the accepted way. In the work realm, this orientation toward individualism leads individuals to seek intrinsic rewards and to place less emphasis on status and income.

3. *A participatory orientation.* This orientation leads individuals to participate critically in groups, associations, and other collectivities. It leads one to challenge traditional patterns of hierarchical authority in the family, the work place, the community, and the polity.[15]

Cummings argues that both preschool socialization and interactions with peer groups tend to facilitate and reinforce the internalization of

13. Ibid., pp. 29–39. For analysis of the American Occupation authorities' policy toward higher education, see Pempel, *Patterns of Japanese Policymaking*, pp. 35–51.
14. Cummings is the principal proponent of this idea. Other scholars, notably Rohlen, believe that the influence of the JTU has been exaggerated. See Thomas P. Rohlen, *Japan's High Schools* (Berkeley: University of California Press, 1983), esp. p. 238 n. 12.
15. Cummings, *Education and Equality*, pp. 177–78.

the egalitarian values. In his view, child-rearing practices and interpersonal relations have become "relatively egalitarian" in the postwar period, thus predisposing contemporary Japanese children "to expect egalitarian relations in other social situations."[16] Moreover, participation in "largely school-based extracurricular activities" by middle-school children further bolsters such democratic values as "participation, expressiveness, and cooperation."[17]

Cummings finds redeeming features even in the fierce competition in entrance examinations. He notes, for example, that entrance into top-rated universities in Japan is based solely on universalistic criteria, namely, one's scores in entrance examinations. Contrast this with the situation in the United States, where a multitude of particularistic criteria, such as being offspring of a rich alumnus or a generous contributor, enter into the equation. This implies that the examination competition serves to guarantee equality of opportunity.[18] On the other hand, Cummings acknowledges that one's chances of success in entrance examination are enhanced to a significant extent by "the consumption of various forms of extra-education, such as attendance at *juku,* special high schools, *yobikō,* and lessons from household tutors."[19] Because all of these things cost a considerable amount of money, not everybody can afford them, hence equality of opportunity is appreciably eroded.

A somewhat different picture emerges from a study of high schools by Thomas P. Rohlen. Although Rohlen shares the views of Cummings and other non-Japanese observers[20] that the achievements of Japan's basic education—in terms of the proportion of school-age population that complete schooling, levels of knowledge and skills learned by students, results of achievement tests in science and mathematics, and other statistical indicators—are quite impressive, he does not share Cummings's thesis that schools help students acquire egalitarian values. As Rohlen puts it:

> Japanese high schools are not training grounds for democracy, Japanese traditional values, or a new egalitarian order. Rather, they are best

16. Ibid., p. 96.
17. Ibid., pp. 98–99.
18. Ibid., p. 218. Strictly speaking, it is not just scores in entrance examinations but also those in uniform preliminary examinations administered by the state, known as *kyōtsū ichiji* (common preliminary), that help determine the outcome for applicants to national and public universities.
19. Ibid., p. 224.
20. See, for example Ezra F. Vogel, *Japan As Number One* (New York: Harper Colophon Books, 1980), pp. 158–83.

understood as shaping generations of disciplined workers for a technomerit-ocratic system that requires highly socialized individuals capable of per-forming reliably in a rigorous, hierarchical, and finely tuned organizational environment.[21]

These two views, however, are not as irreconcilable as they may appear at first glance. As Rohlen himself points out, the differing perspectives may be a function of the levels of schools studied: primary versus high schools.[22] It is possible that although Japanese children become exposed to and even internalize egalitarian values in primary schools, by the time they enter high schools these values are no longer salient concerns, being eclipsed by the overriding goal of preparing for university entrance examinations. What count most at this stage are "diligence, sacrifice, mastery of detailed information, endurance over the many preparatory years, willingness to postpone gratification, and competitive spirit."[23]

Depending on the potency with which the primary-school experience propagates egalitarian values, one cannot rule out the possibility that they may survive the rigors of high-school years. Early socialization frequently proves to be more efficacious than what follows later. In short, it can be hypothesized that two sets of values, one egalitarian and the other instrumental, dominate the preadult socialization stage in Japan and that the two are not mutually exclusive.

AN INTERNATIONAL COMPARISON

Finally, to gain some comparative perspective let us examine selected results of a world youth-survey project. Initiated in 1972, the project has collected data on the attitudes of youth between the ages of eighteen and twenty-four in eleven different countries at periodic intervals. The survey utilized the same set of questions as well as national probability samples, hence the data lend themselves to cross-national comparison to an unusual degree.[24]

---

21. Rohlen, *Japan's High Schools,* p. 209.
22. Ibid., p. 6.
23. Ibid., p. 109.
24. For a complete description of the project, including its chronology, methodology, questionnaire, and responses, see Sōrifu, Seishōnen Taisaku Honbu, ed., *Sekai no seinen tono hikaku kara mita Nihon no seinen: Sekai seinen ishiki chōsa (dai 3-kai) hōkokusho* [Japanese Youths As Compared with the Youth of the World: Report on the Survey of the Attitudes of the World Youth (the Third Survey)] (Tokyo: Ōkurashō, Insatsukyoku, 1984).

TABLE 24   *Attitudes Toward Country and Society
Among Youths in Japan, the United States, Great
Britain, West Germany, and France*

Percentage of Respondents Who—	Japan		U.S.	G. Brit.	W. Ger.	France
	1977	1983	1983	1983	1983	1983
Expressed pride in their country[a]	70.7	70.4	96.3	82.6	56.9	61.7
Indicated a willingness to sacrifice their own interests for their country[b]	16.3	20.3	67.6	46.0	41.5	22.6
Expressed satisfaction with "the way things are in their country"[c]	40.7	35.2	59.9	50.7	88.8	31.4
Said their foremost goal in life is to "work on behalf of society"	3.7	6.8	9.5	8.6	7.5	3.4
N	2,010	1,021	1,134	1,035	1,032	1,000

SOURCE: Sōrifu Seishōnen Taisaku Honbu, ed., *Sekaino seinen tono hikaku kara mita Nihon no seinen* (Tokyo: Ōkurashō, Insatsukyoku, 1984).
NOTE: Respondents were aged 18–24.
    [a]The respondents were asked to agree or disagree with the statement "I am proud to be a [citizen of X country]."
    [b]The statement read: "In order to serve [name of country] I wouldn't mind sacrificing my own interests."
    [c]The two responses, "Yes, satisfied," and "More or less satisfied," were combined for this table.

Table 24 presents some measures of patriotism and commitment to or alienation from one's country and society. In terms of "pride" in one's own country, young people in Japan occupy a middle position among the five industrialized democracies. On the other hand, Japan ranks lowest in the proportion of youths expressing willingness to sacrifice their own personal interests for their country. Note, in particular, the gap between the United States and Japan. The proportion of Japanese youths who are either satisfied or more or less satisfied with "the way things are in [their] country" is only 35 percent, as compared with 89 percent for West Germany and 60 percent for the United States. Finally, whereas in all five countries only a tiny fraction of the respondents said their number-one goal in life was "to work on behalf of society," the proportion of such youth in Japan was among the lowest. One way of interpreting these data is to conclude that Japanese youths have become remarkably self-centered, even more so than their counterparts in the United States and Western Europe. To the extent that preoccupation with one's personal interests bespeaks individualism, one can also argue that Japanese youths are in some ways more individualistic than their counterparts in other industrialized democracies. It is worth noting, however, that such attitudes apparently declined, rather than increased, between 1977 and 1983.

Turning to attitudes toward parents, we see in table 25 that the picture is somewhat murky in Japan. On the one hand, Japan has the lowest proportion of respondents who acknowledged having "real

TABLE 25   *Attitudes Toward Parents Among Youths in Japan, the United States, Great Britain, West Germany, and France*

Percentage of Respondents Who—	Japan		U.S.	G. Brit.	W. Ger.	France
	1977	1983	1983	1983	1983	1983
Said they have had "real clashes" with their father and/or mother in the last two or three years	19.2	15.8	24.4	28.7	35.1	21.4
Preferred a father who is strict with his children	36.7	32.3	24.9	13.6	6.1	13.4
Preferred a father who tries to be friends with his children	48.2	53.6	67.8	78.4	76.0	77.5
Preferred a father who lets his children do what they want	54.1	48.4	36.4	29.6	25.2	44.1
Said they would support their parents in old age, "no matter what the circumstances"	35.0	34.5	38.6	30.3	33.9	54.3
N	2,010	1,021	1,134	1,035	1,032	1,000

SOURCE: Sōrifu Seishōnen Taisaku Honbu, ed., *Sekaino seinen tono hikaku kara mita Nihon no seinen* (Tokyo: Ōkurashō, Insatsukyoku, 1984).

TABLE 26   *Perceptions of Success and University Education Among Youths in Japan, the United States, Great Britain, West Germany, and France*

Percentage of Respondents Who—	Japan 1977	Japan 1983	U.S. 1983	G.Brit. 1983	W.Ger. 1983	France 1983
Said "personal abilities" were one of the two most important things for "becoming successful"	50.0	48.5	59.1	64.7	60.7	48.0
Mentioned "personal effort" as one of the two most important things for "becoming successful"	73.9	68.2	70.0	63.9	56.6	57.3
Mentioned "good education" as one of the two most important things for "becoming successful"	7.8	14.1	42.9	37.3	11.4	19.4
Mentioned "family position and social rank"	3.2	4.8	13.3	11.4	21.9	37.5
Said what "people generally value in college graduates" most is— "having gone to a top-rated college"	22.8	26.0	15.9	18.2	9.4	25.0
"school performance and school record"	8.5	10.8	36.1	43.4	47.1	14.7
"major field of study"	35.6	32.7	24.9	15.2	8.5	25.5
N	2,010	1,021	1,134	1,035	1,032	1,000

SOURCE: Sōrifu Seishōnen Taisaku Honbu, ed., *Sekaino seinen tono hikaku kara mita Nihon no seinen* (Tokyo: Ōkurashō, Insatsukyoku, 1984).

clashes" with their parents and the highest proportion of respondents preferring a strict father. On the other, not only is the latter proportion (32 percent in 1983) relatively small, but it is also eclipsed by the proportion of those preferring "a father who tries to be friends with his children" (54 percent in 1983). Moreover, a greater proportion of

Japanese youth endorse a permissive father than do the youth in the four Western countries. Finally, it is rather surprising to see Japanese youth in the third place in expression of filial piety, behind their counterparts in France and the United States. Can all this be viewed as further evidence of the rise of egalitarian sentiment among Japanese youth?

If, as noted previously, universalistic values are stressed in Japanese education, is this reflected in the attitudes of Japanese youths? Slightly less than half of the Japanese youth surveyed in 1983 cited "personal abilities" as one of the two most important ingredients of success in life, but seven in ten mentioned "personal effort." The belief that hard work can reinforce innate ability and even compensate for the lack of it seems to be widely shared among the youths of the five countries. The differential perception of the relative importance of "family position and social rank" between Japanese youths and that of the other countries is perhaps indicative of the salience of universalistic criteria in Japan. The surprisingly low proportion of Japanese youths who mentioned "good education" as one of the top two requirements for success, however, should be balanced against their responses concerning the perceived value of "having gone to a top-rated college."[25] That more Japanese youths were sensitive to the importance of "major field of study" than were the youths of the other countries simply reflects a well-known fact of life in Japan: graduation from a faculty of law, particularly that of Tōdai, can provide that crucial margin of success in close matches.

All in all, the attitudes displayed by Japanese youths closely parallel those of their counterparts in the United States and the three European countries. The data do not indicate in any way that the Japanese youth are more authoritarian than the youths of the other four countries.

SOCIALIZATION IN TŌDAI'S FACULTY OF LAW

The preceding chapters have documented the preponderant position of the University of Tokyo in Japan's higher civil service. In 1986, six out of ten civil servants occupying the position of section chief or higher in the national government were Tōdai graduates (see table 21). The

25. In a 1984 survey of 3,948 Japanese high-school students applying for admission to universities, conducted by the Japan Recruit (*sic*) Center, 68.2 percent of the respondents agreed with the statement that "it will be difficult to get a job with a first-rate company (*ichiryū kigyō*) unless one has gone to a first-rate university." *Asahi shinbun*, 1 Feb. 1985.

proportion increases to 76 percent at the bureau-chief level and to 86.7 percent at the vice-ministerial level. What is more, an overwhelming majority of these Tōdai graduates (about three-quarters) were products of its faculty of law (*hōgakubu*). Overall, close to half of all the senior bureaucrats were graduates of Tōdai's law faculty, the proportion rising to 65.5 percent at the bureau-chief level and to 72.7 percent at the vice-ministerial level (see table 22).

That Tōdai's law faculty is the single most important source of Japan's administrative elite is indisputable. Before one jumps to the conclusion that its principal mission is to train future elite bureaucrats, however, one needs to inquire into the career paths taken by its graduates. Of 1,218 Tōdai law graduates whose occupations could be verified in 1900, 33 percent were in the legal profession and 31 percent were "administrative officials" (*gyōsei kanri*). Nearly three-quarters of the former were "judicial officials" (judges, prosecutors, and the like), hence the actual proportion of bureaucrats increases to 55 percent. Of 9,413 Tōdai law alumni about whom information was available in 1926, 25.3 percent were in the legal profession, and a majority of them (1,215 out of 2,194) were serving as "judicial officials." Administrative officials numbered 2,046 or 21.7 percent of the total. But nearly four in ten Tōdai law alumni were found to be working either in banks or in private firms. By 1958, the proportion of Tōdai law alumni in banking and private firms had increased to 43.8 percent (10,681 out of 24,366), whereas their proportion in the legal profession had declined to 12.8 percent. Judicial officials still outnumbered attorneys (1,776 as against 1,345). Meanwhile, the proportion of administrative officials remained virtually unchanged from 1926 at 22.6 percent.[26]

Of 574 persons who graduated from Tōdai's law faculty in the spring of 1976, only 9 percent were bound for careers in the legal profession. That bespoke not the latter's decline in popularity over the years but the extreme difficulty of passing the judicial examination, a prerequisite for admission to the Judicial Training Institute, which in turn is a sine qua non for becoming a full-fledged lawyer. The proportion of those opting for civil-service careers in the national government was 21.8 percent, which was consistent with the trend noted above. When we add those hired by public corporations and local governments, the proportion of civil servants increases to 29.3 percent, by far the largest category. The next-largest category was banking, which accounted for nearly a quarter of the law graduates.[27]

26. Shimizu, *Tōkyō Daigaku Hōgakubu*, p. 48.
27. *Tōkyō Daigaku shinbun*, 28 June 1976.

What emerges from the preceding analysis is that the principal mission of Tōdai's law faculty is neither to train lawyers nor to produce elite administrators. Rather, it is to produce Japan's future leaders in a wide range of fields, most of which are in the private sector. Nonetheless, the faculty does serve as a major training ground of Japan's administrative elite. In fact, that was its original mission when it was first established in the early Meiji period. To paraphrase Hata Ikuhiko, a 1956 graduate of Tōdai's law faculty and a former bureaucrat in the Finance Ministry, it is as natural for a Tōdai law graduate to choose a career in the government bureaucracy as it is for a graduate of an arts school to become a painter and for a graduate of a merchant-marine school to become a ship's officer.[28]

The historical dimension merits a little more elaboration. The University of Tokyo was created in 1877, the tenth year of the Meiji reign, by the merger of Tokyo Kaisei School and Tokyo Medical School. At first, there were only four faculties—law, science, literature, and medicine—but those of engineering and agriculture were added after the name of the university was changed to the Imperial University (Teikoku Daigaku) in 1886. Actually, the term "faculty" (*gakubu*) was replaced by "college" (*daigaku*) from 1886 to 1919, when *gakubu* reappeared. In 1887 the Imperial University's college of law (Hōka Daigaku) was elevated to a privileged position: the president of the entire university was required by law to serve concurrently as its dean, and he was empowered to supervise the five other law schools that had sprung up in Tokyo. This latter power, however, was rescinded after a little more than a year. More important, graduates of the Imperial University college of law were exempt from the bar examination (later the judicial examination) as well as from administrative (higher civil-service) examinations. With the establishment of a second imperial university in Kyoto in 1897, Tōdai's name was changed to Tokyo Imperial University. The privilege of exemption from the judicial examination was extended to Kyoto law graduates until it was abolished in 1923. Meanwhile, the privilege of exemption from the administrative examinations was terminated in 1894.[29]

During the American Occupation, Tōdai was reorganized. Apart from the deletion of the adjective "Imperial" from its name, there was a

---

28. Hata, *Kanryō no kenkyū*, p. 224.
29. "Tōkyō Daigaku no hyakunen" Henshū Iinkai, *Tōkyō Daigaku no hyakunen, 1877–1977*, pp. 85–92; on the privileges of imperial-university law graduates, consult Spaulding, *Imperial Japan's Higher Civil Service Examinations*, pp. 39, 59–60, 91–98, 129–130, and 156.

Theodore Lownik Library
Illinois Benedictine College
Lisle, Illinois 60532

fundamental restructuring of Tōdai's curriculum, of which the single most important component was the introduction of a two-year "general-education" (*kyōyō*) sequence. A new faculty of general education (*kyōyō gakubu*) was established in Komaba by merging the First Higher School (Daiichi Kōtō Gakkō) and Tokyo Higher School.[30]

All entering students are required to spend two years on the Komaba campus taking courses in "general education" before moving to their respective faculties in Hongo. For those who choose to get their degrees in "general education," however, a wide array of advanced courses in the humanities, area studies, social sciences, and natural sciences is available in Komaba. In other words, not only does the faculty of general education serve as a preparatory school for all Tōdai students but it has also become a full-fledged faculty in its own right. During their two years in Komaba, all students are required to take a minimum of two courses each in the "human and literary sciences" (*jinbun kagaku*), the social sciences (*shakai kagaku*), and the natural sciences (*shizen kagaku*). In addition, they are required to take two foreign languages, including English. The "human and literary sciences" encompass not only philosophy, history, and literature but also psychology, anthropology, geography, and education, and the social sciences include law, political science, economics, statistics, sociology, history of social thought, and international relations.[31]

As a general rule, students aspiring to enter the faculty of law must have passed entrance examinations for Humanities Group 1 (*bunka ichirui*), one of six groups into which all entering students are divided. In terms of difficulty of admission, Humanities Group 1, which has a quota of 630, shares the top position with Science Group 3 (*rika sanrui*), whose students are bound for the faculty of medicine. Whereas all Humanities Group 1 students who wish to do so automatically advance to the faculty of law upon completion of two years of required work in Komaba, others must face stiff competition. Only ten or so outsiders (those from the other groups) are admitted on the basis of their grade-point average during the first three terms in Komaba.[32]

30. *Tōkyō Daigaku no hyakunen*, p. 97; Tōkyō Daigaku Kyōyō Gakubu, *Kyōyō Gakubu no sanjūnen, 1949–1979* [Thirty Years of the Faculty of General Education, 1949–1979] (Tokyo: Tōkyō Daigaku Shuppankai, 1979); Sakurai Tsuneji, *Tōdai seikatsu, 1953-nenban* [Life at the University of Tokyo, 1953 Edition] (Tokyo: Gendai Shichōsha, 1952), pp. 41–46.

31. Daigaku Sōgō Kenkyū Shirizu Kikaku Henshū Iinkai, ed., *Tōkyō Daigaku sōgō kenkyū* [A Comprehensive Study of the University of Tokyo] (Tokyo: Nihon Rikurūto Sentaà Shuppanbu, 1979), pp. 68–71; Tōkyō Daigaku Kyōyō Gakubu, *Kyōyō Gakubu no sanjūnen*, pp. 158–59.

32. *Tōkyō Daigaku sōgō kenkyū*, pp. 74–76; Kokuritsu Daigaku Kyōkai et al., eds.,

Strictly speaking, specialized training begins not in the third year but in the second year for most students. Those who are bound for the faculty of law, for example, start taking such courses as constitutional law, criminal law, and civil law as early as in their third semester. When they move to the Hongo campus, they must choose among three departments in the faculty of law: the First Department (private law), the Second Department (public law), and the Third Department (political science). None of these departments has a quota, and students are allowed to transfer from one to another freely. Generally speaking, those aspiring to a career in law join the First Department and those aiming for a civil-service career opt for the Second Department. These two departments usually draw the largest number of students.[33]

In order to graduate from the faculty of law, all students must complete at least ninety units (one unit typically consists of one hour of classroom work per week for fifteen weeks), including all of the required courses (*hisshu kamoku*) and four units of "elective required courses" (*sentaku hisshu kamoku*). Table 27 comprises all of the required courses for the three departments in the faculty. Only five courses, totaling eighteen units, are required of all students regardless of their departmental affiliation: Constitutional Law I and II and Civil Law I, II, and III. Beyond that, requirements reflect the differing foci of the three departments. The First Department, whose students major in private law, requires the whole gamut of laws except administrative law and international law, whereas the Second Department, with its focus on public law, requires eight units each of administrative law and international law, in addition to four units each of criminal law and political science. Students of the Third Department are freed from any further requirements in law courses; instead, they are asked to concentrate on political science, political and diplomatic history, public administration, and public finance.

As for "elective required courses," all students are required to take four units from a specified group of courses. Private-law majors must choose from a set of Anglo-American Law I, French Law I, and German

---

Kokkōritsu daigaku gaidobukku 1985 [Guide Book for National and Public Universities, 1985] (Tokyo: Kokuritsu Daigaku Kyōkai, Kōritsu Daigaku Kyōkai, Daigaku Nyūshi Sentaà, 1984), pp. 224–25.
33. *Tōkyō Daigaku Ichiran* [Catalogue of the University of Tokyo] (Tokyo: Tōkyō Daigaku Shuppankai, 1953), pp. 141–59; *The University of Tokyo Catalogue 1980–81* (Tokyo: University of Tokyo, 1980), pp. 47–54; Sakurai, *Tōdai seikatsu,* pp. 146–48; Tōkyō Daigaku, *Hōgakubu benran, kyōran-yō* [A Handbook of the Faculty of Law, Display Copy] (Tokyo: Tōkyō Daigaku, 1987), pp. 83–84 and 100–101.

TABLE 27   *Required Courses in the University of Tokyo Law Faculty*

| | | Department | | |
Course	Unit	I	II	III
Constitutional law I	4	4	4	4
Constitutional law II	2	2	2	2
Civil law I	4	4	4	4
Civil law II	4	4	4	4
Civil law III	4	4	4	4
Civil law IV	4	4		
Commercial law I	4	4		
Commercial law II	4	4		
Criminal law I	4	4	4	
Criminal law II	4	4		
Civil procedure I	4	4		
Civil procedure II	4	4		
Criminal procedure	4	4		
Administrative law I	4		4	
Administrative law II	4		4	
International law I	4		4	
International law II	4		4	
Political science	4		4	4
Political process	4			4
Japanese politics and diplomatic history	4			4
Public administration	4			4
European political history	4			4
Public finance	4			4
TOTAL UNITS REQUIRED		50	42	42

SOURCES: Tōkyō Daigaku, *Hōgakubu benran, kyōran-yō* (Tokyo: Tōkyō Daigaku, 1987), pp. 85–101; *The University of Tokyo Catalogue 1980–81* (Tokyo: University of Tokyo 1980), pp. 50–53. This was the most recent catalogue in English as of Dec. 1987.
NOTE: One unit entails one hour of classroom work per week for fifteen weeks.

Law I, each of which is worth four units. Public-law majors are also given the preceding three courses and two additional ones: Public Administration and Public Finance. Finally, political-science majors have the least amount of latitude, for they must choose either Principles of Economics or Modern Economic Theory.[34]

Once these two sets of requirements are out of the way, students may take virtually any courses that are offered in the faculty, although, technically, elective courses are grouped into two categories for students

34. Tōkyō Daigaku, *Hōgakubu benran*, 1987, pp. 90–95.

in each department. Because of the large number of courses listed and their variety, students are given ample choices. Basically, the whole gamut of law-related courses as well as courses in political science and economics are available to students. Hence they not only receive varying doses of legal training but also become exposed to the historical, theoretical, and institutional underpinnings of the Japanese and foreign political and economic systems.

What we have described above are the formal requirements and options that Tōdai law students face. Whether and to what extent these opportunities for learning will actually enrich their intellectual repertoire, broaden their horizons, and shape their values will hinge on such factors as the motivation of individual students and the amount of effort expended. An important stumbling block to intellectual growth appears to be the paucity of stimuli for independent thinking. Most courses are delivered in large lecture halls that provide few opportunities for individual contacts between instructors and students. Some of the required courses are conducted in rooms capable of accommodating five hundred or more students, in which the use of a microphone by the instructor is a necessity. In this respect, according to a former Tōdai law student, the situation in Tōdai's law faculty is as bad as or perhaps worse than that at private universities that are notorious for their "mass production" approach to education.[35]

To be fair, opportunities for student-teacher interaction and for independent research are not totally absent. For example, a sizable number of seminars (*enshū*) are offered each semester on analysis of court decisions in the various branches of law, readings in foreign-language scholarly books, and research on specialized topics. Because the size of these seminars is deliberately kept small, enrollment can sometimes be difficult. The official handbook of Tōdai's faculty of law underscores the importance of these seminars, even though all of them are optional.[36]

Insofar as motivation and effort are concerned, there is one overarching reality: preoccupation with grades and examinations. By most accounts, Tōdai law students tend to be predominantly career-oriented. Because grades earned in college have a direct bearing on the probability of landing attractive jobs upon graduation, there is a keen competition

35. Ikeda Shin'ichi, "Binbōnin no ko wa Tōdai ni hairenai" [Children of the Poor Cannot Get into the University of Tokyo] in *Kyōiku tokuhon: Tōkyō Daigaku* [Readings on Education: The University of Tokyo] (Tokyo: Kawade Shobō Shinsha, 1983), p. 199.
36. Tōkyō Daigaku, *Hōgakubu benran*, 1987, pp. 98–99.

to earn as many *yū* (A) as possible.[37] This means that unlike the situation in Komaba, classes on the Hongo campus are well attended, even though attendance is never taken. In classes that begin at 8:30 A.M., many students arrive early in order to get choice front-row seats.

Closely related to this is the preoccupation with national examinations. A majority of Tōdai law students take either the judicial examination or the higher civil-service examination or both, which require a great deal of preparation. As noted previously, the judicial examination is so difficult that only a handful of students pass it on their first try. Hence it calls for a prolonged period of intensive study. Although the higher civil-service examination is appreciably less demanding, it too requires careful planning and disciplined preparation. Because there is a considerable overlap in the subjects covered by both examinations, many students prepare for and take both. The price they pay is said to be a "triangular pattern of life" (*sankakukei no seikatsu*) that is bounded by the classrooms, the library, and the boarding house. Daily routines for these students consist of going to classes, studying in the library until it closes at night, and returning to the boarding house, where more time is spent on study.[38]

As seasoned veterans of "examination wars" (*juken sensō*), most Tōdai law students can not only survive the rigors of such life but also thrive on it. Nonetheless, their "triangular" life leaves very little room for extracurricular activities and can be excruciatingly tedious. Small wonder that Tōdai's law faculty is often referred to as a desert (*hōgakubu sabaku*).[39] But the skills that are necessary to win such "examination wars" are not necessarily creative thinking and critical

---

37. Tōdai law students refer to *yū* (A) as *shō* (victory) and *ryō* (B) as *hai* (defeat). See Masuda Reiko, "Shin hana monogatari: Tōdai Hōgakuba joshi gakusei no tabiji" [New Tale of Flowers: Journey of a Woman Student in the University of Tokyo Faculty of Law] in Konaka Yōtarō, ed., *Tōdai Hōgakubu: Sono kyozō to jitsuzō* [The University of Tokyo Faculty of Law: Myths and Reality] (Tokyo: Gendai Hyōronsha, 1978), p. 85; Shimizu, *Tōkyō Daigaku Hōgakubu,* p. 134. There are five grades at Tōdai's Law Faculty: *yū* (A), *ryōjō* (B+), *ryō* (B), *ka* (C), and *fuka* (fail). Tōkyō Daigaku, *Hōgakubu benran,* 1987, p. 88.

38. Mikawa Yōichirō, "Tōdaisei ga mite kita Tōdaisei" [University of Tokyo Students As Observed by a University of Tokyo Student], in Itō Satoru, ed., *Tōdaisei hakusho* [White Paper on University of Tokyo Students] (Tokyo: Sobokusha, 1981), p. 182; Yamane Kazurō, "Aru gakusei seikatsu" [The Life of a Certain Student] in Konaka, ed., *Tōdai Hōgakubu,* p. 70. See also the articles by four former Tōdai law students in Juken Shinpō Henshūbu, ed., *Watashi no totta kokka jōkyū shiken toppahō,* pp. 60–71, 110–21, 134–57.

39. Masuda, "Shin hana monogatari," p. 83; Y. N. Sei, "Hongo karano tsūshin: Hōgakubu hen" [News from Hongo: The Faculty of Law] in Itō, ed., *Tōdaisei hakusho,* p. 107.

modes of analysis but good memory and problem-solving ability. Even though it is committed to the lofty objective of "producing individuals who are equipped not only with broad perspectives linking the past and the future to the present but also with knowledge that is at once deep and erudite,"[40] Tōdai's law faculty may actually turn out narrow-minded technicians well versed in the fine points of legal theories and interpretation and supremely adept at taking examinations. As one writer put it, Tōdai law graduates who become elite bureaucrats "can see the trees but not the forest."[41]

Two caveats are in order. First, these are broad generalizations to which numerous exceptions can be found. Second, they pertain primarily to the last two years of Tōdai law students, for the first two years on the Komaba campus offer abundant opportunities for extracurricular activities. Not only are there numerous clubs and circles encompassing a wide array of interests and hobbies, but the academic work load is said to be relatively light.[42] Moreover, for Humanities Group 1 students, who are virtually assured of admission to the faculty of law after two years, there is little or no pressure to earn good grades in their courses. On the other hand, many students must work part time, typically as private tutors to high-school students preparing for university entrance examinations, and that is bound to impose constraints on their time. This condition may last throughout their university years.

Generally speaking, however, Tōdai students tend to come from relatively affluent families. Children of professional and managerial people are vastly overrepresented in the Tōdai student body, whereas those of farmers and sales people are grossly underrepresented. This reflects the fact that preparing for Tōdai's entrance examinations is an expensive proposition, frequently necessitating attendance at supplementary (*juku*) and preparatory schools (*yobikō*) and hiring private tutors. A recent survey by Tōdai's Office of Student Affairs showed that over half of Tōdai students had some experience with *juku, yobikō,* or private tutors. Moreover, the list of the top ten or twenty high schools that produced successful applicants to Tōdai in recent years is dominated by private high schools and schools attached to national universi-

40. *Tōkyō Daigaku sōgō kenkyū,* p. 86; Yamane, "Aru gakusei seikatsu," p. 41.
41. Ōkura Hisarō, "Ōkurashō to Tōdai Hōgakubu" [The Finance Ministry and the University of Tokyo Faculty of Law] in Konaka, ed., *Tōdai Hōgakubu,* p. 145.
42. For a list of student "circles" at Tōdai, see Itō, ed., *Tōdaisei hakusho,* pp. 160–67. Table 3 (pp. 162–67) shows that nearly three-quarters of the circles are affiliated with the Faculty of General Education in Komaba.

ties, all of which tend to be appreciably more expensive than public high schools.[43] On the other hand, the cost of attending Tōdai or any other national university is generally lower than that of attending a private university. In 1987, the estimated mean expenses of first-year students were 1,550,000 yen for national universities and 1,950,000 yen for private universities.[44]

Given their social background, it is not surprising that the values of Tōdai students tend to be somewhat status-quo affirming. The data presented in the first column of table 28 are based on a survey of first-year Tōdai students who were enrolled in a political-science course on the Komaba campus. According to the instructor of the course, most of them were bound for the faculty of law. The table shows that there is a discernible conservative trend: whereas the Japan Socialist party was the favorite among the 1977 sample, the Liberal-Democratic party emerged at the top among the 1983 group. Although over half of the 1983 group who were willing to express a preference for a political party chose the ruling party, the proportion still lagged behind that of the general public, not to mention the bureaucrats.

The second half of the table is based on self-identification by the respondents. Here again, comparison of the first two columns discloses a conservative trend, with the proportion of Todai students describing themselves as either "progressive" or "somewhat progressive" declining by 33 percent. On the other hand, the 1983 group was evenly split between self-styled liberals and conservatives. Moreover, compared with the general public, the 1983 students were both more liberal and more conservative at the same time, for the general public chose by and large to describe their political orientation as "moderate."[45]

Other parts of the survey not summarized in the table merit brief mention. Regarding Japan's security policy—specifically, military

43. Ikeda, "Binbōnin no ko," pp. 199–201; Inoguchi Takashi and Kabashima Ikuo, "Tōdai ichinensei no seiji ishiki: Genjō kōtei no hensachi sedai" [Political Consciousness of University of Tokyo Freshmen: "Hensachi" Generation That Affirms the Status Quo], *Chūō kōron*, Dec. 1983, pp. 63–64. "Hensachi" literally means "the value of deviations." It refers to a type of standardized score that can predict a student's chances of passing entrance examinations to specific high schools and universities. For a discussion of "hensachi," see NHK Shuzaihan, *Nihon no jōken, 11: Kyōiku, 2—hensachi ga Nihon no mirai o shihai suru* [Japan's Condition, 11: Education, 2—Hensachi Dominates the Future of Japan] (Tokyo: Nihon Hōsō Shuppan Kyōkai, 1983).

44. *Asahi shinbun*, 19 Jan. 1987. Since the exchange rate between the Japanese yen and the U.S. dollar fluctuated between 120:1 and 150:1 in 1987, these figures were equivalent to $10,333–$12,916 and $13,000–$16,250, respectively.

45. The Japanese term for "moderate" used in the survey was *chūdō*, which literally means "the middle road."

TABLE 28   *Party Identification and Political Orientation*
of University of Tokyo Students (Percentages)

	Freshmen 1983 Entrants	Law Faculty 1977 Entrants	Bureaucrats Who Graduated from Tōdai	General Public
Party				
LDP	28.5	9.4	60.0	37.0
JSP	10.5	30.2	3.6	13.9
Kōmeitō	0.4	0.0	0.0	4.5
DSP	2.5	1.9	10.9	5.8
JCP	6.9	5.7	0.0	3.9
NLC	5.1	7.5	0.0	1.2
Shaminren	1.8	13.2	0.0	0.0
Independents	44.4	32.1	25.5	33.1
TOTAL	100.1	100.0	100.0	99.4
N	277	53	55	1,769
Political orientation				
Progressive	7.9	30.8	0.0	6.7
Somewhat progressive	32.4	42.3	15.8	17.3
Moderate	18.3	7.7	26.3	42.2
Somewhat conservative	27.3	17.3	45.6	20.8
Conservative	14.2	1.9	12.3	12.9
TOTAL	100.1	100.0	100.0	99.9
N	268	52	57	1,495

SOURCE: Inoguchi Takeshi and Kabashima Ikuo, "Tōdai ichinensei no seiji ishiki: Genjō kōteino hensachi sedai," *Chūō kōron*, Dec. 1983, p. 66.
NOTE:

LDP	Liberal Democratic party
JSP	Japan Socialist party
Kōmeitō	Clean Government party
DSP	Democratic Socialist party
JCP	Japan Communist party
NLC	New Liberal Club
Shaminren	United Social Democratic party

spending and security cooperation with the United States—and the status of the Emperor in the political system, Tōdai students expressed an overwhelming approval of the status quo. In fact, the degree to which they opposed any change in the status quo was much higher than that of the general public. Ninety-six percent of Tōdai students opposed the idea of giving the Emperor a substantial say in politics, whereas only about 40 percent of the general public did so. Almost a third of the latter had no opinion on the matter. On issues dealing with the rights of workers, social welfare, and sexual equality, however, the students tended to be somewhat more conservative than the general public. Whereas 62 percent of the general public favored giving more decision-making powers to workers in matters that are important to them, 57 percent of Tōdai students did so. On pensions and medical care for the aged, 72 percent of the general public thought that they should receive top priority regardless of budgetary constraints; 55 percent of Tōdai students concurred in this view. Finally, whereas 37 percent of the general public agreed with the statement that "the government ought to have a special mechanism for increasing the number of women in higher positions and better jobs," only 28 percent of Tōdai students did so.[46]

The preceding data, it should be stressed, do not indicate that Tōdai students hold conservative views in an absolute sense. Rather, the data show that while the students tend to be somewhat more conservative than the general public on most issues, their overall position cannot be characterized as conservative. On social issues they tend to take fairly progressive positions. It may even be argued that the students display egalitarian values. Unfortunately, the data cited here do not permit us to make any inferences about the actual impact of the socialization experiences of Tōdai students in general and of Tōdai law students in particular.

POST-ENTRY SOCIALIZATION

Having survived the rigors of Japan's educational system, with its emphasis on entrance examinations, and having cleared the hurdle of the higher civil-service examination, Japan's elite-track bureaucrats bring to their tasks an impressive array of skills: a basic understanding of the broad spectrum of human knowledge, an exceptional ability in memorization and problem solving, and a mastery of at least one field of specialization. The practice of decentralized recruitment whereby those who have passed the higher civil-service examination must be hired by individual ministries and agencies implies, furthermore, that each appointee brings with him or her those qualities that are particularly valued by the ministry or agency concerned. To a striking extent, the process resembles an arranged marriage: inasmuch as both sides are making commitments that are expected to endure for at least a few

46. Inoguchi and Kabashima, "Tōdai ichinensei," pp. 71–72.

decades, they must scrutinize each other's qualifications with utmost care. In most cases there are other options, making the final selection contingent upon the convergence of perceptions of mutual benefit.

Notwithstanding the above, the need for postentry socialization remains. From the standpoint of the government as a whole, the adverse effects of decentralized hiring practices need to be neutralized. The new civil servant must be persuaded to view himself not as an employee of the ministry or agency that has hired him but as an employee of the nation as a whole (*kuni no shokuin*). So far as the individual ministries and agencies are concerned, the new recruits must be guided step by step to internalize their organizational goals, values, and norms. In addition, the new recruits must be taught the specific skills that may be necessary or useful for the performance of their tasks during the coming years. Broadly speaking, the types of postentry socialization can be divided into two categories: on-the-job training and off-the-job training. The latter in turn consists of several subtypes: training programs run by the National Personnel Authority, sometimes in conjunction with the prime minister's office; training programs provided by individual ministries and agencies; and training that takes place in educational institutions in Japan and abroad.

ON-THE-JOB TRAINING

As noted previously, an important part of the backdrop against which postentry socialization takes place is the convergence of perceptions of mutual benefit by both parties, the novice bureaucrat and his employer. What is known as "self-selection" is operative here. As Armstrong puts it, "If young men may choose alternative careers, and if they have a reasonably accurate perception of the demands of those careers, each career will tend to attract those men whose personalities are best adapted to the specific career demands."[47]

A *Mainichi shinbun* survey of 109 persons who were about to embark on the elite track in 1979, for example, showed that almost half (47.7 percent) chose a civil-service career out of a desire to serve the public. Thirty-seven percent also cited "an interest in the affairs of the nation" as a key motive. In terms of career prospects, 74 percent expected to rise above the rank of section chief, 35 percent anticipated an eventual promotion to the rank of bureau chief, and 6 percent to

47. Armstrong, *The European Administrative Elite*, p. 94.

that of administrative vice-minister. Three percent thought that they would ultimately become cabinet ministers.[48] Although the low return rate (46 percent) of this survey dictates caution in interpreting its findings, it is nonetheless striking that the values articulated by Japanese youth who have opted for a public-service career differ sharply from those of Japanese youth in general.

"Self-selection," however, does not tell the whole story, for the selection of a civil servant is obviously a two-way process. The hiring organization tends to select only those who measure up to its own standards and criteria of excellence. The latter not only vary from agency to agency but also change in the course of time. The Ministry of International Trade and Industry (MITI), for example, is said to have alternated its preference between "aggressive action-oriented types" and "internationally oriented gentleman types" over the years. One quality that MITI has consistently valued in its new recruits for the elite track is said to be boundless energy, a willingness to work harder than any other civil servant. When those who have passed the first stage of the higher civil-service examination make their customary rounds in Kasumigaseki in search of prospective employers, they are said to get a blunt message from MITI: "Anyone who doesn't like to work overtime, please look elsewhere." Only those who answer enthusiastically that they love overtime work will be given opportunities to explore further.[49]

48. Mainichi Shinbun Shakaibu, *Kanryō: Sono fushoku no kōzō* [Bureaucrats: Structure of Their Corrosion] (Tokyo: Tairiku Shobō, 1980), pp. 41–46. Note the contrast between the results of this survey and those of the youth survey reported in table 24. The contrast, in my view, underscores both the self-selection mechanism and the "select" nature of the 109 persons questioned in the *Mainichi* survey. Nonetheless, the validity of the responses summarized here is open to question.

49. "Kanchō daikaibō, 1: This Is Tsūsan-shō!" [Great Autopsy on Government Agencies, 1: This Is MITI], *Shūkan Yomiuri*, 18 Nov. 1984, p. 29. Although working overtime is a way of life for all higher civil servants, MITI does seem to stand out among the crowd. MITI bureaucrats have renamed their ministry *Tsūjō Zangyōshō* in lieu of the official *Tsūshō Sangyōshō*. The former means the Ministry of Regular Overtime. See Kakuma Takashi, *Dokyumentō Tsūsanshō, part I: Shin Kanryō no jidai* [Document on the Ministry of International Trade and Industry, Part I: The Era of New Bureaucrats] (Tokyo: PHP Kenkyūjo, 1979), pp. 62–63. Legally, civil servants are entitled to receive compensation for overtime work at either 25 or 50 percent above the regular rate. The latter applies to work performed between 10:00 P.M. and 5:00 A.M. See art. 16 of the Law Concerning the Compensation of Regular Service Employees in Jinji-in, *Ninmen kankei hōreishū*, 1984 ed., p. 63. Although civil servants above the rank of section chief are not entitled to overtime pay, they receive special allowances for managerial positions (*kanri shoku teate*), which can amount to 25 percent of their basic salary. Koitabashi, "Sengo umare" erīto kanryō no sugao, pp. 63 and 98.

Aspirants for positions in the Ministry of Home Affairs, on the other hand, are allegedly screened on the basis of their ability to listen to other people with empathy while managing to get their position across and their ability to lead other people effectively. Although the ministry minimizes the importance of grades earned in college and in the higher civil-service examination, it nonetheless attracts people with high grade-point averages. Of the fifteen persons who were hired by the ministry in 1985, thirteen were graduates of Tōdai's law faculty with outstanding scholastic records: on average, 70 percent of their grades were A's. According to knowledgeable observers, a conspicuous attribute of Home Ministry bureaucrats is their ability to change colors according to the dictates of the situation: when they are serving as responsible officials of local governments, in accordance with the policy of rotation, they become ardent spokesmen for local interests, criticizing the policies of the national government to such an extent that even progressive Diet members cannot match their zeal. Even when they serve in the ministry headquarters, they continue to advocate the viewpoints of localities. In their own dealings with local governments, however, the Home Ministry bureaucrats undergo a metamorphosis, becoming "rulers" who interfere in all phases of local government.[50]

Although the degree to which on-the-job training is structured varies widely, one common denominator appears to be the policy of rotation. The general idea behind the policy seems to be to give the novice bureaucrats the widest possible exposure to the organization, its structure, personnel, tasks, and modus operandi. As we saw in the preceding chapter, the Ministry of Finance processes its elite-track entrants through a fairly well-structured training course lasting six to seven years. A unique feature of the Finance Ministry training program is that every first-year career bureaucrat is paired with someone who is one year senior to him. The *senpai* (senior) becomes the novice's guide, teacher, companion, and patron. Not only does the *senpai* provide guidance on the job but he is expected to entertain his *kōhai* (junior) after working hours as well, buying meals and drinks. By custom, the *senpai* even buys the *kōhai*'s lunches until the latter receives his first monthly salary. The financial burden of all this on the *senpai* is by no

50. "Kanchō daikaibō, 10: This Is Jichi-shō!" [Great Autopsy on Government Agencies, 10: This Is the Ministry of Home Affairs!], *Shūkan Yomiuri*, 28 Apr. 1985, p. 142.

means light; the *kōhai*, who must reverse roles in the following year, must plan ahead, saving part of his meager salary throughout the first year for the anticipated expenses in the second year.[51]

Another interesting aspect of the Finance Ministry's training program is the practice of using members of its freshman class as "question-takers" in the National Diet. Specifically, when the Diet convenes its annual session, attention is focused on the interpellations of government officials by Diet members in the budget committee. Because the sessions are frequently televised and receive wide coverage in the press, no cabinet minister or his ranking deputy wants to be caught off guard. Hence every effort is made to anticipate questions and to prepare for them as fully as possible.

Whereas all other ministries and agencies rely on seasoned veterans for their respective intelligence-gathering operations in the Diet, the Finance Ministry is unique in having its freshman career bureaucrats perform the thankless task. The latter serve stints of two weeks on a rotating basis. With the help of five "noncareer" Finance Ministry bureaucrats who are stationed in the Diet full time, these novices roam around, talking with various Diet members in an effort to learn what questions the latter are planning to ask. For their part, many Diet members find it expedient or gratifying to let the bureaucrats know the general thrust of their questions in advance. The Diet members call their talks with Finance Ministry freshman bureaucrats *reku* (lecture), maintaining the lofty posture of teacher vis-à-vis the bureaucrats. Such experiences are indeed designed to perform an important teaching function for the bureaucrats: to enable them to learn firsthand about the politics of the Diet at the beginning of their careers.[52]

We have already noted that in the second year most Finance Ministry trainees are dispatched to the field to learn about "front-line work" in internal revenue and finances as "inspectors" (*chōsakan*). Chiefs of tax bureaus in the localities and other senior officials play the role of mentor, frequently "preaching to" the trainee about various matters over drinks in the evenings. In the third year, all trainees are expected to devote full time to study. A few of them are selected to go abroad to pursue graduate study, but the majority undergo formal training at home. Their focus of study is economics. The faculty, drawn from the outside, is said to be superb, and the program of study exceedingly

51. Jin, *Ōkura kanryō*, p. 98; Mainichi Shinbun, *Kanryō*, pp. 21–22.
52. Ibid., pp. 19–21.

rigorous. Finance Ministry officials claim that the one-year training program is comparable to a graduate program in economics leading to a master's degree in economics. The ministry takes this theoretical training so seriously that the trainees are left undisturbed throughout the year; even during the ministry's busiest period, September through December, when work on the next year's budget requires all the help it can muster, the ministry allows the third-year civil servants to concentrate on their studies exclusively.[53]

After receiving further exposure to substantive work of the ministry in Tokyo, first as a senior member of a sub-section (*shunin*) and then as chief of a subsection (*kakarichō*), the trainee assumes in the sixth and final year of formal on-the-job training (*minarai kikan*) the position of chief of a local tax office (*zeimushochō*). For the first time, the trainee is put in charge of a government office in the field that not only has several dozen employees but also performs a significant function. As such, he becomes part of the local establishment and must interact with leaders in various walks of life as an equal. To be the head of an organization, however small, is a challenge of considerable proportions for a novice bureaucrat still in his twenties. A former Finance Ministry bureaucrat writes that it was the most memorable experience of his life.[54]

Aware of the risks involved, the Finance Ministry takes pains to minimize them. For one thing, the privilege is denied to women bureaucrats on its career track. According to the Finance Ministry's reasoning, in view of the fact that most localities in Japan tend to lag behind metropolitan areas in social change, few are ready for a woman tax chief. Nonetheless, a "noncareer" woman in the Finance Ministry, with thirty-seven years of service in the National Tax Administration Agency, was appointed a local tax chief in 1981.[55]

Another precaution taken by the ministry is to select as the novices' training ground only those localities where there are no major problems in tax collection. Additionally, the ministry makes certain that the tax offices chosen have deputy directors and chiefs of general-affairs sections who are particularly suited to serve as "guardians" (*omamori yaku*) of their prospective young bosses. These are veteran "noncareer" civil servants. The other people in the localities concerned usually make

---

53. Sakakibara, *Nihon o enshutsu suru shin kanryōzō*, pp. 41–44; Kanayama Bunji, "Sei'iki no okite: Kanryōdō no kenkyū" [Laws of a Sanctuary: A Study of the Ways of Bureaucrats], *Chūō kōron*, July 1978, p. 234.
54. Sakakibara, *Niho o enshutsu suru*, p. 47.
55. Sano, *Josei kanryō*, pp. 97–134 and 138.

the young trainees feel both welcome and important, for they are well aware that the trainees may one day become bureau chiefs and even vice-ministers. So far as the trainees themselves are concerned, what they get out of this experience is not only an exercise in leadership but also self-confidence and a heightened consciousness of their elite status.[56] Not only do the actual experiences of trainees vary from case to case, but the timing of appointment as a local tax-office chief also varies from class to class and sometimes within the same class. In the 1950s it occurred in the seventh year. From 1958 to 1962 it occurred in the sixth year for most trainees. Since 1963, it has occurred in the fifth year more often than not.[57]

A major feature of the on-the-job training appears to be self-learning, of which the Finance Ministry's use of first-year bureaucrats as "question-takers" in the Diet is a notable example. That is to say, one is sometimes dispatched to the "combat zone" alone and compelled to fend for oneself. What undoubtedly eases the anxiety of the Finance Ministry freshmen bureaucrat, however, is the *senpai-kōhai* system mentioned earlier. In the case of the Diet assignment, the availability of "noncareer" veterans provides another cushion.

Novices in other ministries, however, point to the need for surreptitious learning. As a first-year career woman in MITI confided, "when one is in the dark as to how things should be done, one should not ask someone but try to figure them out on one's own or observe how other people do things. For example, one can learn what kind of work others are doing by looking at the files left on their desks in the evening when everyone has left and by studying the material one is asked to duplicate." Conceding that such behavior resembles that of a "cat that steals" (*dorobō neko*), she argued that "there is no other way." Her views are echoed by a first-year career man in the Home Ministry, who says that he was compelled to learn about the flow and handling of documents entirely on his own and to eavesdrop on telephone conversations in order to learn how to handle telephone inquiries.[58]

---

56. Kanayama, "Sei'iki no okite," pp. 235–36. The care with which the Finance Ministry selects local tax offices for its trainees is reminiscent of a similar practice in France. The Ecole Nationale d'Administration takes pains to ensure that the prefectures to which its first-year students are dispatched for prolonged on-the-job training are capable of giving them a meaningful learning experience. A *département* headed by a particularly capable prefect who is enthusiastic about the training program will be entrusted with two trainees, notwithstanding the rule of one trainee per *département*. See Parris, "Twenty Years of l'Ecole Nationale d'Administration," pp. 309–10.

57. These impressions are based on a review of the career background of Finance Ministry officials listed in *Shōwa 62-nenban Ōkurashō meikan*.

58. "Kōmuin to natte: Jōkyū shiken saiyōsha zadankai" [On Becoming Civil Servants:

In all of the on-the-job training programs, either structured or unstructured, an overriding aim is to instill in the minds of the novice bureaucrats a sense of identification with the organization that they have joined. This is frequently accompanied by the inculcation of a sense of pride, a goal whose attainment will hinge to a great extent on the relative prestige of the organization concerned. Regardless of their relative prestige, however, all government agencies seem to have a large measure of success in generating a sense of commitment and loyalty to them. In a significant sense, this may be a function of sheer necessity on the part of the bureaucrats: having made long-term commitments based on considerations of expediency as well as other factors, they have a stake in the well-being of their new employer. On the other hand, too strong a sense of identification with individual ministries can be dysfunctional for the government as a whole. We now turn to programs designed to foster supraorganizational loyalties and cross-organizational friendships.

OFF-THE-JOB TRAINING

The number of off-the-job training programs has increased dramatically over the years. In 1972 there were 4,790 such programs, in which 16.6 percent of all regular-service (*ippan shoku*) national civil servants participated. By 1977 the number of programs had increased to 6,241 and the proportion of regular-service participants to 20.8 percent. In 1986, there were 9,725 programs, in which 38.5 percent of all regular-service national civil servants participated.[59] But what interests us most are those programs that are specifically tailored to elite-track civil servants. Since 1956, four such programs have been initiated and conducted by the national government, each of which is available to civil servants at different stages of their career: (1) new appointees, (2) subsection chiefs, (3) assistant section chiefs, and (4) section chiefs.

Joint Training of New Appointees   Conducted annually since 1967 under the joint auspices of the National Personnel Authority and the Bureau of Personnel (which had been part of the prime minister's office

A Roundtable Discussion of Appointees Who Have Passed the Higher (Civil-Service) Examination], *Jinji-in geppō* 312 (Feb. 1977): 6–7.

59. "Kokka kōmuin kenshū no kihon mondai ni kansuru kentō kekka no hōkoku" [A Report on the Results of an Investigation into the Basic Problems in the Training of National Civil Servants], *Jinji-in geppō* 347 (Jan. 1980): 19; Jinji-in, *Nenji hōkokusho*, 1983, p. 108; Jinji-in, *Kōmuin hakusho*, 1988, p. 108.

until 1984, when it was absorbed by the Management and Coordination Agency), the joint training of new appointees (*kyōdō shonin kenshū*) is the only program that brings together all elite-track civil servants in the same stage of their careers. It has the dual aim of helping them to realize that they are the servants of the entire nation (*kokumin zentai no hōshisha*) and of generating a sense of solidarity among its participants. Taking place in the first week of April, this program is tantamount to an orientation for the new appointees, who spend four days together during which they follow a tight schedule. The schedule includes listening to lectures on various topics by senior officials, retired officials, and scholars; participating in small group discussions; visiting the Diet and the prime minister's residence; and taking part in recreational and athletic activities.[60]

The reaction to the program by former participants has been generally favorable. In an evaluation survey conducted in the first class ($N = 685$), 59 percent indicated that the experience had been "meaningful" and that the duration of the program had been "just right." The same sentiment was echoed by a number of new appointees in a round-table discussion ten years later. One found the experience "morale-boosting," and another indicated that the experience of spending "five days [*sic*] with persons in entirely different fields" had been very rewarding. On the other hand, the brevity of the program was criticized by some former participants (20 percent of the first class), and others voiced the hope that there would be more emphasis on small group discussion and informal interactions among the participants. One even complained of the total ban on alcoholic beverages, even during the evening hours, a ban that is imposed by the regulations of the Olympic Youth Center, where the trainees are housed.[61]

Training of Sub-Section Chiefs   Initiated in 1956, the "administrative training" (*gyōsei kenshū*) of subsection chiefs is the oldest of the four programs. Whereas the program for new appointees is all-inclusive, this program accommodates only about 30 percent of the eligible bureaucrats. Until 1984, it was held three times a year, each session lasting eight weeks. As in the other training programs, the participants, who average about eighty per session, spend all of their time together in the training camp, which is the National Personnel Authority's Public-service Training Institute (*Kōmuin Kenshūjo*) located in Iruma city,

60. "Dai ikkai kyōdō shonin kenshū o jisshi shite" [Implementation of the First Joint Training of New Appointees], *Jinji-in geppō* 197 (July 1967): 20–23.
61. Ibid., pp. 21–22; "Kōmuin to natte," p. 6.

Saitama prefecture. In addition to the twin goals of inculcating a sense of mission to the nation as a whole (transcending the parochial perspectives of individual ministries and agencies) and of fostering a sense of solidarity and a network of friendship among the participants, this program aims at imparting specialized knowledge to the fledgling higher civil servants. Until its reorganization in 1985, the program consisted of two tracks: course A for persons with expertise in law, economics, the humanities, and the social sciences and course B for specialists in the natural sciences and engineering. A sizable number of lectures, seminars, and joint research projects were common to both tracks; they dealt with such topics as administrative law, international relations, national security, economic theory, economic planning, fiscal and monetary policies, international economy, public administration and citizens, population problems, policy science, public management, personnel management, and labor relations. The lecturers were predominantly from the academic world, with a sprinkling of senior officials.[62]

Judging from the comments of its participants, the program seems to accomplish its intended purposes. Not only does it provide a broadening experience, in terms of one's perspectives, intellectual horizons, and network of friends and acquaintances, but it also furnishes a welcome relief from the pressure-cooker atmosphere of Kasumigaseki. In a rustic setting far removed from the hustle and bustle of Tokyo, the participants can relax both their minds and their bodies, enjoying the luxury of reflection and study. The allocation of almost equal amounts of time to lectures and seminars, moreover, ensures that the participants have ample opportunities to think on their own and to interact intellectually with their peers and instructors.[63] In an evaluation survey administered to seventy participants in March 1984, all but three indicated that the program had been worthwhile, and half of the respondents said that it had been "unusually productive." Moreover, 91 percent said that when they became section chiefs, they would make every effort to send their subordinates to the training program even if it should interfere with the work of the section.[64] *Mainichi shinbun* reporters who interviewed

---

62. Okada Maki, "110 tai 102: Gyōsei kenshū (kakarichō kyū) inshōki" [110 vs. 102: Impressions of Administrative Training (Subsection-Chief Level)], *Jinji-in geppō*, 356 (Oct. 1980): 21–25. The numbers refer to 110 hours of lectures vs. 102 hours of seminars (*enshū*).

63. Ibid., pp. 21–23.

64. "Shōwa 58-nendo gyōsei kenshū no jisshi jōkyō: Tai 81-kai gyōsei kenshū (kakarichō kyū) o chūshin to shite" [The Situation Regarding the Implementation of Administrative Training in Fiscal Year 1983: With Emphasis on the 81st Administrative Training Session (Subsection-Chief Level)], *Jinji-in geppō* 401 (June 1984): 6–7.

trainees in January 1979 found that the program was indeed engendering the feeling of *Kasumigaseki ikka* (one Kasumigaseki family), namely, cross-organizational solidarity among the participants. "The biggest harvest of all is making acquaintance with people from all kinds of ministries and agencies" was a sentiment shared by all the trainees. Some even expressed the desire for a longer training period, lasting six months instead of two.[65]

As noted previously, the program was reorganized in 1985. Its length was shortened from eight to four weeks, and the frequency of its sessions was reduced from three to two per year. In lieu of courses A and B, three new tracks dealing respectively with public administration, law, and economics were established. This was in response to the requests of many ministries and agencies for more specialized training. The duration having been cut in half, the training became more intensive than before. All three tracks have in common segments on the "administrative process," dealing primarily with public policy; "administrative management"; "administrative environment"; physical fitness; general education (*kyōyō*); and individualized research. The amount of training time devoted to individualized research varies from 27 to 45 hours (out of 122 hours) depending on one's track. In addition, a separate training program for subsection chiefs who are not on the traditional elite track was created. This seems to be a major concession to the "noncareer" civil servants, who constitute over 95 percent of all national civil servants. Known as the basic course in administrative training (subsection-chief level) (*gyōsei kenshū kiso katei* [*kakarichō kyū*]), the new program is open to civil servants who have passed the lower and intermediate civil-service examinations, have compiled outstanding records of performance, and show promise of leadership. Its session lasts about five weeks.[66]

Training of Assistant Section Chiefs   Under the 1985 reorganization plan, the training of assistant section chiefs was given the principal emphasis. Whereas in the past only about 20 percent of the eligible persons received government-wide training at this level, the new plan calls for the eventual accommodation of practically all eligible persons. The number of participants thus doubled in fiscal year 1985, from 150

---

65. Mainichi Shinbun, *Kanryō*, pp. 32–35.
66. "Shōwa 60-nendo Jinji-in kenshū no jisshi keikaku" [A Plan for the Implementation of Training Programs Administered by the National Personnel Authority in Fiscal Year 1985], *Jinji-in geppō* 412 (May 1985): 10–14; Jinji-in, *Kōmuin hakusho*, 1987, pp. 135–37.

to 300, and the frequency of sessions also increased, from three to six per year. On the other hand, the length of each session was reduced from four to three weeks. The rationale for that reduction was that the pivotal role played by assistant section chiefs in their respective units made it impractical to prolong their absence from work. In terms of curriculum, there is an increased emphasis on the "environment of public administration," which has become more complex and multifaceted than ever before.[67]

An interesting feature of this program is that it occasionally invites participants from the private sector. Of the 50 persons who participated in the program's forty-third session in May 1981, for example, 4 were employees of major corporations: Toyota Motor Company, Shin Nippon Steel Company, Mitsubishi Shoji, and Toshiba Electric Company. In a jointly authored article, the four private-sector participants gave rave reviews to the program. They praised the timeliness of the topics covered and the pedagogy used, particularly the emphasis on seminars in which individualized research and small group discussion play the major part. Of 120 hours devoted to study, only 21 were consumed by straight lectures. On the average, each participant was required to serve as a discussion leader three or four times during the session. The layout of the dormitory, which contained both single rooms and Japanese-style rooms accommodating three persons, facilitated close interpersonal relationships. Rooms and roommates were changed every week. Extracurricular activities, such as softball and tennis tournaments, contributed to the development of camaraderie.[68]

All in all, this program, too, performs useful functions for its participants: it simultaneously broadens their intellectual horizons and helps them forge personal ties with their peers in the other parts of the national government and, occasionally, in the private sector as well.

Training of Section Chiefs   The training program for section chiefs, known as "managers' study session" (*kanrisha kenkyūkai*), accommodates only 10 percent of all eligible persons. Initiated in 1963, the program is open to civil servants who are serving as section chiefs or their equivalents in the national-government ministries and agencies. It is held about four times a year and, like the program for assistant section chiefs, allows the participation of private-sector personnel who

67. "Shōwa 60-nendo Jinji-in kenshū," pp. 10–11. In fiscal year 1986, a total of 258 assistant section chiefs took part in this program in six separate sessions. Jinji-in, *Kōmuin hakusho*, 1987, pp. 137–38.

68. Imai Fukuzō et al., "'Moeru shūdan' ni mi o tōjite" [Joining a "Burning Group"], *Jinji-in geppō* 366 (July 1981): 12–17.

hold equivalent positions. Each session lasts about three weeks, of which ten days are spent on individualized research and a week on group activities. Only during the final week do the participants live together in a camp. A typical session has between twenty and twenty-five participants and a common theme. The range of topics covered by individualized research, however, is somewhat broader. The ninety-first session, held from 17 September to 4 October 1986, for example, focused on the theme of "procedural guarantees in public administration," but the participants prepared research papers on "theories of management" (*kanrisha ron*). In addition, there were lectures and discussions on such topics as "the recent international situation," "the ideology of business management" (*kigyō keiei no rinen*), "the economic situation," "theories of modern society," and "mental hygiene in the workplace."[69]

The small size of each class may compensate for the brevity of the session. Former participants cite as one of the principal benefits of the program the establishment of horizontal linkages with their peers in the other ministries and agencies. An official of the Construction Ministry recalls, for example, that as a section chief in charge of budgetary matters, he was able to call up a Finance Ministry official who had been a fellow trainee and obtain valuable assistance. Other participants state that learning about what their peers in other parts of the government are doing and being able to exchange ideas with them did indeed help engender a sense of solidarity and an awareness of their status as "public servants of the entire nation" (*kuni no kōmuin*).[70]

Other Training Programs   A number of ministries and agencies conduct off-the-job training programs on their own. A few of them even have their own training institutes, notably the Finance Ministry, the Foreign Ministry, the prime minister's office, and the Environment Agency. Most of these programs are geared to specialized training in such fields as accounting and finance, statistics, environmental pollution, and foreign languages.[71]

---

69. "Shōwa 58-nendo Jinji-in kenshū no jisshi keikaku (kaiyō)" [A Plan for the Implementation of Training Programs by the National Personnel Authority in Fiscal Year 1983 (Outline)], *Jinji-in geppō* 388 (May 1983): 6; "Shōwa 60-nendo Jinji-in kenshū," p. 14; Jinji-in, *Kōmuin hakusho*, 1987, pp. 139–40.

70. "Zadankai: Kōmuin kenshū no arikata" [Roundtable Discussion: Ideal of Civil Servants' Training], *Jinji-in geppō* 317 (July 1977): 13–21.

71. "Shōwa 58-nendo Jinji-in kenshū," p. 29; Jinji-in, *Jinji gyōsei sanjūnen no ayumi*, pp. 323–40.

Specialized training is also provided by educational institutions outside the Japanese government. Graduate schools at Tsukuba and Saitama universities have been utilized for the training of elite-track civil servants in management, policy science, and other subjects. Initiated in 1976, this program allows those who meet the standards of both their respective agencies and the graduate schools to work toward master's degrees for two years. During the twelve-year period from 1976 to 1987, a total of 114 civil servants took part in the program.[72]

Finally, foreign institutions and experiences can provide both specialized training and socializing influences to Japan's administrative elite. There are both long-term and short-term programs. The former, initiated in 1966, allows selected individuals to study abroad for two years, usually in pursuit of master's degrees, and the latter, initiated in 1974, allows about 30 civil servants a year to do research on specific topics in foreign countries for six months.[73]

From 1966 to 1988 a total of 680 persons participated in the long-term overseas-training program. Over 60 percent of them studied in major graduate schools in the United States, and the remainder attended major institutions of higher learning in Britain, France, West Germany, Canada, and Australia. Candidates must survive a stringent selection process, including recommendation by their respective ministries or agencies and an examination conducted by the National Personnel Authority. Arrangements are made with foreign educational institutions in accordance with the preferences of both candidates and their agencies as well as the candidates' linguistic ability. Candidates usually undergo a brief training in Japan prior to their departure for their destinations. They are also encouraged to go to their chosen countries two months prior to the commencement of their studies in order to receive intensive language training. Despite such careful preparations, many of them encounter a substantial language barrier during the first several months.[74]

With the exception of those who go to European countries in which educational systems differ substantially from Japan's, however, nearly all of the trainees succeed in earning master's degrees. Besides knowledge and skills, they also gain an understanding of foreign cultures and a network of friends and acquaintances abroad. The government's

72. Jinji-in, *Kōmuin hakusho*, 1987, pp. 146–47.
73. Ibid., pp. 143–46.
74. Ibid., 1988, pp. 117–18; "Ichinen tatta zaigai kenkyū no jōkyō" [The Condition of Overseas Research After One Year], *Jinji-in geppō* 203 (Jan. 1968): 10–13.

objective of turning out higher civil servants capable of functioning effectively in the international arena appears to be succeeding.[75]

The short-term overseas-research program differs from the long-term program in that the participants are affiliated not with universities but with government agencies, international organizations, and, occasionally, research institutes. Since its inception in 1974, a majority of the participants have chosen the United States as the site of their research, the remainder going to Western Europe, Canada, and Australia. They have investigated a wide range of problems. The short-term visitors to the United States have investigated such problems as U.S. policy toward technology transfer, the treatment and rehabilitation of drug abusers, land-use policy, deregulation of the airlines industry, conflict resolution in inner cities, and judicial activism and judicial restraint.[76] Its short duration notwithstanding, the program does expose its participants to ways of life that are different from their own and allows them to study an aspect of foreign society in reasonable depth. At a minimum, it can generate a comparative perspective of sorts and broaden the intellectual horizons of the participants to some degree.[77]

In addition to the above, there is an informal but nonetheless effective method of acquiring education abroad. Civil servants can make their own arrangements, subject to the approval of their superiors. Both short-term and long-term stays abroad can be arranged. To give a few examples of self-arranged training abroad: a woman assistant section chief in the prime minister's office, a Tōdai graduate and an eleventh-year career civil servant, went to Harvard in 1980 to do research on American women executives for eight months. The Japanese government paid for her round-trip air fare but the remaining expenses were her own responsibility. Another woman graduate of Tōdai, in her second year at the Finance Ministry, won a French-government scholarship on her own and studied economics in France for six months in 1967. Still another woman, also a Tōdai graduate in the Finance Ministry, obtained a scholarship from Brown University in her third year, earning a master's degree there after three years of study

75. "Ninenkan o furi kaette: Kikoku shita zaigai kenkyūin dai nikaisei no kaikō" [Looking Back Upon Two Years: Recollections of the Second Group of Returned Overseas Research Students], *Jinji-in geppō* 227, (Jan. 1970): 24–26; Ueyama Shin'ichi, "Purinsuton Daigaku no ninenkan" [Two Years at Princeton University], ibid. 412 (May 1985): 21–23.
76. "Tanki zaigai kenkyūin seido" [The Short-term Overseas Researcher System], *Jinji-in geppō* 401 (June 1984) 29–32.
77. See, for example, Nakajima Sachiko, "Watashi no kaimamita Igirisu" [The England I Caught a Glimpse of], *Jinji-in geppō* 365 (May 1981) 21–24; Fujii Ryōko, "Amerika zakkan" [Miscellaneous Impressions of America], ibid., 378 (July 1982) 22–24.

(1979–82).[78] In the Finance Ministry, almost as many third-year civil servants go abroad for graduate study on scholarships obtained on their own as they do on Japanese-government scholarships.[79]

For obvious reasons, opportunities to study abroad are highly sought after by Japanese civil servants. In the *Mainichi shinbun* survey of new appointees cited earlier, almost half of the respondents indicated a wish to study abroad after they entered the government service.[80] In reality, only a small minority have their wish fulfilled, for the total number of long-term and short-term overseas trainees, both official (that is, government-sponsored) and unofficial, rarely exceeds one hundred a year. For those who make it, however, the rewards seem to be substantial. A steady increase in the pool of elite bureaucrats who can deal effectively with their counterparts in other parts of the world, moreover, is a welcome development for the Japanese government as a whole. If foreign experience helps to increase empathy on the part of Japan's administrative elite, as seems likely, then it can have only salutary effects on the conduct of Japan's public policy in this era of internationalization (*kokusaika jidai*).

CONCLUSION

Although no abstract model can represent the complexity and subtleties of Japanese reality, the progressive-equal-attrition model nonetheless highlights a major dimension of that reality: the probability of induction into Japan's administrative elite diminishes to a vanishing point for an overwhelming majority of Japanese youth at the successive stages of their progression in the educational system. Consequently, the relevant socialization experiences of Japan's administrative elite include (1) their preadult socialization, (2) socialization in universities, and (3) socialization in the postinduction stage.

Among the various agents of preadult socialization, schools play a particularly potent role in Japan. In primary schools, there is an overwhelming emphasis on the inculcation of egalitarian values, notably an egalitarian orientation to jobs, an orientation toward individualism, and a participatory orientation. In high schools, on the other hand, instrumental values become more salient. The latter include diligence, sacrifice, mastery of detailed information, perseverance, asceticism, and a competitive spirit. These values are internalized in the course of the

78. Sano, *Josei kanryō*, pp. 28, 104–5, and 127–29.
79. Jin, *Ōkura kanryō*, pp. 99–101.
80. Mainichi Shinbun, *Kanryō*, p. 42.

students' single-minded pursuit of an overriding goal: passing entrance examinations to "first-rate" universities.

The extent to which these two sets of values are embraced by the Japanese youth, of course, varies widely from individual to individual and among different subsets of the population. Data collected in a world youth-survey project show that the Japanese youth do indeed display a pronounced degree of individualistic and instrumental orientation. The data suggest that they are virtually indistinguishable from their counterparts in the United States, Britain, France, and West Germany in their commitment to universalistic values, aversion to authoritarianism, and preoccupation with individualistic pursuits.

In trying to understand socialization in universities, we have focused our attention on the faculty of law of the University of Tokyo, the single most important training ground of Japan's administrative elite. In terms of formal requirements, all Tōdai law students receive two years of "general education" consisting of courses in the humanities, the social sciences, the natural sciences, and foreign languages. As for specialized training, the number of law-related courses one takes is a function of one's career plans; those contemplating entry into the legal profession take the most, and those leaning toward "political" or other careers (political-science majors) take the fewest. Most students who aspire for careers in the civil service not only take a large number of law-related courses but also immerse themselves in law and other subjects on their own for a prolonged period of time in order to prepare for the higher civil-service examination.

Preparing for examinations, either judicial or administrative or both, is so arduous, in fact, that it necessitates a "triangular pattern of life" that revolves around classrooms, the library, and the boardinghouse. The numerical preponderance of students following such routines contributes to the "desertlike" atmosphere of Tōdai's law faculty. Although opportunities for seminars do exist, most courses permit little interaction between professors and students. In short, the qualities that tend to be accentuated in Tōdai's law faculty are not so much creative thinking and critical modes of analysis as discipline, hard work, good memory, and problem-solving ability.

Those who are inducted into Japan's administrative elite, after passing the exceedingly competitive higher civil-service examination, then, can be presumed to possess an array of substantive skills essential for their prospective duties: an understanding of a broad spectrum of human knowledge, a proven ability in memorization and problem-solving, and a mastery of a chosen field of specialization. The practice of decentralized hiring implies, further, that their role perceptions have been judged to be consistent with the preferences of their employers.

Nonetheless, there remains the need for inculcating a sense of identification with the ministry or agency they have joined and teaching them the fundamentals of its mores and modus operandi. Given the notorious "sectionalism" of the various governmental agencies, moreover, the national government sees a pressing need to bring home to the inductees the primacy of their transorganizational bonds and loyalty. No less important is the need to expose the civil servants in the various stages of their careers to developments both in the operational environment of the Japanese government and in the research frontiers in the relevant disciplines. The opportunity to escape from the daily grind of Kasumigaseki—to collect one's thoughts and reflect on issues, large and small, and to enjoy the companionship of one's peers in other parts of the government and, occasionally, in the private sector as well—is deemed to be of value in its own right. All this has led to the proliferation of training programs for civil servants, conducted by the individual ministries, the National Personnel Authority, and institutions of higher learning.

In fact, in terms of the sheer quantity of in-service training programs and the proportion of civil servants who participate in them, Japan probably has few rivals. To what extent their intended goals materialize, however, remains uncertain. Surveys conducted by the government as well as testimony of participants indicate that the goal of encouraging the development of cross-organizational bonds is being attained to some degree.

Regarding the overall effectiveness of the multitude of training programs, however, Tsuji Kiyoaki, a leading expert on Japanese bureaucracy with wide experience on the postentry training programs, is highly skeptical. He finds that the substantive contents of training programs, that is, courses offered, do not really reflect the cutting edge of research and practice but duplicate the curriculum of faculties of law and economics in Japanese universities, thus turning the programs into "minicolleges of law and economics" (*mini hōkei daigaku*). Tsuji also believes that there is need to increase the proportion of seminars at the expense of lectures. As for the selection of trainees, Tsuji feels that the "horizontal-type training" (*suihei-gata kenshū*) in which all the participants are of the same rank, should be replaced by a "vertical-type training" (*suichoku-gata kenshū*) in which participants will represent a mix of different ranks. In his view, the latter reproduces the reality of Japanese bureaucracy more faithfully and will be conducive to effective training. Finally, Tsuji underscores the value of practical training on the pattern of the French Ecole Nationale d'Administration. As he sees it, most of what happens in Japan is not so much practical training (*jitchi kenshū*) as "practical observation" (*jitchi kengaku*).[81]

Let us examine the Western patterns briefly. If we focus on direct socialization, that is, efforts to transmit a set of values and skills to those who have opted for a public-service career, then we find variations among the industrialized democracies in a number of dimensions—timing, duration, contents, and relative emphasis. As for timing, whether training takes place before or after induction into the public service depends on how "induction" is defined. If it is defined legalistically to refer to formal appointment as an official, then most training programs occur in the preinduction period. Japan and Britain depart from the pattern in that official training programs in these countries do not begin until after formal appointment. From a substantive standpoint, however, the difference in timing may be minimal, for nearly all of the preappointment trainees in France, West Germany, and the United States go on to become full-fledged officials upon completion of their training.

As we have already seen, in West Germany the preinduction training for an aspiring higher civil servant includes (1) university education, normally in law, followed by the passing of a state examination and (2) two-and-a-half years of preparatory service under the auspices of the Lander administrations, capped by the passing of a second state examination. All this leads to certification as a full-fledged jurist and an assessor, which in turn allows the candidate to seek an appointment as a probationary official. Only after a probationary period of one-and-a-half to five years will the candidate be formally admitted to the higher civil service.[82]

It is theoretically possible for nonlaw graduates to enter the higher service in West Germany. Those who have completed their university studies in the social sciences must enter a preparatory service, during which they receive an "in-service training [that] is specifically tailored to public administration." They must spend one semester at the Graduate School of Administrative Sciences in Speyer in the state of Rhineland-Palatinate. The curriculum at Speyer includes formal

    81. Tsuji Kiyoaki, "Kōmu kenshū" [Public-Service Training], in Tsuji Kiyoaki, ed., *Gyōseigaku kōza, dai 4-kan: gyōsei to soshiki* [Lectures on Public Administration, vol. 4: Public Administration and Organization] (Tokyo: Tōkyō Daigaku Shuppankai, 1976), pp. 285–91. Emphasis added.
    82. Johnson, *State and Government in the Federal Republic of Germany*, pp. 182–83.

courses, discussion groups (colloquia), seminars, and visits to "important government agencies or organizations of special interest." Students are also required to engage in an in-depth study of "an unusual administrative problem or undertaking," during which they are given a chance to study all the available documents and hear lectures from key participants in the case under study. At the end of their training, which lasts two and a half years, the nonjurist applicants for the higher service must take a "career examination." In practice, the demand for nonjurists is rather low, hence the phenomenon of *Juristenmonopol* persists.[83]

In France, training for the higher civil service takes place under the auspices of the Ecole Nationale d'Administration (ENA), which supervises a two-and-a-half-year training program for a select group of 150 or so students a year. This number, as we saw in chapter 4, was scheduled to be cut in half by 1987. The program places a heavy emphasis on practical training, rotation of assignments, and group projects. Given its stringent entrance examinations, the ENA has structured its curriculum on the assumption that the entering students have already acquired a thorough grounding in theoretical matters and need primarily to be exposed to the practical world of administration. Hence, during their first year, students are dispatched to local-government units for practical training. This means, in most cases, apprenticeship in a prefecture in the provinces. Some students spend part of the first year in foreign countries such as West Germany, Britain, Spain, Canada, and the United States, learning the operation of local-government agencies in those countries. A novel aspect of the ENA curriculum is the requirement that all students spend about three months in a nongovernmental organization, usually a business firm. With respect to study, emphasis is on quantitative analytic techniques, problem solving, and policy analysis. As part of a seminar, students, in groups of ten, must carry out in-depth studies of a policy problem and submit a sixty-page report recommending and justifying a fresh policy option. Preparation of the seminar report takes about six months, during which students must interview officials and other types of people and reach a consensus among themselves. Learning to work together in a group is said to be a significant side benefit of this experience. In

83. Klaus Konig, "Education and Advanced Training for the Public Service in the Federal Republic of Germany," *International Review of Administrative Sciences* 49, no. 2(1983): 204–9; Fritz Morstein Marx, "German Administration and the Speyer Academy," *Public Administration Review* 27, no. 5(Dec. 1967): 406–08. See also Becker and Kruger, "Personnel Administration," p. 259.

addition to the group research project, there is even a group examination in some courses.[84]

As for the United States, Presidential Management Intern Program (PMIP), inaugurated in 1977, is the single most important training program for higher civil servants. Inasmuch as all PMIs have received graduate training in management or related fields, the two-year internship program consists entirely of practical training. All interns must be hired by individual agencies but are nonetheless exposed to common experiences: "an initial orientation, evening seminars, a three-day seminar at the end of the first and second years, and cluster group meetings which are held several times a year." Led by high-level federal managers, cluster-group meetings "seek to provide a unique perspective on how federal programs are managed and to give interns insight into the application of management techniques within the working environment." At the agency level, the interns design their own "Development Plan," of which the principal component tends to be on-the-job training in a specific functional area as well as on a rotational basis. Just as finalists in the PMIP competition must obtain a Federal position on their own to begin their internship, so those who successfully complete the internship, too, must take the initiative in finding permanent employment in the federal government. It is in this sense that initial appointment as PMIs can only be characterized as tentative; hence the training received by the interns technically occurs prior to permanent appointment.[85]

As noted, Great Britain deviates from the preceding patterns by relying on postentry training. Notwithstanding their title, administrative trainees (ATs) should be viewed as inductees into the higher civil service for all practical purposes. Their number has gradually declined over the years. In the early 1970s, when the AT program was first launched, about 300 ATs were recruited each year, but by the latter part of the decade the number had declined to 160. With the restructuring of the program in the early 1980s, the number of ATs plummeted: in 1982 there were only 44 AT entrants.[86]

84. Tashiro Kū, "Nihon gyōseikan kenkyū—gyōseikan no ikusei: Kakkoku betsu ni mita sono seido" [A Study of Japanese Public Administrators: Systems in Various Countries], *Kankai*, Oct. 1981, p. 76; "Furansu jōkyū kōmuin no shonin kyōiku: Rainichi no Kokuritsu Gyōsei Gakuin (ENA) sei ni kiku" [Early Education of French Higher Civil Servants: Interview with Students of the Ecole Nationale d'Administration Who Are Visiting Japan], *Jinji-in geppō* 266(July 1981): 6–11; Parris, "Twenty Years of l'Ecole Nationale d'Administration," pp. 308–11.

85. U.S. Office of Personnel Management, *The Presidential Management Intern Program Bulletin* (Washington: Government Printing Office, 1984), pp. 1–9.

86. Geoffrey K. Fry, *The Changing Civil Service* (London: George Allen & Unwin, 1985), p. 56.

What has remained constant, however, is that all ATs receive a two-year probationary appointment. Initially assigned to individual departments, ATs until 1981 participated in ten-week-long training programs at the Civil Service College at Sunningdale, England, at the end of their first and second years. During their probationary period, they were given at least three different types of work, and their performance was evaluated by their superiors. On the basis of evaluation, about a third of ATs were "fast-streamed" and the remainder became "mainstreamers." The former in effect became an elite among the elite, with vastly enhanced opportunities for interesting assignments and the assurance of a fast-paced promotion. Since 1981, however, all ATs have become fast-stream entrants and their course of training at the Civil Service College has been changed. It now consists of twelve "modules" requiring a total of twenty-two weeks of training. The training begins earlier than before, for ATs can take "an induction course in administration" after about three months in their departments. The course consists of three modules dealing, respectively, with "communication and the use of information (one week), Parliament, government and the civil service (two weeks), and finance and control of public expenditures (one week)." After their second year of service, ATs can take up to six modules: "quantitative skills (two weeks), economics, government and the administrator (two weeks), principles of accounts (one week), the social role of government (three weeks), government and industry (three weeks), and international relations and the United Kingdom interests (three weeks)." Three more modules focusing on resource management may be taken in the fifth year of service. It is noteworthy that attendance at any of these courses is not mandatory, and "there is a high rate of withdrawal from courses because of the demands of the work—it is usually work in a minister's private office."[87]

The variations among the four countries analyzed above are closely bound up with the idiosyncrasies of their educational systems, their methods of recruiting higher civil servants, and budgetary and other constraints in each country. Cross-national comparison of the "effectiveness" of training programs, then, becomes singularly elusive. The relevant question to ask appears to be: to what extent are the goals of training in each system being attained? Viewed in this light, the Japanese system may not be as ineffectual as its domestic critics would have us believe.

87. Ibid., pp. 63–69; Tashiro, "Nihon gyōseikan kenkyū—gyōseikan no ikusei," p. 77; Kellner and Crowther-Hunt, *The Civil Servants*, pp. 138–46. The quoted passages are from Fry, *The Changing Civil Service*, p. 68.

CHAPTER SEVEN

Modes of Interaction

Conventional wisdom assigns to bureaucrats the twin functions of policy making and implementation. Although they are seen as all but monopolizing the function of policy implementation, their role in policy making is generally viewed as one of coparticipation with politicians. In this chapter we shall examine how Japanese bureaucrats interact with politicians and other groups in performing their key function of policy making. We shall first delineate the salient modes of interaction among the principal players in the policy arena. We shall next discuss differing perspectives on the relative influence of bureaucrats and politicians in Japan's policy-making process. Finally, we shall make an overall assessment, placing the Japanese case in comparative perspective.

SALIENT FEATURES OF
THE POLICY-MAKING PROCESS

BUREAUCRATS AND POLITICIANS: FOUR IMAGES

In their comparative study of bureaucrats and politicians in Western democracies, Joel D. Aberbach and his colleagues posit four possible "images" of the relationship between the two sets of players in the political arena. The oldest and simplest of the four is image I: "politicians make policy; civil servants administer. Politicians make decisions; bureaucrats merely implement them."[1] Although this image was propagated by classical writers on bureaucracy and public administration, it has relatively few adherents today. The boundary line between politics and administration is far from clear-cut in the real world.

Somewhat more credible is image II, which "assumes that both politicians and civil servants participate in making policy, but that they make distinctive contributions." Civil servants contribute "neutral expertise," emphasizing "the technical efficacy of policy," whereas politicians contribute "political sensitivity," focusing on the "responsiveness [of policy] to relevant constituencies."[2] If this image comes closer to portraying the reality than the preceding one, it still leaves something to be desired as an adequate account of the division of labor between politicians and bureaucrats; it fails, for example, to take into account either the growing expertise of politicians in substantive policy areas or the politicization of bureaucrats.

Images III and IV aim at rectifying this shortcoming. Image III posits that "both bureaucrats and politicians engage in policy making, and both are concerned with politics." There is nonetheless a division of labor between them: "whereas politicians articulate broad, diffuse interests of unorganized individuals, bureaucrats mediate narrow, focused interests of organized clienteles."[3]

Image IV goes farther than any of the preceding ones in blurring the distinction between the roles of politicians and bureaucrats; it suggests that developments in the last few decades, notably a "politicization" of the bureaucracy and a "bureaucratization" of politics, have helped to produce a "pure hybrid." This image, caution Aberbach and his associates, is highly speculative. Whether such hybrids have actually become the dominant players in Western-style democracies remains to be verified.[4]

---

1. Joel D. Aberbach, Robert D. Putnam, and Bert A. Rockman, *Bureaucrats and Politicians in Western Democracies* (Cambridge: Harvard University Press, 1981), p. 4. Three other scholars also collaborated in the study: Thomas J. Anton, Samuel J. Eldersveld, and Ronald Inglehart.
2. Ibid., p. 6.
3. Ibid., p. 9.
4. Ibid., pp. 16–19.

THE ROLE OF THE SECTION

Which of the preceding four images best illuminates the Japanese reality? Because we are interested primarily in higher civil servants, we can readily dismiss image I. Only at the lowest rungs of Japanese bureaucracy can a dichotomy between policy (or politics) and administration be sustained; for most civil servants, particularly those in the intermediate and high echelons, participation in policy making in some capacity is taken for granted.

To ascertain which of the remaining three images is most appropriate for Japan, we need to delineate the outstanding features of the policy-making process in the Japanese government. To consider how policy proposals are prepared for submission to the Diet, we must first note the centrality of the section (*ka*) of a ministry, which does most of the spadework, including the drafting of a proposal. This does not mean, however, that ideas for a policy necessarily originate at that level. Even when they originate at higher levels, as they frequently do, the burden of preparing the paperwork and conducting the preliminary consultation falls on the section.[5]

Within the section the task of preparing the draft proposal is typically given to an assistant section chief (*kachō hosa*) who is a "noncareer" man. Because "career" civil servants—those on the elite track—tend to be rotated frequently, their level of substantive expertise is relatively low. By contrast, "noncareer" civil servants stay on the same job for a prolonged period of time; for most of them the position of assistant section chief may be the ultimate destination. They are therefore living repositories of institutional memory and substantive expertise on whom the section relies for the performance of such key functions as preparing drafts of proposed legislation.[6]

RINGISEI

When a draft is prepared, it takes the form of a formal internal document known as *ringisho*. The circulation of such documents upward through the chain of command for approval is known as *ringisei*.[7] Given its notoriety, *ringisei* merits further elaboration. Ac-

5. Murakawa Ichirō, *Seisaku kettei katei* [Policy-Making Process], *Gyōsei kikō shirizu* [Administrative Organization Series], no. 121 (Tokyo: Kyōikusha, 1979), p. 125.
6. Ibid., pp. 126–29.
7. The standard source on *ringisei* is Tsuji, *Shinpan Nihon kanryōsei no kenkyū*, pp. 155–72; see also Tsuji, "Decision-Making in the Japanese Government: A Study of

cording to Tsuji Kiyoaki, it was first introduced by private business firms in the Meiji era but has since gained wide acceptance by public and private organizations alike. He notes three distinguishing features of the system. First, *ringisho* is drafted by a rank-and-file official (*mattan no jimukan*) who lacks any decision-making authority. Tsuji suggests that even officials at the rank of subsection chief (*kakarichō*) or below are sometimes given the responsibility.[8]

Second, in principle *ringisho* is discussed and evaluated separately by the officials of the section, division, and bureau concerned; it does not necessitate a collective discussion in a conference of all relevant administrators. Third, although the head of the organization concerned—for example, the minister in a government ministry—has the sole legal authority to approve *ringisho*, it is customary for him to ratify the result of prolonged evaluation by his subordinates.[9]

In Tsuji's view, *ringisei* has both advantages and disadvantages. On the credit side of the ledger, he lists the opportunity the system provides for participation in decision making by many persons, thus ensuring their cooperation at a later stage and the preservation of a record of decision making. On the debit side, Tsuji sees three problems. First, the system breeds inefficiency, because the process can take a long time. Sometimes delays are caused by the absence of the appropriate officials or by their negligence. At other times delays may stem from deliberate stalling by officials who, although unhappy about the document, find it difficult to propose revisions.[10]

Another shortcoming Tsuji cites has to do with the diffusion of responsibility. Because officials other than the minister or the head of an organization see their role in the process as laying the groundwork for the final decision, they seldom feel a sense of responsibility for the outcome. As for the minister, endowed with neither expertise nor a staff that can provide an independent assessment, he usually ends up rubber-stamping the document; as a result, his sense of responsibility is equally weak.[11]

Ringisei," in Ward, ed., *Political Development in Modern Japan*, pp. 457–75; Miyake, *Gyōseigaku to gyōsei kanri*, pp. 315–34. Miyake's book contains an informative discussion of *ringisei* as practiced in the private sector, based on survey data.
  8. Tsuji, *Shinpan Nihon kanryōsei no kenkyū*, pp. 155–56.
  9. Ibid.
  10. Ibid., pp. 158–59.
  11. Ibid., pp. 159–60.

Finally, Tsuji faults *ringisei* for stifling the exercise of leadership. When higher civil servants or their political superiors, such as a minister, feel inclined to take the initiative, they often find themselves stymied by the rigidity of *ringisei*. A policy proposal by a minister, for example, must first go to the lowest echelon and then travel upward through the *ringi* system, causing the usual delays. Any attempt by a higher official to short-circuit the process, according to Tsuji, triggers shock waves throughout the organization, sometimes resulting in his ouster. Tsuji mentions the case of Kobayashi Ichizō, who was forced to resign as minister of commerce and industry in the prewar period, after his attempts to introduce changes, bypassing the established modus operandi, had alienated his vice-minister, Kishi Nobusuke, and other bureaucrats of the ministry.[12]

It appears, however, that either Tsuji overemphasizes the rigidity of *ringisei* or it has undergone significant change over the years. According to Ojimi Yoshihisa, a former administrative vice-minister of the Ministry of International Trade and Industry (MITI):

> We consider the *ringi* document as part of office equipment along with pencils and paper. The *ringi* document is rarely written at the section-chief level. More commonly it is written by the person in charge of a certain matter below that level. . . . The simplest routine matters are simply written on a standard printed form as a *ringi* document. And at the other extreme, covering important matters, decisions are made before the *ringi* is ever written and passed around. Of course, *ringi* does serve to make the content of the decision clear, to put things on record, and to keep people in various parts of the organization mutually informed.[13]

Ojimi also informs us that although there is reluctance to revise the *ringi* document as it moves up the ladder of bureaucratic hierarchy, some administrators do propose revisions from time to time. Moreover, he states that "there are no matters where the power of subordinates is greater than that of superiors. . . . Subordinates give their opinions freely and generously but there are no cases where the actions of the subordinates do not reflect the intentions of their superiors."[14] From this account of how *ringisei* works, Ezra F. Vogel concludes that the "*ringi* system is often an *ato ringi* system, in which the leaders make the

---

12. Ibid., pp. 160–61.
13. Yoshihisa Ojimi, "A Government Ministry: The Case of the Ministry of International Trade and Industry" in Vogel, ed., *Modern Japanese Organization and Decision-Making*, pp. 109–10.
14. Ibid., pp. 110 and 103. The quotation is from p. 103.

major decisions and then encourage lower levels to draft documents in line with the decision."[15]

More compelling evidence underscoring the instrumental nature of *ringisei* is provided by Yung H. Park. Based on interviews with nearly two hundred former bureaucrats, politicians, cabinet ministers, and other individuals with first-hand knowledge of the situation, Park demonstrates that the notion that the *ringi* system gives subordinate officials "tyrannical powers" over superiors is a myth. He quotes, for example, Kobayashi Yukio, a former administrative vice-minister of the Ministry of Education, as saying:

> A *ringisho* is prepared by a [section] only after careful consultations with its bureau director. During the consultations he may give his approval or instructions as to how the proposal on hand should be prepared or modified. . . . Thus, a *ringisho* is a written version of what transpires between the bureau director and the [section]. Hence it is not necessarily synonymous with the ideas originally entertained by the [section].[16]

Kobayashi also told Park that a standard operating procedure is for the bureau chief to "consult with and seek approval from his superiors—[the administrative vice-minister] and, especially, the minister." The bureau chief also takes pains to clear the matter with the relevant organs of the Liberal-Democratic party (LDP), namely the division (*bukai*) of its Policy Affairs Research Council (PARC, or Seimu Chōsakai) having jurisdiction over the ministry.[17]

CONSULTATIONS WITH OTHER MINISTRIES

While decision making is under way within a ministry, consultations occur not only between the ministry and the LDP but also between the ministry and other ministries and agencies. Because jurisdictional boundaries are seldom clear-cut and because most issues encroach upon the bailiwicks of several ministries and agencies, interministerial consultations and coordination are a sine qua non. All proposals for legislation and ordinances need a stamp of approval from the cabinet legislation

15. Ezra F. Vogel, "Introduction: Toward More Accurate Concepts," in ibid., p. xvii. "Ato ringi" may be translated as "prearranged *ringi*."
16. Park, *Bureaucrats and Ministers in Contemporary Japanese Government*, p. 21. In his original text Park uses the word "division" for *ka*. I have substituted "section" for "division" to maintain consistency.
17. Ibid., pp. 21–22.

bureau (Naikaku Hōseikyoku), which acts as legal advisor for the executive branch.[18]

Any proposal for new policy requiring an expenditure of funds must also be cleared with the Ministry of Finance. Whereas consultations with these two agencies leave relatively little room for compromise, those with other ministries and agencies usually involve a symmetry of power. If compromise proves to be elusive, mediation by a third party may become necessary. Occasionally, the ministry asks its PARC counterpart in the LDP to assume the role of mediator. In short, the three most important external organizations in the decision-making process are the cabinet legislation bureau, the Finance Ministry, and the PARC division of the LDP.[19]

INTRAMINISTERIAL DECISION MAKING

With regard to intraministerial decision making, there are a number of mechanisms for reaching a consensus, such as bureau conference (*kyokugi*), leaders' conference (*kanbu kaigi*), interbureau liaison conference (*kakukyoku renraku kaigi*) and ministry conference (*shōgi*). Although specific forms used vary from ministry to ministry, the aim of these conferences is to enable responsible officials at various levels to exchange ideas, iron out differences, and form a common outlook and approach.[20]

In the Finance Ministry, bureau conference is subdivided into regular (*kyokugi*) and "important" (*jūyō kyokugi*). The latter, which serves as the highest decision-making body of each bureau, is attended by the bureau chief, his deputy, section chiefs, and assistant section chiefs. Occasionally, even subsection chiefs and senior members of subsections (*shunin*) are invited. To promote free discussion by all participants, one bureau is said to impose fines on those who fail to speak up.[21] The regular bureau conference is presided over by the assistant bureau chief. The supreme decision-making organ of the Finance Ministry as a whole is leaders' conference. Held every Monday, this "summit conference" is

---

18. On the role of the Cabinet Legislation Bureau, consult Kyōikusha, *Kaikei Kensa-in, Jinji-in, Naikaku Hōseikyoku*, pp. 119–63.

19. Murakawa, *Seisaku kettei katei*, pp. 128–29.

20. Ibid., pp. 132–37; Ojimi, "A Government Ministry," p. 102.

21. Sakakibara, *Nihon o enshutsu suru shin kanryōzō*, p. 56; Kuribayashi, *Ōkurashō shukeikyoku*, p. 53.

attended by the administrative vice-minister, the assistant vice-minister for financial affairs (*zaimukan*), chiefs of the seven main bureaus (*honshō shichikyoku*), and the chief of the minister's secretariat. Occasionally, the director general of the Tax Administration Agency (Kokuzeichō chōkan), the chief of the Mint Bureau, and the chief of the Printing Bureau also join the select group. In addition, section chiefs of the minister's secretariat observe the proceedings. The difficult task of reconciling conflicting positions, however, is performed in advance of a leaders' conference through consultations and negotiations among senior section chiefs representing the various bureaus.[22]

The Role of the LDP   When the minister officially gives his final approval, the policy proposal formally becomes that of the ministry. After the cabinet legislation bureau and the Finance Ministry have officially endorsed it, the proposal is submitted to the appropriate PARC division of the LDP. There are seventeen PARC divisions, each of which supervises one or more ministries and agencies.[23] All members of the divisions are LDP Diet members, who are required by party rules to belong to at least one division.[24] The chairmanships of the divisions usually go to LDP Diet members who have been elected at least three times, most of whom have previously served as directors (*riji*) of Diet standing committees, parliamentary vice-ministers, or deputy chairmen of PARC divisions.[25] According to Yung H. Park:

> PARC divisional chairmanship is a key policy-making office. In the area of divisional jurisdiction, the chairman is one of the most powerful actors. . . .

22. Jin, *Ōkura kanryō*, pp. 171–72.
23. The divisions are (1) Cabinet, (2) Local Administration, (3) National Defense, (4) Justice, (5) Foreign Affairs, (6) Finance, (7) Education, (8) Social Affairs [*Shakai Bukai*], (9) Labor, (10) Agriculture and Forestry, (11) Fisheries, (12) Commerce and Industry, (13) Transportation, (14) Communications, (15) Construction, (16) Science and Technology, and (17) Environment. *Seiji handobukku* [Handbook of Politics], February 1987 (Tokyo: Seiji Kōhō Sentaà, 1987), pp. 179–82.
24. Inoguchi Takashi and Iwai Tomoaki, *"Zoku giin" no kenkyū* [A Study of "Tribal Diet Members"] (Tokyo: Nihon Keizai Shinbunsha, 1987), pp. 103–4. Because all LDP Diet members, except those serving as cabinet ministers and parliamentary vice-ministers, automatically belong to the PARC divisions that are counterparts of the Diet standing committees of which they are members, they are allowed to join two additional divisions. This means that most LDP Diet members belong to three divisions.
25. Satō Seisaburō and Matsuzaki Tetsuhisa, *Jimintō seiken* [The Regime of the Liberal Democratic Party] (Tokyo: Kōdansha, 1986), pp. 39 and 85–86. According to Inoguchi and Iwai, most divisional chairmen have been elected to the Diet four times. See their *"Zoku giin" no kenkyū*, p. 121.

As far as the ministry under the division's supervision is concerned, he is the first and, most likely, the foremost party figure who must be persuaded in support of its major policy programs. Without his blessings, no agency policy can get party authorization. Hence he plays a major role in agency policy and budgetary processes and even in agency personnel decisions. He is a principal medium through whom the party influences ministry decisions.[26]

As mentioned earlier, consultations between the ministry and the PARC division usually precede the formal submission of the ministry's legislative proposal, hence the deliberations in the division are sometimes a mere formality. The relatively large size of divisions also serves to inhibit an in-depth evaluation of legislative proposals by them. Some divisions have over a hundred members. As of March 1986, for example, the Agriculture and Forestry Division had 149 members. Substantive decisions are frequently made in informal meetings of Diet members that have become specialists in the subject matter at hand; known as *zoku giin* (literally, "tribal Diet members"), these include the chairmen of PARC divisions. Officials of the ministries concerned usually participate in such informal meetings.[27]

Most of the deliberations in formal sessions of PARC divisions take less than one and a half hours. Thanks to painstaking preparatory work, known as *nemawashi*, the ministry's proposal is approved intact in nine out of ten cases. Because all of the division members also belong to the Diet standing committee having jurisdiction over the same ministry, their participation in this stage of policy making helps them become better prepared for the task of defending the bill against attacks by opposition Diet members in the legislative stage.[28]

The PARC Deliberation Commission (Seimu Chōsakai Shingikai), to which the policy proposal goes next, consists of about thirty members, including the chairman and vice-chairmen of the PARC. Whereas in the preceding stage the responsibility of defending the proposal rested with the bureau chief and section chiefs of the ministry, in the Shingikai phase the ball is carried by the chairman of the PARC division, who sometimes seeks the assistance of bureaucrats when questions become too technical or specific. In rare cases where a division of opinion

26. Park, *Bureaucrats and Ministers*, p. 38.
27. Satō and Matsuzaki, *Jimintō seiken*, pp. 91–93.
28. Murakawa, *Seisaku kettei katei*, pp. 146–51. For an explanation of *nemawashi*, see Vogel, "Introduction: Toward More Accurate Concepts," pp. xxii–xxiii.

persists, direct negotiations between the PARC chairman and the minister concerned may become necessary.[29]

The final hurdle within the LDP is the Executive Council (Sōmukai). One of the three officially designated "decision making organs" of the LDP—the other two being the party conference and the assembly of all Diet members—the Executive Council consists of thirty "executors" (*sōmu*), of whom fifteen are elected by members of the House of Representatives (Shūgiin), seven are elected by members of the House of Councillors (Sangiin), and eight are appointed by the president of the LDP. Given their prestige and power, the selection of *sōmu*, especially those appointed by the party president, is handled with great care; the need to maintain interfactional balance and other political considerations enter into the equation. Normally, only seasoned politicians, with at least four terms in the House of Representatives (fewer in the case of the upper house) and experience as parliamentary vice-ministers and committee chairmen in the Diet, can hope to win that honor.[30]

The principal criterion employed by the Executive Council is political. Will the proposed policy benefit the interests of the LDP as a whole? By the time the proposal reaches the council, its need and technical feasibility will have been thoroughly examined and certified, hence the only question that remains to be asked is "will it fly?" Will there be any adverse political fallout? If so, will the anticipated benefits outweigh them? Participating in its deliberations are not only its members but also other leaders of the party—the secretary-general (*kanjichō*), the chairman of the PARC, and the chairman of the Diet strategy committee (Kokkai Taisaku Iinchō). The job of explaining and, if necessary, defending the proposal at hand is performed by the chairman of the responsible PARC division. Although most of the proposals are approved rather routinely, some become bogged down from time to time. When that happens, there are two options: either remand the case to the PARC or refer it to the weekly meeting of top party leaders (*yakuinkai*), which is attended by the LDP president (*sōsai*), the vice-president, the secretary general, the chairmen of the Executive Council, the PARC,

---

29. Murakawa, *Seisaku kettei katei,* pp. 152–54.

30. Thayer, *How the Conservatives Rule Japan,* pp. 237–57. In Feb. 1987 the Executive Council consisted of twenty-eight executors. All eight who were appointees of the LDP President had one of three titles: president, acting president, and vice-president. Six had been elected by LDP members of the House of Councillors. *Seiji handobukku,* Feb. 1987, p. 179.

and the Diet strategy committee, and other leaders.[31] Approval by the Executive Council is all but synonymous with approval by the LDP as a whole. The LDP Diet strategy committee deals not with any substantive issues but with those of procedure and strategy. To decide when and how to introduce the bill in the Diet, the committee hears reports on informal consultations with opposition parties as well as explanations from bureaucrats.[32]

AVM CONFERENCE AND CABINET MEETINGS

The Conference of Administrative Vice-Ministers (Jimujikan Kaigi) takes up the bill after its approval by the LDP Executive Council. Convened twice a week, the AVM conference is attended by all the officials who carry the title of *jimu jikan,* namely, the highest career officials of the twelve ministries (*shō*) and those of eight cabinet-level agencies (*chō*). It is also attended by the deputy director general of the cabinet secretariat (Naikaku Kanbō fuku chōkan), the director general of the Police Agency (Keisatsuchō chōkan), and the deputy director general (*jikan*) of the cabinet legislation bureau.[33]

Although the AVM conference is widely perceived as the real decision-making organ in the executive branch, its short duration belies its reputation. The conference, in the form of working breakfasts, usually lasts less than an hour. Like most meetings in Japan, it too is preceded by extensive *nemawashi,* which obviates the need for further negotiation. According to Tahara Soichirō, who interviewed a number of participant observers, the AVM conference has become a mere formality; one of his informants went so far as to call it a "completely skeletonized" thing (*kanzenni keigaika shite iru*).[34]

31. Murakawa, *Seisaku kettei katei,* pp. 154–56. On the role of the leaders' meeting, consult Fukui, *Party in Power,* pp. 93–95.

32. Murakawa, *Seisaku kettei katei,* pp. 157–58. On the role of the Executive Council, consult Fukui, *Party in Power,* pp. 89–92; on the role of the Diet Strategy Committee, consult Baerwald, *Japan's Parliament,* pp. 84–86.

33. Tahara, *Nihon no kanryō,* pp. 9–13; Murakawa, *Seisaku kettei katei,* pp. 159–61. The eight cabinet-level agencies are Management and Coordination, Hokkaido Development, Defense, Economic Planning, Science and Technology, Environment, Okinawa Development, and National Land. The Management and Coordination Agency (*Sōmuchō*) was established in July 1984 by merging part of the Prime Minister's Office (*Sōrifu*) with the Administrative Management Agency (*Gyōsei Kanrichō*). See "Kasumigaseki toppu no kao: Jimu jikan" [Faces of the Top Men in Kasumigaseki: Administrative Vice-ministers], *Kankai,* Sept. 1985, an unpaged pictorial essay.

34. Tahara, *Nihon no kanryō,* p. 13.

Officially, the highest decision-making organ in the executive branch is the cabinet meeting (*kakugi*). There are three types of cabinet meetings: (1) *teirei* (ordinary), (2) *rinji* (extraordinary), and (3) *mochimawari* (literally, carrying around). Ordinary cabinet meetings are held twice a week, usually on Tuesdays and Fridays, although their frequency may be reduced during the summer. Extraordinary cabinet meetings are convened whenever there is urgent business. Finally, *mochimawari kakugi* is not really a meeting, for it entails the dispatch of officials to all members of the cabinet to collect their signatures on a document. Two things make such a procedure both necessary and feasible: the lack of time to call an extraordinary meeting and the relative unimportance of the issues involved.[35]

In addition to all members of the cabinet, who number around twenty, the two deputy directors general of the cabinet secretariat (*naikaku kanbō seimu fuku chōkan* and *naikaku kanbō jimu fuku chōkan*) and the director general of the cabinet legislation bureau (*naikaku hōseikyoku chōkan*) also attend cabinet meetings, although the latter three sit apart from cabinet members in a corner of the conference room. By custom, a veil of secrecy surrounds cabinet meetings. Not even "photo opportunities" are allowed in the cabinet room itself. Nor are official minutes kept. A gist of what has transpired, however, is released to the press by the director general of the cabinet secretariat. The rule of unanimity governs the meetings, including *mochimawari kakugi*.[36]

Although, as a rule, only those matters that have been finally approved by the LDP Executive Council come before the cabinet meeting, once in a while matters that are still in the LDP pipeline may be taken up to expedite the decision-making process. Such matters are considered in the form of "items outside the agenda" (*ankengai*) and given provisional approval.[37] Given the overlap in the memberships of the cabinet and LDP policy organs, there is only a slight chance that policy proposals that have survived the rigors of LDP scrutiny will generate a fresh controversy and unanticipated problems in the cabinet meeting. In a sense, what happens in that forum is anticlimactic, for all the hard work has already been completed, and all the significant battles have been fought. If the stakes are high, the senior politicians that make

---

35. *Asahi shinbun*, 28 July 1985.
36. Ibid.; Naikaku Seido Hyakunen-shi Hensan Iinkai, ed., *Naikaku hyakunen no ayumi*, pp. 22–23; Murakawa, *Seisaku kettei katei*, pp. 161–63.
37. Ibid., pp. 162–63.

up the cabinet will already have made their inputs in the preceding phases of the policy process, in their capacities as ministers and as party leaders.

DIFFERING PERSPECTIVES ON THE PROCESS

THE QUESTION OF RELATIVE INFLUENCE

The picture of policy making sketched above is both incomplete and misleading. For one thing, there are other players in the game, such as advisory councils, interest groups, opposition parties, and the media. For another, the actual dynamics of decision making vary considerably depending on the issues and stakes involved, the idiosyncrasies of the ministries and agencies, and many other variables. Moreover, the preceding picture glosses over the controversy regarding the relative weights of bureaucrats and politicians in the policy equation. It is the last-mentioned question that we propose to explore briefly. Whether one subscribes to the elitist perspective, of which the most popular version posits a triple alliance of the LDP, the bureaucracy, and big business, or to the pluralist perspective, which stresses a diversity of participants, a fragmentation of power, and a complexity of options, there is general agreement that the bureaucracy and the LDP are the two most powerful institutions in the policy-making process.[38]

Opinion is divided about which of these two institutions is more influential. Although there is a growing tendency among scholars to view the controversy as sterile, we should nonetheless take note of two contending schools of thought: the "bureaucratic-dominance school" (*kanryō yūiron*) and the "party-dominance school" (*seitō yūiron*).

"BUREAUCRATIC-DOMINANCE" SCHOOL

Perhaps the leading exponent of the "bureaucratic-dominance school" is Tsuji Kiyoaki, a distinguished student of Japanese public administration. Tsuji argues that three developments have helped to bolster

---

38. For an overview, see Haruhiko Fukui, "Studies in Policymaking; A Review of the Literature" in T. J. Pempel, ed., *Policymaking in Contemporary Japan* (Ithaca: Cornell University Press, 1977), pp. 22–59. See also Bradley M. Richardson, "Policymaking in Japan: An Organizing Perspective" in ibid., pp. 239–68 and T. J. Pempel, "Conclusion" in ibid., pp. 318–23.

bureaucratic power in Japan. First, the decision of the Allied powers to rule postsurrender Japan indirectly meant that the government bureaucracy through which indirect government would be conducted would retain its erstwhile influence.[39] Because the other groups that had exercised power in prewar and wartime Japan—the military and financial cliques (*gunbatsu to zaibatsu*)—were dismantled by the Occupation authorities, the bureaucracy's power position actually improved after the Japanese defeat in World War II.[40]

Second, the bureaucrats benefited immensely from a strong conviction on the part of the Japanese people that bureaucracy was a neutral instrument, a conviction bordering on religion (*isshu no shinkō*). Unwilling to recognize legislators and party politicians as legitimate wielders of authority, the people sought consolation from the "fantasy" of bureaucratic neutrality.[41] Third, the weaknesses of other political forces, particularly party politicians, further contributed to the ascendancy of bureaucrats.[42]

To the preceding list, Chalmers Johnson, a leading American student of Japanese bureaucracy, would add a fourth reason for the expansion of bureaucratic influence: "the requirements of economic recovery led to a vast ballooning of the bureaucracy." The upshot of all this, in Johnson's words, is that "although it is influenced by pressure groups and political claimants, the elite bureaucracy of Japan makes most major decisions, drafts virtually all legislation, controls the national budget, and is the source of all major policy innovations in the system."[43] In a more recent study, however, Johnson writes that "during the late 1970s a subtle combination of events started an apparent decline in the power of the bureaucracy and a concurrent rise in the power of the LDP—or, as the Japanese press puts it, a trend away from the *kanryō shudo taisei* (bureaucratic leadership structure) toward the *to shudo taisei* (party leadership structure)."[44] We shall address this theme in the next section.

Nonetheless, the bureaucracy's virtual monopoly on bill-drafting is indisputable. Throughout the postwar period, nearly nine of every ten

39. Tsuji, *Shinpan Nihon kanryōsei no kenkyū*, pp. 273–75.
40. One of the first observers to note this phenomenon was John M. Maki. See his article, "The Role of Bureaucracy in Japan," *Pacific Affairs*, 20(Dec. 1947): 391.
41. Tsuji, *Shinpan Nihon kanryōsei no kenkyū*, pp. 275–77.
42. Ibid., pp. 277–81.
43. Johnson, *MITI and the Japanese Miracle*, pp. 44 and 20–21.
44. Chalmers Johnson, "Tanaka Kakuei, Structural Corruption, and the Advent of Machine Politics in Japan," *Journal of Japanese Studies*, 12, no. 1(Winter 1986): 24.

bills enacted into law by the Japanese Diet have originated in the cabinet, meaning the bureaucracy. Although the proportion of cabinet-sponsored bills has begun to decline slightly since the 1970s, it still exceeds the 80-percent mark.[45]

Moreover, as T. J. Pempel has demonstrated, the success rate of cabinet-sponsored (hence bureaucracy-drafted) bills was higher than 75 percent between December 1955 and December 1970, whereas that of bills sponsored by individual members of the Diet ranged between 11 and 14 percent during the same period.[46] The success rate of cabinet bills has remained high in recent years; in the 1980s it has ranged from 72 percent in the 108th Diet (December 1986–May 1987) to 95 percent in the 96th Diet (December 1981–August 1982).[47] The preponderance of the bureaucracy in drafting legislation continues unabated.

As for the bureaucracy's control over the national budget, a careful study by John C. Campbell has shown that although the Ministry of Finance exerts a powerful influence in Japan's budget-making process, it nonetheless shares power with the LDP. Even when the latter does not intervene directly, Finance Ministry bureaucrats try to anticipate LDP reactions. However, "the most striking aspect of Japanese budgeting, to those familiar with other budget systems, is that the major party organization intervenes routinely at nearly all stages of the budgetary process." On the other hand, the real impact of LDP organs, such as PARC, is diluted by their need to depend on the bureaucracy and sometimes on interest groups for information. The lack of sufficient time further hampers the exercise of effective party control.[48]

Three other indicators of "bureaucratic dominance" merit brief mention: (1) the prevalence of former bureaucrats in the LDP, (2) the quasi-legislative powers of the bureaucracy, and (3) de facto bureaucratic control over advisory commissions. A significant development in postwar Japan has been the entry of a large number of former bureaucrats into the political arena, a development that has been aided by the custom of early retirement for higher civil servants as well as by

45. For relevant statistics, see Domoto Seiji, "Seisaku keisei katei no shisutemu: Hōan seitei katei ni miru seifu yotō kan chōsei" [The Policy-Making Process: Mutual Adjustment Between the Government and the Ruling Party in the Legislative Process], *Jurisuto*, special issue, no. 29 (Winter 1983): 57, and Satō and Matsuzaki, *Jimintō seiken*, pp. 277–79.

46. T. J. Pempel, "The Bureaucratization of Policymaking in Postwar Japan, *American Journal of Political Science* 18, no. 4 (Nov. 1974): 650, table 1.

47. *Asahi shinbun*, 28 May 1987.

48. Campbell, *Contemporary Japanese Budget Politics*, pp. 137–43, 2, and 127–28. The quotation is from p. 2.

their political ambition. As a result, about 25 percent of LDP Diet members have been former bureaucrats. Inasmuch as LDP Diet members constitute virtually the exclusive source of cabinet members and prime ministers, this has meant that about 40 percent of the former and 53 percent of the latter (nine out of seventeen) have been former bureaucrats.[49] The entry of so many former bureaucrats into the Diet implies that its perceived power is great. In other words, it can be treated as a sign not of bureaucratic ascendancy but of the Diet's dominance.

So far as the quasi-legislative powers of the bureaucracy are concerned, the executive branch, acting either as a group or as individual ministries and agencies, is empowered to issue ordinances and communications having the force of law. In fact, most laws contain provisions delegating ordinance powers to specific bureaucratic agencies.[50] These ordinances outnumber laws by the ratio of nine to one.[51]

Finally, the proliferation of advisory commissions (known generically as *shingikai*) has not really encroached upon bureaucratic power. On the contrary, they have actually become "tools of bureaucratic control." Bureaucrats exercise a large amount of influence over the selection of *shingikai* members, control "the areas of investigation," provide the staff and expertise for investigation, and draft the reports.[52]

"PARTY-DOMINANCE SCHOOL"

Just as journalistic exposés have played a considerable part in popularizing the concept of "bureaucratic domination" (*kanryō shihai*), so

49. Jung-Suk Youn, "Recruitment of Political Leadership in Postwar Japan, 1958–1972," Ph.D. diss., University of Michigan, 1977, Chap. 5; Peter P. Cheng, "The Japanese Cabinets, 1885–1973; An Elite Analysis," *Asian Survey* 14, no. 12 (Dec. 1974): 1066; Key Sung Ryang, "Postwar Japanese Political Leadership—A Study of Prime Ministers," ibid. 13, no. 11 (Nov. 1973): 1010–20. For more recent data, consult such standard references as *Kokkai benran* [National Diet Handbook] (published semiannually by Nihon Seikei Shinbunsha) and *Seiji handobukku* [Political Handbook] (published by Seiji Kōhō Sentā). Of the 304 LDP members elected to the House of Representatives in the "double" parliamentary election of 6 July 1986, 70 (23 percent) were former bureaucrats. The proportion in the 1983 election had been 22 percent (N = 57). *Asahi shinbun*, 8 July 1986.

50. Chalmers Johnson, "Japan: Who Governs? An Essay on Official Bureaucracy," *Journal of Japanese Studies*, 2 (Autumn 1975): 11. According to Spaulding, "the bureaucracy's ordinances powers, though still important, have been significantly narrowed. Under the 1889 Constitution, there were two main categories of executive ordinances: those implementing laws passed by the Diet and those dealing with the numerous 'imperial powers' over which the Diet had no control whatever. The second category was abolished by the 1947 constitution." Robert M. Spaulding, Jr., prepublication review of an earlier version of this study, May 1987.

51. Pempel, "The Bureaucratization of Policymaking," pp. 654–57.

52. Pempel, *Patterns of Japanese Policymaking*, pp. 70–71.

investigative reporters have been instrumental in alerting the public to what they perceive as the ascendancy of the LDP over the bureaucracy. Three examples will suffice. In a long-running series on bureaucracy begun in July 1977, *Asahi shinbun* brought to the reader's attention a steady diminution of bureaucratic influence. The paper noted that budgets prepared by Finance Ministry bureaucrats were no longer being rubber-stamped by the Diet and that in such key policy areas as setting the price of rice and health insurance, LDP politicians were clearly playing the dominant role. The paper declared that a trend toward the "predominance of politics" (*seiji no yūisei*) had become discernible since the 1960s.[53]

Another year-long series on bureaucracy in *Mainichi shinbun* in 1979–80 also documented the growing power of politicians over bureaucrats. Symptomatic of the latter's vulnerability, according to the paper, was the saying that "[the tenure of] bureau chiefs can be counted in days, [that of administrative] vice-ministers in hours." The implication was that bureaucrats in these top-level positions could lose their jobs should they antagonize key politicians in the ruling political party.[54] In a 1980 book based on serialized reports in the weekly magazine *Shūkan bunshun*, Tahara Sōichirō underscored the changing nature of the relationship between bureaucrats and politicians in Japan. He quoted Finance Ministry bureaucrats as acknowledging the erosion of their power. They told Tahara that three distinct eras could be identified in the relative power position of the Finance Ministry: the era of unipolarity (*ikkyoku kōzō jidai*), the era of bipolarity (*nikyoku kōzō jidai*), and the era of tripolarity (*sankyoku kōzō jidai*).[55]

The era of unipolarity was coterminous with the American Occupation (1945–52). During the "golden days" of the Occupation, Finance Ministry bureaucrats enhanced their power vis-à-vis other bureaucrats, the Diet, and opposition parties by invoking the name of "GHQ," that is, the General Headquarters of the Supreme Commander for the Allied Powers (SCAP). Given the absolute authority of SCAP, no one could argue with what was claimed to be a GHQ order. In their dealings with

---

53. Asahi Shinbun "Kanryō" Shuzaihan, *Kanryō: Sono seitai* [Bureaucrats: Their Mode of Life] (Tokyo: Sangyō Nōritsu Tanki Daigaku Shuppanbu, 1978), esp. pp. 143–52.
    54. Mainichi Shinbun Shakaibu, *Kanryō: Sono fushoku no kōzō*, passim. The quotation is from p. 59.
    55. Tahara, *Nihon no kanryō*, pp. 140–48.

SCAP, on the other hand, Finance Ministry bureaucrats discovered that they could have their way by alleging a strong opposition by the Diet and other ministries. Acquisition of decision-making powers by the Finance Ministry in preparing the national budget, in monetary policy, and in other areas was also facilitated by its virtual monopolization of strategic information and by the complexity of the issues involved.[56]

With the end of the Occupation, however, came an increasing assertiveness of other ministries and agencies, with which the Finance Ministry was compelled to share power. The era of bipolarity had thus begun. However, it came to an end in the latter half of the 1960s, when a new era, one of tripolarity, commenced. The third pillar of power was the LDP (notably its PARC divisions), which had acquired its own expertise in budgetary matters as well as in substantive policy areas.[57]

In the scholarly community, the most articulate proponents of "party dominance" are probably Muramatsu Michio and Yung H. Park. In his study of the perceptions of 251 bureaucrats and 101 members of the Diet, Muramatsu found substantial evidence that lends support to the journalistic impressions noted above. Table 29 indicates that all four groups with firsthand knowledge of the policy-making process chose party politicians as the most influential group in greater proportion than they did bureaucrats. To be sure, senior bureaucrats were almost evenly divided in their assessment of the relative influence of politicians and bureaucrats, but the margin is substantial among middle-level bureaucrats, whose perceptions are no less important than those of their seniors.

That LDP Diet members picked party politicians over bureaucrats by a margin of more than two to one may reflect the tendency of politicians everywhere to inflate their own importance. Because "party politicians"—actually, the Japanese term used in the interview was simply "political party" (*seitō*)[58]—implied LDP members, the responses of opposition Diet members were probably untainted by such ego-related needs. On the other hand, the impact of ideology on the latter's

56. Ibid., pp. 143–45.
57. Ibid., pp. 145–46. For a study of the role of the Finance Ministry in budget making that shows the increasing influence of both other ministries and politicians, see Kuribayashi, *Ōkurashō shukeikyoku.* Kuribayashi calls other ministries the "Second Finance Ministry" (*daini no Ōkurashō;* p. 250). For his discussion of the LDP's role, see pp. 252–54.
58. Muramatsu, *Sengo Nihon no kanryōsei,* p. 27.

TABLE 29 *Perceived Influence in Policy Making*

Groups Perceived As Most Influential	Respondents							
	Senior Bureaucrats		Middle-level Bureaucrats		LDP Diet members		Opposition Diet members	
	N	%	N	%	N	%	N	%
Party politicians	26	47.3	88	44.9	34	68.0	22	43.1
Bureaucrats	25	45.5	79	40.3	15	30.0	21	41.2
Big-businessmen	—		10	5.1	—		7	13.7
Agriculture, medicine, and other groups (excld. labor)	—		6	3.1	—		—	
Mass media	2	3.6	7	3.6	1	2.0	—	
Citizen groups	—		1	0.5	—		—	
Other	—		4	2.0	—		1	2.0
No response	2	3.6	1	0.5	—		—	
TOTAL	55	100.0	196	100.0	50	100.0	51	100.0

SOURCE: Adapted from Muramatsu Michio, *Sengo Nihon no Kanryōsei* (Tokyo: Tōyō Keizai Shinpōsha, 1981), p. 27.
NOTE: Respondents were asked to choose the three most influential groups in Japan's policy-making process. Only their first choices are reported in this table. Groups that appeared on the list but did not receive any endorsement as *the* most influential policy maker were (1) judges, (2) labor unions, (3) scholars and intellectuals, and (4) religious organizations.
"Senior bureaucrats" included administrative vice-ministers, chiefs of bureaus and minister's secretariat (*kyoku chō* and *kanbōchō*), and councillors (*shingikan*).
"Middle-level bureaucrats" included both junior and senior section chiefs (*kachō*).

TABLE 30 *Perceived Influence of Politicians and Bureaucrats[a] in Policy Making, by Country*

Group	Great Britain		West Germany		United States		Japan	
	CS	MP	CS	MP	CS	MP	CS	MP
Members of Parliament	2	12	13	22	58	—	16	35
Party leaders	44	45	81	61	20	—	55	49
Cabinet ministers	91	85	59	63	54	—	49	40
Higher civil servants	44	58	5	17	41	—	43	41
Minimum N	126	108	138	128	126	—	99	103

SOURCE: Compiled from Akira Kubota, "Kokusaitekini mita Nihon kōkyū kanryō, 7: Ōbei oyobi Nihon no kōkyū kanryō no kangaete iru seifu ritsuan katei," *Kankai*, Sept. 1978, pp. 118 and 124; ibid., "10," *Kankai*, Dec. 1978, pp. 115, 117, 120–21.
NOTE: CS refers to [higher] civil servants, MP to members of parliament.
[a]Entries are percentages of respondents from each sample who said the group in question was "extremely influential" in policy making.

perceptions is shown by the relative frequency with which "big businessmen" (*zaikai, daikigyō*) were mentioned.[59]

Table 30 displays data from another source. Compiled from a study by Akira Kubota, the table shows several interesting things.[60] First, looking at the last two columns, we find that higher civil servants in Japan rated party leaders and cabinet ministers as more influential in policy making than themselves. Interestingly, members of parliament (the Diet), while expressing an inflated estimate of their own influence, tend to be slightly more subdued in measuring the influence of party leaders and, particularly, cabinet ministers. Nonetheless, if we set aside members of the Diet, the overwhelming impression is one of bureaucrats and politicians sharing power on a more or less equal basis.

Second, comparison of Japan with the other three countries shows that the relative position of bureaucrats vis-à-vis politicians is stronger in Japan than in the other countries. Although, at first glance, the perceived influence of higher civil servants in Britain is higher than that of their Japanese counterparts, the gap between civil servants and cabinet ministers is appreciably wider in Britain than it is in Japan.

Third, the table confirms that parliament plays only a modest role in policy making in parliamentary systems; however, its perceived influence is greater in Japan than in Britain and West Germany. As

59. In interpreting these data, it may be instructive to keep in mind John C. Campbell's observation that "nearly everyone involved with Japanese budgeting finds it in his interest to magnify the role played by the majority party." Bureaucrats in both line ministries (i.e., all ministries except the Finance Ministry) and the Finance Ministry can blame the LDP for gaps, deficiencies, and problems in the budget. "Journalists find 'political interference' a dependable source of picturesque copy. LDP leaders and members also like to think of themselves as influential and surely wish to convince interest groups and constituents of their efficacy in obtaining financial benefits. Even the objective scholarly observer will tend to play up the role of the majority party, because its direct participation in decision making is one of the most distinctive features of the Japanese budgetary system." Campbell, *Contemporary Japanese Budget Politics,* pp. 137–38.

60. Kubota's study is reported in the following sources: Kubota Akira, "Seiji erīto no kokusai hikaku" [An International Comparison of Political Elites], *Kankai,* Oct. 1976, pp. 158–63; Kubota Akira and Tomita Nobuo, "Nihon seifu kōkan no ishiki kōzō: Sono kokusaiteki dōshitsusei to ishitsusei" [The Value Structure of Japanese Higher Civil Servants: Its International Homogeneity and Heterogeneity], *Chūō kōron,* Feb. 1977, pp. 190–96; Kubota Akira, "Kokusaitekini mita Nihon no kōkyū kanryō" [Japan's Higher Civil Servants in International Perspective], 20 parts, *Kankai,* Mar. 1978–Oct. 1979. The study was part of a multinational comparative research project based at the University of Michigan. The Japanese phase of the project was undertaken by Kubota (University of Windsor), Tomita Nobuo (Meiji University), and Ide Yoshinori (University of Tokyo). The book by Aberbach and his colleagues cited at the outset of this chapter (see n. 1) is basically a report of the larger research project; it, however, omits the Japanese portion of the project altogether.

might be expected, parliament (Congress) is perceived as having the greatest amount of influence in the United States.

As noted earlier, Yung H. Park's study, published in 1986, is based on interviews with more than two hundred politicians, bureaucrats, and other knowledgeable persons. He attributes an increase in the relative influence of cabinet ministers and LDP politicians to several factors, of which the most notable are the "specialization" of politicians and the "partisanization" of former bureaucrats who enter politics.[61]

The specialization of politicians refers to "the accumulation of vast administrative knowledge and experience in the hands of politicians," which has been brought about by the prolonged rule of the LDP and the multiplication of opportunities for LDP Diet members to serve as parliamentary vice-ministers, ministers, and members of Diet standing committees and PARC divisions. LDP Diet members with specialized knowledge operate in informal policy groups known as *zoku* (literally, tribe).[62]

The growing prominence of *zoku* Diet members may indeed be the single most important indicator of a shift in the balance of power in Japan's policy-making arena, a shift the Japanese press has dubbed *tōkō kantei* (the ascendancy of party and the decline of bureaucracy) and *tōkō seitei* (the ascendancy of party and the decline of politics). The party (*tō*) in these phrases refers to the LDP.[63]

Becoming a member of *zoku,* of which there were eleven in 1987—commerce and industry, agriculture and forestry, fisheries, transportation, construction, social welfare, labor, education, posts and telecommunications, finance, and national defense—however, is not

61. Park, *Bureaucrats and Ministers,* pp. 29–54. Spaulding reminds us that "in the United States, [the specialization of politicians] has been augmented by a huge increase in the size of the Congressional *staff,* so that even a Congress member lacking specialized knowledge has access to it without relying on the executive branch." Spaulding, prepublication review of an earlier version of this study, May 1987. Although the Japanese Diet, too, has an independent research staff—in the form of research offices (*chōsa shitsu*) attached to standing committees, legislation bureaus (*hōsei kyoku*) in both houses, and the Investigation and Legislative Research Bureau of the National Diet Library—it pales in comparison with the resources available to members of the American Congress in terms of size and importance.

62. Park, *Bureaucrats and Ministers,* p. 30. The importance of *zoku* is also explained in Kawaguchi Hiroyuki, "Jimintō habatsu to kanryō, joron: Kyōson suru habatsu to 'zoku'" [Liberal-Democratic Party Factions and Bureaucrats, Introduction: The Coexistence of Factions and "Tribes"], *Kankai,* Mar. 1983, pp. 98–109. Campbell also mentions *zoku* but implies that their role is relatively marginal; he defines them as "numbers of LDP members who get together only at budget time to press for greater expenditures in some policy area." Campbell, *Contemporary Japanese Budget Politics,* pp. 118–19.

63. Inoguchi and Iwai, *"Zoku giin" no kenkyū,* pp. i–iii and 1–40.

easy. An LDP Diet member must fulfill the requirements of seniority, experience, and expertise before he is accepted as a full-fledged member of a *zoku*. Generally speaking, appointment as chairman of a PARC division signifies such a status. This in turn requires not only four terms as a Diet member but also the acquisition of expertise in a substantive policy area through previous participation in policy making in that area.[64] An additional factor in the selection of divisional chairmen is factional balance. The seventeen LDP Diet members who were appointed as divisional chairmen in November 1987 following the inauguration of the Takeshita administration were divided as follows: four from the Takeshita faction, three each from the Miyazawa, Abe, and Nakasone factions, one from the Kōno faction, and three from the House of Councillors.[65]

Thanks to prolonged immersion in their chosen field of specialization, members of *zoku* can frequently boast more expertise in their field of specialization than senior bureaucrats, who are subject to frequent rotation in assignments. Even former bureaucrats, who constitute a sizable proportion of the LDP Diet contingent, undergo a socialization process during which they internalize the goals and values of the LDP, becoming politicized and "partisanized." Yung H. Park argues that this serves to undercut the widely held assumption that former bureaucrats in the Diet and the cabinet are "Trojan horses" that augment the influence of their erstwhile colleagues.[66]

"Partisanization" occurs not only among former bureaucrats who enter politics but also among incumbent bureaucrats, particularly those at the bureau-chief level, who interact most frequently with politicians. All this spawns the phenomenon known as the "politicization of administration" (*gyosei no seijika*). Government ministries are depicted as being mere "support arms" for the LDP and its *zoku* or "junior partners" with the LDP or as "suffocating" under LDP pressure.[67]

In table 30 we saw that, with the notable exception of the U.S. Congress, parliaments are perceived as having only modest influence in policy making; however, the Japanese Diet received higher marks than either the British Parliament or the West German Bundestag. Both Muramatsu and Park show that the influence of the Diet as perceived by bureaucrats and politicians alike is far greater than conventional

64. Ibid., pp. 120–21 and 293–304.
65. *Asahi shinbun*, 13 Nov. 1987.
66. Park, *Bureaucrats and Ministers*, pp. 33–47.
67. Ibid., pp. 95–96.

wisdom suggests. Eight percent of Muramatsu's respondents said that the Diet played a decisive role in enacting legislation, whereas 68 percent said that it exercised a fair amount of influence (*kanari eikyō ari*).[68] According to Park, the "importance of the contemporary Diet is most visible . . . in its reactive roles of amending, delaying, and rejecting government-LDP bills."[69] In fact, 22 percent of the bills enacted by the House of Representatives (266 out of 1,208) during the 1967–75 period (the 56th through the 76th Diet) and 17.6 percent of those enacted by the House of Representatives (178 out of 1,009) during the 1976–86 period (the 77th through the 104th Diet) were amended during the legislative stage.[70]

Hans H. Baerwald, a leading authority on the Diet, also rejects "the concept of the Diet as an absolute nullity." In his words, "substantive decisions, to be sure, are made outside the Diet, but if they are to be effectuated (that is, generally accepted as being legitimately a part of the law of the land) their proponents must take into account the balance of forces present in the Diet at a given point of time. . . . The Diet's most crucial role is to reflect the divisions of opinion and the pluralistic groups of the Japanese society."[71]

Finally, the proponents of the "party-dominance school" underscore the growing importance of interest groups. Although the respondents in Muramatsu's survey rarely chose interest groups as the most influential factor in policy making (see table 30), they mentioned interest groups much more frequently as their second and third choices.[72] As Park puts it, "interest groups have become increasingly multitudinous and assertive, performing, with a growing vigor, functions of initiating, amending, and rejecting, thus limiting the traditional discretion of bureaucratic policymakers." He adds that interest groups also make life difficult by taking their case directly to LDP politicians.[73]

As mentioned previously, Chalmers Johnson has taken note of the preceding developments. He attributes the "apparent trend" toward the consolidation of "party leadership structure" not only to the professionalization of politicians but also to "excessive 'sectionalism' and

68. Muramatsu, *Sengo Nihon no kanryōsei*, p. 182, table 5-2.
69. Park, *Bureaucrats and Ministers*, p. 110.
70. These statistics were computed from the data in Satō and Matsuzaki, *Jimintō seiken*, pp. 282–85.
71. Baerwald, *Japan's Parliament*, p. 140.
72. Muramatsu, *Sengo Nihon no kanryōsei*, p. 28, table 1-4. For an extended analysis of interest groups, see ibid., pp. 207–56.
73. Park, *Bureaucrats and Ministers*, pp. 126–27.

jurisdictional infighting within the bureaucracy" and "a shift in the recruitment of political leadership away from ex-bureaucrats and toward long-incumbent pure politicians." He shows that former Prime Minister Tanaka Kakuei has played a major role in "bring[ing] the bureaucracy to heel" and that in so doing Tanaka has helped to set off a trend toward "a genuine democratization"—"in the sense that the previously very large gap between the real power and the legal authority of political officeholders in Japan is narrowing."[74]

In a provocative study published in 1987, Yamaguchi Jirō argues that a milestone event that marked the beginning of the end of bureaucratic dominance was the 1965 decision of the Japanese government to abandon the balanced budget and start financing deficits with government bonds. A decisive factor in this policy change, according to Yamaguchi, was political resolve (*seijiteki ketsudan*), specifically that of Fukuda Takeo, who became finance minister in June 1965. Increased revenues led to stepped-up competition for funds by the various ministries and agencies, a marked growth in interest-group activities, and, most important, an escalation of intervention by LDP politicians in the budgetary process. The politicization of the budgetary process was further fueled by the deliberate policy of the Finance Ministry's Budget Bureau to restrain government spending through what it hoped would be checks and balances of political competition. In Yamaguchi's view, however, the end of bureaucratic dominance does not necessarily imply the advent of the era of an unquestioned party, that is, LDP, supremacy. Rather, the two sets of actors, bureaucrats and LDP politicians, interact and cooperate with each other to a higher degree than ever before.[75]

AN ASSESSMENT

Given the complexity of the real world, which is susceptible to neither sweeping generalizations nor simplistic conceptualization, we cannot settle the controversy regarding who governs Japan in any conclusive manner. As Chalmers Johnson has pointed out, "political rivals to bureaucratic power . . . existed both before and after the war, but it would require detailed ministry-by-ministry analysis to determine

---

74. Johnson, "Tanaka Kakuei," pp. 24–28.
75. Yamaguchi, *Ōkura kanryō shihai no shūen*, pp. 16 and 123–329.

which power was ascendant where in either the prewar or postwar periods."[76]

If the various case studies that have been published thus far prove anything, it is that there is no single dominant pattern. The configuration of forces varies from case to case, to such an extent that what figures prominently in one case becomes all but irrelevant in another. Interest groups, for example, played a pivotal role in a number of cases and were strikingly ineffectual in others. In some cases, notably Japan's decision to normalize relations with the People's Republic of China, even opposition politicians played a prominent part.[77] Just how complex the reality can be is underscored by Bradley M. Richardson, who is able to conceptualize seven different patterns of policy making in the space of a single year and by T. J. Pempel, who identifies three distinct patterns of policy making in the same policy area, namely, higher education.[78]

Notwithstanding all this, the proposition that change has occurred in the course of time—that there has been a steady increase in both the influence and expertise of LDP politicians—seems plausible enough.[79] Most often, however, LDP politicians and bureaucrats have a remarkable harmony of interests. As Nathaniel Thayer has pointed out, they should not be regarded as mutually antagonistic; more often than not, they are partners.[80] This is not very far removed from what happens in other industrialized democracies, although it represents a drastic change from prewar Japanese attitudes. According to Aberbach et al.: "Although the relationship between politicians and bureaucrats in Western polities has competitive features, it is *not* fundamentally one of zero-sum conflict, in which any gain for politicians is a loss for bureaucrats and vice versa. Both can make important contributions to public policy and, conversely, both can be weak and ineffective."[81]

In comparative terms, the predominance of bureaucrats in policy initiation is "a pervasive. . . phenomenon rather than the exception."[82]

76. Johnson, "Japan: Who Governs?", p. 14.
77. See the cases analyzed in Fukui, *Party in Power*, pp. 173–262; Hiroshi Itoh, trans. and ed., *Japanese Politics—An Inside View* (Ithaca: Cornell University Press, 1973), pp. 49–87; Pempel, *Policymaking in Contemporary Japan*, chaps. 3–6.
78. Ibid., pp. 239–307.
79. Even Chalmers Johnson, who until 1986 was perceived as a leading critic of the party-dominance school, agreed in 1982 that "ever since the creation in 1955 of the Liberal Democratic Party, politicians slowly had been rising in power as rivals to the bureaucrats, although the bureaucrats were not fully attuned to what was happening." Johnson, *MITI and the Japanese Miracle*, p. 247.
80. Thayer, *How the Conservatives Rule Japan*, p. 226.
81. Aberbach et al., *Bureaucrats and Politicians*, p. 251.
82. Ibid., p. 245.

Hence image I, which denies an activist role for civil servants in policy development, can be dismissed as a mirage. On the other hand, bureaucrats do function, in Japan and Western democracies alike, as the principal source of expertise, whereas politicians inject into policy making a large dose of "political sensitivity." Image II, in other words, does seem to capture a large measure of the reality. Its chief problem, however, is the assumption that bureaucrats are apolitical, that their expertise comes in a politically neutral form. The evidence to support that view is rather thin.

Image III overcomes the problem by positing that "bureaucrats and politicians are both active participants in the policy process, but each responds to an audience different both in character and in size, and each imparts a distinctive orientation to the policy process."[83] Aberbach and his associates add:

> Bureaucrats are integrators, preferring tranquility, predictability, manageability, and tidiness. Politicians, on the other hand, are partisans who bring both visionary and particularistic elements to the process. They bring general direction, but rarely a concern for detail. Bureaucrats at times must persuade politicians to confront vague goals with intractable facts, and politicians, in turn, sometimes must stretch the incrementalist instincts of bureaucrats. These distinctions express the contemporary division of labor between bureaucrats and politicians.[84]

Although these generalizations appear broadly applicable to Japan, there is one key difference: whereas in Western democracies "bureaucrats, in fact, have more contact with organized interests than do politicians,"[85] the reverse is true in Japan. Of all the groups with which the higher civil servants in his study came into contact, Kubota found that "representatives of clientele groups" ranked at the bottom, whereas they were in the middle of the politicians' list.[86] In sum, image III seems to reflect the situation in Western democracies to an appreciably greater degree than it does the Japanese case.

Image IV, too, finds some, but not overwhelming, support in Japan and some Western democracies. As we have seen, there is evidence of

---

83. Ibid., p. 93.
84. Ibid.
85. Ibid., p. 213.
86. Kubota, "Kokusaitekini mita Nihon no kōkyū kanryō," parts 5, 6, and 8, *Kankai*, July, Aug., Oct. 1978. Because Kubota does not provide data on the actual frequency of contacts between bureaucrats and representatives of clientele groups, a precise comparison cannot be made. Nonetheless, both his indexes and narrative analysis leave no doubt about the points being made here.

both a politicization of bureaucrats and a "bureaucratization" of politicians, in the sense of the latter's acquiring substantive expertise in specific policy areas. When this is seen in conjunction with the entry of a large number of former bureaucrats into the political arena, the proposition that the boundary line between bureaucrats and politicians has become blurred, spawning "pure hybrids," does not appear to be completely off the mark.

Insofar as the actual penetration of the political arena, principally parliament, by bureaucrats is concerned, it occurs in Japan, France, and West Germany but not in Britain and the United States. In some ways the phenomenon is more significant in France and West Germany than it is in Japan, for in the former, bureaucrats need not resign to run for elective offices.[87] Nonetheless, "pure hybrids" remain a distinct minority in all three countries. Hence image IV illuminates but a small part of the complex reality

To sum up, then, although none of the four images is fully satisfactory, image III comes closer than the others to capturing the most conspicuous aspects of the reality. However, it seems to have a better fit with Western democracies than it does with Japan. What is common to all these polities is that "bureaucrats and politicians are interdependent participants in the policy process."[88] To the extent that they have not become interchangeable, however, their distinct modes of operation pose dilemmas: bureaucratic policy making poses the dilemma of "power without responsibility," whereas policy making by politicians generates the dilemma of "power without competence." In the words of Aberbach et al, "excessively bureaucratic policymaking may lead to a crisis of legitimacy, but excessively political policymaking threatens a crisis of effectiveness."[89] The obvious challenge, then, is to find a happy medium, a means of mutual accommodation that can maximize the strengths of both bureaucrats and politicians, while minimizing their weaknesses. Whether Japan has found such a creative solution remains to be seen.

87. In prewar and wartime Japan, higher civil servants had the option of "transfer[ring] from the bureaucracy to appointive positions in the House of Peers, an option not available after 1947." Spaulding, prepublication review of an earlier version of this study, May 1987.
88. Aberbach et al., *Bureaucrats and Politicians*, p. 252.
89. Ibid., p. 255.

CHAPTER EIGHT

Rewards

In order to attract and keep qualified men and women, bureaucracy needs to have an adequate system of rewards. The rewards may be either tangible or intangible, immediate or deferred. Tangible rewards include salary and fringe benefits, and intangible rewards encompass a sense of service, the prestige and power of office, and the like. If, in addition to all this, service in government bureaucracy can facilitate subsequent career advancement, then it generates long-term rewards.

In this chapter we shall examine both the immediate and the deferred rewards of Japanese bureaucracy. We shall first note a few salient aspects of the compensation system. Second, we shall touch briefly on the question of corruption among Japanese civil servants. Third, we shall discuss the reemployment of retired higher civil servants. Finally, we shall try to place the Japanese case in comparative perspective.

COMPENSATION

SALARY SCHEDULES

As we saw in chapter 4, Japan's national public employees are divided into a number of different categories; for purposes of compensation, the two most important categories are (1) employees who are subject to the regular compensation law (*kyūyohō shokuin*) and (2) those governed by the special compensation law (*kyūyo tokureihō shokuin*). Because the latter consist mainly of postal employees, however, we shall be concerned primarily with the former.

The regular-compensation-law employees are divided into seventeen salary schedules (*hōkyūhyō*). Table 31 displays selected attributes of each schedule. First, by far the largest is the Administrative Service (*gyōsei shoku*) I, which accounts for nearly half of all public employees covered by the regular-compensation law. As we have previously noted, the higher civil servants with whom this study deals belong for the most part to this category.

Second, in terms of average age, the Designated Service (*shitei shoku*) surpasses all the others, because this category consists of administrative vice ministers and their equivalents, bureau chiefs, university presidents, directors of research institutes and hospitals, and other high-ranking officials. Given the rule of lifetime employment, it is not surprising that average age and average length of service are highly correlated.

Third, the proportion of college graduates varies widely from schedule to schedule. The top three categories are the Designated Service; the Medical Service (*iryō shoku*) I, which is made up of physicians and dentists; and the Educational Service (*kyōiku shoku*) I, which consists of college professors. Overall, the level of educational attainments is quite high; one of every three civil servants is a college graduate, and well over half have had at least two years of college.

Finally, the proportion of women, too, varies widely from schedule to schedule. Although there are no women in the Marine Service (*kaiji shoku*) II, they all but monopolize the Medical Service III, which is made up of midwives, nurses, and nursing assistants.

Each of these salary schedules encompasses a number of grades, each of which in turn subsumes a number of steps. Until 1985 the Administrative Service I salary schedule consisted of eight grades. Effective 1 July 1986 the number of grades increased to eleven. Table 32 presents basic data on the revised structure of the Administrative Service I. Whereas, in the old system, the lowest grade was 8 and the highest 1, the new system has reversed the order: the higher the grade level, the larger the number.

The number of steps within grades ranges from fifteen to twenty-eight, which accounts for the wide range in monthly salaries within each grade. Step 16 in grade 1, for example, pays more than step 1 in grade 3; step 28 in grade 4 pays more than step 1 in Grade 10; and step 24 in grade 6 pays more than step 1 in grade 11, the highest grade. This type of pay structure is designed to benefit "noncareer" civil servants, whose

TABLE 31 *Attributes of Japanese Civil Servants, by Salary Schedule, 1987*

Salary Schedule	Mean Age	Mean Length of Service (yrs.)	Col.	J.C.	H.S.	M.S.	Women (%)	N
					(%)			
Administrative service I	39.6	19.6	28.0	9.6	58.8	3.6	14.7	227,725
Administrative service II	47.5	27.0	1.2	2.0	36.2	60.6	28.6	33,100
Specialized adm. service	38.4	16.6	40.6	31.6	26.7	1.1	2.7	6,232
Taxation service	37.1	17.5	25.6	5.1	68.3	1.0	8.9	50,137
Public security service I	38.0	16.7	28.9	3.6	60.8	6.7	3.4	18,265
Pub. security service II	40.7	20.3	29.8	22.6	37.3	10.3	3.1	20,643
Marine service I	42.7	21.3	51.3	17.8	17.0	13.9	0.5	630
Marine service II	42.4	25.0	0.3	2.2	32.9	64.6	—	1,435
Educational service I	44.3	20.5	96.3	2.8	0.8	0.1	6.6	52,619
Educational service II	39.8	17.0	87.3	11.2	0.9	0.6	30.6	2,131
Educational service III	39.1	16.5	93.0	6.6	0.4	—	22.6	3,456
Educational service IV	44.8	21.6	77.8	20.6	1.4	0.2	14.8	3,642
Research service	42.9	20.2	80.5	7.1	11.7	0.7	6.7	10,033
Medical service I	42.5	17.8	97.1	2.9	—	—	8.0	4,989
Medical service II	38.6	16.0	28.8	59.8	10.1	1.3	30.5	9,153
Medical service III	35.7	13.9	4.9	71.6	22.6	0.9	98.0	41,481
Designated service	56.9	33.4	96.7	2.8	0.4	0.1	0.4	1,357
TOTAL	40.2	19.3	34.6	14.6	43.8	7.0	20.3	487,028

SOURCE: "Sankō shiryō (kyūyo kankei)," *Jinji-in geppō* 440 (Sept. 1987): 30–31.
NOTE:
Col.	four-year college
J.C.	junior (two-year) college
H.S.	high school
M.S.	middle school

TABLE 32   *Administrative Service I Salary Schedule,*
1987–88

Grade Level	Number of Steps	Corresponding Position	Monthly Salary Range (yen)	N
1	16	subsection member	96,500–143,300	19,036
2	19	subsection member	117,900–196,700	27,488
3	28	senior subsection member (*shunin*)	137,400–261,400	43,879
4	28	subsection chief	167,600–312,800	44,555
5	26	senior subsection chief	183,200–328,300	22,784
6	24	assistant section chief	200,600–359,400	33,980
7	22	assistant section chief	217,700–368,300	14,699
8	21	senior assistant section chief	236,200–389,800	15,324
9	18	section chief	265,200–422,100	3,301
10	15	senior section chief	298,900–443,400	1,446
11	15	assistant bureau chief	341,300–503,600	1,233

SOURCES: *Jinji-in geppō* 440 (Sept. 1987): 14 and 33; *Asahi shinbun,* 12 Dec. 1987.

promotional opportunities are limited. Noncareerists tend to stay in the same grade substantially longer than "career" civil servants, hence they have a chance to climb to the highest step within each grade. Thus a veteran noncareerist who is a subsection chief usually draws a higher salary than a careerist section chief to whom he reports, and a veteran assistant section chief may be better off financially than a careerist assistant bureau chief.[1]

A few other aspects of the compensation system emerge from a review of statistics on civil-servants' compensation in two different years, 1958 and 1976.[2] First of all, if we control for the level of educational attainments, we find a linear relationship between seniority and pay. Although no comparable data are available for the 1980s, there is no reason to assume that the situation has changed to any appreciable degree. Second, in both 1958 and 1976, women lagged behind men in compensation. What is striking is that the discrepancy appears after the effects of education have been neutralized. Becuase the salary schedules per se make no distinctions between the sexes, the data

1. The Designated Service Salary Schedule, to which bureau chiefs and administrative vice-ministers belong, has twelve steps and the monthly salary range of 468,000 yen and 1,065,000 yen. *Jinji-in geppo* 440 (Sept. 1987): 28.
2. Jinji-in, *Nenji hōkokusho,* 1958, pp. 48–49; Jinji-in, Kyūyokyoku, *Kokka kōmuin kyūyotō jittai chōsa hōkokusho,* 15 Jan. 1976, pp. 38–39.

suggest that women are concentrated on the lower rungs of the ladder and receive stepwise promotions within grades at a slower pace than men.

On the other hand, the gender gap in compensation became somewhat narrower by the latter part of the 1970s than it was in the late 1950s. More important, the gap was closed completely for women with two years or less of service. It needs to be stressed, however, that the data on which these observations are based pertain to the civil service as a whole. If we look at the Administrative Service I only, the gender gap remains. Although no data are available for 1958, those for 1976 show that women lagged behind men in all categories of seniority; the first two categories nonetheless showed the smallest gaps: 0.98 for one year or less and 0.964 for one to two years.[3] The lack of more recent data prevents us from knowing whether there has been further progress on this front.

Finally, it should be pointed out that the monthly salary figures shown in table 32 and discussed in the preceding paragraphs pertain only to the basic salary (honpō). When the various allowances are added, the figures increase by 10 to 20 percent. The allowances include the dependents' allowance (fuyō teate), the housing allowance (jūkyo teate), the commuter allowance (tsūkin teate), and the adjustment allowance (chōsei teate) paid to civil servants assigned to areas where living costs are unusually high.[4] In addition, there are overtime pay and bonuses.

Although higher civil servants express embarrassment at their relatively meagre income, financial reward does not appear to figure prominently in their incentive structure. When Koitabashi Jirō, a free-lance journalist, interviewed twenty section chiefs in the various ministries and agencies, all belonging to the postwar generation, in 1985, he found that very few could cite reasonably accurate figures for their salaries, an indication of the relative unimportance of the issue. Most reported, however, that their income was between a half and two-thirds of what their peers (former college classmates) in major private firms were making. According to a section chief in the Transport

3. Ibid., pp. 40–41. Because comparable data are not available for 1958, all civil servants, instead of those in the Administrative Service (I), were used as the data base for the preceding discussion.
4. "Kōmuin kyūyo no gaiyō" [An Outline of the Compensation of Civil Servants], Jinji-in geppō 402 (July 1984): 24 and 26; "Kokka kōmuin kyūyoto jittai chōsa" [An Investigation into the Actual Conditions of National Civil Servants' Compensation and Related Matters], ibid., 420 (Jan. 1986): 7–11.

Ministry, bureaucrats sometimes earned extra money by writing magazine articles using the name of their superior, such as a bureau chief, not to enrich themselves but to generate funds with which to purchase meals at night for their unit, which is a far cry from the affluent world of private-sector managers who have the perquisities of expense accounts and business-related entertainments.[5]

THE RECOMMENDATION SYSTEM

A novel feature of the compensation system for Japanese civil servants has to do with the role of the National Personnel Authority (Jinji-in) in the determination of salary schedules. Both the national public-service law (*kokka kōmuinhō*) and the law concerning the compensation of regular service employees (*ippan shoku no shokuin no kyūyo ni kansuru hōritsu*) require the National Personnel Authority to conduct surveys to determine whether salary rates for public employees are appropriate and to report simultaneously to the Diet and the cabinet on its recommendations for revision should an adjustment of 5 percent or more either upward or downward be deemed necessary.[6]

The right, or obligation, to submit recommendations directly to both the Diet and the cabinet is significant, for no other agency belonging to the executive branch of the Japanese national government enjoys such a privilege. This was designed to bolster the independence of the National Personnel Authority in carrying out its mandate; the principal rationale for the recommendation system, which was initially imposed by the American Occupation authorities on the Japanese government, was to compensate for the restrictions on the exercise of constitutional rights by civil servants. Although article 28 of the Japanese constitution explicitly guarantees "the right of workers to organize and to bargain and act collectively,"[7] civil servants were forbidden to bargain collectively for their salary rates and, especially, to engage in strikes. It was therefore considered imperative to have a mechanism under which the right of civil servants to have a fair and equitable system of compensation would be protected. The recommendation system, in other words,

---

5. Koitabashi, *"Sengo umare" erīto kanryō no sugao*, pp. 52–66.
6. See art. 67 of the National Public Service Law and art. 2, para. 3 of the Compensation Law in Jinji-in, Nin'yokyoku, ed., *Ninmen kankei hōreishū*, 1984 ed., pp. 25 and 52.
7. See the English version of the constitution in Suekawa, ed., *Iwanami kihon roppō*, 1974 ed., p. 114.

was devised in part as a functional equivalent to wage determination by collective bargaining.[8]

The compensatory function of the recommendation system was explicitly recognized by the Japanese Supreme Court in April 1973. The court noted that the guarantee of fundamental rights for workers in article 28 of the constitution was not an end in itself but a means to the advancement of the workers' economic position, hence it could be restricted in the common interest of all the citizens. When that occurs, however, "compensatory measures" (*daishō sochi*) become necessary. According to the court, detailed regulations regarding civil servants' status, appointments, dismissals, compensation, and other conditions of work and the establishment of a central personnel administrative agency endowed with quasi-judicial powers to oversee the implementation of these regulations, particularly those relating to compensation, constituted such compensatory measures. Two judges held in a supplementary opinion that civil servants had a right to engage in limited "dispute behavior" (*sōgi kōi*) to the extent that the preceding compensatory measures failed to perform their intended functions. All the responsible authorities had an obligation to make sincere efforts within the limits of law and available resources to make the system work, they added.[9] This latter principle was reaffirmed in a more recent ruling by the Tokyo Higher Court, which held in November 1985 that the nonimplementation of the National Personnel Authority's recommendation on compensation might under certain circumstances justify strikes by civil servants.[10]

Under the recommendation system the National Personnel Authority has conducted surveys of compensation in the private sector every year with the aim of ascertaining whether government pay rates are

8. Asai Kiyoshi, "Omoide no ki: Kokka kōmuinhō no seitei to dai ikkai kyūyo kankoku" [Reminiscences: The Enactment of the National Public Service Law and the First Recommendation on Compensation], in Jinji-in, *Jinji gyōsei sanjūnen no ayumi*, pp. 38–42; Sakaiya Taiichi and Utsumi Hitoshi, "Taidan: Kōmuin kyūyo o kangaeru" [Conversation: Thinking About Civil Servants' Compensation], *Jinji-in geppō* 402 (July 1984): 4–5.

9. For excerpts from the Supreme Court decision, see *Jinji-in geppō* 402 (July 1984): 11–13. For a discussion of the case and its implications, see "Shinso o saguru: Ima magari kado ni tatsu Jinji-in" [In Search of Truth: The National Personnel Authority at a Turning Point], *Kankai*, Oct. 1984, pp. 134–43. Written by the editorial department of the magazine, this article construes the drastic cuts in the authority's recommended pay increases in the early 1980s as a sign of its decline in power.

10. *Asahi shinbun*, 20 Nov. 1985 (evening ed.). For excerpts from the decision, see ibid., p. 2.

comparable to private-sector pay rates for the same levels of work. In 1985, for example, the authority collected data on compensation from 40,660 places of work (*jigyōsho*) with fifty or more full-time workers that were part of enterprises employing at least one hundred full-time workers. All told, data were collected on more than half a million persons spanning ninety-one different occupational categories.[11] As was the case in previous surveys, the data showed that government pay rates lagged behind private-enterprise pay rates.

On the basis of detailed comparisons, controlling for type of jobs, position level, education, and age, the authority recommended an average pay increase of 5.74 percent for civil servants, effective 1 April 1986. In December 1985 the cabinet formally approved the recommendation on condition that the new rates enter into force on 1 July instead of 1 April 1986.[12] This meant, in effect, that the authority's recommendation would be diluted by 25 percent.

The record of the authority in having its recommendations implemented is somewhat mixed. Since the adoption of the recommendation system in 1948, the authority's recommendations were totally rejected twice, in 1949 and 1982, and revised six times. During the early 1950s the revisions were relatively minor: 1 percent reduction in 1950, 11 percent reduction in 1951, and 5.1 percent reduction in 1952. In 1953, there was an unprecedented upward revision, although the increase was negligible (0.02 percent).

It was in the 1980s that the authority suffered major setbacks. As noted, its recommendation was rejected in toto in 1982. The authority's proposal in 1983 for a 6.47-percent increase was scaled down to 2.03 percent, a reduction of 69 percent. In 1984, the recommended rate was cut by 48 percent, from 6.44 to 3.37 percent. The year 1985 saw a de facto reduction of 25 percent. On the other hand, during the remaining years the authority's recommendations on the upward adjustment of pay rates were implemented in full, although some of its other recommendations were occasionally amended. In August 1986 the authority recommended that an average increase of 2.31 percent be granted to civil servants, retroactive to 1 April. Although this was the lowest rate of increase ever recommended by the authority since 1960,

---

11. "Kyūyo ni kansuru hōkoku to kankoku (zenbun)" [Report and Recommendations on Compensation (Full Text)], *Jinji-in geppō* 416 (Sept. 1985): 50.

12. For reports on the handling of the National Personnel Authority's recommendations on compensation, see *Asahi shinbun*, 23 Aug., 13 Sept., 14 and 22 Oct., 5 and 6 Nov. (editorial), and 6 Dec. 1985.

the record was broken in 1987, when it recommended and the Diet approved an average increase of a mere 1.47 percent. The increase was implemented retroactively to 1 April 1987. The rates of increase recommended by the authority have ranged from none (1954) to 29.64 percent (1974).[13]

CORRUPTION

Before turning to the civil servants' retirement benefits and postretirement employment, let us examine briefly the issue of corruption. Logically, compensation and corruption are interrelated, for inadequate compensation can increase incentives for illicit financial gains. Empirically, however, the linkage between the two remains to be established. According to statistics published by the National Personnel Authority, the frequency of corruption among Japanese civil servants is remarkably low.

Table 33 presents data on two categories of behavior that pertain to corruption: embezzling public funds and accepting bribes. Other types of behavior, even when they involve public funds, were excluded from the table because they involve mistakes rather than intentional misappropriation of funds. Note also that the table pertains to all civil servants; in fact, the absence of any breakdown by rank in these data constitutes a major deficiency.

The four types of disciplinary action taken against the offending civil servants correspond with the relative severity of the breaches involved. If we look at those cases that led to the dismissal of the offenders, we find not only that their numbers are extremely small but also that they have declined over the years. On the other hand, the proportion of these most serious cases to the total cases has steadily grown: whereas they constituted less than half of the total in the 1960s, they exceeded three-quarters in the 1980s. The last column in the table shows that the decline in the frequency of corruption has not only been absolute but relative as well: whereas, in 1960, 6 of every 10,000 civil servants were disciplined for corrupt behavior, by 1975 the ratio had dropped to 2 of every 10,000, stabilizing at that level in subsequent years.

---

13. For basic facts regarding the disposition of the Authority's recommendations on composation, see Jinji-in, *Kōmuin hakusho,* 1987, pp. 198–27; "Kōmuin seido no shikumi" [The Plan of the Civil-Service System], *Jinji-in geppō* 365(temporary, expanded issue; 1981): 36–37. For the 1987 recommendation, see "Kyūyo kankoku no kosshi" [The Gist of the Recommendation on Compensation], *Jinji-in geppō* 440 (Sept. 1987): 2, and *Asahi shinbun,* 12 Dec. 1987.

TABLE 33   *Disciplinary Action Against Civil Servants for Corrupt Practices, by Type and Year*

Year and Type of Offense	Type of Disciplinary Action					Total as % of All Civil Servants
	Dismiss	Suspend	Reduce Pay	Reprimand	Total	
1960						
Embezzlement	213	98	38	16	365	0.05000
Bribery	7	15	30	28	80	0.01000
Subtotal	220	113	68	44	445	0.06000
1965						
Embezzlement	151	64	28	5	248	0.03000
Bribery	68	10	88	62	228	0.02000
Subtotal	219	74	116	67	476	0.05000
1970						
Embezzlement	163	50	16	4	233	0.03000
Bribery	44	4	17	20	85	0.01000
Subtotal	207	54	33	24	318	0.04000
1975						
Embezzlement	124	22	5	0	151	0.02000
Bribery	16	6	13	4	39	0.00458
Subtotal	140	28	18	4	190	0.02234
1980						
Embezzlement	135	20	2	4	161	0.02000
Bribery	5	1	10	5	21	0.00245
Subtotal	140	21	12	9	182	0.02130
1985						
Embezzlement	104	11	2	0	117	0.01000
Bribery	9	2	1	0	12	0.00142
Subtotal	113	13	3	0	129	0.02000

SOURCE: Jinji-in, *Nenji hōkokusho*, 1960, 1965, 1970, 1975, 1980, and 1985 (Tokyo: Ōkurashō, Insatsukyoku, 1961–86).

Because we are primarily interested in the higher civil servants, however, we need to know whether this overall picture can be extrapolated to that subset of the civil service. The available evidence bearing on this question is fragmentary. One study conducted by a research institute attached to the Ministry of Justice shows that a total of 204 civil servants were either indicted or received suspended indictments (*kiso yūyo shobun*) in 1976 for bribery; of these, 31 were national civil servants. Of the latter, 8 were section chiefs or above. In other words, the higher civil servants constituted about a quarter of the total. Of the 173 prefectural and local civil servants, however, 65 (37.6 percent) held the rank of section chief or higher.[14]

Another indication that corrupt behavior among the higher civil servants is rare is that it literally makes headlines when it does occur. When a section chief in the Ministry of International Trade and Industry (MITI) and a subsection chief in the Medium and Small Enterprises Agency, one of the external bureaus (*gaikyoku*) of MITI, were arrested in March 1986 on suspicion of having accepted bribes from an industrial organization, the news became the lead story in *Asahi shinbun*'s evening edition on the same day. The newspaper noted that this was the first time in twelve years that a leading official of a key ministry or agency (*kikan kanchō no kanbu*) had been arrested on charges of corruption. The significance attached to the event was reflected in the prompt public apology by the chief government spokesman: on the same day Chief Cabinet Secretary Gotoda Masaharu apologized for "having produced arrestees," pledging to step up efforts "to establish discipline among civil servants and to restore their credibility."[15] Although the arrested civil servants faced a prolonged legal process before their guilt or innocence could be conclusively determined, the government was clearly embarrassed by the episode.

In sum, notwithstanding their modest compensation, Japanese civil servants are remarkably free of corruption, and this is particularly true of the higher civil servants. It should be stressed that what has been discussed above pertains to *personal* corruption among the bureaucrats. As Chalmers Johnson points out, however, "structural corruption" has plagued the Japanese political system throughout the postwar period, and among the many causes of the phenomenon is the reemployment of retired bureaucrats by private firms, a topic to which we now turn.[16]

RETIREMENT AND REEMPLOYMENT

Monetary compensation for civil servants is only part, albeit a significant part, of the rewards they receive. They also receive various psychological rewards as well as deferred ones. The latter include separation pay and pension and also opportunities to find postretire-

14. Sase Minoru, *Nippon kōmuin jijō* [The Condition of Japanese Civil Servants] (Tokyo: Nihon Jitsugyō Shuppansha, 1978), p. 108.

15. *Asahi shinbun*, 26 Mar. 1986 (evening ed.).

16. Johnson, "Tanaka Kakuei," pp. 1–28.

ment careers—the so-called "second careers" (*daini no jinsei*). Two facts make such reemployment opportunities particularly important in the Japanese context: (1) Japanese higher civil servants retire relatively early and (2) their retirement benefits are seldom sufficient.

AN OVERVIEW OF RESIGNATIONS

Although a mandatory retirement system did not take effect until March 1985, most civil servants, particularly higher civil servants, retired at relatively early ages. Before focusing on the latter, however, let us first look at the overall picture. Table 34 contains some relevant statistics. Note that this table pertains to the Administrative Service I only. If the other salary schedules were added, the total numbers of resignations in the last column would increase about fourfold in the years covered.

TABLE 34   *Resignations by Year, Age, and Sex:*
Administrative Service I Only

					Age		
	29 or Below		30–54	55–59	60 or Above	All Ages	
Year	All	Women	All	All	All	All	Women
1973							
N	2640	1,296	3,128	1,447	1,267	8,482	
%	31.1	15.3	36.9	17.1	14.9	100.0	
1976							
N	1435	779	2,218	1,539	1,571	6,763	1,328
%	21.2	11.5	32.8	22.8	23.2	100.0	19.6
1979							
N	1206	535	2,684	2,263	1,653	7,896	1,269
%	15.2	6.8	34.4	29.0	21.2	100.1	16.3
1982							
N	1097	450	2,944[a]	3,524	1,369	8,934	1,305
%	12.3	5.1	33.0	39.4	15.3	100.0	14.6
1985							
N	1143	415	3,274[b]	4,378	72	8,867	1,338
%	12.9	4.7	36.9	49.4	0.8	100.0	15.1

SOURCE: Jinji-in, *Nenji hōkokusho*, 1974, 1977, 1980, 1983, and 1986 (Tokyo: Ōkurashō, Insatsukyoku, 1975–87).
   [a]Of this number, 1,772 (19.8%) were between the ages of 45 and 54.
   [b]Of this number, 1,993 (22.5%) were between the ages of 45 and 54.

Several things are apparent from the table. First of all, disproportionately large numbers of women resign from the civil service before age twenty-nine. Although, overall, women constitute between 15 and 20 percent of all those who resign, they account for between 36 and 55 percent of those who resign in their twenties. This is no doubt related to the difficulty of combining marriage and career in the early years.[17] On the other hand, not only has there been a steady decline in the proportion of younger resignees as a whole, but women's share of the below twenty-nine group has dwindled markedly.

Also noteworthy is that in the 1970s the single largest age group among resignees was the thirty–fifty-four-year group. Further breakdown is available for recent years only, and it shows that, although resignations occur more frequently between the ages of forty-five and fifty-four, they also occur in significant numbers between the ages of thirty and forty-four. Another notable trend has to do with a steady increase in the proportion of resignees in the fifty-five–fifty-nine-year group. The proportion of resignees in the over-sixty group remained fairly high until 1985, when a law mandating retirement at age sixty entered into force. If we look at the age distribution of incumbent civil servants in the Administrative Service I, we find that the proportion of the over-sixty group has declined precipitously from 11.9 percent in 1973 to 0.9 percent in 1985.[18]

In the pre-1985 period, early retirement was a function of cultural norms, pressure from superiors, and financial incentives. A key cultural norm is a strong sense of equality among cohorts: all members of the same entering class in the same ministry share such a keen sense of equality that they cannot function in any hierarchical relationship among themselves. As we have previously noted, when one member of an entering class reaches the pinnacle of the career civil service, administrative vice-ministership, all of the remaining classmates feel compelled to resign. Given the limited opportunities for advancement, however, "noncareer" civil servants seldom face similar constraints.

---

17. A survey of 1,598 civil servants who resigned before reaching the age of 30, conducted by the National Personnel Authority in 1964, found that 55.4 percent of women ($N = 960$) cited marriage as the reason for their resignation. "Marriage" also included childbirth, rearing children, and other family-related matters. The most important reason cited by men, on the other hand, was alternative employment in the private sector (31.2 percent). See Kondō Masaru, "Shokai: Jakunen taishokusha no jittai" [Introduction: the Realities of Young Resignees], *Jinji-in geppō* 186 (Aug. 1966): 6–9.

18. Jinji-in, *Nenji hōkokusho*, 1973, in *Kanpō* [Official Gazette], extra ed., no. 72, 19 Aug. 1974, p. 15; idem., *Kōmuin hakusho*, 1987, p. 46.

Pressure from superiors, on the other hand, affects all civil servants, particularly those who are not on the elite track. Known officially as *taishoku kanshō* (encouraging retirement) and unofficially as *kata tataki* (a tap on the shoulder), this procedure typically involves not only a suggestion that the civil servant in question should retire but also assistance in arranging reemployment for him.[19] There is an additional inducement: the lump-sum retirement allowance increases by one-third for those who retire in this fashion.[20]

Available evidence suggests that nine out of ten civil servants who retire after the age of fifty-five do so after receiving *kata tataki*.[21] With the introduction of a mandatory retirement system in 1985, however, the proportion of "encouraged resignations" will probably decline sharply. As noted, the new system designates sixty as the mandatory retirement age for most civil servants. Those who are exempt from this rule include physicians and dentists (whose retirement age is set at sixty-five), guards (whose retirement age is set at sixty-three), and other persons who are specifically exempted by the rules of the National Personnel Authority.[22] Although some observers have expressed fear that the mandatory retirement system may lead to a de facto increase in the retirement age of higher civil servants,[23] its actual impact on higher civil servants may well be minimal.[24]

RETIREMENT OF HIGHER CIVIL SERVANTS

The single most important factor affecting the retirement patterns of higher civil servants will no doubt continue to be the culturally rooted norm that decrees that one should avoid the embarrassment of taking

19. Asahi Shinbun "Kanryō" Shuzaihan, *Kanryō: Sono seitai*, pp. 90 and 130–31.
20. For example, those who retire after twenty years of service receive 28.875 times their monthly salary at the time of retirement, whereas the regular rate is twenty-one times the monthly salary. For those with thirty years of service, the difference between "encouraged retirement" and retirement at personal convenience is 54.45 times the monthly salary versus 41.25 times the monthly salary. See "Komuin no taishoku teate to nenkin" [Civil Servants' Retirement Allowance and Annuity], *Jinji-in geppō* 402 (July 1984): 22.
21. The National Personnel Authority has published statistics on "encouraged resignations" for the years 1968 through 1972 only. They show that their proportion ranged from 89 to 96 percent. See Jinji-in, *Nenji hōkokusho, 1969–1973*.
22. Jinji-in, *Kōmuin hakusho, 1982*, pp. 44–45.
23. Katō, *Kanryō desu, yoroshiku*, pp. 180–81. Katō is a former higher civil servant in the Home Ministry.
24. This assessment was given to the author by Nakajima Sachiko, a counselor (*sanijikan*) in the Appointments Bureau (*Nin'yōkyoku*) of the National Personnel Authority in an interview on 7 June 1985.

orders from one's peers. With rare exceptions, therefore, the promotion of a member of one's entering class to the position of administrative vice-minister will continue to trigger resignations by his classmates; by the same token, the failure to be promoted to the position of bureau chief or its equivalent with one's classmates is a signal that the time for retirement has arrived, even if no *kata tataki* may have occurred.

For these reasons the average age of higher civil servants at various stages in their career suggests when most resignations are likely to occur. Table 35 shows that the average age has steadily increased across the board over the years. The sole exception is section chiefs: according to the table, their average actually decreased by 1.4 years between the early 1970s and the mid-1980s. The average age of senior section chiefs in 1986, however, was 2.2 years higher than that of all section chiefs.

If we look at bureau chiefs, we find that their average age increased by nine years between 1949 and 1986. Equally striking is the steady aging of administrative vice-ministers: whereas they were still in their late forties in 1949 and 1954, they were in their late fifties by 1986. More relevant for our purposes is the average age of newly appointed administrative vice-ministers, for that is the age when the remaining

TABLE 35   *Average Age of Higher Civil Servants, by Rank and Year*

Year	Section Chief		Division Chief		Bureau Chief		Administrative Vice-Minister	
	Age	*N*	*Age*	*N*	*Age*	*N*	*Age*	*N*
1949	39.8	110	43.9	122	44.2	117	49.2	46
1954	42.1	96	45.8	92	46.2	120	49.9	39
1959	43.4	90	48.2	89	48.2	155	51.8	40
1972–73	47.7	671	—	—	52.8	154	54.1	43
1986	46.3ᵃ	758	50.8	57	53.4	144	56.5	22

SOURCES: The 1949–59 data are from Akira Kubota, *Higher Civil Servants in Postwar Japan* (Princeton: Princeton University Press, 1969), p. 74; the 1972–73 data are from B. C. Koh and Jae-On Kim, "Paths to Advancement in Japanese Bureaucracy," *Comparative Political Studies* 15, no. 3 (Oct. 1982): 294; the 1986 data are based on an analysis of a random sample of higher civil servants listed in *Seikai kanchō jinji roku, 1987-nenban* (Tokyo: Tōyō Keizai Shinpōsha, 1986).

ᵃThe average age of "senior" section chiefs—that is, chiefs of sections in the minister's secretariat and of principal sections in bureaus—was 48.5. There were 119 persons in that subgroup.

members of their respective entering classes retire. We have data for three time periods: 1972–73: 53.6 ($N = 34$), 1981–83: 56.5 ($N = 42$), and 1984–87: 56.0 ($N = 50$).[25]

What all this suggests is that the average retirement age of higher civil servants has steadily increased over the years. As we saw in chapter 5, nearly all careerists advance to the rank of section chief, hence the moment of truth arrives just before promotion to the rank of bureau chief. For, given the nature of the bureaucratic pyramid, only a handful of positions are available at this exalted level. Those who are passed over must leave, and they are in the majority. It is not surprising, then, to learn that the average retirement age for all higher civil servants approximates the average age of bureau chiefs: it was 52.9 in 1972–73 and 55.2 in 1985.[26]

REEMPLOYMENT PATTERNS

Even if retirement benefits were adequate, those who retire in their fifties would find it necessary to seek reemployment or something useful to do. For most people, however, the retirement benefits are far from adequate. Until 31 March 1986, for example, a civil servant with thirty years of service was entitled to a separation allowance amounting to about four and half years of pay and an annuity totaling 55 percent of salary.[27] Effective 1 April 1986, a new system of annuities went into effect; under its extremely complicated provisions the retirement benefits of civil servants were expected to increase slightly.[28] Most higher civil servants, therefore, seek reemployment either by choice or by necessity.

25. The figure for 1972–73 is from B. C. Koh and Jae-on Kim, "Paths to Advancement in Japanese Bureaucracy," *Comparative Political Studies* 15, no. 3 (Oct. 1982): 304, table 6. The figures for the 1980s were calculated from a data set compiled by the author from the following sources: *Kankai*, May 1981–Sept. 1987; *Asahi shinbun*, May 1986–Sept. 1987; *Yomiuri nenkan bessatsu, bun'ya betsu jinmei roku* [Separate Volume Supplement to Yomiuri Yearbook, Who's Who by Fields], 1985 (Tokyo: Yomiuri Shinbunsha, 1985); *Seikai kanchō jinji roku, 1987-nenban*; ibid., *1988-nenban*.

26. See Koh and Kim, "Paths to Advancement," p. 304, for the 1972–73 average; for the 1985 figure, see *Jinji-in geppō* 425 (June 1986): 5.

27. "Kōmuin no taishoku teate to nenkin," p. 22. The computational formula for annuity consists of multiplying the retiree's last salary by a rate determined by his length of service. For the first twenty years the rate is 0.4. Each additional year thereafter earns a credit of 0.015. The maximum rate is 0.7. The amount of separation allowance is a function of both length of service and the reason for separation. A civil servant who resigns voluntarily after twenty years of service will receive twenty-one times his last monthly salary, whereas a thirty-year veteran will get 41.25 times his last monthly salary.

There are a number of options for those seeking postretirement jobs. One is to find employment in the private sector. This move from the ostensibly exalted position of a higher civil servant to an employee of a private, profit-making firm is known as *amakudari* (descent from heaven).[29] As Gerald L. Curtis notes, however, what happens may not necessarily be descent but ascent; the former bureaucrat may actually enjoy more affluence and prestige than ever before.[30]

The second option is to land a job in a public corporation, known collectively as "special legal entities" (*tokushu hōjin*). Unlike the first option, this does not involve any legal restrictions. That is to say, there is no need to seek permission. The third option is to become a member of the Diet, which of course requires winning an election.[31] Although there are other possibilities, such as teaching, research, and working for a local-government body, the three options noted above seem most important. Let us examine them in more detail.

AMAKUDARI

As noted, *amakudari* in a narrow sense is subject to some legal restrictions.[32] Article 103 of the national public-service law stipulates a

---

28. For a comprehensive review of the new system, see Kokka Kōmuin Nenkin Seido Kenkyūkai, ed., *Kokka kōmuintō no shin kyōsai nenkin seido no shikumi* [The Plan of the New Cooperative Annuity System for National Civil Servants and Others] (Tokyo: Zaikei Shōhōsha, 1986) and Jinji-in, Taishoku Teate Nenkin Seido Kenkyūkai, ed., *Kōmuin no tameno taishoku teate nenkin gaidobukku* [Retirement Allowance and Annuity Guidebook for Civil Servants] (Tokyo: Ōkurashō, Insatsukyoku, 1986). Under the new system, civil servants are subject to a dual system of annuities. First, they are required to enroll in *kokumin nenkin* (citizens' annuity plan) along with all other citizens; this requires monthly payment of premiums. Second, the civil servants continue to participate in *kyōsai nenkin* (cooperative annuity plan), which, too, requires monthly contributions on the part of its participants. The formula for computing benefits, however, has become so complicated that at least five different tables need to be used; in addition, the calculation of the average monthly salary during one's entire civil-service career, which becomes the constant in the equation, is beyond the capability of individuals. It will be done by computers in the Social Insurance Agency. In computing the average monthly salary, adjustments are made to neutralize the effects of inflation and other factors.

29. For an informative analysis of this and related matters, see Johnson, "The Reemployment of Retired Government Bureaucrats in Japanese Big Business," pp. 953–65.

30. If that is the case, then a more accurate term would be *amaagari* (ascending to heaven). See Gerald L. Curtis, "Big Business and Political Influence," in Vogel, ed., *Modern Japanese Organization and Decision-Making*, p. 44, no. 32.

31. Johnson, "The Reemployment of Retired Government Bureaucrats," pp. 953–54; Ino Kenji and Hokuto Man, *Amakudari Kanryō: Nihon o ugokasu tokken shūdan* [Bureaucrats Who Descend from Heaven: A Privileged Group That Moves Japan] (Tokyo: Nisshin Hōdō, 1972), pp. 91–92.

two-year moratorium on the reemployment of retired civil servants in profit-making enterprises if the government organs in which they have served during the preceding five years have had a "close connection" (*missetsu na kankei*) with such enterprises. However, the article adds that this prohibition shall not apply should a recommendation for exemption by the government organ concerned be approved by the National Personnel Authority.[33]

Depending on how it is interpreted and applied, then, article 103 has the potential of preventing conflicts of interest. In 1963, the Diet appended a requirement to article 103: the National Personnel Authority was enjoined to report annually to both the Diet and the cabinet regarding the number and details of all the exemptions it granted in the preceding year. Officially known as the "Annual Report on Approval of Employment in Profit-Making Enterprises" (*Eiri kigyō e no shūshoku no shōnin ni kansuru nenji hōkoku*), the report has been dubbed the *amakudari* white paper by the mass media. Table 36 presents summary statistics from these reports in selected years.

Note that the numbers shown in the table refer to cases rather than individuals. From time to time, an individual may seek approval for employment in more than one position; occasionally, therefore, the number of cases exceeds that of individuals. Even though table 36 displays statistics for selected years only, we shall also refer, in the following discussion, to the years not covered in the table.

First, we can see a marked increase in the total numbers over the years. The 1986 total is almost double that of 1965. There was actually a notable decline in 1986 from the previous year, when the total had climbed to 320. Second, it is remarkable that a handful of ministries have dominated the scene throughout the period; although the five ministries have continued to account for an overwhelming majority of all the cases, their degree of dominance actually decreased in the 1970s compared with the late 1960s. Beginning in 1977, the Ministry of Posts and Communications joined the five ministries listed in the table as a

---

32. In a narrow sense, *amakudari* refers to the reemployment of retired government officials in private, profit-making enterprises only. Their reemployment in public corporations is called *yokosuberi* (side slip). However, the broad meaning of *amakudari* encompasses both. Although Johnson makes the distinction, Ino and Hokuto do not. For a reference to *yokosuberi*, see "Shinso or saguru: Kareinaru amakudari no urade ugomeku yokubō" [In Search of Truth: The Desire That Squirms Behind the Splendid Descent from Heaven], *Kankai*, May 1982, p. 140.

33. See paragraphs 2 and 3 of art. 103 of the law in Jinji-in ed., *Ninmen kankei hōreishū*, 1984 ed., p. 33.

TABLE 36   *Approvals of Reemployment of Retired*
Officials in the Private Sector, by Year and Ministry

Ministry

Year	Finance	MITI	Const.	Agric.	Trans.	Other	Total
1965	30	28	14	10	19	27	128
1968	34	18	14	17	13	40	136
1971	44	17	10	18	22	56	167
1974	59	18	21	12	15	64	189
1977	49	18	21	16	17	77	198
1980	46	25	27	17	25	88	228
1983	51	32	27	32	23	102	267
1986	54	25	29	25	20	99	252

SOURCES: *JInji-in geppō,* 182 (Apr. 1966): 21 and 437 (June 1987): 7; Murobushi Tetsuro, "Kōkyū kanryō—riken no kōzō," *Sekai,* Feb. 1980, p. 56; Jinji-in, *Nenji hōkokusho,* 1976–1986 (Tokyo; Ōkurashō, Insatsukyoku, 1977–87).

major player in the game. In 1986 it surpassed both MITI and the Ministry of Agriculture, with twenty-eight exemptions.

Third, the Ministry of Finance has been the indisputable leader: in all eight years covered in the table, it was number one, accounting for an average of 24 percent of the total exemptions. Although the number-two position goes to MITI, the other ministries are not very far behind. What all these ministries have in common is their close linkage with the strategic sectors of the Japanese economy. The close patterns of interaction between them and their respective clientele groups make retiring higher civil servants valuable assets to their prospective employers in the private sector: not only do the retirees possess managerial ability and substantive expertise but they can also measurably facilitate interactions with the government bureaucracy. To ascertain whether the National Personnel Authority actually performs the function of obviating or, at least, minimizing conflicts of interest, we need to know details of specific cases, which are not available. Fragmentary evidence suggests, however, that the authority is not a rubber stamp: in the 1970s, it rejected between 3.0 and 7.4 percent of the requests for exemption.[34]

Table 37 discloses another notable trend in *amakudari:* the growing number of technical officials. Whereas they accounted for only four of

34. Murobushi Tetsurō, "Kōkyū kanryō—riken no kōzō" [Higher Civil Servants: The Structure of Interests], *Sekai,* Feb. 1980, p. 56.

TABLE 37   *Approvals of Reemployment of Retired Officials in the Private Sector, by Year and Type of Officials*

	Type of Officials					
	Technical		Administrative		Total	
Year	N	%	N	%	N^a	%
1965	33	25.8	95	74.2	128	100.0
1970	93	48.2	100	51.8	193	100.0
1975	75	42.6	101	57.4	176	100.0
1980	118	51.8	110	48.2	228	100.0
1985	178	56.0	140	44.0	318	100.0

SOURCE: Jinji-in, *Nenji hōkokusho*, 1965–1985 (Tokyo: Ōkurashō, Insatsukyoku, 1966–86).

[a]The numbers in this table refer to persons rather than cases. In 1985, for example, there were 320 cases involving 318 persons.

every ten cases in 1965, their share nearly doubled by 1970. After declining slightly in 1975, the proportion of technical officials surpassed that of administrative officials in 1980. Their lead widened in 1985. All this suggests that a major reason that former government bureaucrats are hired by private firms may be the substantive expertise they bring to their jobs in addition to other assets.

As noted, even though all the cases included in the annual *amakudari* white papers pertain to former bureaucrats with the rank of section chief or its equivalent and above, only a handful of them actually occupied key positions in the headquarters of the ministries and agencies. Of the 318 persons who were granted exemptions by the National Personnel Authority in 1985, for example, only 49 (15.4 percent) were in that category (*honshōchō kachō shoku ijō*). Of this number, 13 held the rank of bureau chief or above.[35] In 1986, 38 (15.3 percent) of the 248 persons receiving exemptions were in the same category, of whom only 7 had held the rank of bureau chief or above.[36]

To examine briefly the destinations of the 20 highest-ranking retirees in these two years, the largest proportion of the group (7, or 35 percent)

35. *Asahi shinbun*, 28 Mar. 1986.
36. "Shōwa 61-nen eiri kigyō eno shūshoku no shōnin ni kansuru nenji hōkoku" [1986 Annual Report on Approval of Employment in Profit-making Enterprises], *Jinji-in geppō* 437 (June 1987): 6.

went to banks, all but one being appointed as advisers (*komon*). The lone exception became vice president (*fuku tōdori*). In fact, *komon* is the title most commonly given to these people, accounting for 8 of the 20 titles. Technically, they are not of the directorial rank (*yakuin*); therefore, approval of reemployment is believed to be almost pro forma. In most cases, they will be elevated to directorial positions after a lapse of two years. Should a change in status occur earlier, however, approval by the National Personnel Authority is required de novo. Exactly half of the group landed *yakuin* positions immediately: one presidency (*torishimari yaku shachō*), one vice-presidency (*fuku tōdori*), two managing directorships (*senmu torishimari yaku*), one executive directorship (*jōmu torishimari yaku*), four directorships (*riji*), and one consulting directorship (*torishimari yaku sōdan yaku*). Also noteworthy is that a recently privatized company, Nippon Telegraph and Telephone (formerly the Japan Telegraph and Telephone Corporation, or Nihon Denshin Denwa Kōsha), hired 5 of the top group, 1 of them as an executive director and 2 as directors.[37]

Inasmuch as the Ministry of Finance is the single largest source of *amakudari*, let us examine the destinations of its high-level retirees. In 1984, 29 persons at the rank of section chief or above in the ministry (*honshō kachō-kyū ijō*) retired. Of this total, only 1, a former administrative vice minister, did not seek immediate reemployment. The destinations of the remainder were as follows: government-affiliated financial institutions, 6; public corporations, 9; private banks, 2; private firms, 8; licensed tax accountants (*zeirishi*), 3. In terms of position titles, 16 became directors, and 5 became advisers. On the other hand, of those who entered the private sector, only a few landed jobs in what may be described as first-rate companies, which included Mitsui Trust Bank, Japan Air Lines, and Mitsubishi Shoji.[38]

The number of retirees in the same category in 1985 was 35. Of this total, 1 died and 1 was preparing to run for the House of Representatives in the next election. Five became licensed tax accountants, and the remainder went to either public corporations or private banks and firms. Although 11 became directors, none was hired by a really prestigious firm. Officials in charge of finding reemployment for the Finance Ministry's retirees complained of a growing scarcity of suitable landing spots; noting they had to "lower their heads" to find reemployment

37. For destinations of these and other high-ranking retirees, see *Asahi shinbun*, 28 Mar. 1986, and 28 Mar. 1987.
38. Ibid., 19 Feb. 1985.

positions for their retirees, they pointed out that it was difficult to call their ministry a "first-rate government agency" (*ichiryū kanchō*) any longer.[39]

The situation in 1986, however, was far from gloomy. All but two of the Finance Ministry's 32 high-level retirees found employment in that year. The 2 who did not apparently chose not to seek immediate reemployment; one of these was former administrative vice-minister. Although the destinations of the 30 varied widely, the largest number, 7, went to public corporations. Three went to private banks, 2 to insurance companies, and 5 to other private firms. Three went into private practice as either an attorney or a licensed tax accountant. One entered the Judicial Training Institute with the aim of entering the legal profession. Among the more notable destinations were the Tokyo Stock Exchange (executive director), the Mitsubishi Trust Bank (adviser), the Japan Foundation (executive director), and the Sumitomo Life Insurance Company (adviser).[40]

All in all, the record of the Finance Ministry in finding postretirement employment for its elite-track bureaucrats seems solid. It is plain that the ministry remains the premier government agency insofar as *amakudari* is concerned. No other ministry or agency, for example, has produced so many directors and presidents of banks.[41] As we shall see below, moreover, the Finance Ministry is the leading source of candidates for the Diet as well.

YOKOSUBERI

The movement from ministry or agency to a public corporation is known as a "side slip" (*yokosuberi*).[42] Most writers, however, use the term *amakudari* to encompass this form of reemployment by retired officials as well.[43] Unlike *amakudari* as strictly defined, *yokosuberi* allows the retired government bureaucrat to remain in the public sector; what happens is equivalent to a transfer from the mainstream of the

---

39. Ibid., 16 Feb. 1986.
40. Ibid., 8 Mar. 1987.
41. For examples of and statistics pertaining to *amakudari* of retired Finance Ministry bureaucrats to the various banks and financial institutions, see Takamoto, *Ōkura kanryō no keifu*, pp. 159–95; *Asahi shinbun*, 22 May 1986; "Kasumigaseki konhidenshāru," *Bungei shunjū*, July 1986, p. 163.
42. Johnson, "The Reemployment of Retired Government Bureaucrats," p. 953.
43. Although Chalmers Johnson differentiates between the two terms in his *Asian Survey* article cited above, he blurs the distinction in his study *Japan's Public Policy Companies* (Washington: American Enterprise Institute for Public Policy Research, 1978). In the latter Johnson defines *amakudari* as the "practice of employing retired government officials as chief executives or members of boards of directors of *public and private*

government to its periphery, for he will be reemployed by one of the hundred-odd "special legal entities." In 1980, there were 111 such entities, of which 3 were *kōsha* (public corporations), 16 were *kōdan* (public units), 19 were *jigyōdan* (enterprise units), 10 were *kōko* (public finance corporations), 2 were *tokushu ginkō* (special banks), 2 were *kinkō* (depositories), 1 was *eidan* (corporation), 11 were *tokushu kaisha* (special companies), and the remainder were called by a wide variety of names. These entities employed nearly a million persons, of whom fewer than 800 were in executive positions (*yakuin*).[44] In 1985, however, 2 of the 3 *kōsha* were privatized, and the third was scheduled to follow suit in 1986.[45]

Because *yokosuberi* is not subject to any legal restrictions, the government does not publish any comprehensive data on it. Nonetheless, a labor federation, to which labor unions comprising employees of special legal entities belong, collects data on its own and publishes annual reports. According to its report published in 1987, 379 of 489 *yakuin* in eighty-three special legal entities it studied in 1986 were retired higher civil servants. This amounted to 77.5 percent of the total. MITI had produced the largest number of the subgroup ($N = 54$), followed by the ministries of Agriculture, Forestry, and Fisheries ($N = 46$), Finance ($N = 34$), and Construction ($N = 30$).[46]

Yokosuberi differs from *amakudari*, narrowly construed, in another sense: the same individual can experience it more than once. The retired higher civil servant who moves from one *yokosuberi* post to another, collecting generous separation allowances in the process, is known as *wataridori* (migratory bird). According to information disclosed by opposition-party members in the House of Representatives in May 1969, of 363 retired higher civil servants serving as *yakuin* in 108 special legal entities at the time, 75 (20.7 percent) had experienced *yokosuberi* three times or more. Of the latter, 15 had experienced it four times, and 1 five times. Separation allowances collected by these people during each transition were equal to 65 percent of their total earnings

corporations" (p. 5, emphasis added). Elsewhere in the study, however, he mentions the difference between the two terms (p. 102). For another definition of *amakudari* that subsumes *yokosuberi*, see "Shinso o saguru: Kareinaru amakudari," p. 144.

44. For a complete list and definitions of these "special legal entities," see *Gyōsei kanri benran* [Handbook of Administrative Management], 1980 (Tokyo: Gyōsei Kanri Kenkyū Sentā, 1980), pp. 28–39. The English translations were taken from Johnson, *Japan's Public Policy Companies*, pp. 5–7 (Glossary of Japanese Terms).

45. See "Shinso o saguru: NTT, min'eika no sono ato" [In Search of Truth: Nippon Telegraph and Telephone in the Wake of Privatization], *Kankai*, May 1986, pp. 164–73.

46. *Asahi shinbun*, 5 Apr. 1987.

during their tenure in each job. Although the percentage was lowered to 45 in 1970 and to 36 in 1978, the comparatively high salaries of *yakuin* in public corporations make the separation allowance quite generous.[47] In 1986, about a quarter of the 379 former bureaucrats occupying leadership positions in the special legal entities were *wataridori*.[48]

A leading example of *wataridori* is Funayama Masakichi, who retired as administrative vice-minister of the Finance Ministry in 1953. He first served as a director of the Bank of Japan and then became the deputy governor of the Japan Monopoly Corporation. His next job was with the Japan Export-Import Bank, where he was deputy governor. Finally, he was appointed the governor of the Smaller Business Finance Corporation. The separation allowances he had collected prior to his last appointment amounted to over 27.5 million yen, a considerable sum in the 1950s and 1960s.[49]

ENTERING POLITICS

The option of running for a seat in the Diet is available only to the select few among retired higher civil servants. Whereas *amakudari,* broadly defined, is typically arranged by the prospective retiree's ministry or agency, running for election is something one must arrange on one's own. Because virtually all retired higher civil servants run as candidates of the Liberal-Democratic party, they find it necessary to affiliate themselves with one of the factions within the party in order to win official endorsement. Factional affiliation is also necessary to help finance the campaigns, which cost astronomical sums.

As we saw in the preceding chapter, in the double election of 6 July 1986, a total of 80 former higher civil servants were elected to the House of Representatives, accounting for 23.3 percent of the 300 successful LDP candidates. Of the 72 LDP candidates who were elected to the House of Councillors in the same election, 24 (33.3 percent) were former bureaucrats. Another former bureaucrat who ran as a Democratic Socialist party candidate was also elected to the upper house.[50]

47. Murobushi, "Kōkyū kanryō," pp. 59–60. The formula for calculating the amount of separation allowance is as follows: monthly salary at the time of separation × number of months served × 0.36. Sekiguchi Takeshi, *Kōmuin tengoku!!* [Civil Servants' Heaven] (Tokyo: Arō Shuppansha, n.d.), p. 161. Although this book does not show any publication date, it appears to have been published in 1978. The copy that I used had been purchased by the U.S. Library of Congress on 14 July, 1978.

48. *Asahi shinbun,* 5 Apr. 1987.

49. Ino and Hokuto, *Amakudari kanryō,* p. 22; for other examples of *wataridori,* see ibid., pp. 22–24, and Sekiguchi, *Kōmuin tengoku!!,* pp. 162–63.

50. *Asahi shinbun,* 7 July 1986 (evening ed.) and 8 July 1986.

The broad picture given above, however, pertains to all former higher civil servants. Table 38 is therefore aimed at showing what happens to those retired civil servants who elect the political option. It is plain that throwing one's hat into the political arena is not as easy as it sounds: in the 1986 election, only 4 of every 10 former bureaucrats who had not previously been elected to the Diet achieved their goals. The probability

TABLE 38   *A Statistical Profile of Former Higher Civil Servants Who Ran for the House of Representatives for the First Time in the Election of 6 July 1986*

Characteristic	Number of Candidates	Number Elected	Percentage Elected
Age			
Below 39	4	1	25.0
40–44	5	1	20.0
45–49	6	2	33.3
50–54	9	5	55.6
55–59	2	2	100.0
TOTAL	26[a]	11	42.3
Former Rank			
Administrative vice-minister[b]	2	2	100.0
Bureau chief	1	1	100.0
Division chief[c]	6	4	66.7
Section chief	10	2	20.0
Below section chief	4	2	50.0
Unknown	3	0	0.0
TOTAL	26	11	42.3
Ministry			
Finance	8	3	37.5
MITI	6	2	33.3
Agriculture	4	3	75.0
Construction	2	1	50.0
Welfare	2	1	50.0
Foreign Affairs	2	0	0.0
Home Affairs	1	1	100.0
Police Agency	1	0	0.0
TOTAL	26	11	42.3

SOURCES: Tsuchiya Shigeru, "Kanryō shusshin rikkōhosha sōtenken," *Kankai*, May 1986, pp. 142–51; *Asahi shinbun*, 8 July 1986.

[a]All but three of these candidates ran as Liberal Democrats. Two ran as independent and one as a nominee of the United Social Democratic Party. All of the non-LDP candidates were defeated.

[b]One of the two had served as director-general of the Social Insurance Agency.

[c]Two individuals whose last title had been councillor (*shingikan*) were included in this category.

of success varied inversely with age: those in their fifties were more than twice as likely to succeed as those in their forties and thirties.

Although the relationship between rank and the probability of electoral success is somewhat murky because of missing data, the two nonetheless seem to covary to an appreciable degree. Whereas 7 of the 9 persons who had attained the rank of division chief or higher won their bids, only 2 of the 10 former section chiefs did so. On the other hand, the success rate of those who had not even attained the section-chief rank is quite good, although because of the small numbers involved, caution is called for in drawing any conclusions.

Finally, it is interesting to note that the ministries that contribute most to *amakudari* also produce the largest number of candidates for the House of Representatives. The success rates of the top two, Finance and MITI, however, are mediocre at best.[51]

Let us now consider briefly the situation regarding the House of Councillors. Of the twenty-five former bureaucrats elected to the upper house on 6 July 1986, six were freshmen. A comparison of the backgrounds of the six freshmen with those of the eleven novice members of the House of Representatives yields some interesting results. To begin with similarities, all are Liberal-Democrats. And, by a remarkable coincidence, all are graduates of the University of Tokyo. However, the upper-house members are considerably older: their average age is 58.2; in fact, half are in their early sixties. By contrast, the average age of the lower-house group is 50.4, and none is in his sixties. Another striking difference has to do with their former bureaucratic ranks: whereas only three of the eleven representatives had attained the rank of bureau chief or above, all of the councillors had done so. Half of the latter had retired as either administrative vice-minister or director general (*chōkan*).[52]

AN ASSESSMENT OF REEMPLOYMENT PATTERNS

As noted, the need for reemployment of retired higher civil servants is rooted in the twin realities of early retirement and insufficient retire-

---

51. For a discussion of the motives of young Finance Ministry bureaucrats who resign to run for elective offices, see Kuribayashi, *Ōkurashō shukeikyoku,* pp. 203–24.

52. Biographical data on the candidates, both successful and unsuccessful, were gleaned from Tsuchiya Shigeru, "Kanryō shusshin rikkōhosha sōtenken" [A Complete Examination of Candidates Who Are Former Bureaucrats], *Kankai,* Apr. 1986, pp. 160–71; May 1986, pp. 142–51; and June 1986, pp. 145–57; *Asahi shinbun,* 7 July 1986 (evening ed.) and 8 July 1986. Of the twenty-five former bureaucrats elected to the upper house in July 1986, nine had served as administrative vice-ministers and two as directors general (*chōkan*). Only one had retired as a section chief. The remainder had been bureau chiefs. In terms of educational background, twenty were graduates of the University of

ment benefits. Of the two, the former may be a more potent cause of *amakudari*, broadly defined, than the latter. Unless the practice of early retirement ceases, therefore, the need for reemployment will persist. However, there are no signs that the practice will change to any notable degree.

Hallowed by tradition, early retirement is sustained by the interaction of organizational dynamics and cultural norms. The progressive diminution of positions in the upper levels of the organizational pyramid dictates a pruning of the ranks among the old-timers. Moreover, a strong sense of equality among peers defined by the year of entry expedites resignations by those who fall behind leaders in the unacknowledged but nonetheless real race toward administrative vice-ministership.

Amakudari in a narrow sense, that is, reemployment by a private firm, can occur in three distinct ways. The most common mode is for the ministry or agency to take charge and arrange a landing spot for the retiree. Another mode takes the form of what the Japanese call "scouting." In this mode it is the private firm that takes the initiative: the firm seeks out a higher civil servant who has the kind of expertise, experience, and contacts that it needs most. In a variant of this mode, a firm may ask a ministry or agency to recommend a suitable candidate. In a third and final mode, the civil servant is rewarded for past services rendered to a firm; the initiative in such cases usually emanates from the retiring civil servant himself. All three modes may require approval by the National Personnel Authority.[53]

No matter what form it may take, *amakudari* entails mixed consequences. On the positive side, it contributes to the optimal utilization of talent, facilitates communication between government bureaucracy and private business, and "enhance[s] the effectiveness of administrative guidance."[54] On the negative side, *amakudari* may

Tokyo, four were graduates of Kyoto University, and one was a graduate of a technical high school.

53. Ino and Hokuto, *Amakudari kanryō*, pp. 169–71. According to Ojimi Yoshihisa, a former administrative vice-minister of MITI, "From the point of view of private companies, there is a need for these men [retired higher civil servants]. Requests frequently come to the personnel division of the ministry. Thus, placement is usually taken care of by the personnel division." See Ojimi, "A Government Ministry," p. 110.

54. Johnson, "The Reemployment of Retired Government Bureaucrats," p. 964. See also Curtis, "Big Business and Political Influence," p. 45; Kazuo Noda, "Big Business Organization," in Vogel, ed., *Modern Japanese Organization and Decision-Making*, p. 133; Akimoto Hideo and Kanai Hachirō, "Taidan: Kōmuin rinri to 'amakudari' mondai o megutte" [Conversation: Concerning the Ethics of Civil Servants and the Problem of "Descent from Heaven"], *Jinji-in geppō* 377 (June 1982): 4; Hayashi, *Nihon Kanryō kenkoku ron*, pp. 61–71.

compromise the independence and integrity of government bureaucracy, breed corruption, and confer unfair advantages on the firms that hire retired higher civil servants. It also has demoralizing effects on those members of the private firms whose promotional opportunities are undercut by the lateral entry of outsiders. To a large extent, however, the potential for corruption is offset by the modus operandi of Japanese organizations, which, by accentuating consensual decision making and diffusing authority and responsibility, makes it difficult for any individual to do favors for clientele.[55] As we have seen already, this is borne out by the actual record. Not only is corruption among incumbent higher civil servants rare, but the behavior of retired officials who have landed *amakudari* positions has not been marred by any scandals.[56]

The entry of former bureaucrats into the political arena via the ballot box, too, can be viewed from the standpoint of resource utilization. The expertise and experience they bring to their roles as members of the Diet can theoretically enhance the latter's capability to formulate policy and monitor policy implementation. On the other hand, the necessity to plan ahead—to find a patron, to align oneself with a faction, and to build a political base, no matter how rudimentary it may be—may conceivably interfere with a dispassionate discharge of bureaucratic responsibilities. The potential for compromising the bureaucrat's objectivity and neutrality is ever present.

On balance, then, the reemployment of retired higher civil servants is neither an unmitigated evil nor a cause for satisfaction. It represents a pragmatic response to real needs of individual bureaucrats, the government bureaucracy as a whole, and private business.[57] So long as the needs remain, the practice is likely to persist. The real challenge for the Japanese government remains how to prevent flagrant abuses, how to minimize patent conflicts of interests, and how to retain the trust and confidence of its citizens in the basic integrity of higher civil servants.[58]

---

55. Akimoto and Kanai, "Taidan: Kōmuin rinri," p. 5.

56. This last point is stressed by a former bureau chief in the National Personnel Authority. See Shima Yotsuo, "Kaisōbun: Amakudari mondai' arekore" [Reminiscences: Aspects of the "Problem of Descent from Heaven"] in Jinji-in, *Jinji gyōsei sanjūnen no ayumi*, p. 394.

57. Johnson, "The Reemployment of Retired Government Bureaucrats," p. 965.

58. In a survey of a national sample of 2,445 adults conducted by the prime minister's office in 1973, 65 percent of the respondents thought retired civil servants were either well off or relatively well off, citing their annuity, separation allowance, and reemployment in that order. Thirty-seven percent disapproved of *amakudari*, and 31 percent endorsed it. Of those who disapproved of the practice, 63 percent said it should not be allowed even after a lapse of several years. See Sōrifu, Naikaku Sōri Daijin Kanbō, *Kōmuin ni kansuru*

A COMPARATIVE PERSPECTIVE

To what extent, if any, are the patterns sketched above unique to Japan? The basic structure of compensation appears to be broadly similar among all industrialized democracies. The stratification of civil-service employees is reflected in the stratification of pay schedules. The discrepancy between the public and private sectors, the former perennially lagging behind the latter, is a universal phenomenon. Equally universal is the concern for narrowing the gap, for approximating the idea of "comparability" between government and private-sector salaries.

Both the United States and the United Kingdom have mechanisms for periodic review of government pay schedules. Under the Postal Revenue and Federal Salary Act of 1967, a nine-member commission is appointed every four years in the United States by the president, the chief justice of the Supreme Court, and the speaker of the House of Representatives; the commission submits a report to the president, who in turn makes his own recommendation to Congress. Until 1977 the president's proposal automatically took effect thirty days after transmittal to Congress "unless in the meantime either house had formally voted disapproval or Congress had enacted a statute establishing alternative pay rates." The law was revised in 1977 to require roll-call votes by Congress. That is, unless the president's proposal is explicitly enacted into law, it does not take effect.[59]

In Great Britain the government conducts periodic surveys of compensation, but the task of making specific recommendations for higher civil servants' pay adjustments is assigned to a commission appointed by the prime minister. Unlike the situation in both the United States and Japan, however, the commission's recommendations to the prime minister are implemented without revision.[60] Although a major rationale for empowering the National Personnel Authority to make annual recommendations on civil servants' pay was the restrictions on civil servants' right to engage in collective bargaining and in strikes,

seron chōsa, Shōwa 48-nen 9-gatsu [Opinion Survey Concerning Civil Servants, September 1973] (Tokyo: Sōrifu, Naikaku Sōri Daijin Kanbō Kōhōshitsu, 1973), pp. 10–13 and 20–21.

59. Robert W. Hartman and Arnold R. Weber, eds., *Rewards of Public Service: Compensating Top Federal Officials* (Washington: Brookings Institution, 1980), pp. 76–87.

60. Hashidachi Eiji, "Shō gaikoku kōmuin no kyūyo seido no gairyaku" [An Outline of Civil Servants' Compensation Systems in Various Foreign Countries], I, *Jinji-in geppō* 297 (Nov. 1975): 15.

such restrictions are by no means confined to Japan. In fact, none of the four Western democracies with which Japan has been compared in this study permits strikes by their civil servants.[61]

Provisions regarding the retirement of civil servants vary somewhat in the four countries. The most common age for mandatory retirement seems to be sixty-five. Eligibility for annuity typically requires the attainment of sixty years of age. Interestingly, the practice of encouraging retirement that we noted earlier is found in Britain as well: it is applied to civil servants who have passed the age of sixty.[62]

Retirement annuities in these countries are a function of the civil servant's salary and length of service. In the United States, a federal employee becomes eligible for voluntary retirement with full annuity after either thirty years of service and attaining the age of fifty-five or twenty years of service and attaining the age of sixty. Since 1970, federal employees have contributed 7 percent of their entire salary to the retirement system. The amount of annuity is computed by multiplying "the highest average salary during any three consecutive years of employment" by credits based on the number of years of service. "Each of the first five years of service earns a 1.5 percent credit for the worker; each of the next five earns him or her 1.75 percent, and each year of service above ten adds another 2 percent." The maximum annuity is 80 percent of the average salary. Under the preceding formula, a federal employee with thirty years of service receives credits of 56.25 percent.[63]

A British civil servant with at least ten years of service who attains the age of sixty is eligible for an annuity, which is equal to the average of his last three years of salary × one-eightieth × the number of years of service. A retiree with thirty years of service will thus receive 37.5 percent of his average salary. Although this is substantially less than what his American counterpart would get, the gap is reduced to some extent by a lump-sum separation allowance equal to three times the annuity. The British civil servant contributes about 8 percent of his salary to his pension scheme.[64]

61. "Kakkoku kōmuin seido no hikaku (10): Fukumu, shokuin dantai" [A Comparison of Civil Service Systems in Various Countries (10): Duties and Employee Organizations], *Jinji-in geppō* 112 (June 1960): 8–10.
62. Yoshida Kōzō, "Eikoku ni okeru kōmuin taishoku seisaku no genjō to tenbō" [The Present Situation and Future Prospects of Britain's Policy toward Civil Servants' Retirement], *Jinji-in geppō* 345 (Nov. 1979): 6–10.
63. Robert W. Hartman, *Pay and Pensions for Federal Workers* (Washington: Brookings Institution, 1983), pp. 16–17.
64. Shimoda Akiko, "Igirisu kōmuin no nenkin seido" [British Civil Servants' Annuity System] I, *Jinji-in geppō* 420 (Jan. 1986): 29–30.

In the French civil service one must have at least fifteen years of service to be eligible for pension; the minimum age for drawing pension is either fifty-five or sixty, depending on circumstances. The amount of annuity is computed by multiplying the preretirement salary by two-one-hundredths times the number of years of service; in no case, however, may the amount exceed 75 percent of the last salary. Thus a civil servant with thirty years of service will receive 60 percent of his salary; he will have contributed 6 percent of his salary to the pension fund during his civil-service career.[65]

A distinctive feature of the West German pension system is that it is completely state-financed; the civil servant need not make any contributions during his career. At least ten years of service are required, however, before he is eligible to draw pension. A credit of 35 percent is awarded for the first ten years of service, and a credit of 2 percent is added for each of the next fifteen years. Beyond that, each additional year earns a credit of 1 percent. In no case may the total exceed 75 percent. A civil servant with thirty years of service will thus receive 70 percent of his salary upon retirement.[66]

In comparative terms, then, the annuity of Japanese civil servants is on a par with that of their American counterparts. If the lump-sum separation allowance is added, it is probably comparable to that of the French civil servant as well. It is substantially better than that of the British civil servant. The clear winner is the West German civil servant, who enjoys the most-generous benefits at no cost.

What of the reemployment of retired civil servants? Although no statistics are available, it does not appear to be a major problem in Britain and West Germany. France, however, has its own version of *amakudari*. Known as *pantouflage*, this involves primarily the movement of elite administrators, mostly products of the Ecole Nationale d'Administration (ENA) and relatively young, from the public to the private sector. Those who choose this option are either "men with great family wealth who have entered the [government] service primarily for experience in managing large affairs" or "men who simply find private salaries irresistibly attractive."[67] Unless they have fulfilled their obligation to serve in the government for ten years, ENA graduates who move

65. Nomura Nario, "Furansu Kyōwakoku kanri no onkyū seido" [The Pension System of the Officials of the French Republic] I, *Jinji-in geppō* 315 (May 1977): 4–8.

66. Okada Jin, "Kakkoku kōmuin no onkyū seido" [The Pension System of Civil Servants in Various Countries] II, *Jinji-in geppō* 86 (Apr. 1958): 4–6.

67. Armstrong, *The European Administrative Elite*, p. 221.

to the private sector must reimburse the government the entire expense of their three-year education. In most cases the firms that hire them will pick up the tab.[68]

In the United States there is an extraordinarily high degree of mobility in all aspects of employment, both public and private. The closest thing to *amakudari* may therefore be the phenomenon of the revolving door—the movement of managerial-level personnel from government to private business and vice versa. Although it occurs in all government agencies, it is particularly prevalent in the Department of Defense. According to the *New York Times,* about a thousand people pass through the revolving door at the Pentagon each year. To illustrate, in 1985 an assistant secretary of defense for manpower and logistics resigned to assume a new position at Raytheon Company, a manufacturer of missiles, and a senior vice president at Northrop Corporation, a major defense contractor, became under secretary of defense for research engineering.[69]

All four countries have laws regulating the reemployment of former government officials. In the United States, former Federal employees are forbidden by law to return to "their agencies as supplicants for their new employers. But the restrictions are narrowly drawn to catch clear conflicts of interests. There are few prosecutions."[70] Former British civil servants must obtain approval from the government if, during two years following their retirement, they wish to work for firms with which the government is involved in any kind of financial transaction. This means that the British law is much more restrictive than its Japanese counterpart; the latter applies only to cases where the civil servant's own agency, not any government agency, has had a close connection with a prospective employer. Approval is required as well for reemployment in profit-making firms in both France and West Germany.[71]

As for entering the political arena, civil servants in France and West Germany enjoy the extraordinary privilege of running for elective

68. Shimizu Kunio, "Kanryō okuni-buri (6), Furansu: Banjaku no cho-erīto shugi" [Bureaucrats in Different Countries (6), France: An Unshakable Super-elitism], *Kankai,* Mar. 1981, p. 87.

69. *New York Times,* 25 Aug. 1985.

70. Ibid. Efforts to enact a new law that would "for two years prohibit officials leaving the Pentagon from going to work for a contractor over which they had 'personal and substantial' decision-making responsibility" have thus far been unsuccessful. Although passed by the House, the bill faced opposition in the Senate; the opponents argued that "it would hurt recruitment by the Pentagon, reduce opportunities for officials usefully forced out of Government and damage a helpful 'cross-fertilization' among military experts." See "Close the Pentagon's Revolving Door," ibid., 6 Sept. 1986, editorial.

71. "Kakkoku kōmuin seido no hikaku (10): Fukumu, shokuin dantai," pp. 6–7.

offices without first resigning from their jobs, and a sizable number of them do run for their respective parliaments. If successful, they are allowed to take what amount to leaves of absence to serve in parliament.[72] However, the phenomenon of retired bureaucrats running for national legislatures in any conspicuous numbers is not duplicated outside Japan.

In sum, although Japanese higher civil servants are not alone in suffering from relatively meager financial rewards, particularly in relation to their counterparts in the private sector, their custom of early retirement may be unique in its scale and clocklike regularity. Likewise, the pattern of reemployment by retired Japanese bureaucrats does seem to have some unusual features.

72. Ibid., pp. 5–6.

CHAPTER NINE

Conclusion

JAPAN'S ADMINISTRATIVE ELITE: AN OVERVIEW

What are the most outstanding characteristics of Japan's administrative elite? First and foremost, one is struck by the extent to which higher civil servants indeed constitute an "elite" in Japan. The traditionally high prestige of "career" bureaucrats has helped to make Japan's higher civil-service examinations the most competitive of their kind among industrialized democracies; those who survive the competition tend to be among the best that Japan's educational system has to offer to that country's prospective employers. Given the stratification of Japanese universities, this translates into the dominance of a few elite universities in the recruitment process.

Such an elitist complexion of Japanese bureaucracy persists despite the genuinely open nature of Japan's higher civil-service examinations, which, unlike their counterparts in Western democracies, lack any formal educational requirement. Just as the openness of civil-service examinations in imperial China did not necessarily imply a true equality of opportunity for all, regardless of social class or wealth,[1] so the absence of educational prerequisites in the Japanese system have thus far failed to neutralize the disadvantages of those without elitist educational credentials.

One aspect of the recruitment process that seems to play a role in perpetuating the elitist nature of the Japanese higher civil service is the

---

1. Ichisada Miyazaki, *China's Examination Hell: The Civil Service Examinations of Imperial China,* trans. Conrad Schirokauer (New Haven: Yale University Press, 1963).

decentralization of hiring. Those who pass the higher civil-service examination must apply to individual ministries and agencies on their own; because, overall, only about half of the candidates eventually receive appointments and because competition to enter such ministries as Finance and MITI is particularly intense, most ministries and agencies have considerable leeway in making their final selections. It is generally assumed that products of elite universities enjoy a competitive edge at this stage of the game, an assumption that is buttressed by evidence showing that the proportion of elite-university graduates, particularly those of Tōdai, is much higher among those who are actually hired than it is among those who pass the higher civil-service examination.

Nonetheless, it would be neither an exaggeration nor a distortion of the reality to characterize Japan's administrative elite as a "meritocratic elite"—an elite chosen on the basis of the universalistic criteria of performance in open, competitive examinations and, indirectly, of educational attainments.

Having said this, we must note that ascriptive features are not totally absent in Japan. For one thing, one's chances of success in Japan's highly stratified and fiercely competitive educational system do not depend exclusively on one's own talents and efforts; they are also affected to a significant degree by the quantity and quality of preparations for entrance examinations to schools at succeeding levels that one can purchase, which obviously is a function of the financial status of one's parents. But there is another sense in which quasi-ascriptive criteria creep into the equation, and this must be viewed as a second distinctive feature of Japan's administrative elite.

Whether or not one can join the coveted ranks of Japan's administrative elite in a narrow sense—that is, those who occupy the positions of section chief or its equivalent and above in the national government—is critically dependent on one's mode of entry into the government bureaucracy. In other words, mode of entry, which is based on a confluence of achievement and quasi-ascriptive factors (for example, the quality and quantity of education one has purchased) exerts an enduring influence on one's career progression in the civil service. Only those who are hired by the various ministries and agencies after passing the higher civil-service examination have a better-than-even chance of being promoted to section chief and beyond. Called "career" civil servants, these cadets for elite administrative positions have been included in the broad definition of Japan's administrative elite in this study.

What is more, it is not simply whether but when one has passed the higher civil-service examination that becomes controlling. For example, someone who passes the higher examination after he has already entered the civil service via other routes, typically the intermediate examination, is not accorded a fullfledged "career" status but relegated to membership in a "separate-list group" (*beppyō-gumi*), an anomalous category that lies midway between the "career" and "noncareer" groups. It should be made plain that promotion to the rank of section chief and above is within the reach of both noncareer and *beppyō-gumi* civil servants. Nonetheless, not only is there a patently unequal distribution of probabilities of promotion that corresponds to the civil servants' mode of initial entry into the bureaucracy but their career paths, in terms of opportunities encountered and psychic satisfactions experienced, also diverge markedly.

The relative importance of seniority may be listed as a third characteristic of Japan's administrative elite. Although merit is by no means neglected, it does not really become a criterion of promotion until a cohort of civil servants has reached a certain level, typically assistant section chief or section chief. Among career civil servants, the year of entry, which is bound up with the year of graduation from university, becomes all but sacrosanct in personnel assignments in the sense that a bureau chief will have more seniority than an assistant bureau chief, and so on down the line. As Sahashi Shigeru, a former administrative vice-minister of MITI put it, the concept of "ability" is totally nullified.[2]

A fourth feature of Japan's administrative elite that merits special mention is the predominance of law graduates in its ranks. Although about one in seven successful candidates in the higher civil-service examination in recent years has chosen law as his field of specialization in the examination, one in four or five of those who are ultimately hired by the government from the pool of successful candidates has been a "specialist" in law. The predominance of law graduates becomes particularly pronounced in the upper rungs of Japanese bureaucracy, namely among its administrative elite in a narrow sense. Between six and seven in ten elite administrators have been law graduates in the postwar period.

In a strict sense, a law "specialist" and a law graduate are distinct categories, for it is theoretically possible for a nonlaw graduate to become a law "specialist" by opting for the field of law in the higher civil-service examination. In practice, the two overlap to a striking

2. Sahashi Shigeru, "Kanryō shokun ni chokugen suru" [Talking Straight to Bureaucrats], *Bungei shunjū*, July 1971, p. 110.

degree. More important, unlike the situation in most Western democracies, being a law graduate in Japan does not necessarily imply possession of a license to practice law. To qualify for membership in the legal profession, one must pass an exceedingly competitive judicial examination, in which the failure rate averages 98 percent; undergo two years of postgraduate training at the state-run Judicial Training Institute; and pass its graduation examination. For these reasons, the typical law graduate in Japan, who possesses both a fair amount of substantive knowledge of law and a bachelor-of-law degree (*hōgakushi*), is regarded as a generalist rather than a specialist.

This leads us to a fifth characteristic of Japan's administrative elite, which is a corollary of the phenomenon noted above: the ascendancy of administrative generalists (*jimukan*) over technical specialists (*gikan*). Even though the term "administrative" elite implies the exclusion of technical personnel, we have actually used it to refer to all higher civil servants in this study; hence it is not tautological to note the predominance of "administrative generalists" among Japan's administrative elite. In fact, technical officials outnumber administrative ones by six to four at the entry level, that is, in the realm of elite-track higher civil servants. It is at higher levels that we discern a reversal of roles; when we focus on those who have crossed the threshold into the administrative elite in a narrow sense, administrative officials emerge as a majority, whereas technical officials become a minority: between six and seven in ten of the senior civil servants are administrative officials. At the level of administrative vice-ministers, a technical specialist is even harder to find. Of the twelve ministries of the national government, only one, the Ministry of Construction, provides equal opportunity for advancement to all of its elite-track bureaucrats: by custom, the top career position is rotated between administrative and technical officials.

The ascendancy of generalists is linked with and sustained by the policy of frequent rotation in the career progression of Japan's administrative elite. Rotation between the headquarters and the field, including overseas posts, and among a wide range of units within the same ministry or agency, is bound to be a broadening experience, allowing the bureaucrat to gain a feel for the diversity of functions and tasks performed by his ministry or agency and enabling him to approach his problems with the interests of the larger organization in view as he moves up the ladder of authority.

Such a policy, even if successful, does not prevent Japan's administrative elite from engaging in jurisdictional rivalries both within and between their respective organizations. Within the same ministry, different bureaus jealously guard their turfs, and across ministerial boundaries disputes routinely erupt concerning each other's jurisdictions and clienteles as well as over policy issues. Known as "sectionalism," this phenomenon, although by no means confined to Japan, can be viewed as a sixth characteristic of Japan's administrative elite. According to Sahashi Shigeru, sectionalism frequently leads to the subordination of national interests to those of one's ministry (*kokka yori shōga yūsen*).[3] Among its many consequences are the obvious waste of resources, duplication of effort, occasional paralysis of government action, and erosion of bureaucratic power.

A well-known feature of Japanese organizations in the private and public sectors alike is consensual decision making; we shall list it as a seventh attribute of Japan's administrative elite. Two devices that are utilized in building consensus are *ringisho* and *nemawashi*. Although it is typically drafted by a relatively low-level bureaucrat and then circulated upward, the *ringisho* is seldom a brainchild of its drafter. It may have originated elsewhere, such as at higher levels of the bureaucracy. *Nemawashi*, a painstaking process of touching bases with all important persons who probably will impinge upon a decision, occurs both within and across organizational boundaries.

In comparative terms, Japan's administrative elite may be among the most powerful in industrialized democracies; hence its extraordinary power may be listed as an eighth characteristic. Paradoxically, the American Occupation played a key role not only in perpetuating but also in bolstering the power of Japanese government bureaucracy. For one thing, the principal rivals of bureaucrats, the military and the zaibatsu, were decimated. Furthermore, the purge program, though it temporarily incapacitated a large number of politicians, hardly touched the bureaucrats. Finally, SCAP's program of civil-service reform ultimately enhanced the position of bureaucrats by spawning a central personnel agency charged with the multiple functions of safeguarding the merit principle, protecting the interests of civil servants, and promoting the goals of democracy, efficiency, and equity in personnel management.

During the first three decades of the postwar era, Japan experienced a system of government in which formal authority lagged behind actual power; in Chalmers Johnson's phrase, politicians "reigned," whereas bureaucrats "ruled."[4] Among the many factors undergirding bureaucratic power was a national consensus regarding the primacy of

3. Ibid., p. 108.
4. Johnson, *MITI and the Japanese Miracle*, pp. 34–35 and 316.

developmental goals, which, along with an institutional legacy of the prewar and wartime era, helped to sustain a "developmental state." The adoption of an "industrial policy" and the use of "market-conforming methods of state intervention" in the economy, including "administrative guidance," were further sources, or perhaps symptoms, of the formidable power of Japan's administrative elite.[5]

Although the power of the administrate elite has been waning gradually since the mid-1970s, as LDP politicians acquired more expertise and became more assertive in the exercise of their constitutional authority, reinforced by electoral mandates, senior bureaucrats have by no means relinquished their power. In an important sense, they continue to play a pivotal role in policy formulation, while virtually monopolizing the power of policy implementation.

Finally, we must note the retirement patterns of Japan's administrative elite. Although guaranteed "lifetime employment," the careers of Japanese higher civil servants tend to be remarkably brief; nearly all of them retire in their mid-fifties, and a sizable number retire even earlier. Rooted in the culturally reinforced custom whereby members of the same entering class shun hierarchical relationships among themselves and thus resign when a classmate reaches the top of the career ladder, this phenomenon also serves the organizational need for periodic turnover of personnel in high echelons, thus ensuring the relative youth and vitality of its leadership.

The civil servants who retire in their prime of life do not fade away; most of them find productive "second careers" in private enterprises, public corporations, politics, and other fields. In an overwhelming number of cases, finding a postretirement landing spot is the responsibility not of the retiring civil servant but of his ministry or agency. The options available to the bureaucrats vary, depending on such factors as the nature of linkage between their organization and the private sector, the number and type of public corporations under its jurisdiction, their preretirement rank, and the marketability of their experience and skills. In general, the higher one's last rank, the greater the range of options. Judging from the number of exemptions (that is, waivers of rules proscribing employment that might entail conflicts of interest) granted by the National Personnel Authority, the Finance Ministry has consistently outperformed all others in the reemployment of retirees in the private sector. The Finance Ministry is also the largest source of former bureaucrats who run for the Diet.

5. Ibid., esp. pp. 17–34.

These, in brief, are the most notable features of Japan's administrative elite. We shall take a further look at most of them by exploring patterns of continuity and change, the universality and particularity of the Japanese experience, and implications of the Japanese model.

CONTINUITY AND CHANGE

Nearly all of the attributes noted in the preceding section have their antecedents in the prewar period. As we saw in chapter 2, the prewar Japanese bureaucracy was thoroughly elitist, enjoying high prestige, vast powers, and conspicuous perquisites and dominated by graduates of elite universities, notably Tokyo Imperial University. Moreover, it embraced a virtual caste system in which there were distinctly unequal classes, the sharpest distinction being drawn between ordinary and higher officials. Inasmuch as the mode of initial entry served as the primary basis for differentiation between the two groups, the prewar system, too, was quasi-ascriptive to some extent.

The domination by law graduates, known as *hōka bannō*, was much more pronounced in the prewar period than it is in the postwar era. So, too, was the preferential treatment of generalist administrators over technical specialists. Practices that gave rise to "sectionalism" originated in the prewar period: decentralized hiring of officials, lifetime employment, and the low frequency of interministerial transfers. Also traceable to the prewar bureaucracy is the custom of early retirement, which was rooted in the same considerations that govern its postwar practice: the need to obviate a conflict between the cultural norm of equality among peers and the bureaucratic norm of hierarchical authority based on rank regardless of age or length of service. Since the mean retirement age may have been slightly lower in the prewar period—retirement in the late forties as compared with the mid-fifties in the 1980s—the need to find "second careers" was equally present. *Amakudari* in a narrow sense, that is, descending onto private firms, however, appeared to have been less frequent in the prewar era than it is today.

If there are striking continuities in broad patterns, one can also detect slight but nonetheless significant changes. Most of these have to do with a decline in some of the prewar tendencies rather than their complete disappearance. Particularly noteworthy in this connection are a slight decline in elitism and a slow but steady increase in the number of women.

A decline in elitism can be seen in a number of trends: (1) a strong showing of universities other than Tōdai and Kyōdai in the higher civil-service examination, (2) a notable increase in the proportion of private-university graduates who enter the higher civil service, and (3) advancement of "noncareer" bureaucrats to elite administrative positions.

Although Tōdai and Kyōdai have consistently maintained their positions as the first- and second-largest sources, respectively, of successful candidates in the higher civil-service examination throughout the postwar period, their combined share of the total has frequently fallen short of 50 percent. In the eighteen-year period from 1970 to 1987, for example, the two top universities' share fell below the 50-percent mark eleven times (see table 9 in chapter 4). This means that the majority of successful candidates in the higher civil-service examination came from other institutions of higher learning in those years. In the 1980s, private universities surpassed the 10-percent mark for the first time, reaching 12.6 percent by 1986 and 13 percent in 1987. In the ten-year period from 1976 to 1985 the number of private-university graduates who passed the higher civil-service examination increased 3.5 times.[6]

If we examine the situation at the hiring stage, we find the same trend: a steady increase in the proportion of private-university graduates. Since 1980, private-university graduates who passed the higher civil-service examination had a greater probability of being hired than graduates of national universities. In 1983 and 1984, six in ten of the former, as compared with four in ten of the latter, were hired. In the ten-year period from 1976 to 1985, the number of private-university graduates who entered the higher civil service quadrupled.[7]

A slight decline in the elitist character of Japan's higher civil service is suggested by a steady increase in the number of "noncareer" civil servants who advance to elite administrative positions. As we saw in chapter 4 (table 8), graduates of the intermediate civil-service examination began to appear in grade-1 positions (assistant bureau chief, division chief, and senior-level section chief) in increasing numbers since 1974; in 1981, a graduate of the lower examination attained grade 1 for the first time, and a small but growing number of others followed in his footsteps in subsequent years. By 1986, the National Personnel Author-

6. "Komuin Q & A" [Questions and Answers About Civil Servants], *Jinji-in geppō* 426 (July 1986): 11.
7. Ibid.

ity disclosed that two in ten civil servants at the rank of section chief or its equivalent and above in the national government had not gone beyond junior colleges, implying that they were "noncareer" bureaucrats.[8]

Women were allowed to compete in the higher civil-service examination for the first time in 1909, and beginning in 1928 a handful of women passed its judicial section and one passed its administrative section. The lone woman, however, was never offered an appointment to the higher civil service. In contrast to this dismal picture, the postwar period is a paradise for women. The proportion of women among successful candidates in the higher civil-service examination has ranged from 3.3 to 8.7 percent; in absolute numbers, between 42 and 160 women have passed the higher examination each year (see table 14). There has been a steady increase during the 1980s in women's share, in both absolute and proportional terms; in 1986, 128 women, accounting for 7.5 percent of the total, passed the higher examination. In 1987, however, women's share declined slightly, to 116 successes (6.8 percent).

These developments have been reflected in a steady infusion of women into the higher civil service in recent years. Since the mid-1970s, between 3 and 4 percent of all new appointees to elite-track administrative service I positions have been women. However, only a handful of women have attained the rank of section chief or above in most ministries and agencies. Although a few of them have advanced to the rank of bureau chief, the ultimate prize of administrative vice-ministership has thus far eluded them.

In sum, although there are striking continuities between the prewar and postwar periods insofar as the elite of Japanese-government bureaucracy is concerned, that bureaucracy is by no means a static institution. It has demonstrated a capacity for change, and the incremental changes that have occurred in the past two or three decades point toward a steady democratization of Japan's higher civil service.

UNIVERSALITY AND PARTICULARITY

To what extent are the salient attributes of Japan's administrative elite shared by the government bureaucracies of other industrialized democracies? In what ways are they idiosyncratic? Although none of the attributes is duplicated in identical form or to the same degree in the

8. Ibid.

four advanced industrial democracies with which Japan has been compared in this study, a few of them come very close to being common denominators. One is elitism. In three of the four Western democracies—Britain, France, and West Germany—careers in the higher civil service are sufficiently well regarded to attract the cream of the crop among their university-educated youth. In two of those countries—Britain and France—products of elite educational institutions outnumber those of lesser institutions. In all three, merit as demonstrated in examinations, whether competitive or qualifying, plays a decisive role in the recruitment of their higher civil servants. In sum, the phrase, "meritocratic elite," is no less apt for the latter than for those in Japan.

The situation in the United States is different. Although the competition for the presidential management internship is keen, the successful candidates are distributed among a large number of institutions without domination by a few elite universities. Nor can it be said that either the government service in general or the PMIP in particular necessarily attracts "the best and the brightest" among the age cohort in the United States. Moreover, the extensive use of political appointees in the high and intermediate echelons of the American federal bureaucracy dilutes its meritocratic complexion to a significant degree.

Another quasi-common denominator appears to be the ascendancy of generalists, particularly its twin phenomenon of rotation of higher civil servants among a wide range of assignments. One can find similar practices in the three European democracies. A major difference, however, is that rotation occurs across organizational boundaries far more frequently in Europe than it does in Japan.[9] Members of the *grands corps* in France are notable for the versatility of their contributions in a wide array of organizations, including private enterprises. West German higher civil servants move back and forth between the federal government and Lander administrations. Once again, the American practice differs from the Western European pattern; there is marked emphasis on specialized career paths, in terms of both function and organization.

A third feature that may approximate a common denominator is the power of the administrative elite. Senior civil servants in all four Western countries wield considerable influence; their actual power

9. According to Spaulding, "generalism and rotation were hallmarks of the oldest examination, the Chinese imperial, and the Chinese precedent may have had more influence (centuries later) on Europe than on Japan (which may have adopted the two principles because the Germans had)." Robert M. Spaulding, Jr., prepublication review of an earlier version of this study, 27 May 1987.

tends to be appreciably greater than their formal authority. In a fundamental sense, this is a function of the indivisibility of policy and administration; because no policy is self-executing, those who are charged with the task of executing it must necessarily use their judgment and discretion, which more often than not translates into the exercise of power. Another major source of bureaucratic power is their expertise, an indispensable ingredient of public policy in the contemporary era. In all three European democracies, the responsibility for drafting legislation rests primarily on the shoulders of bureaucrats. The relative power of administrative elites varies from country to country; it tends to be greater in a developmental nation such as Japan than in a regulatory state such as the United States. Another important variable in the equation is the power of competing institutions, notably parliament. Its relative weakness in Japan serves to bolster bureaucratic power, and its relative strength in the United States helps to diminish bureaucratic power.

Another phenomenon that finds its echo in the Western democracies is the underrepresentation of women. In none of the four countries have women attained full equality, in the sense of numerical parity with men at upper levels of the higher civil service. However, the degree of women's underrepresentation varies widely: whereas the United States displays near parity in the key recruitment channel, the PMIP, Britain hovers around the 10-percent mark in its administrative-trainee program. One in four or five candidates who enter the French Ecole Nationale d'Administration is a woman. On this score, the Japanese record, which, as noted, has improved markedly in the postwar period, still falls short of the Western norm.

Finally, the propensity of Japanese bureaucrats to engage in territorial disputes is by no means unique. Jurisdictional disputes occur among bureaucratic organizations everywhere. What is nonetheless noteworthy is their frequency and scope in Japan. Their manifestation not merely *between* but also *within* organizations does seem to be peculiarly Japanese. As noted, decentralized hiring, coupled with lifetime employment within single organizations, accentuates that universal bureaucratic tendency.

These seem to exhaust the list of the more notable aspects of bureaucratic elites that are more or less common to the industrialized democracies. There is at least one facet of the Japanese case that is replicated in another industrialized democracy, namely, the dominant position of law graduates. If anything, the phenomenon is more pronounced in West Germany than it is in Japan, where, as previously noted, it shows signs of tapering off in the postwar period. The occurrence of the same phenomenon in the two countries seems to reflect the German influence on the Japanese system a century ago as well as the relative continuity in both during the ensuing years.

The characteristics that set Japan apart from the Western democracies the most appear to be the quasi-ascriptive nature, consensual decision making, and retirement practices of its administrative elite. To be sure, Japan is not alone in having a highly stratified government bureaucracy; all three European democracies have distinct groups and classes within their respective civil services. In terms of their relative rigidity, however, only West Germany resembles Japan. But the West German system is considerably more permeable than the Japanese one.

The consensual mode of decision making noted earlier is clearly a distinctive Japanese phenomenon. There is nothing in the Western repertoire of administrative practices that resembles the *ringisei*. If touching bases with other players in the decision-making arena is fairly widespread in all advanced industrial democracies, very few if any can rival Japan in the thoroughness with which such preparatory work is carried out. The *nemawashi*, in other words, does seem to be uniquely Japanese.

The early retirement of Japan's administrative elite is not duplicated elsewhere. Nor is the reemployment of retired senior bureaucrats in private firms and public corporations matched in the other democracies in terms of its scope. Only in the area of bureaucratic penetration of the political arena, notably parliaments, do two of the four Western democracies, France and West Germany, parallel or surpass Japan.

In sum, then, Japan shares many attributes of its bureaucracy with the three advanced industrial countries in Western Europe, although there are significant variations in degree. Nonetheless, very few of the attributes can be characterized as universal, because the United States either does not exhibit them at all or exhibits them to a negligible degree. On the other hand, a few practices do appear to be either idiosyncratic to or more pronounced in Japan: the rigidity of the multiple-track system, consensual decision making, and the early retirement and reemployment of elite administrators.

AN ASSESSMENT OF THE JAPANESE MODEL

Whether there is a Japanese model of government bureaucracy worthy of emulation is open to debate. If the existence of a normative Japanese model is debatable, however, the reality of an analytic or empirical model is undeniable. To contribute to the debate on the normative implications of the Japanese experience, let us essay a tentative and necessarily subjective assessment of the strengths and weaknesses of the empirical model of Japanese bureaucracy sketched in the preceding pages.

Most aspects of Japanese bureaucracy or Japan's administrative elite appear to have multiple consequences, some positive and some negative. We shall, however, delineate the positive side of the coin first. Perhaps the most noteworthy is the exceptional caliber of Japan's administrative elite, broadly defined. They are the veritable cream of the crop—extraordinarily competent, highly dedicated, and singularly hard-working. As T. J. Pempel points out, this, along with internal structural features and the mode of interaction between bureaucrats and politicians, may go a long way toward explaining the apparent efficiency of Japanese-government bureaucracy and the efficacy of Japan's public policies.[10]

The policy of frequently rotating elite-track and elite administrators and the preferential treatment of generalists, too, have their positive side: they help facilitate the task of coordination, particularly, within the various ministries and agencies. Consensual decision making undoubtedly enhances the sense of participation and commitment among the bureaucrats concerned; it also contributes to the implementation of decisions that, theoretically, most of the key players have played a part in shaping.

The character of the nexus between bureaucrats and politicians can also be listed as a strength of the Japanese model. The modes of interaction between the two groups, the bureaucratization of politics, and the politicization of bureaucracy in Japan result in an unusually high degree of cooperation between them, which can be construed as functional not only for the government bureaucracy but for the larger society as well.

The early retirement of Japan's administrative elite performs a manifest organizational function: it enables each organization to sustain a healthy rate of personnel turnover, not only infusing new blood but also promoting relatively young members to leadership positions on a continuing basis. If this helps to make the Japanese government bureaucracy a repository of vitality and fresh outlook, its outputs, both in terms of policy and implementation, can benefit the citizenry at large. So, too, can one accentuate the positive aspects of *amakudari*. For the penetration of former elite bureaucrats into the private sector, the public corporations, and the political arena can bolster the ability of Japanese society as a whole to function smoothly. Their valuable experience,

10. Pempel, "Organizing for Efficiency," pp. 72–106.

expertise, and connections can both increase the efficiency of the various organizations in which the retired bureaucrats have relocated themselves and facilitate the interaction of the myriad structures to a striking degree.

The much-maligned "sectionalism," too, is not without its virtues. For example, it contributes crucially to the curbing of bureaucratic power. By competing against each other, by jealously guarding their respective turfs, and by exposing the excesses of their rivals, bureaucratic agencies, in effect, perform the much-needed function of checking and balancing each other.[11]

As already noted, most of these features also have negative consequences. The price Japan pays for the high caliber of its administrative elite is the stifling rigidity of the multiple-track system, a system in which there are second-class citizens, lack of representativeness, and demoralization of "noncareer" bureaucrats who, in fact, not only devote their entire careers to government service but also bear a great share of the burden in public administration.

No less serious is the problem of discrimination against technical specialists. The lack of an equal opportunity for this numerical majority in Japan's higher civil service is not only an anomaly but also a betrayal of the goal of democracy to which Japanese bureaucracy is officially committed. It may also lead to bureaucratic inefficiency and create increasing problems for the Japanese government in this technological age.

Consensual decision making has two obvious shortcomings: it is time-consuming and it stifles individual initiative. The key question here is how to weigh the benefits and the costs. It is possible that, in the Japanese context, the benefits generally outweigh the costs, although each organization and each case may well entail a different mix of both.

The question of the net balance of benefits over costs is also germane to the other features of Japanese bureaucracy, such as early retirement, *amakudari,* and "sectionalism." Early retirement, for example, may mean the loss of valuable talent for the organization concerned. The accumulated experience and wisdom of the retiring bureaucrat may well be more valuable to the organization than to his postretirement destination. This is true because a person in his mid-fifties in Japan, which boasts the longest life expectancy in the world, is probably still in the prime of life.[12]

---

11. Johnson, *MITI and the Japanese Miracle,* p. 78.
12. In 1985, the life expectancy of the Japanese male was 74.78 years, whereas that of the Japanese female was 80.48. *Asahi shinbun,* 26 Mar. 1987.

Reemployment of retired bureaucrats may, in one sense, signify the redeployment of talent or reallocation of human resources. From the standpoint of society at large, there may not be a net loss at all; on the contrary, it may lead to a healthy circulation, and hence wider utilization, of available talent. Nonetheless, the phenomenon is not without costs, of which the most obvious is a conflict of interest. Neither the existing law nor actual practice appears to be effective in curbing such conflicts. Another cost is the "presumably inevitable increase in (a) average age and (b) number of people in high-level positions in the public corporations and some private corporations." A rigorous evaluation of this cost, however, would necessitate an inquiry into "which positions are functional and which are sinecures"—something that is beyond the scope of this study.[13]

If "sectionalism" helps to spawn the phenomenon of checks and balances in the rough and tumble of the bureaucratic world, it also leads to a wasteful expenditure of energy and resources. In its intraorganizational manifestation, sectionalism sets bureau against bureau; in its larger incarnation, sectionalism engenders a displacement of goals in which the ultimate loser may well be the country as a whole and hence the citizenry at large.

In sum, the empirical model of Japanese bureaucracy is so intermingled with both positive and negative features as to preclude an unambiguous verdict on its normative implications. If one chooses to accentuate the positive or to assume that the positive features tend to eclipse the negative ones, that choice can probably be defended with a fair amount of cogency. If the proof of the pudding is in the eating, any objective observer cannot but be struck by the amazing development of the Japanese economy and, by implication as well as on the strength of direct evidence, of the Japanese government. The latter in turn bespeaks the high efficiency of Japanese-government bureaucracy.

Nothwithstanding all this, the unmistakable lesson of the Japanese experience in bureaucratic organization and administration is that the Japanese have paid a high price for their success. They have also demonstrated an unsurpassed aptitude and capacity for creative adaptation of structures and practices developed in alien settings. Moreover, one sees in the Japanese record a powerful confirmation of the tenacity of culture—of the enduring effects of culture over structure.[14]

13. Spaulding, prepublication review of an earlier version of this study.
14. A notable example is "consensual decision-making both in the bureaucracy and elsewhere." According to Spaulding, it "reflect[s] a very ancient Japanese preference traceable all the way back to Shinto legends in the Kojiki and Nihongi and visible throughout centuries of changes in political and economic systems." Ibid.

Bibliography

Aberbach, Joel, Robert D. Putnam, and Bert A. Rochman. *Bureaucrats and Politicians in Western Democracies*. Cambridge: Harvard University Press, 1981.

Akimoto Hideo and Kanai Hachirō. "Taidan: Kōmuin rinri to 'amakudari' mondai o megutte" [Conversation: Concerning the Ethics of Civil Servants and the Problem of "Descent from Heaven"]. *Jinji-in geppō* [Monthly Bulletin of the National Personnel Authority] 377 (June 1982): 1–8.

Armstrong, John A. *The European Administrative Elite.* Princeton: Princeton University Press, 1973.

Asahi Shinbun "Kanryō" Shuzaihan. *Kanryō: Sono seitai* [Bureaucrats: Their Mode of Life]. Tokyo: Sangyō Nōritsu Tanki Daigaku Shuppanbu, 1978.

Asai Kiyoshi. *Shinpan kokka kōmuinhō seigi* [Detailed Commentaries on the National Public Service Law, New Edition]. Tokyo: Gakuyō Shobō, 1970.

Ashitate Chūzō. "Kōhei shinsa no omoide" [Recollections of the Equity Process]. *Jinji-in geppō* 274 (December 1973): 18–19.

Baerwald, Hans H. *Japan's Parliament: An Introduction*. London: Cambridge University Press, 1974.

――――. *The Purge of Japanese Leaders Under the Occupation*. Berkeley: University of California Press, 1959.

Bartholomew, James R. "Japanese Modernization and the Imperial Universities, 1876–1920." *Journal of Asian Studies* 37, no. 2 (February 1978): 251–72.

Becker, Ulrich, and Berend Kruger. "Personnel Administration and Personnel Management." In Klaus Konig et al., eds., *Public Administration in the Federal Republic of Germany*, pp. 247–62. Antwerp: Kluwer-Deventer, 1983.

Bessatsu kokkai benran: Shiryō sōshūhen [Separate-Volume Supplement to the National Diet Handbook: Complete Collection of Materials]. Tokyo: Nihon Seikei Shinbun Shuppanbu, 1975.

Beyme, Klaus von. *The Political System of the Federal Republic of Germany.* New York: St. Martin's Press, 1983.

Black, Cyril E., et al. *The Modernization of Japan and Russia.* New York: Free Press, 1975.

Brecht, Arnold. "Personnel Management." In Edward H. Litchfield et al., *Governing Postwar Germany,* pp. 263–93. Ithaca: Cornell University Press, 1953.

Campbell, John C. *Contemporary Japanese Budget Politics.* Berkeley: University of California Press, 1977.

———. "Policy Conflict and Its Resolution Within the Governmental System." In Ellis S. Krauss et al., eds., *Conflict in Japan,* pp. 294–334. Honolulu: University of Hawaii Press, 1984.

Chapman, Brian. *The Profession of Government: The Public Service in Europe.* London: George Allen and Unwin, 1959.

Cheng, Peter P. "The Japanese Cabinets, 1885–1973: An Elite Analysis." *Asian Survey,* 14, no. 12 (December 1974): 1055–71.

Corson, John J., and R. Shale Paul. *Men near the Top: Filling Key Posts in the Federal Service.* Baltimore: Johns Hopkins Press, 1966.

Craig, Albert M. "Functional and Dysfunctional Aspects of Government Bureaucracy." In Ezra F. Vogel, ed., *Modern Japanese Organization and Decision-Making,* pp. 3–32. Berkeley: University of California Press, 1975.

———, ed. *Japan: A Comparative View.* Princeton: Princeton University Press, 1979.

Cummings, William K. *Education and Equality in Japan.* Princeton: Princeton University Press, 1980.

Curtis, Gerald L. "Big Business and Political Influence." In Ezra F. Vogel, ed., *Modern Japanese Organization and Decision-Making,* pp. 33–70. Berkeley: University of California Press, 1975.

"Dai ikkai kyōdō shonin kenshū o jisshi shite" [Implementation of the First Joint Training of New Appointees]. *Jinji-in geppō* 197 (July 1967): 20–23.

Daigaku Sōgō Kenkyū Sirizu Kikaku Henshū Iinkai, ed. *Tōkyō Daigaku sōgō kenkyū* [A Comprehensive Study of the University of Tokyo]. Tokyo: Nihon Rikurūto Sentā Shuppanbu, 1979.

Deutsch, Karl, and Lewis Edinger. *Germany Rejoins the Powers.* Stanford: Stanford University Press, 1959.

Dogan, Mattei, ed. *The Mandarins of Western Europe: The Political Role of Top Civil Servants.* Beverly Hills, Calif.: Sage Publications, 1975.

Domoto Seiji. "Seisaku keisei katei no shisutemu: Hōan seitei katei ni miru seifu yotō kan chōsei" [The Policy-making Process: Mutual Adjustment Between the Government and the Ruling Party in the Legislative Process]. *Jurisuto,* special issue, 29 (Winter 1983): 56–63.

Donnelly, Michael W. "Conflict over Government Authority and Markets: Japan's Rice Economy." In Ellis S. Krauss et al., eds., *Conflict in Japan,* pp. 335–74. Honolulu: University of Hawaii Press, 1984.

Dyson, Kenneth H. F. *Party, State, and Bureaucracy in Western Germany.* Beverly Hills, Calif.: Sage Publications, 1977.

Ebato Tetsuo. *Kasumigaseki no kōbō: Ōkurashō, Yūseishō, Keisatsuchō, Gaimushō* [The Rise and Fall of Kasumigaseki: The Finance Ministry, the Posts and Telecommunications Ministry, the Police Agency, and the Foreign Ministry]. Tokyo: Tsukuma Shobō, 1987.

Edinger, Lewis J. *Politics in Germany: Attitudes and Processes.* Boston: Little, Brown, 1968.

Esman, Milton J. "Japanese Administration—A Comparative View." *Public Administration Review* 7, no. 2 (Spring 1947): 100–12.

Fry, Geoffrey K. *"The Administrative Revolution" in Whitehall: A Study of the Politics of Administrative Change in British Central Government since the 1950s.* London: Croom Helm, 1981.

_____. *The Changing Civil Service.* London: George Allen and Unwin, 1985.

_____. "The Development of the Thatcher Government's 'Grand Strategy' For the Civil Service: A Public Policy Perspective." *Public Administration* (London) 62, no. 3 (Autumn 1984): 322–35.

_____. *Statesmen in Disguise: The Changing Role of the Administrative Class of the British Home Civil Service, 1853–1966.* London: Macmillan, 1969.

Fujii Ryōko. "Amerika zakkan" [Miscellaneous Impressions of America]. *Jinji-in geppō* 378 (July 1982): 22–24.

Fukui, Haruhiro. *Party in Power: the Japanese Liberal-Democrats and Policymaking.* Berkeley: University of California Press, 1970.

_____. "Studies in Policymaking: A Review of the Literature." In T. J. Pempel, ed., *Policymaking in Contemporary Japan,* pp. 22–59. Ithaca: Cornell University Press, 1977.

Fukumoto Kunio. *Kanryō* [Bureaucrats]. Tokyo: Kōbundō, 1959.

"Furansu jōkyū kōmuin no shonin kyōiku: Rainichi no Kokuritsu Gyosei Gakuin (ENA) sei ni kiku" [Early Education of French Higher Civil Servants: Interview with Students of the Ecole Nationale d' Administration Who Are Visiting Japan]. *Jinji-in geppō* 266 (July 1981): 6–11.

Garon, Sheldon H. "The Imperial Bureaucracy and Labor Policy in Postwar Japan." *Journal of Asian Studies* 43, no. 3 (May 1984): 441–58.

Gerth, Hans, and C. Wright Mills, trans. and eds. From *Max Weber: Essays in Sociology.* New York: Oxford University Press, 1946.

Gillis, John R. *The Prussian Bureaucracy in Crisis, 1840–1860: Origins of an Administrative Ethos.* Stanford: Stanford University Press, 1971.

Gordon, Leonard V., and Akio Kikuchi. "The Measurement of Bureaucratic Orientation in Japan." *International Review of Applied Psychology* 19, no. 2 (October 1970): 133–39.

Great Britain. Committee Under the Chairmanship of Lord Fulton. *The Civil Service.* Vols. I, II, III (1), III (2), IV, V (1), V (2). London: H.M. Stationery Office, 1968.

Gyōsei kanri benran [Handbook of Administrative Management], 1980. Tokyo: Gyōsei Kanri Kenkyū Sentā, 1980.

Gyōsei Kanrichō. *Gyōsei kanri no genjō: Gyōsei kaikaku no dōkō* [The Present Condition of Administrative Management: Trends in Administrative Reform], 1984. Tokyo: Ōkurashō, Insatsukyoku, 1984.

_____. *Shingikai sōran, Shōwa 54-nendo* [Directory of Advisory Councils, 1979 Edition]. Tokyo: Ōkurashō, Insatsukyoku, 1979.

88-nenban isshu kokka kōmuin shiken [Type-I National Civil-Service Examinations, 1988 Edition]. Tokyo: Hitotsubashi Shoten, 1986.

88-nenban isshu nishu (jōkyū, chūkyū) kōmuin mensetsu shiken [Types I and II (Higher-Level and Intermediate-Level) National Civil-Service Oral Examinations, 1988 Edition]. Tokyo: Hitotsubashi Shoten, 1986.

Hartman, Robert W. *Pay and Pensions for Federal Workers.* Washington: Brookings Institution, 1983.

Hartman, Robert W., and Arnold R. Weber, eds. *Rewards of Public Service: Compensating Top Federal Officials.* Washington: Brookings Institution, 1980.

Hashidachi Eiji. "Shō gaikoku kōmuin no kyūyo seido no gairyaku" [An Outline of Civil Servants' Compensation Systems in Various Foreign Countries], 2 parts. *Jinji-in geppō* 297 (November 1975): 11–15, and 298 (December 1975): 8–13.

Hashimoto Gorō. "Kankai jinmyaku chiri: Kōseishō no maki" [Who's Who in Government: The Ministry of Health and Welfare]. *Kankai,* December 1981, pp. 37–47.

Hata Ikuhiko. *Kanryō no kenkyū: Fumetsu no pawa, 1868–1983* [A Study of Bureaucrats: Immortal Power, 1868–1983]. Tokyo: Kōdansha, 1983.

_____. *Senzenki Nihon kanryōsei no seido, soshiki, jinji* [Japan's Prewar Bureaucracy: System, Organization, and Personnel]. Tokyo: Tōkyō Daigaku Shuppankai, 1981.

Hayashi Shūzō. *Nihon kanryō kenkoku ron* [On State Building by Japanese Bureaucrats]. Tokyo: Gyōsei Mondai Kenkyūjo, 1982.

_____.."Shiken jigoku iroiro" [Aspects of an Examination Hell]. *Jinji-in geppō* 236 (October 1970): 4–5.

Heady, Ferrel. *Public Administration: A Comparative Perspective.* Englewood Cliffs, N.J.: Prentice-Hall, 1966.

Hetzner, Candace. "Social Democracy and Bureaucracy: The Labour Party and Higher Civil Service Recruitment." *Administration and Society* 17, no. 1 (May 1985): 97–128.

Honda Yasuharu. *Nihon neo kanryō ron* [On Japan's New Bureaucrats], 2 vols. Tokyo: Kōdansha, 1974.

"Ichinen tatta zaigai kenkyū no jōkyō" [The Condition of Overseas Research After One Year]. *Jinji-in geppo* 203 (January 1968): 10–13.

Ide, Yoshinori. "Administrative Reform and Innovation: The Japanese Case." *International Social Science Journal* 21, no. 1 (1969): 56–67.

_____. *Nihon kanryōsei to gyōsei bunka* [Japanese Bureaucracy and Administrative Culture]. Tokyo: Tōkyō Daigaku Shuppankai, 1982.

Ide, Yoshinori, and Ishida Takeshi. "The Education and Recruitment of Governing Elites in Modern Japan." In Rupert Wilkinson, ed., *Governing Elites: Studies in Training and Selection.* New York: Oxford University Press, 1969.

Ikeda Toyoharu. "Kankai jinmayku chiri: Hōmushō Kensatsuchō no maki"

[Who's Who in Government: the Ministry of Justice and the Public Prosecutor's Office]. *Kankai,* March 1981, pp. 30–41.

Imai Fukuzō et al. "'Moeru shūdan' ni mi o tōjite" [Joining a "Burning Group"]. *Jinji-in geppō* 366 (July 1981): 12–17.

Ino Kenji and Hokuto Man. *Amakudari kanryō: Nihon o ugokasu tokken shūdan* [Bureaucrats Who Descend from Heaven: A Privileged Group That Moves Japan]. Tokyo: Nisshin Hōdō, 1972.

Inoguchi Takashi and Iwai Tomoaki. *"Zoku giin" no kenkyū* [A Study of "Tribal Diet Members"]. Tokyo: Nihon Keizai Shinbunsha, 1987.

Inoguchi Takashi and Kabashima Ikuo. "Tōdai ichinensei no seiji ishiki: Genjō kōtei no hensachi sedai" [Political Consciousness of University of Tokyo Freshmen: "Hensachi" Generation That Affirms the Status Quo]. *Chūō kōron,* December 1983, pp. 62–76.

Inoki, Masamichi. "The Civil Bureaucracy." In Robert E. Ward and Dankwart A. Rustow, eds., *Political Modernization in Japan and Turkey,* pp. 284–300. Princeton: Princeton University Press, 1964.

Institute of Administrative Management. *Organization of the Government of Japan, 1986.* Tokyo: Gyōsei Kanri Kenkyū Sentā, 1987.

Ishii, Masashi. "Kankai jinmyaku chiri: Ōkurashō no maki" [Who's Who in Government: The Ministry of Finance]. *Kankai,* October 1981, pp. 38–53.

Itō Daiichi. "Kōmuin no kōdō yōshiki" [The Behavior Patterns of Civil Servants]. In Tsuji Kiyoaki, ed., *Gyōseigaku kōza dai 4-kan: Gyōsei to soshiki* [Lectures on Public Administration, vol. IV: Public Administration and Organization], pp. 209–45. Tokyo: Tōkyō Daigaku Shuppankai, 1976.

Itō Satoru, ed. *Tōdaisei hakusho* [White Paper on University of Tokyo Students]. Tokyo: Sobokusha, 1981.

Itoh Hiroshi, trans. and ed. *Japanese Politics—An Inside View.* Ithaca: Cornell University Press, 1973.

Jacob, Herbert. *German Administration Since Bismarck: Central Authority Versus Local Autonomy.* New Haven: Yale University Press, 1963.

"Jimu jikan kenkyū" [A Study of Administrative Vice-ministers]. *Kankai,* January 1982–June 1983.

Jin Ikkō. *Jichi kanryō* [Home Ministry Bureaucrats]. Tokyo: Kōdansha, 1986.

―――. *Ōkura kanryō: Cho-erīto shūdan no jinmyaku to yabō* [Finance Ministry Bureaucrats: The Personal Connections and Ambitions of a Super-Elite Group]. Tokyo: Kōdansha, 1982.

"Jinji yōgo haya wakari: Senkō" [A Quick Guide to Personnel Terms: Evaluation]. *Jinji-in geppō* 87 (May 1958): 17.

Jinji-in. *Jinji gyōsei nijūnen no ayumi* [The Path of Twenty Years of Public Personnel Administration]. Tokyo: Ōkurashō, Insatsukyoku, 1968.

―――. *Jinji gyōsei sanjūnen no ayumi* [The Path of Thirty Years of Public Personnel Administration]. Tokyo: Ōkurashō, Insatsukyoku, 1978.

―――. *Kōmuin hakusho* [White Paper on Civil Servants]. Tokyo: Ōkurashō, Insatsukyoku, annual.

―――. *Nenji hōkokusho* [Annual Report]. Tokyo: Ōkurashō, Insatsukyoku, annual. *Kōmuin hakusho* is identical to *Nenji hōkokusho,* the only difference being the years for which each is designated. For example, *Nenji hōkokusho,* 1986, is the same as *Kōmuin hakusho,* 1987.

_____. *Ninmen kankei hōreishū* [Collection of Laws and Ordinances Concerning Appointments and Dismissals], 1984 ed. Tokyo: Ōkurashō, Insatsukyoku, 1984.

_____. Kanrikyoku, Kenshū Shingishitsu. *Shinpan: Shinyū shokuin no jōshiki* [Essential Information for New Government Employees, New Edition]. (3d rev. ed.); Nihon Jinji Gyōsei Kenkyūjo, 1983.

_____. Kenshū Tantōkan Kaigi. *Kokka kōmuin kenshū kyōzai* [Teaching Materials for the Training of National Civil Servants]. 5 vols. Tokyo: Nihon Jinji Gyōsei Kenkyūjo, 1981.

_____. Kyūyokyoku. *Kokka kōmuin kyūyotō jittai chōsa hōkokusho* [Report on an Investigation into the Actual Conditions of National Civil Servants' Compensation and Related Matters], 15 January 1976. Tokyo: Ōkurashō, Insatsukyoku, 1976.

_____. Kyūyokyoku. "Kyū kanri seidoka ni okeru kōtōkan no keireki chōsa no kekka gaiyō" [A Summary of the Results of an Investigation into the Background of Higher Officials Under the Old Bureaucratic System]. *Kikan jinji gyōsei* [Public Personnel Administration Quarterly] 25 (August 1983): 94–109.

_____. Taishoku Teate Nenkin Seido Kenkyūkai, ed. *Kōmuin no tameno taishoku teate nenkin gaidobukku* [Retirement Allowance and Annuity Guidebook for Civil Servants]. Tokyo: Ōkurashō, Insatsukyoku, 1986.

Johnson, Chalmers. "Japan: Who Governs? An Essay on Official Bureaucracy." *Journal of Japanese Studies* 2 (Autumn 1975): 1–28.

_____. *Japan's Public Policy Companies.* Washington: American Enterprise Institute for Public Policy Research, 1978.

_____. *MITI and the Japanese Miracle: The Growth of Industrial Policy, 1925–1975.* Stanford: Stanford University Press, 1982.

_____. "The Reemployment of Retired Government Bureaucrats in Japanese Big Business." *Asian Survey* 14, no. 11 (November 1974): 953–65.

_____. "Tanaka Kakuei, Structural Corruption, and the Advent of Machine Politics in Japan." *Journal of Japanese Studies* 12, no. 1 (Winter 1986): 1–28.

Johnson, Nevil. "Change in the Civil Service: Retrospect and Prospects." *Public Administration* 63, no. 4 (Winter 1985): 415–33.

_____. *State and Government in the Federal Republic of Germany: The Executive at Work.* Oxford: Pergamon Press, 1983.

Juken Shinpō Henshūbu. *Gaikōkan shiken mondaishū* [Collection of Questions in the Foreign-Service Examination]. Tokyo: Hōgaku Shoin, 1987.

_____. *Kōmuin shiken mondai to taisaku: Jōkyū shiken, '85-nenban* [Questions and Strategies for Civil Service Examination: The Higher Examination, 1985 Edition]. Tokyo: Hōgaku Shoin, 1984.

_____, ed. *Watashi no totta kokka jōkyū shiken toppahō, 86-nenban* [How I Passed the National Higher (Civil-Service) Examination, 1986 Edition]. Tokyo: Hōgaku Shoin, 1984.

"Kakkoku kōmuin seido no hikaku (10): Fukumu, shokuin dantai" [A Comparison of Civil Service Systems in Various Countries (10): Duties and Employee Organizations]. *Jinji-in geppō* 112 (June 1960): 8–10.

Kakuma Takashi. *Dokyumento Tsūsanshō, part I: Shin kanryō no jidai* [Document on the Ministry of International Trade and Industry, Part I: The Era of New Bureaucrats]. Tokyo: PHP Kenkyūjo, 1979.

Kanayama Bunji. "Seiiki no okite: Kanryōdō no kenkyū" [Laws of a Sanctuary: A Study of the Ways of Bureaucrats]. *Chūō kōron*, July 1978, pp. 230–45.

"Kanchō daikaibō" [Great Autopsy on Government Agencies]. 13 parts. *Shūkan Yomiuri*. 18 November 1984–16 June 1985.

"Kankai jinmyaku chiri" [Who's Who in Government]. *Kankai*, January 1981–December 1986.

"Kanryō shusshin seijika genzan: fujin no chii kōjō ni kakeru" [Interview with Bureaucrats-Turned-Politicians: Gambling on the Improvement of the Position of Women]. *Kankai*, November, 1985, pp. 88–96.

"Kasumigaseki kanryō dēta banku, 5: Josei kachō rokunin no kojin jōhō" [Kasumigaseki Data Bank, 5: Personal Information on Six Women Section Chiefs]. *Kankai*, March, 1985, pp. 210–13.

"Kasumigaseki konhidensharu" [Confidential Report from Kasumigaseki]. *Bungei shunjū*, a monthly column.

Katō Eiichi. *Kanryō desu, yoroshiku* [I Am a Bureaucrat, Pleased to Meet You]. Tokyo: TBS Buritanika, 1983.

Katō Hisabumi. *Jinji-in: Nihon no shihai kikō* [The National Personnel Authority: An Organization That Controls Japan]. Tokyo: Rōdō Junpōsha, 1966.

Kawaguchi Hiroyuki. "Jimintō habatsu to kanryō, joron: Kyōson suru habatsu to 'zoku'" [Liberal-Democratic Party Factions and Bureaucrats, Introduction: the Coexistence of Factions and "Tribes"]. *Kankai*, March, 1983; pp. 98–109.

———. *Kanryō shihai no kōzō* [The Structure of Bureaucratic Domination]. Tokyo: Kōdansha, 1987.

Kawana Hideyuki. "Kankai jinmyaku chiri: Kensetsushō no maki" [Who's Who in Government: The Ministry of Construction]. *Kankai*, January 1986, pp. 36–48.

Kawanaka Nikō. *Gendai no kanryōsei—kōmuin no kanri taisei* [Modern Bureaucracy—the Management System of Civil Servants]. Revised, expanded edition. Tokyo: Chūō Daigaku Shuppanbu, 1972.

Keeling, Desmond. "The Development of Central Training in the Civil Service 1963–70." *Public Administration* 49 (Spring 1971): 51–71.

Kellner, Peter, and Lord Crowther-Hunt. *The Civil Servants; An Inquiry into Britain's Ruling Class*. London: MacDonald Futura Publishers, 1980.

Kelsall, R. K. *Higher Civil Servants in Britain*. London: Routledge and Kegan Paul, 1955.

Kim, Paul S. "Japan's National Civil Service Commission: Its Origin and Structure." *Public Administration* 48 (Winter 1970): 405–21.

Kobayashi Ken'ichi. "Kankai jinmyaku chiri: Kensetsushō no maki" [Who's Who in Government: The Ministry of Construction]. *Kankai*, September 1982, pp. 32–41.

Koh, B. C. "The Recruitment of Higher Civil Servants in Japan: A Comparative

Perspective." *Asian Survey* 25, no. 3 (March 1985): 292–309.

──── . "Stability and Change in Japan's Higher Civil Service." *Comparative Politics* 11, no. 3 (April 1979): 279–97.

Koh, B. C.; and Jae-On Kim. "Paths to Advancement in Japanese Bureaucracy." *Comparative Political Studies* 15, no. 3 (October 1982): 289–313.

──── . "Correlates of Upward Mobility in Japanese Bureaucracy." *Sociology Working Paper Series* 77, no. 2. Iowa City: University of Iowa, Department of Sociology, 1977.

Koitabashi Jirō. *"Sengo umare" erīto kanryō no sugao* [The Real Faces of Elite Bureaucrats Who Were "Born After the War"]. Tokyo: Kōdansha, 1986.

"Kokka kōmuin kenshū no kihon mondai ni kansuru kentō kekka no hōkoku" [A Report on the Results of an Investigation into the Basic Problems in the Training of National Civil Servants]. *Jinji-in geppō* 347 (January 1980): 9–28.

"Kokka kōmuin kyūyotō jittai chōsa" [An Investigation into the Actual Conditions of National Civil Servants' Compensation and Related Matters]. *Jinji-in geppō* 420 (January 1986): 4–18.

Kokka Kōmuin Nenkin Seido Kenkyūkai. *Kokka kōmuintō no shin kyōsai nenkin seido no shikumi* [The Plan of the New Cooperative Annuity System for National Civil Servants and Others]. Tokyo: Zaikei Shōhōsha, 1986.

"Kokka kōmuin no kenshū jisshi gaiyō" [An Overview of the Implementation of the National Civil Servants' Training Programs]. *Jinji-in geppō* 422 (March 1986): 14–21.

"Kokka kōmuin no shō teate ichiran" [Summary of the Various Allowances for National Civil Servants]. *Jinji-in geppō* 232 (May 1970): 16–21.

"Kokka kōmuinhō no seitei to hensen" [The Enactment and Change of the National Public Service Law]. *Jinji-in geppō* 334 (December 1978): 24–28.

Kokuritsu Daigaku Kyōkai et al., eds. *Kokkōritsu daigaku gaidobukku 1985* [Guide Book for National and Public Universities, 1985]. Tokyo: Kokuritsu Daigaku Kyōkai, Kōritsu Daigaku Kyōkai, Daigaku Nyūshi Sentā, 1984.

"Kōmuin kyūyo no gaiyō" [An Outline of the Compensation of Civil Servants]. *Jinji-in geppō* 402 (July 1984): 9–32.

"Kōmuin no taishoku teate to nenkin" [Civil Servants' Retirement Allowance and Annuity]. *Jinji-in geppō* 402 (July 1984): 20.

"Kōmuin Q & A" [Questions and Answers About Civil Servants]. *Jinji-in geppō* 426 (July 1986): 7–17.

"Kōmuin seido no shikumi" [The Plan of the Civil Service System]. *Jinji-in geppō* 365 (temporary, expanded issue, 1981): 18–45.

"Kōmuin seido to Jinji-in no yakuwari" [The Civil-Service System and the Role of the National Personnel Authority]. *Jinji-in geppō* 365 (temporary, expanded issue, 1981): 15–17.

"Kōmuin shiken gōkaku kara saiyō made" [From Passing the Civil Service Examination to Being Hired]. *Jinji-in geppō* 103 (September 1959): 14–17.

Kōmuin Shiken Jōhō Kenkyūkai, ed. *88 nendo-han kōmuin saiyō shiken shirizu: Isshu kokka kōmuin shiken* [1988 Edition, Civil-Service Examination Series: Type-I National Public-Employee Examination]. Tokyo: Hitotsubashi Shoten, 1986.

"Kōmuin to natte: Jōkyū shiken saiyōsha zadankai" [On Becoming Civil Servants: A Roundtable Discussion of Appointees Who Have Passed the Higher Examination]. *Jinji-in geppō* 312 (February 1977): 1–9.

Konaka Yōtarō, ed. *Tōdai Hōgakubu: Sono kyozō to jitsuzō* [The University of Tokyo Faculty of Law: Myths and Reality]. Tokyo: Gendai Hyōronsha, 1978.

Kondō Masaru. "Shokai: Jakunen taishokusha no jittai" [Introduction: The Real Conditions of Young Resignees]. *Jinji-in geppō* 186 (August 1966): 6–9.

Konig, Klaus. "Education and Advanced Training for the Public Service in the Federal Republic of Germany." *International Review of Administrative Sciences* 49, no. 2 (1983): 204–9.

Konig, Klaus, Hans Joachim von Oertzen, and Frido Wagener, eds. *Public Administration in the Federal Republic of Germany.* Antwerp: Kluwer-Deventer, 1983.

Kosaka, Masataka. *100 Million Japanese: The Postwar Experience.* Tokyo: Kodansha International, 1972.

Kubota, Akira. *Higher Civil Servants in Postwar Japan: Their Social Origins, Educational Backgrounds, and Career Patterns.* Princeton: Princeton University Press, 1969.

————. "Kokusaiteki ni mita Nihon no kōkyū kanryō" [Japan's Higher Civil Servants in International Perspective]. 20 parts. *Kankai,* March 1978–October 1979.

————. "The Political Influence of the Japanese Higher Civil Service." *Japan Quarterly* 28, no. 1 (January–March 1981): 45–55.

————. "Seiji erīto no kokusai hikaku" [An International Comparison of Political Elites]. *Kankai,* October 1976, pp. 158–63.

Kubuta Akira and Tomita Nobuo. "Nihon, seifu kōkan no ishiki kōzō: sono kokusaiteki dōshitsusei to ishitsusei" [The Value Structure of Japanese Higher Civil Servants: Its International Homogeneity and Heterogeneity]. *Chūō kōron,* February 1977, pp. 190–96.

Kuribayashi Yoshimitsu. *Ōkurashō Shukeikyoku* [The Budget Bureau of the Finance Ministry]. Tokyo: Kōdansha, 1986.

————. *Ōkurashō Shuzeikyoku* [The Tax Bureau of the Finance Ministry]. Tokyo: Kōdansha, 1987.

Kusayanagi Daizō. *Kanryō ōkoku ron* [On the Kingdom of Bureaucrats]. Tokyo: Bungei Shunjū, 1975.

————. *Nihon kaitai* [The Dissolution of Japan]. Tokyo: Gyōsei, 1985.

Kyōiku tokuhon: Tōkyō Daigaku [Readings on Education: The University of Tokyo]. Tokyo: Kawade Shobō Shinsha, 1983.

Kyōikusha. *Kaikei Kensa-in, Jinji-in, Naikaku Hōseikyoku* [The Board of Audit, the National Personnel Authority, and the Cabinet Legislation Bureau]. Tokyo: Kyōikusha, 1979.

————. *Kanryō* [Bureaucrats]. Tokyo: Kyōikusha, 1980.

"Kyūyo ni kansuru hōkoku to kankoku (zenbun)" [Report and Recommendations on Compensation (Full Text)]. *Jinji-in geppō* 416 (September 1985): 5–68.

"Land Without Lawyers." *Time,* 1 August 1983, pp. 64–65.

Litchfield, Edward H., et al. *Governing Postwar Germany.* Ithaca: Cornell University Press, 1953.

MacDonald, Lt. Col. Hugh H., and Lt. Milton J. Esman. "The Japanese Civil Service." *Public Personnel Review* 7, no. 4 (October 1946): 213–24.

Machin, Howard, "France." In F. F. Ridley, ed., *Government and Administration in Western Europe,* pp. 67–106. New York: St. Martin's Press, 1979.

Mainichi Shinbun Shakaibu. *Kanryō: Sono fushoku no kōzō* [Bureaucrats: Structure of Their Corrosion]. Tokyo: Tairiku Shobō, 1980.

Maki, John M. "The Role of Bureaucracy in Japan." *Pacific Affairs* 20 (December 1947): 391–406.

Management and Coordination Agency, Statistics Bureau. *Statistical Handbook of Japan 1985.* Tokyo: Japan Statistical Association, 1985.

Masuda Takaharu. *Gakubatsu—Nihon o shihai suru akamon* [School Clique—The Red Gate That Rules Japan]. Tokyo: Yuki Shobō, 1957.

Masujima Toshiyuki. *Gyōsei kanri no shiten* [A Perspective on Administrative Management]. Tokyo: Ryōsho Fukyūkai, 1981.

Miyake Tarō. *Gyōseigaku to gyōsei kanri* [Public Administration and Public Management]. Tokyo: Sakai Shoten, 1974.

Miyazaki, Ichisada. *China's Examination Hell: The Civil Service Examinations of Imperial China.* Trans. Conrad Schirokauer. New Haven: Yale University Press, 1963.

Monbushō, ed. *Waga kuni kyōiku suijun* [The Educational Level of Our Country], *1980.* Tokyo: Ōkurashō, Insatsukyoku, 1981.

Mori Hiroshi and Yazawa Shūjirō. *Kanryōsei no shihai* [Rule by Bureaucracy]. Tokyo: Yūhikaku, 1981.

Morstein Marx, Fritz. "German Administration and the Speyer Academy." *Public Administration Review* 27, no. 5 (December 1967): 403–10.

Mueller, Hans-Eberhard. *Bureaucracy, Education, and Monopoly: Civil Service Reforms in Prussia and England.* Berkeley: University of California Press, 1984.

Murakawa Ichirō. *Seisaku kettei katei* [Policy-Making Process]. Gyōsei kikō shirizu [Administration Organization Series], no. 121. Tokyo: Kyōikusha, 1979.

Muramatsu Michio. *Sengo Nihon no kanryōsei* [The Bureaucratic System in Postwar Japan]. Tokyo: Tōyō Keizai Shinpōsha, 1981.

Murobushi Tetsurō. *Kōkyū kanryō* [Higher Civil Servants]. Tokyo: Sekai Shoin, 1983.

————. "Kōkyū kanryō—riken no kōzō" [Higher Civil Servants—the Structure of Interests]. *Sekai,* February 1980, pp. 54–63.

Nagano Nobutoshi. *Gaimushō kenkyū* [A Study of the Ministry of Foreign Affairs]. Tokyo: Saimaru Shuppankai, 1975.

————. "Kankai jinmyaku chiri: Gaimushō no maki" [Who's Who in Government: The Ministry of Foreign Affairs]. *Kankai,* April 1987, pp. 40–54.

————. *Nihon gaikō no subete* [All About Japanese Diplomacy]. Tokyo: Gyōsei Mondai Kenkyūjo Shuppankyoku, 1986.

————. "Za Kasumigaseki (9): Gaimushō—Nihon gaikō o ugokasu pawa"

[Series on Kasumigaseki (9): The Ministry of Foreign Affairs—The Power That Moves Japanese Diplomacy]. *Kankai,* March 1986, pp. 98–112.

Naikaku Seido Hyakunen-shi Hensan Iinkai, ed. *Naikaku hyakunen no ayumi* [The Path of One Hundred Years of the Cabinet]. Tokyo: K. K. Ōkyō, 1985.

Nakajima Sachiko. "Watashi no kaimamita Igirisu" [The England I Caught a Glimpse Of]. *Jinji-in geppō* 365 (May 1981): 21–14.

Nakane Chie. *Tate shakai no ningen kankei: Tan'itsu shakai no riron* [Human Relations in a Vertical Society: The Theory of a Homogeneous Society]. Tokyo: Kōdansha, 1967.

Nawa, Tarō. "Jimu jikan kenkyū: Tsūsanshō" [A Study of Administrative Vice-Ministers: The Ministry of International Trade and Industry]. *Kankai,* March, 1982: pp. 130–39.

NHK Shuzaihan. *Nihon no jōken, 15: Kyōiku 4—daigaku to daigakusei— kyōiku wa nani o motarashita noka* [Japan's Condition, 15: Education, part 4—Colleges and College Students—What Has Education Accomplished?]. Tokyo: Nihon Hōsō Shuppan Kyōkai, 1985.

———. *Nihon no jōken, 11: Kyōiku 2—hensachi ga Nihon no mirai o shihai suru* [Japan's Condition, 11: Education, part 2—Hensachi Dominates the Future of Japan]. Tokyo: Nihon Hōsō Shuppan Kyōkai, 1983.

Nihon Gyōsei Gakkai, ed. *Gyōseigaku no genjō to katei* [The Present Condition and Tasks of Public Administration]. Tokyo: Gyōsei, 1983.

Nihon Jinji Gyōsei Kenkyūjo, ed. *Kōmuin no tameno taishoku nenkin gaido- bukku* [Guidebook for Civil Servants' Separation Allowance and Annuity]. Tokyo: Ōkurashō, Insatsukyoku, 1986.

Nihon kankai meikan [Who's Who in Japanese Government]. Vols. 24, 25, and 33. Tokyo: Nihon Kankai Jōhōsha, 1972, 1974, and 1981.

Nihon Keiei Kyōkai, ed. *'80-nendai Nihon no gyōsei* [Japanese Public Ad- ministration in the 1980s]. Tokyo: Nihon Keiei Shuppankai, 1981.

Nihon Keizai Shinbunsha. *Kōmuin no chōsen: Dokyumento sarariman* [Civil Servants' Challenge: Document on Salaryman]. Tokyo: Nihon Keizai Sh- inbunsha, 1987.

Nihon no Kanryō Kenkyūkai. *Oyakunin sōjūhō* [How To Handle Government Officials]. Tokyo: Nihon Keizai Shinbunsha, 1971.

Nihon Seiji Gakkai, ed "Gendai Nihon no seitō to kanryō" [Political Parties and Bureaucracy in Modern Japan], *Nenpō seijigaku* [Political Science Annual], 1967. Tokyo: Iwanami Shoten, 1967.

"Ninenkan o furi kaette: Kikoku zaigai kenkyūin tai nikaisei no kaikō" [Looking Back upon Two Years: Recollections of the Second Group of Returned Overseas Research Students]. *Jinji-in geppō* 227 (January 1970): 24–26.

Noda, Kazuo. "Big Business Organization." In Ezra F. Vogel, ed., *Modern Japanese Organization and Decision-Making,* pp. 115–45. Berkeley: Uni- versity of California Press, 1975.

Nomura Nario. "Furansu kanri no nin'yō seido" [The Appointment System of French Officials]. 2 parts. *Jinji-in geppō* 219 (May 1969): 12–15 and 220 (June 1969): 14–17.

———. "Furansu Kyōwakoku kanri no onkyū seido" [The Pension System of the Officials of the French Republic]. 2 parts. *Jinji-in geppō* 315 (May 1977): 4–8 and 316 (June 1977): 5–8.

Nomura Tadao. *Nihon kanryō no genzō* [The Original Portrait of Japanese Bureaucrats]. Tokyo: PHP Kenkyūjo, 1983.

"Nonkyaria no sekai" [The World of Noncareer (Civil Servants)]. *Kankai*, April 1983–February 1984.

Ōe Shinobu. "Nihon ni okeru kanryōsei no kiseki" [The Locus of the Bureaucratic System in Japan]. *Hōgaku semina zōkan, sōgō tokushu shirizu 9: Naikaku to kanryō* [Legal Studies Seminar Extra Issue, Comprehensive Special Series 9: The Cabinet and Bureaucrats], March 1979, pp. 104–11.

Oertzen, Hans Joachim von. "Public Personnel Management in the Federal Republic of Germany." *International Review of Administrative Sciences*, 49, no. 2 (1983): 210–17.

Ojimi, Yoshihisa. "A Government Ministry: The Case of the Ministry of International Trade and Industry." In Ezra F. Vogel, ed., *Modern Japanese Organization and Decision-Making*, pp. 101–12. Berkeley: University of California Press, 1975.

Okada Maki. "110 tai 102: Gyōsei kenshū (kakarichō kyū) inshōki" [110 vs. 102: Impressions of Administrative Training (Subsection-Chief Level)]. *Jinji-in geppo* 356 (October 1980): 21–25.

Ōki Yū. "Igirisu seifu shokuin no nin'yō seido" [The Appointment System of Government Employees in England]. 2 parts. *Jinji-in geppō* 291 (May 1975): 16–19 and 292 (June 1975): 29–32.

Ōkita Saburō. *Nihon kanryō jijō* [Conditions of Japanese Bureaucrats]. Tokyo: TBS Buritanika, 1984.

Ōkita Saburō, Tsuji Kiyoaki, and Tanimura Hirō. "Tokubetsu zadankai: Nihon no kanryōsei no tokushitsu" [Special Roundtable Discussion: Distinguishing Characteristics of Japanese Bureaucracy]. *Kankai*, August 1984, pp. 88–100.

Ono Mitsuru. "Jimu jikan kenkyū: Kensetsushō" [A Study of Administrative Vice-Ministers: The Ministry of Construction]. *Kankai*, December 1982, pp. 76–88.

Owen, David. "Public Sector Pay: Justice Without Inflation." *Public Administration* 64, no. 1 (Spring 1986): 1–11.

Park, Yung H. *Bureaucrats and Ministers in Contemporary Japanese Government*. Berkeley: University of California, Institute of East Asian Studies, 1986.

––––––. "Jimintō to kyōiku kanryō" [The Liberal-Democratic Party and Education Bureaucrats]. *Gakujutsu kokusai kōryū sankō shiryōshū* [Collection of Reference Materials Concerning International Scholarly Exchanges], no. 60. Tokyo: Meiji Daigaku Gakujutsu Kokusai Kōryū Iinkai, September 1980.

––––––. "Kyōiku gyōsei ni okeru Jimintō to Monbushō" [The Liberal-Democratic Party and the Ministry of Education in Education Administration]. In Shinbori Michiya and Aoi Kazuo, eds., *Nihon kyōiku no rikigaku* [Dynamics of Japanese Education]. Tokyo: Yūshindō, 1983, pp. 49–78.

––––––. "Shingikai ron—Nihon ni okeru seifu no shimon iinkai seido no ichi kenkyū" [On Advisory Councils: A Study of the Government Advisory

Commission System in Japan]. 2 parts. *Jichi kenkyū* 48, no. 5 (May 1972): 20–38, and 48, no. 6 (June 1972): 81–96.

Parris, Henry. "Twenty Years of l'Ecole Nationale d'Administration." *Public Administration* 43 (Winter 1965): 395–411.

Pempel, T. J. "The Bureaucratization of Policymaking in Postwar Japan." *American Journal of Political Science* 18, no. 4 (November 1974): 647–64.

———. "Organizing for Efficiency: The Higher Civil Service in Japan." In Ezra N. Suleiman, ed., *Bureaucrats and Policy Making: A Comparative Overview*, pp. 72–106. New York: Holmes and Meier, 1984.

———. *Patterns of Japanese Policymaking: Experiences from Higher Education*. Boulder, Colo.: Westview Press, 1978.

———. *Policy and Politics in Japan: Creative Conservatism*. Philadelphia: Temple University Press, 1982.

———, ed. *Policymaking in Contemporary Japan*. Ithaca: Cornell University Press, 1977.

———. "The Tar Baby Target: 'Reform' of the Japanese Bureaucracy." In Robert E. Ward and Sakamoto Yoshikazu, eds., *Democratizing Japan: The Allied Occupation*, pp. 157–87. Honolulu: University of Hawaii Press, 1987.

Peters, B. Guy. *The Politics of Bureaucracy*. 2d ed. New York: Longman, 1984.

Plowden, William. "What Prospects for the Civil Service?" *Public Administration* 63, no. 4 (Winter 1985): 393–414.

Quermonne, Jean-Louis, and Luc Rouban. "French Public Administration and Policy Evaluation: The Quest for Accountability." *Public Administration Review* 46, no. 5 (September/October 1986): 397–406.

Richardson, Bradley M. "Policymaking in Japan: An Organizing Perspective." In T. J. Pempel, ed. *Policymaking in Contemporary Japan*, pp. 239–68.

Ridley, F. F., ed. *Government and Administration in Western Europe*. New York: St. Martin's Press, 1979.

Ring, Peter Smith, and James L. Perry. "Reforming the Upper Levels of the Bureaucracy: A Longitudinal Study of the Senior Executive Service." *Administration and Society* 15, no. 1 (May 1983): 119–44.

Rohlen, Thomas P. *Japan's High Schools*. Berkeley: University of California Press, 1983.

Roser, Foster. "Establishing a Modern Merit System in Japan." *Public Personnel Review* 11, no. 4 (October 1950): 199–206.

Rōyama, Masamichi. *Gyōseigaku kenkyū ronbunshū* [Collection of Research Papers on Public Administration]. Tokyo: Keisō Shobō, 1965.

Ryang, Key Sung. "Postwar Japanese Political Leadership—A Study of Prime Ministers." *Asian Survey* 13, no. 11 (November 1973): 1010–20.

Sahashi Shigeru. *Ishoku kanryō* [An Exceptional Bureaucrat]. Tokyo: Daiyamondosha, 1967.

———. "Kanryō shokun ni chokugen suru" [Talking Straight to Bureaucrats]. *Bungei shunjū*, July 1971, pp. 108–15.

"Saiyō shiken taikei no saihen seibi ni tsuite" [On the Reorganization and Adjustment of the Recruitment Examination System]. *Jinji-in geppō* 411 (April 1985): 10–17.

Sakaiya Taiichi and Utsumi Hitoshi. "Taidan: Kōmuin kyūyo o kangaeru" [Conversation: Thinking About Civil Servants' Compensation]. *Jinji-in geppō* 402 (July 1984): 1–8.

Sakakibara Eisuke. *Nihon o enshutsu suru shin kanryō-zō* [A Portrait of New Bureaucrats Who Direct Japan]. Tokyo: Yamade Shobō, 1977.

Sakurai Tsuneji. *Tōdai seikatsu, 1953-nenban* [Life at the University of Tokyo, 1953 Edition]. Tokyo: Gendai Shichōsha, 1952.

"Sankō shiryō (kyūyo kankei)" [Reference Material (Related to Salary)]. *Jinji-in geppō* 440 (September 1987): 29–64.

Sano Mitsuko. *Josei kanryō: Sono ishiki to kōdō* [Women Bureaucrats: Their Consciousness and Behavior]. Tokyo: Jihyōsha, 1983.

Sano Shin'ichi. *Kanryō: Fuyu no jidai* [Bureaucrats: Winter Season]. Tokyo: Pureshidentosha, 1985.

Sase Minoru. *Nippon kōmuin jijō* [The Condition of Japanese Civil Servants]. Tokyo: Jitsugyō Shuppansha, 1978.

Sataka Makoto. *Nihon kanryō hakusho* [White Paper on Japanese Bureaucrats]. Tokyo: Kōdansha, 1986.

Satō Seisaburō and Matsuzaki Tetsuhisa. *Jimintō seiken* [The Regime of the Liberal-Democratic Party]. Tokyo: Chūō Kōronsha, 1986.

Satō Tatsuo. *Kokka kōmuin seido* [The National Public-Service System]. Tokyo: Gakuyō Shobō, 1975.

Satō Tomoyuki et al. *Tōdaibatsu* [The University of Tokyo Clique]. Tokyo: Ēru Shuppansha, 1972.

Scalapino, Robert A. *Democracy and the Party Movement in Prewar Japan.* Berkeley: University of California Press, 1962.

————. "Elections and Political Modernization in Prewar Japan." In Robert E. Ward, ed. *Political Development in Modern Japan,* pp. 249–91. Princeton: Princeton University Press, 1968.

Seiji handobukku [Handbook of Politics], February 1987. Tokyo: Seiji Kōhō Sentā, 1987.

Seikai kanchō jinji roku, 1988-nenban [Who's Who in Politics and Government, 1988 Edition]. Tokyo: Tōyō Keizai Shinpōsha, 1987.

Seikai kanchō jinji roku, 1987-nenban [Who's Who in Politics and Government, 1987 Edition]. Tokyo: Tōyō Keizai Shinpōsha, 1986.

Sekiguchi, Takeshi. *Kōmuin tengoku!!* [Civil Servants' Heaven]. Tokyo: Arō Shuppansha, n.d.

"Senkō ni yoru shokuin no saiyō" [Selection of Government Employees By Means of Evaluation]. *Jinji-in geppō* 94 (December 1958): 20–23.

Setō Shūzō. "Jimu jikan kenkyū: Hōmushō" [A Study of Administrative Vice-Ministers: The Ministry of Justice]. *Kankai,* November 1982, pp. 66–75.

Shimizu, Hideo. *Tōkyō Daigaku Hōgakubu: Nihon erīto no manmosu kichi* [The University of Tokyo Faculty of Law: A Mammoth Base of Japan's Elite]. Tokyo: Kōdansha, 1965.

Shimizu, Kunio. "Kanryō okuni-buri (6), Furansu: banjaku no cho-erīto shugi" [Bureaucrats in Different Countries (6), France: An Unshakable Superelitism]. *Kankai,* March 1981, pp. 81–87.

Shimoda Akiko. "Igirisu Kōmuin no nenkin seido" [British Civil Servants' Annuity System], I. *Jinji-in geppō* 420 (January 1986): 29–32.

"Shinsō o saguru: Ima magari kado ni tatsu Jinji-in" [In Search of Truth: The National Personnel Authority at a Turning Point]. *Kankai,* October 1984, pp. 134–43.

"Shinsō o saguru: Kareinaru amakudari no urade ugomeku yokubō" [In Search of Truth: The Desire That Squirms Behind the Splendid Descent from Heaven]. *Kankai,* May 1982, pp. 136–44.

Shirven, Maynard N., and Joseph L. Speicher. "Examination of Japan's Upper Bureaucracy." *Personnel Administration* 14, no. 4 (July 1951): 48–57.

"Shōwa 58-nendo gyōsei kenshū no jisshi jōkyō: Tai 81-kai gyōsei kenshū (kakarichō kyū) o chūshin to shite" [The Situation Regarding the Implementation of Administrative Training in Fiscal Year 1983: With Emphasis on the 81st Administrative Training Session (Subsection Chief Level)]. *Jinji-in geppō* 401(June 1984): 6–9.

"Shōwa 58-nendo Jinji-in kenshū no jisshi keikaku (kaiyō)" [A Plan for the Implementation of Training Programs by the National Personnel Authority in Fiscal Year 1983 (Outline)]. *Jinji-in geppō* 388 (May 1983): 6.

"Shōwa 61-nen eiri kigyō eno shūshoku no shōnin ni kansuru nenji hōkoku" [1986 Annual Report on Approval of Employment in Profit-Making Enterprises]. *Jinji-in geppō* 437 (June 1987): 6–8.

"Shōwa 60-nendo Jinji-in kenshū no jisshi keikaku" [The Plan for the Implementation of Training Programs Administered by the National Personnel Authority in Fiscal Year 1985]. *Jinji-in geppō* 412 (May 1985): 10–18.

Shōwa 62-nenban Ōkurashō meikan [Directory of the Finance Ministry, 1987 edition]. Tokyo: Jihyōsha, 1986.

Shōwa 62-nenban Tsūshō Sangyōshō meikan [Directory of the Ministry of International Trade and Industry, 1987 Edition]. Tokyo: Jihyōsha, 1986.

"Shōwa 41-nendo kokka kōmuin saiyō jōkyū (kōshu, otsushu) shiken gōkakusha no saiyō jōkyō" [The Situation Regarding the Appointment of Those Who Passed the Higher Civil-Service Examinations (Types A and B) in 1966]. *Jinji-in geppō* 197 (July 1967): 10–16.

Silverman, Bernard S. "The Bureaucracy and Economic Development in Japan." *Asian Survey,* 5, no. 11 (November 1965): 529–37.

————. "The Bureaucratic State in Japan: The Problem of Authority and Legitimacy." In Tetsuo Najita and J. Victor Koschmann, eds., *Conflict in Modern Japanese History: the Neglected Tradition,* pp. 226–57. Princeton: Princeton University Press, 1982.

————. "Elite Transformation in the Meiji Restoration: The Upper Civil Service, 1868–1873." In Bernard S. Silverman and H. D. Harootunian, eds., *Modern Japanese Leadership: Transition and Change,* pp. 233–59. Tucson: University of Arizona Press, 1966.

Sōgō Gakusei Mondai Kenkyūjo, ed. *Nihon daigaku taikan* [An Overview of Japanese Universities]. Tokyo: Nihon Gakujutsu Tsūshinsha, 1973.

Sōrifu. Kōhōshitsu. "Seishōnen no shakai sanka" [Participation of the Youth in Society]. *Gekkan seron chōsa,* March 1986, pp. 2–31.

Sōrifu. Kokuritsu Yoron Chōsajo. *Jinji gyosei ni kansuru seron chōsa* [Public Opinion Survey on Public Personnel Management]. Tokyo: Sōrifu, Kokuritsu Seron Chōsajo, 1951.

Sōrifu. Naikaku Sōri Daijin Kanbō. *Kōmuin ni kansuru seron chōsa, Shōwa 48-nen 9-gatsu* [Public Opinion Survey Concerning Civil Servants, September 1973]. Tokyo: Sōrifu, Naikaku Sōri Daijin Kanbō, Kōhōshitsu, 1973.

Sōrifu. Seishōnen Taisaku Honbu, ed. *Sekai no seinen tono hikaku kara mita Nihon no seinen: sekai seinen ishiki chōsa (dai 3-kai) hokokusho* [Japanese Youths As Compared with the Youth of the World: Report on the Survey of the Attitudes of the World Youth (the Third Survey)]. Tokyo: Ōkurashō, Insatsukyoku, 1984.

Southern, David. "Germany." In F. F. Ridley, ed., *Government and Administration in Western Europe*, pp. 107–55. New York: St. Martin's Press, 1979.

Spaulding, Robert M., Jr. "The Bureaucracy as a Political Force, 1920–45." In James W. Morley, ed., *Dilemmas of Growth in Prewar Japan*, pp. 33–80. Princeton: Princeton University Press, 1971.

———. *Imperial Japan's Higher Civil Service Examinations*. Princeton: Princeton University Press, 1967.

Stanley, David T. "Civil Service Reform in the United States Government (1)." *International Review of Administrative Sciences* 48, nos. 3–4 (1982): 305–14.

———. *The Higher Civil Service: An Evaluation of Federal Personnel Practices*. Washington: Brookings Institution, 1964.

Stanley, David T., Dean E. Mann, and Jameson W. Doig. *Men Who Govern: A Biographical Profile of Federal Political Executives*. Washington: Brookings Institution, 1967.

Steel, D. R. "Britain." In F. F. Ridley, ed., *Government and Administration in Western Europe*, pp. 18–66. New York: St. Martin's Press, 1979.

Suekawa Hiroshi, ed. *Iwanami kihon roppō, Shōwa 49-nenban* [Iwanami Six Fundamental Laws, 1974 Edition]. Tokyo: Iwanami Shoten, 1973.

Suleiman, Ezra N., ed. *Bureaucrats and Policy Making: A Comparative Overview*. New York: Holmes and Meier, 1984.

———. *Politics, Power, and Bureaucracy in France: The Administrative Elite*. Princeton: Princeton University Press, 1974.

Sumitomo Tadashi. "Nishi Dōitsu renpō kanri no nin'yō seido" [The Appointment System of West German Federal Officials]. 2 parts. *Jinji-in geppō* 215 (January 1969): 6–9 and 217 (March 1969): 12–15.

Supreme Commander for the Allied Powers. Government Section. *Political Reorientation of Japan*. 2 vols. Grosse Pointe, Mich.: Scholarly Press, 1968. Originally published by the U.S. Government Printing Office in 1949.

Suttmeier, Richard P. "The 'Gikan' Question in Japanese Government: Bureaucratic Curiosity or Institutional Failure?" *Asian Survey* 18, no. 10 (October 1978): 1046–66.

Suzuki Kazuo. "ENA (Furansu Kokuritsu Gyōsei Gakuin) no Kyōiku seido" [The Educational System of ENA (the French National School of Administration)]. 3 parts. *Jinji-in geppō* 320 (October 1977): 24–27; 321 (November 1977): 23–26; and 322 (December 1977): 17–19.

Suzuki Yukio. *Gendai Nihon no kenryoku erīto* [Modern Japan's Power Elite]. Tokyo: Bancho Shobō, 1967.

Tahara Sōichirō. *Nihon no kanryō* [Japan's Bureaucrats]. Tokyo: Bungei Shunjū, 1980.

_____. *Shin naimu kanryō no jidai* [The Era of New Home Ministry Bureaucrats]. Tokyo: Kōdansha, 1984.

Takahashi Hideki. "Kōbun seidoka no shōshin jittai no bunseki" [Analysis of Promotion Patterns Under the (Prewar) Higher Civil-Service-Examination System]. 2 parts. *Jinji-in geppō* 342 (August 1979): 22–25 and 344 (October 1979): 29–33.

Takahashi Yoshiyuki. "Jimintō habatsu to kanryō: 'Tanaka shihai' no nōhau" [Liberal-Democratic Party Factions and Bureaucrats: Techniques of "Tanaka Rule"]. *Kankai,* June 1983, pp. 114–24.

Takamoto Mitsuo. *Ōkura kanryō no keifu: Kareinaru erīto gunzō* [The Genealogy of Finance Ministry Bureaucrats: A Magnificent Elite Group]. Tokyo: Nihon Shoseki Kabushiki Kaisha, 1979.

Takane, Masa'aki. *The Political Elite of Japan: Continuity and Change in Modernization.* Berkeley: University of California, Institute of East Asian Studies, 1981.

Taniai Kenzō. "Kankai jinmyaku chiri: Chūō shōchōhen: Jinji-in no maki" [Who's Who in Central-Government Ministries and Agencies: The National Personnel Authority]. *Kankai,* August 1987; pp. 38–52.

"Tanki zaigai kenkyūin seido" [The Short-term Overseas Researcher System]. *Jinji-in geppō* 401 (June 1984): 29–32.

Tashiro Kū. "Nihon gyōseikan kenkyū" [A Study of Japanese Public Administrators]. 13 parts. *Kankai,* October 1981–October 1982.

Thayer, Nathaniel B. *How the Conservatives Rule Japan.* Princeton: Princeton University Press, 1969.

Tōkyō Daigaku. *Hōgakubu benran, kyōran-yō* [A Handbook of the Faculty of Law, Display Copy]. Tokyo: Tōkyō Daigaku, 1987.

Tōkyō Daigaku ichiran [Catalogue of the University of Tokyo]. Tokyo: Tōkyō Daigaku Shuppankai, 1953.

Tōkyō Daigaku Kyōyō Gakubu. *Kyōyō Gakubu no sanjūnen, 1949–1979* [Thirty Years of the Faculty of General Education, 1949–79]. Tokyo: Tōkyō Daigaku Shuppankai, 1979.

"Tōkyō Daigaku no hyakunen" Henshū Iinkai. *Tōkyō Daigaku no hyakunen, 1877–1977* [Hundred Years of the University of Tokyo, 1877–1977]. Tokyo: Tōkyō Daigaku Shuppankai, 1977.

Tōkyō Daigaku shinbun, 5 July 1976.

Tōkyō Shinbunsha, ed. *Kanchō monogatari* [Tales of Government Agencies]. Tokyo: Chobunsha, 1958.

Tomioka Shōzō. "Hoittoni keikoku shokan' o skūpu" [Getting a Scoop on the "Whitney Warning Letter"]. *Kankai,* July 1986, pp. 188–93.

Tsuchiya Shigeru. "Kanryō shusshin rikkōhosha sōtenken" [A Complete Examination of Candidates Who Are Former Bureaucrats]. *Kankai,* April 1986, pp. 160–71; May 1986, pp. 142–51; June 1986, pp. 145–57.

Tsuji, Kiyoaki. "The Bureaucracy Preserved and Strengthened." *Journal of*

Social and Political Ideas in Japan 11, no. 3 (December 1964): 88–97.

————. "The Cabinet, Administrative Organization, and the Bureaucracy." *Annals of the American Academy of Political and Social Science,* November 1956, pp. 10–17.

————. "Decision-Making in the Japanese Government: A Study of *Ringisei.*" In Robert E. Ward, ed., *Political Development in Modern Japan,* pp. 457–75. Princeton: Princeton University Press, 1968.

————. "Kōmu kenshū" [Public Service Training]. In Tsuji Kiyoaki, ed., *Gyōseigaku kōza, dai 4-kan: gyōsei to soshiki* [Lectures on Public Administration, vol. 4: Public Administration and Organization], pp. 271–93. Tokyo: Tōkyō Daigaku Shuppankai, 1976.

————. ed. *Public Administration in Japan.* Tokyo: University of Tokyo Press, 1984.

————. *Shinpan Nihon kanryōsei no kenkyū* [A Study of Japanese Bureaucracy, New Edition]. Tokyo: Tōkyō Daigaku Shuppankai, 1969.

Tsuji Kiyoaki and Nakamura Takahide. "Taidan: Nihon kanryōsei—sono byōri to kaikau" [Conversation: Japanese Bureaucracy—Its Pathology and Reform]. *Sekai,* March 1980, pp. 187–201.

Tsurutani, Taketsugi. "Academics in Japan's Advisory Council System: The Ambiguity and Danger in Their Role." *Administration and Society* 18, no. 1 (May 1986): 91–109.

Uemoto Ryōhei. "Nonkyaria no sekai: Un'yūshō no maki" [The World of Noncareer (Civil Servants): The Ministry of Transport]. *Kankai,* September 1983, pp. 154–60.

Ueyama Shin'ichi. "Purinsuton Daigaku no ninenkan" [Two Years at Princeton University]. *Jinji-in geppō* 412 (May 1985): 21–23.

The University of Tokyo Catalogue, 1980–81. Tokyo: University of Tokyo, 1980.

U.S. Congress. House of Representatives, Committee on Foreign Affairs. *Government Decisionmaking in Japan: Implications for the United States.* Washington: Government Printing Office, 1982.

U.S. Office of Personnel Management. *The Presidential Management Intern Program: Anniversary Report, 1978–1980.* Washington: Government Printing Office, 1980.

————. *The Presidential Management Intern Program Bulletin.* Washington: Government Printing Office, 1984.

————. *The Presidential Management Intern Program, 1980–1981.* Washington: Government Printing Office, 1981.

Vogel, Ezra F. *Comeback—Case by Case: Building the Resurgence of American Business.* New York: Simon and Schuster, 1985.

————. *Japan As Number One.* New York: Harper Colophon Books, 1980.

————. *Modern Japanese Organization and Decision-Making.* Berkeley: University of California Press, 1975.

Wada Zen'ichi. "Bunkan nin'yō seido no rekishi" [The History of the Appointment System for Civil Officials], 3 parts. *Jinji-in geppō* 95 (January 1959): 10–15; 96 (February 1959): 10–15; 97 (March 1959): 8–13.

Wakasugi Kazuo. *Konna yakunin ga itemo ii: Aru kōkyū kanryō no sōzōteki hakai* [It's Good to Have This Type of Civil Servant: The Creative Destruction of a Higher Civil Servant]. Tokyo: Jihyōsha, 1987.

Ward, Robert E., ed. *Political Development in Modern Japan.* Princeton: Princeton University Press, 1968.

———. "Reflections on the Allied Occupation and Planned Political Change in Japan." In Robert E. Ward, ed., *Political Development in Modern Japan,* pp. 477–533. Princeton: Princeton University Press, 1968.

Warner, Lloyd W., et al. *The American Federal Executive.* New Haven: Yale University Press, 1963.

Watanabe, Yasuo. "Kōmuin no kyaria" [The Career Patterns of Civil Servants]. In Tsuji Kiyoaki, ed., *Gyōseigaku kōza, dai 4-kan: Gyōsei to soshiki* [Lectures on Public Administration, vol. 4: Public Administration and Organization], pp. 169–207. Tokyo: Tōkyō Daigaku Shuppankai, 1976.

———. "Nihon no kōmuinsei" [The Civil-Service System of Japan]. In Tsuji Kiyoaki, ed., *Gyōseigaku kōza, dai 2-kan: Gyōsei no rekishi* [Lectures on Public Administration, vol. 2: The History of Public Administration], pp. 111–60. Tokyo: Tōkyō Daigaku Shuppankai, 1976.

Weber, Max. *The Theory of Social and Economic Organization.* Trans. A. M. Henderson and Talcott Parsons. New York: Oxford University Press, 1947.

Yamaguchi Jirō. *Ōkura kanryō shihai no shūen* [The End of the Domination by Finance Ministry Bureaucrats]. Tokyo: Iwanami Shoten, 1987.

Yamaji Norio. "Kankai jinmyaku chiri—chūō shōchōhen: Rōdōshō no maki" [Who's Who in Central-Government Ministries and Agencies: the Ministry of Labor]. *Kankai,* (August 1985), pp. 36–46.

Yamanaka Einosuke. *Nihon kindai kokka no keisei to kanryōsei* [The Bureaucracy and the Formation of the Modern Japanese State]. Tokyo: Kōbundō, 1974.

Yamanaka Ichirō. *Kanryōsei to hanzai* [Bureaucracy and Crime]. Tokyo: Gakubunsha, 1981.

Yomiuri nenkan bessatsu, bun'ya betsu jinmei roku [Separate Volume Supplement to Yomiuri Yearbook, Who's Who by Fields of Specialization], 1985. Tokyo: Yomiuri Shinbunsha, 1985.

Yoshida, Kōzō. "Eikoku ni okeru kōmuin taishoku seisaku no genjō to tenbō" [The Present Situation and Future Prospects of Britain's Policy Toward Civil Servants' Retirement]. *Jinji-in geppō* 345 (November 1979): 6–10.

Yoshihara Atsuko. *Sukāto o haita kōkyū kanryō* [Higher Civil Servants Who Wear Skirts]. Tokyo: K. K. Kanki Shuppan, 1986.

Youn, Jung-Suk. "Recruitment of Political Leadership in Postwar Japan 1958–1972." Ph.D. diss., University of Michigan, 1977.

"Zadankai: Jinji gyōsei kongo no hōkō" [Roundtable Discussion: The Future Direction of Public Personnel Administration]. *Jinji-in geppō* 154 (December 1963): 4–9.

"Zadankai: Jinji-in no omoide arekore" [Roundtable Discussion: Recollecting Aspects of the National Personnel Authority]. *Jinji-in geppō* 100 (June 1959): 10–15.

"Zadankai: Kōmuin kenshū no arikata" [Roundtable Discussion: Ideal of Civil Servants' Training]. *Jinji-in geppō* 317 (July 1977): 13–21.

"Zadankai: Korekara no jinji gyōsei" [Roundtable Discussion: Public Personnel Administration in the Days Ahead]. *Jinji-in geppō* 274 (December 1973): 2–8.

Index

Abe Shintarō, faction led by, 213
Aberbach, Joel D., 192–193, 216
Administrative elite: definition of, 2, 253; power of, 261; salient characteristics of, 252–258
Administrative guidance, 257
Administrative Management Agency, 63
Administrative officials, 75, 134; ascendancy of, over technical officials (*gikan*), 255, 264. See also *Jimukan*
Administrative reform, 63
Administrative Research Bureau, 41, 45
Administrative Service I, 83, 127, 220, 223, 230, 231; definition of, 71
Administrative vice-minister (AVM), 7, 28, 69, 130, 138, 141, 143, 151, 172, 197, 231, 240, 244, 254, 255, 260; average age of, 233; conference of, 202
Advisory commission (*shingikai*), 204, 206, 207
Agriculture, Forestry, and Fisheries, Ministry of, 106, 237; deviations from unwritten rule on resignations, 130
Amakudari (descent from heaven), 244, 258, 265; consequences of, 245–246; definition of, 235; differences between, and running for elective offices, 242; patterns of, 236–240; positive aspects of, 264; restrictions on, 236; of technical officials, 238; three modes of, 245; white paper on, 236, 238
America, 133
American Occupation of Japan, 60, 205, 208, 209, 224, 256; form of, 35; perception gap between Japanese and American officials during, 41, 42, 66; and policy on educational reform, 152, 153; purge of higher civil servants, 140, 256; reorganization of Tōdai during, 161–162; termination of, 58
Annuity, 234; provisions for, in Western democracies, 248–249
Aoyama Gakuin University, 69, 113
Armstrong, John A., 152, 171; on models of recruitment, 149
Asahi shinbun, 69, 229; on the decline of bureaucratic influence, 208
Asai Kyoshi, 42, 53
Ascriptive features of Japanese bureaucracy, 253
Ashida Hitoshi, government of, 52, 53
Assistant division chief (*bu jichō*), 140
Assistant section chief (*kachō hosa*), 130, 132; role of, in policy making, 194; tasks of, 133; training of, 180–181
Ateken, 131
Australia, 183, 184
Austria, impact of, on Meiji constitution, 14
Autonomy Agency (*Jichichō*), 63

Baerwald, Hans H., 3; on role of Diet in policy making, 214; on SCAP's purge program, 38–39
Bank of Japan, 242
Beppyō-gumi (separate-list group), 144, 254

Compositor: Interactive Composition Corporation
Text: 10/13 Sabon
Display: Sabon
Printer: Braun-Brumfield, Inc.
Binder: Braun-Brumfield, Inc.